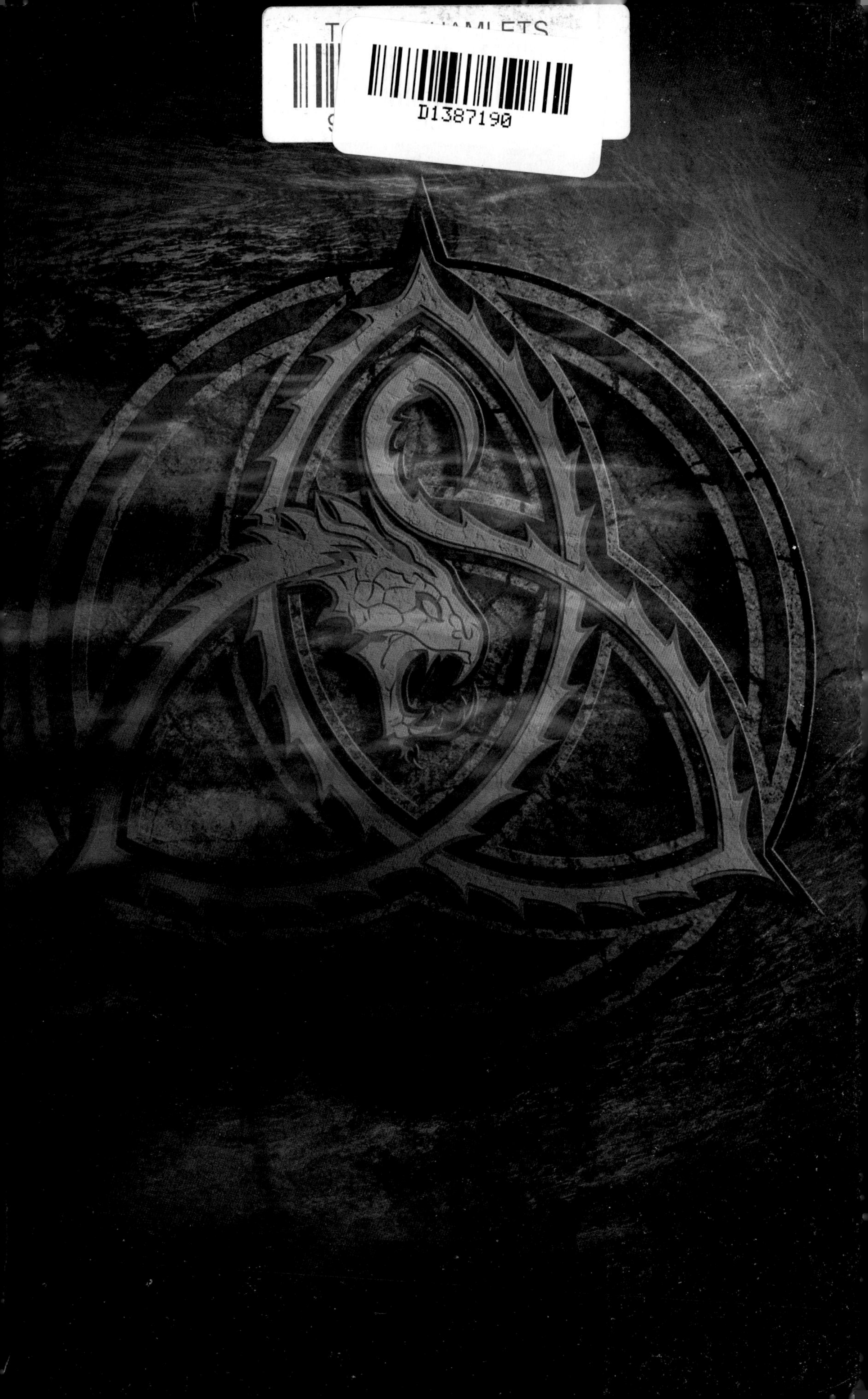

FEAR ITSELF
HEROES
FOR HIRE

WRITERS
DAN ABNETT & ANDY LANNING

PENCILERS
BRAD WALKER (ISSUES #6, #8 & #12)
TIM SEELEY (ISSUE #7)
KYLE HOTZ (ISSUES #9-11)

INKERS
ANDREW HENNESSY (ISSUES #6, #8 & #12)
WITH JOHN LIVESAY (ISSUE #8)
TIM SEELEY (ISSUE #7)
BOB ALMOND (ISSUES #9-11)

COLORIST
JAY DAVID RAMOS

COVER ARTISTS
DOUG BRAITHWAITE & ROB SCHWAGER (ISSUES #6 & #8)
DAVID YARDIN (ISSUES #7 & #12)
JAY ANACLETO & BRIAN HABERLIN (ISSUES #9-11)

LETTERER
VC'S JOE CARAMAGNA

COLLECTION EDITOR: CORY LEVINE
ASSISTANT EDITORS: ALEX STARBUCK & NELSON RIBEIRO
EDITORS, SPECIAL PROJECTS: JENNIFER GRÜNWALD & MARK D. BEAZLEY
SENIOR EDITOR, SPECIAL PROJECTS: JEFF YOUNGQUIST
SENIOR VICE PRESIDENT OF SALES: DAVID GABRIEL
SVP OF BRAND PLANNING & COMMUNICATIONS: MICHAEL PASCIULLO
BOOK DESIGN: JEFF POWELL

EDITOR IN CHIEF: AXEL ALONSO
CHIEF CREATIVE OFFICER: JOE QUESADA
PUBLISHER: DAN BUCKLEY
EXECUTIVE PRODUCER: ALAN FINE

FEAR ITSELF: HEROES FOR HIRE. Contains material originally published in magazine form as HEROES FOR HIRE #6-12. First printing 2012. ISBN# 978-0-7851-5582-9. Published by MARVEL WORLDWIDE, INC., a subsidiary of MARVEL ENTERTAINMENT, LLC. OFFICE OF PUBLICATION: 135 West 50th Street, New York, NY 10020. Copyright © 2011 and 2012 Marvel Characters, Inc. All rights reserved. $19.99 per copy in the U.S. and $21.99 in Canada (GST #R127032852). Canadian Agreement #40668537. All characters featured in this issue and the distinctive names and likenesses thereof, and all related indicia are trademarks of Marvel Characters, Inc. No similarity between any of the names, characters, persons, and/or institutions in this magazine with those of any living or dead person or institution is intended, and any such similarity which may exist is purely coincidental. **Printed in the U.S.A.** ALAN FINE, EVP - Office of the President, Marvel Worldwide, Inc. and EVP & CMO Marvel Characters B.V.; DAN BUCKLEY, Publisher & President - Print, Animation & Digital Divisions; JOE QUESADA, Chief Creative Officer; TOM BREVOORT, SVP of Publishing; DAVID BOGART, SVP of Operations & Procurement, Publishing; RUWAN JAYATILLEKE, SVP & Associate Publisher, Publishing; C.B. CEBULSKI, SVP of Creator & Content Development; DAVID GABRIEL, SVP of Publishing Sales & Circulation; MICHAEL PASCIULLO, SVP of Brand Planning & Communications; JIM O'KEEFE, VP of Operations & Logistics; DAN CARR, Executive Director of Publishing Technology; SUSAN CRESPI, Editorial Operations Manager; ALEX MORALES, Publishing Operations Manager; STAN LEE, Chairman Emeritus. For information regarding advertising in Marvel Comics or on Marvel.com, please contact Niza Disla, Director of Marvel Partnerships, at ndisla@marvel.com. For Marvel subscription inquiries, please call 800-217-9158. **Manufactured between 9/19/2012 and 10/22/2012 by R.R. DONNELLEY, INC., SALEM, VA, USA.**

10 9 8 7 6 5 4 3 2 1

TOWER HAMLETS LIBRARIES	
91000001707793	
Bertrams	08/11/2012
GRA	£14.99
THISBO	TH12001788

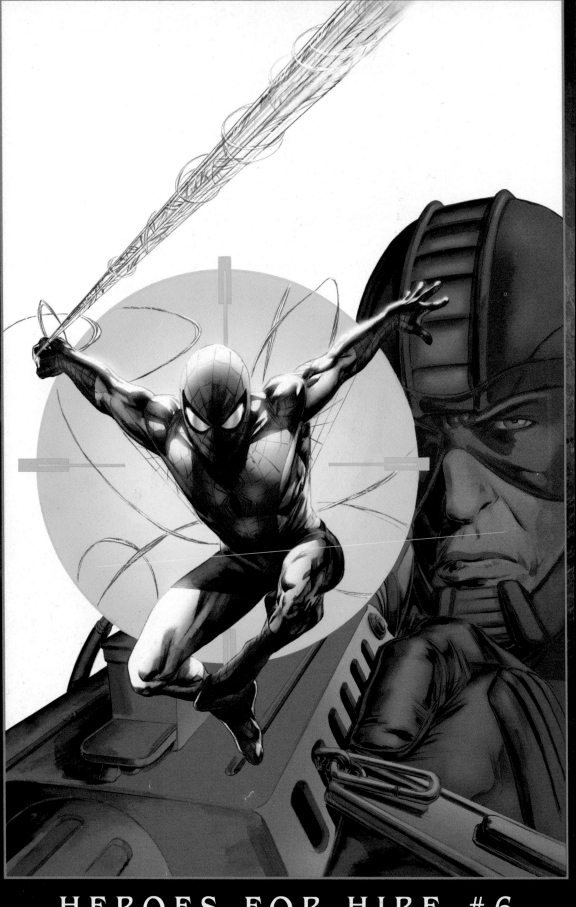

HEROES FOR HIRE #6

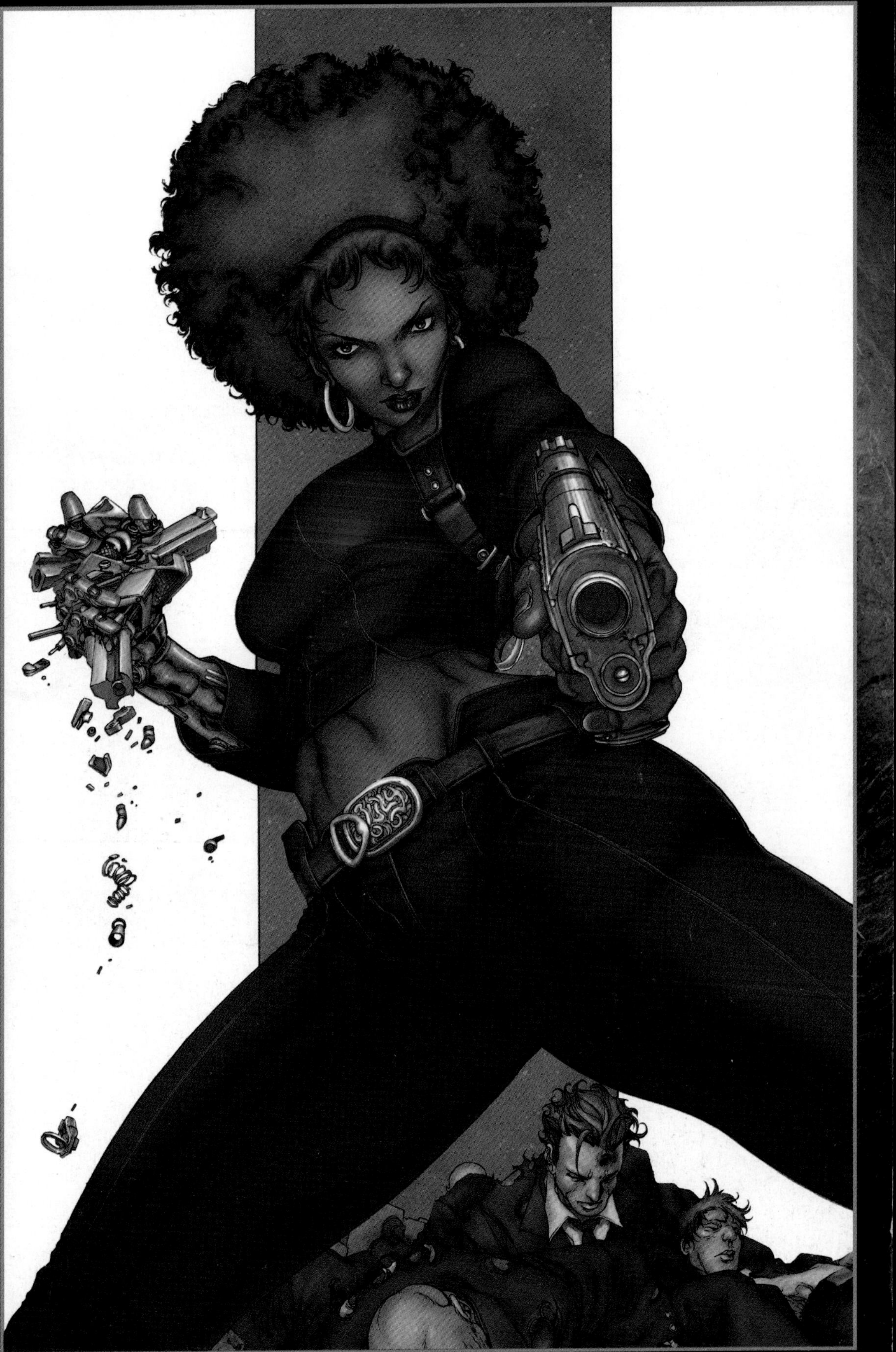

HEROES FOR HIRE #6 VARIANT

Bringing justice to the city's mean streets, bionic detective **MISTY KNIGHT** has reopened the underground mercenary agency, **HEROES FOR HIRE**. From her control room, Knight gets the word out to the right people at the right time so they can do the right thing.

"CONTROL" MISSION LOG.

VILLAIN: PUPPET MASTER

Mission: Manipulate Heroes for Hire to do his bidding.

Mission Status: Failed. Currently in a coma. It appears someone else was pulling his strings.

HERO: MISTY KNIGHT

Mission: Getting her life back in order while searching for the brains behind Puppet Master's operation.

Mission Status: Back in business.

HERO: PALADIN

Mission: Assist Misty in tracking the true culprit behind her capture.

Mission Status: For hire.

After escaping the clutches of the **PUPPET MASTER** and narrowly escaping death at the hands of a mind-controlled **PUNISHER**, Misty is back on her feet, ready to once again pursue her Heroes for Hire venture... this time on her terms!

NEXT MISSION: ACTIVE...

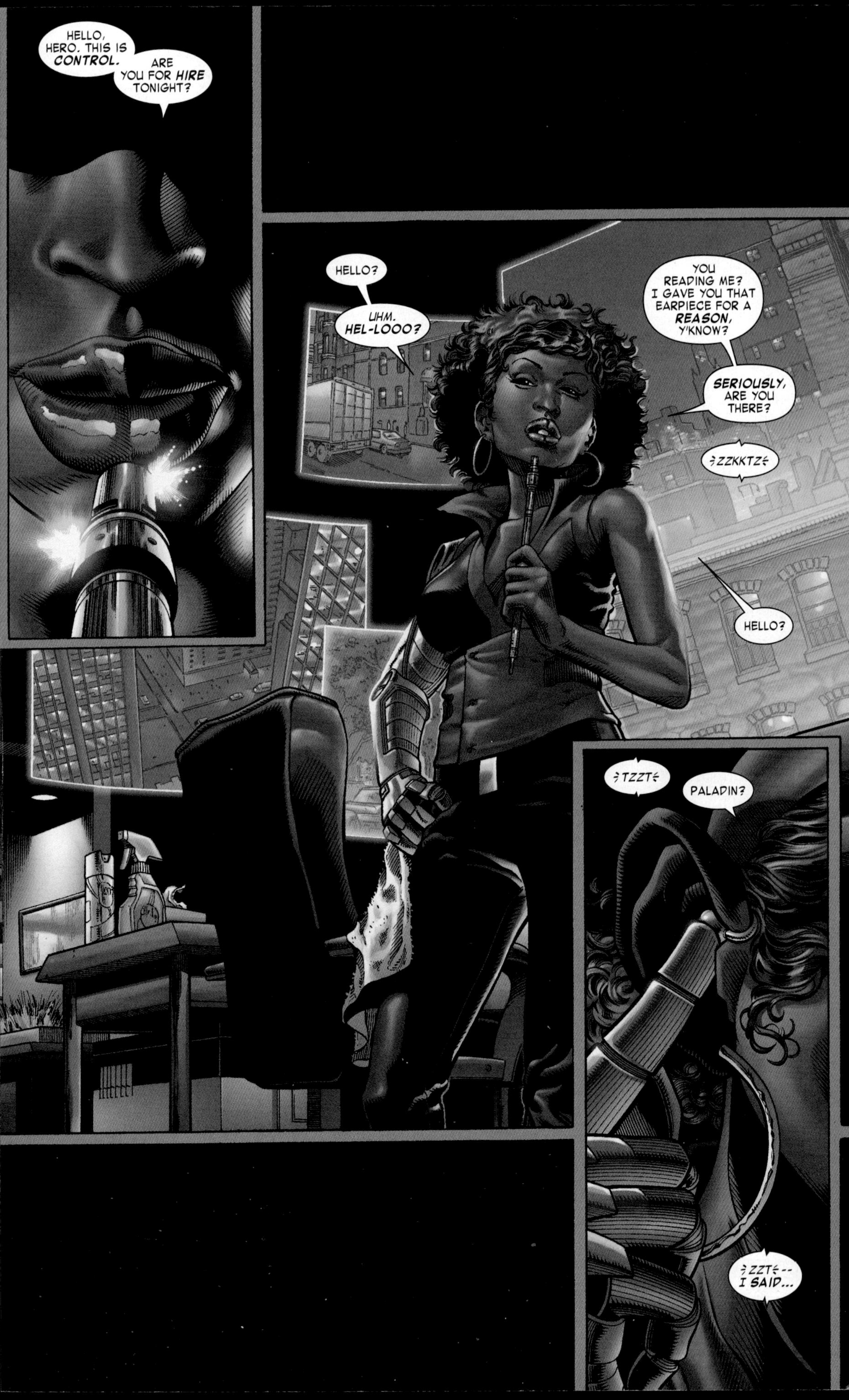
HELLO, HERO. THIS IS CONTROL.
ARE YOU FOR HIRE TONIGHT?
HELLO?
UHM. HEL-LOOO?
YOU READING ME? I GAVE YOU THAT EARPIECE FOR A REASON, Y'KNOW?
SERIOUSLY, ARE YOU THERE?
ZZKKTZ
HELLO?
TZZT
PALADIN?
ZZT-- I SAID...

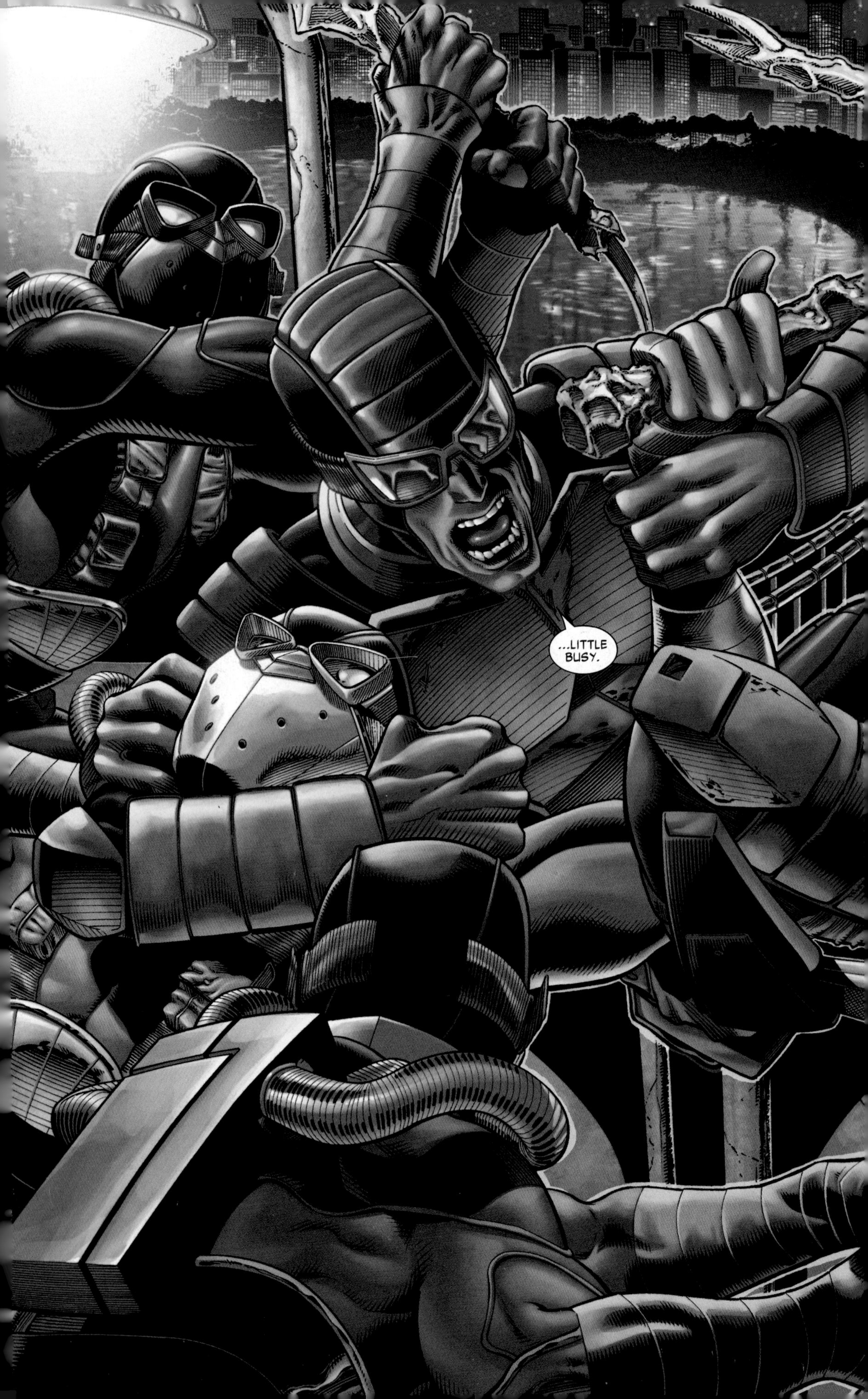
...LITTLE BUSY.

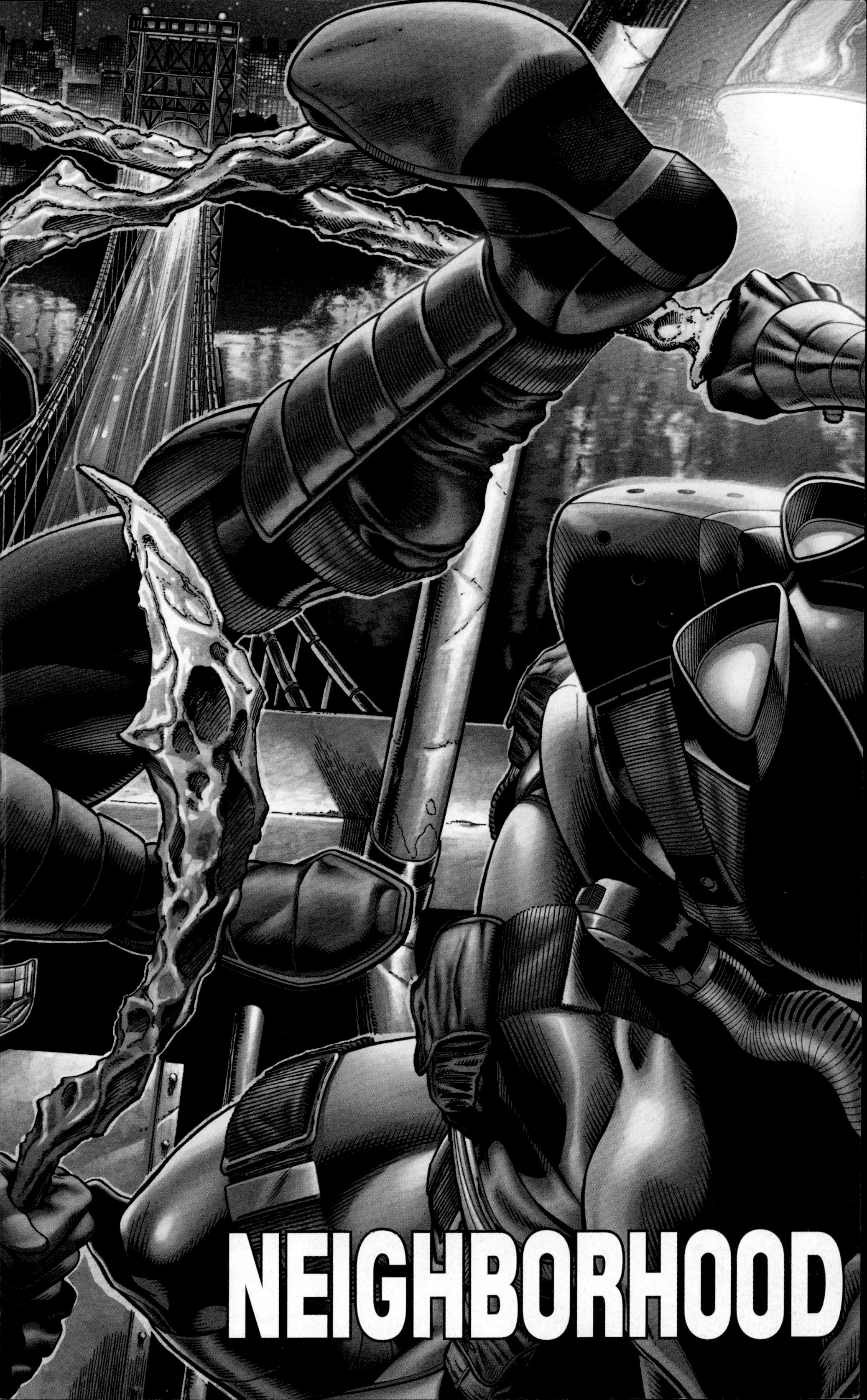
NEIGHBORHOOD

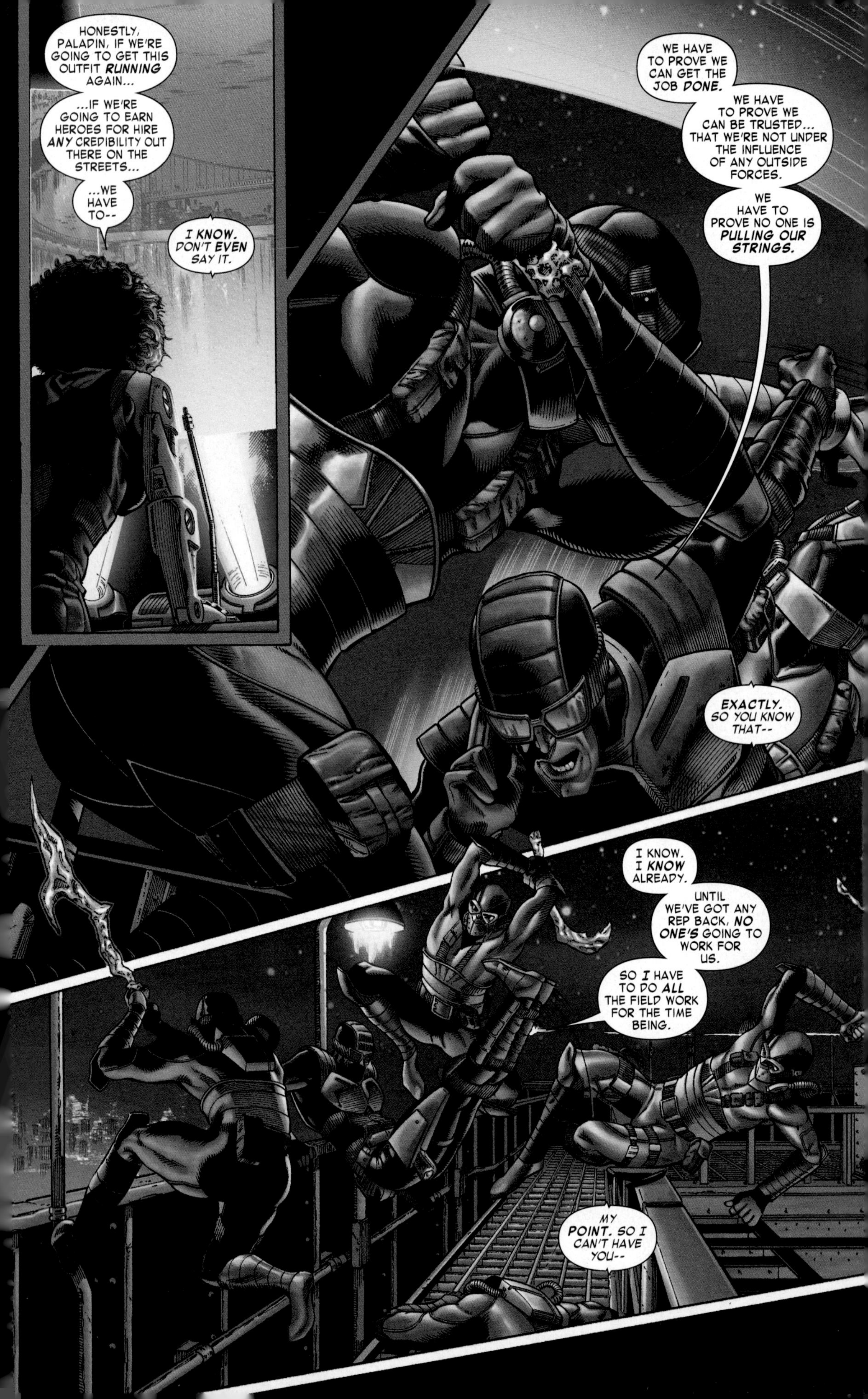
HONESTLY, PALADIN, IF WE'RE GOING TO GET THIS OUTFIT RUNNING AGAIN...
...IF WE'RE GOING TO EARN HEROES FOR HIRE ANY CREDIBILITY OUT THERE ON THE STREETS...
...WE HAVE TO--
I KNOW. DON'T EVEN SAY IT.
WE HAVE TO PROVE WE CAN GET THE JOB DONE.
WE HAVE TO PROVE WE CAN BE TRUSTED... THAT WE'RE NOT UNDER THE INFLUENCE OF ANY OUTSIDE FORCES.
WE HAVE TO PROVE NO ONE IS PULLING OUR STRINGS.
EXACTLY. SO YOU KNOW THAT--
I KNOW. I KNOW ALREADY.
UNTIL WE'VE GOT ANY REP BACK, NO ONE'S GOING TO WORK FOR US.
SO I HAVE TO DO ALL THE FIELD WORK FOR THE TIME BEING.
MY POINT. SO I CAN'T HAVE YOU--

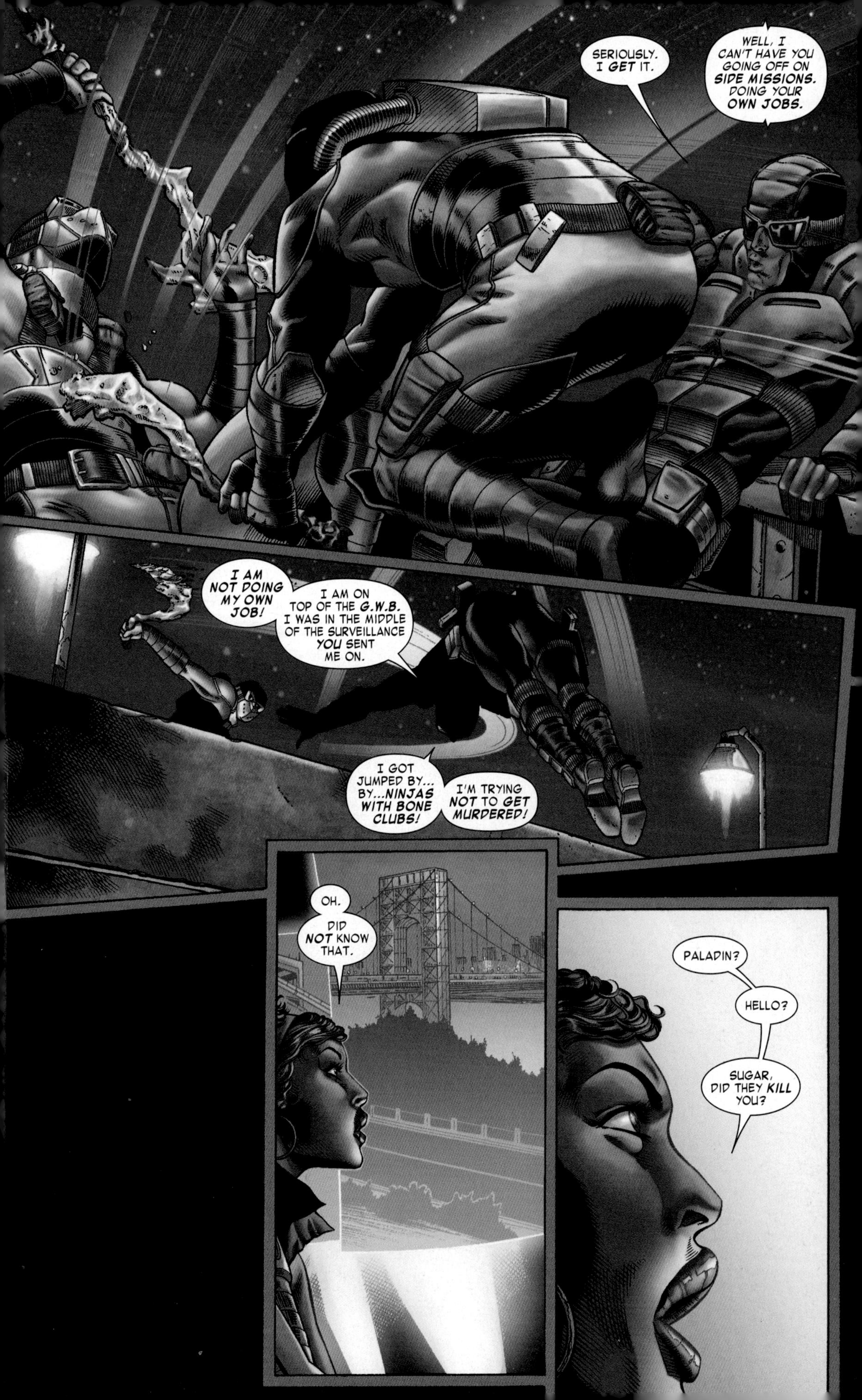
SERIOUSLY. I GET IT.
WELL, I CAN'T HAVE YOU GOING OFF ON SIDE MISSIONS. DOING YOUR OWN JOBS.
I AM NOT DOING MY OWN JOB!
I AM ON TOP OF THE G.W.B. I WAS IN THE MIDDLE OF THE SURVEILLANCE YOU SENT ME ON.
I GOT JUMPED BY... BY...NINJAS WITH BONE CLUBS!
I'M TRYING NOT TO GET MURDERED!
OH.
DID NOT KNOW THAT.
PALADIN?
HELLO?
SUGAR, DID THEY KILL YOU?

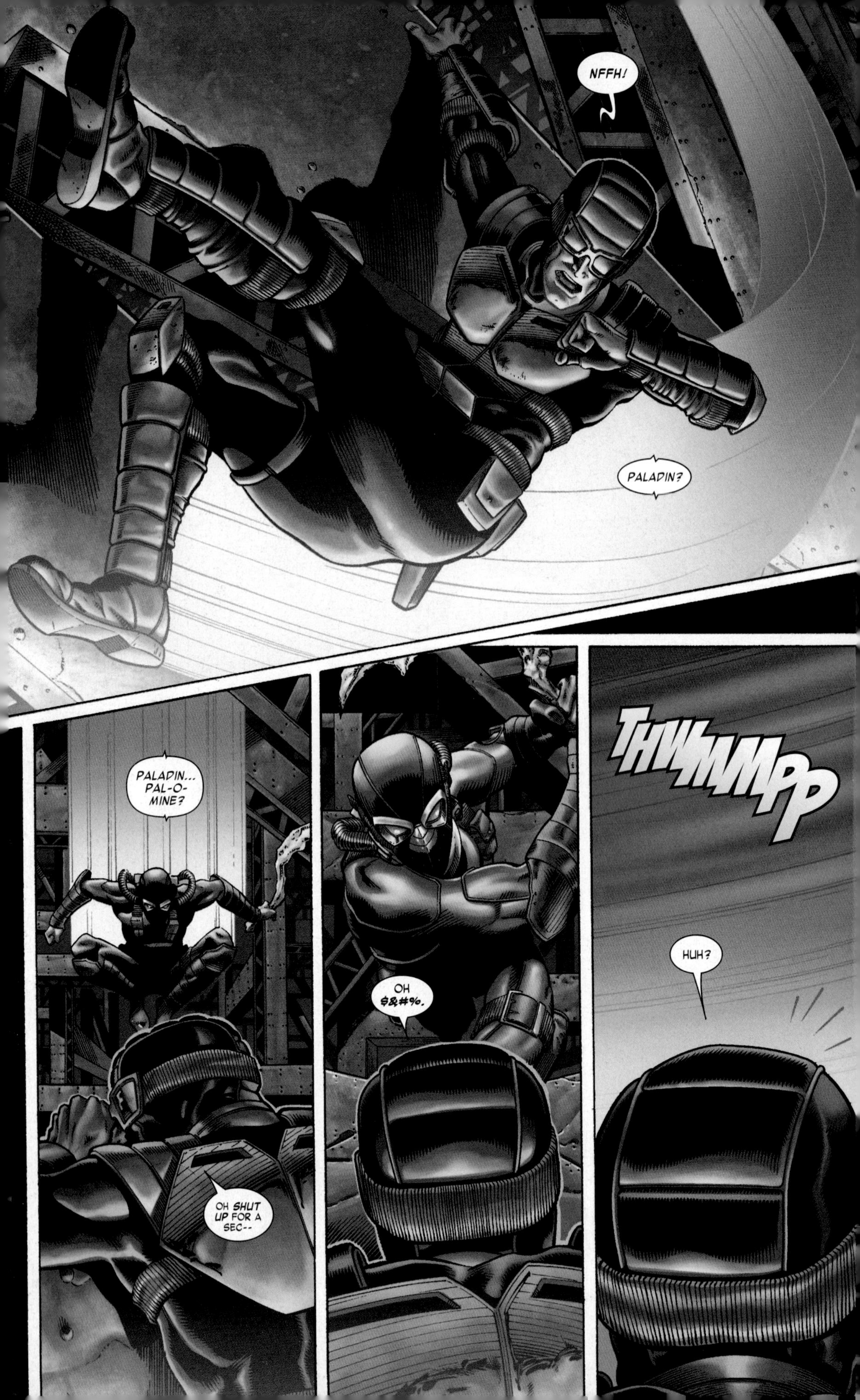
NFFH!
PALADIN?
PALADIN... PAL-O-MINE?
OH SHUT UP FOR A SEC--
OH $&#%.
THWMMPP
HUH?

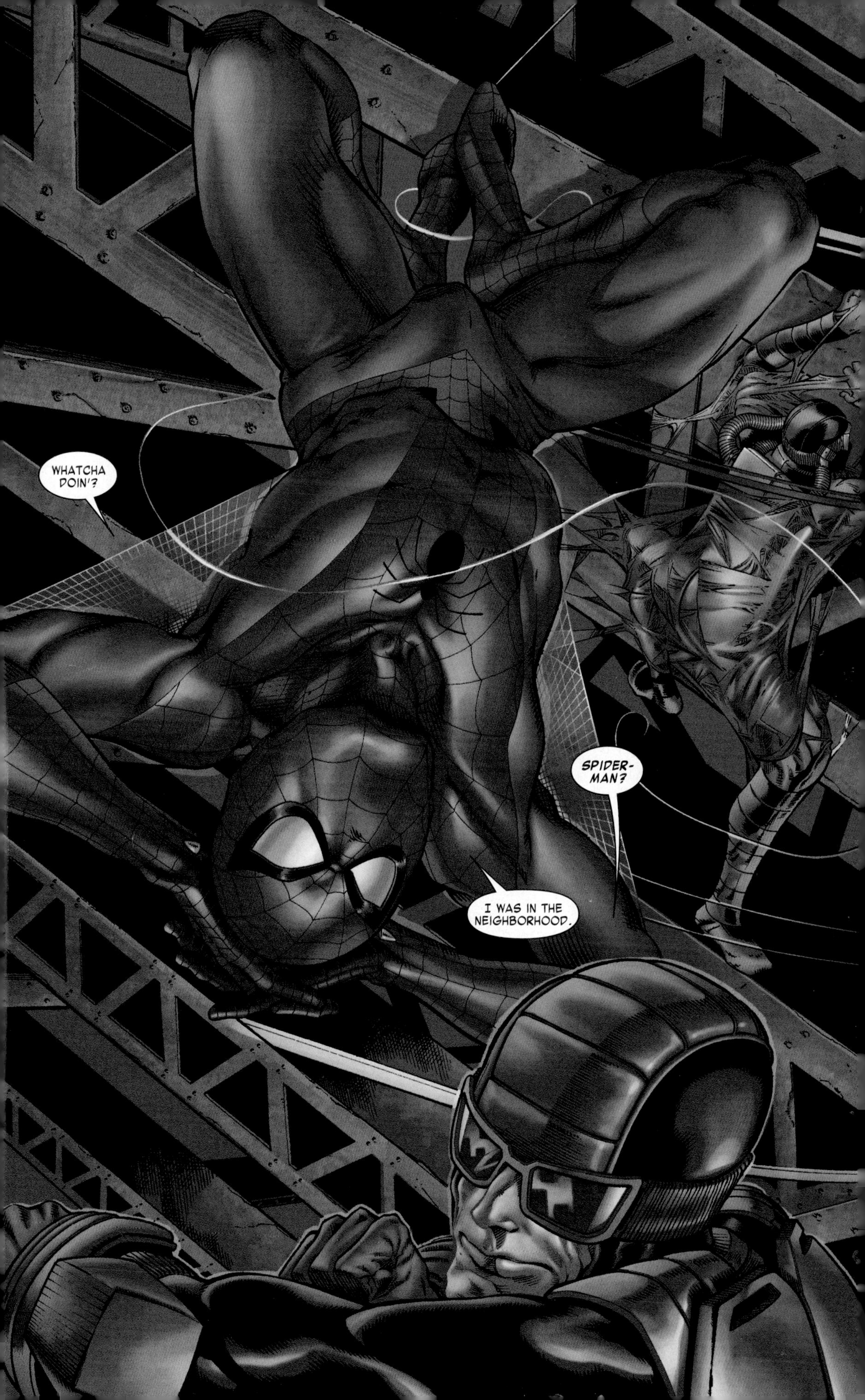
WHATCHA DOIN'?
SPIDER-MAN?
I WAS IN THE NEIGHBORHOOD.

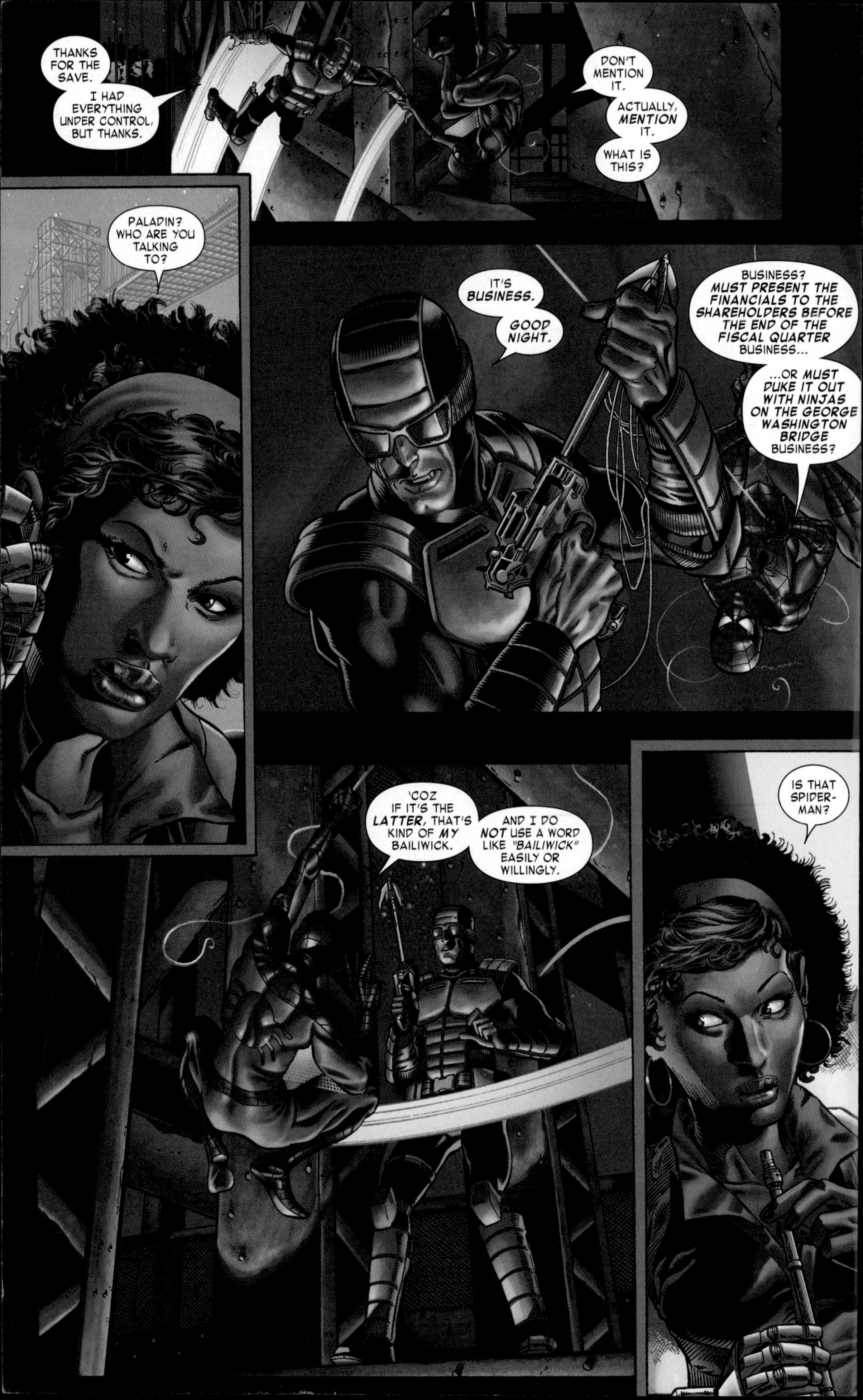
THANKS FOR THE SAVE.
I HAD EVERYTHING UNDER CONTROL, BUT THANKS.
DON'T MENTION IT.
ACTUALLY, MENTION IT.
WHAT IS THIS?
PALADIN? WHO ARE YOU TALKING TO?
IT'S BUSINESS.
GOOD NIGHT.
BUSINESS? MUST PRESENT THE FINANCIALS TO THE SHAREHOLDERS BEFORE THE END OF THE FISCAL QUARTER BUSINESS...
...OR MUST DUKE IT OUT WITH NINJAS ON THE GEORGE WASHINGTON BRIDGE BUSINESS?
'COZ IF IT'S THE LATTER, THAT'S KIND OF MY BAILIWICK.
AND I DO NOT USE A WORD LIKE "BAILIWICK" EASILY OR WILLINGLY.
IS THAT SPIDER-MAN?

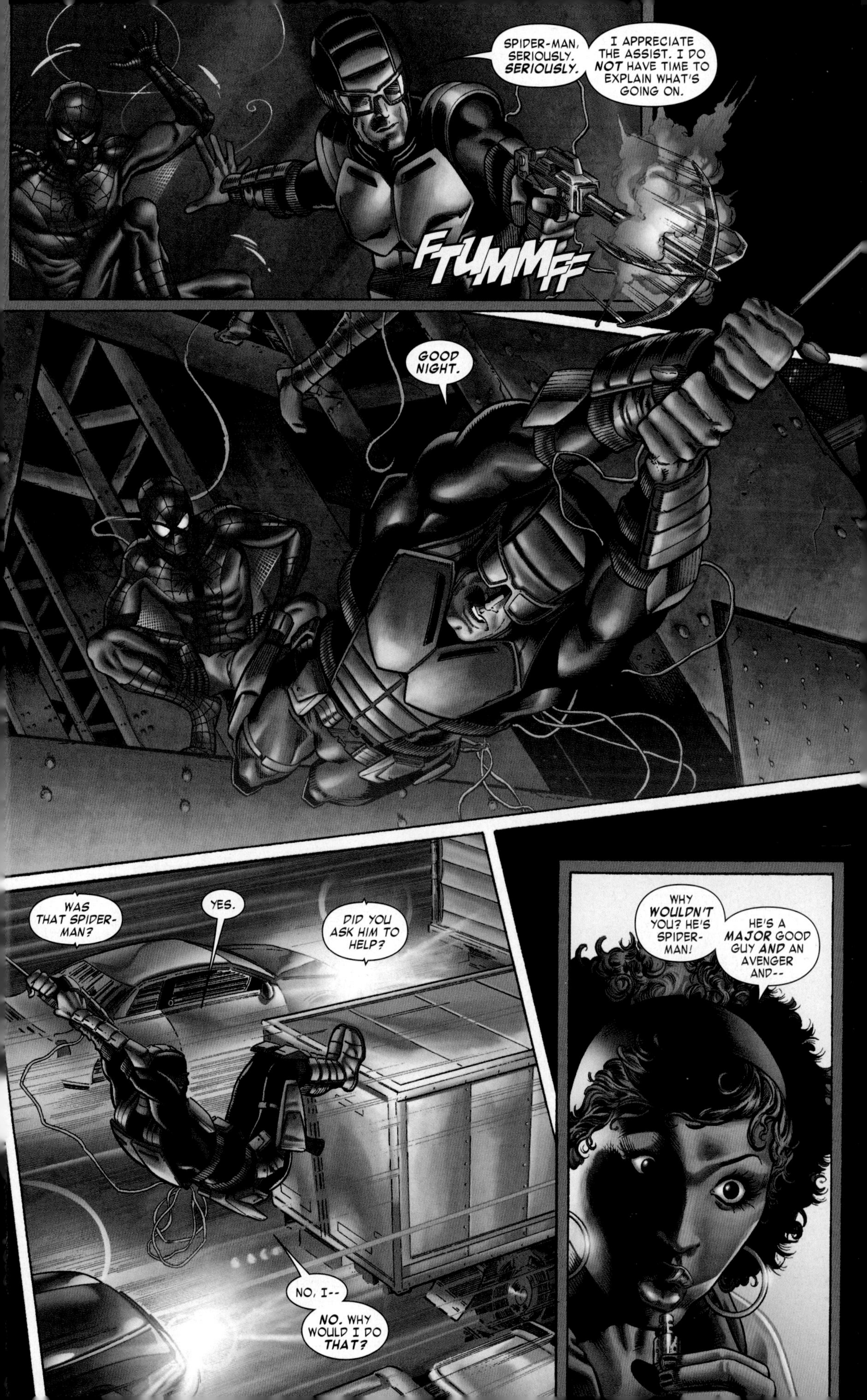
SPIDER-MAN, SERIOUSLY. SERIOUSLY.
I APPRECIATE THE ASSIST. I DO NOT HAVE TIME TO EXPLAIN WHAT'S GOING ON.
FTUMMFF
GOOD NIGHT.
WAS THAT SPIDER-MAN?
YES.
DID YOU ASK HIM TO HELP?
NO, I--
NO. WHY WOULD I DO THAT?
WHY WOULDN'T YOU? HE'S SPIDER-MAN!
HE'S A MAJOR GOOD GUY AND AN AVENGER AND--

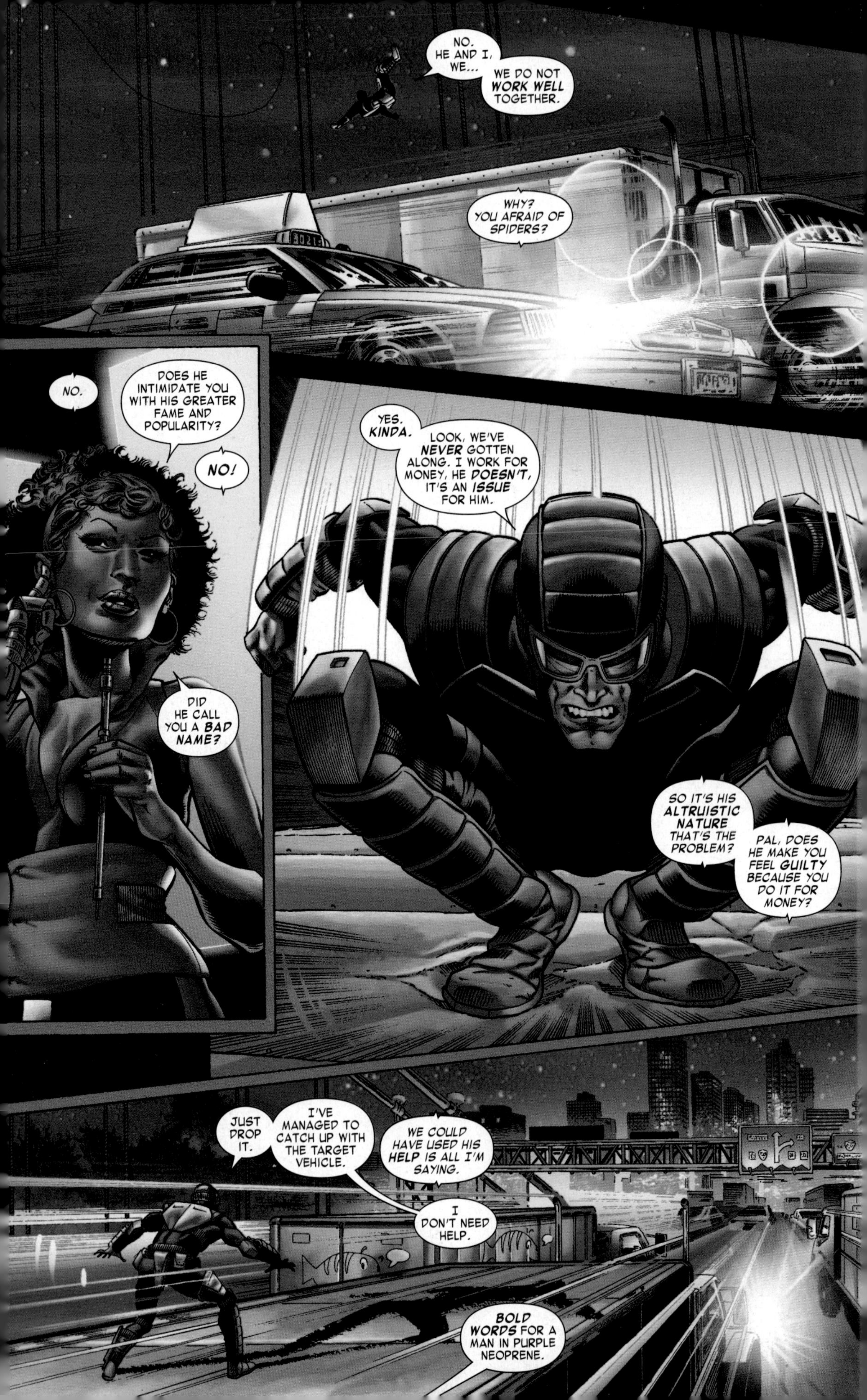
NO. HE AND I, WE...
WE DO NOT WORK WELL TOGETHER.
WHY? YOU AFRAID OF SPIDERS?
NO.
DOES HE INTIMIDATE YOU WITH HIS GREATER FAME AND POPULARITY?
NO!
DID HE CALL YOU A BAD NAME?
YES. KINDA.
LOOK, WE'VE NEVER GOTTEN ALONG. I WORK FOR MONEY, HE DOESN'T, IT'S AN ISSUE FOR HIM.
SO IT'S HIS ALTRUISTIC NATURE THAT'S THE PROBLEM?
PAL, DOES HE MAKE YOU FEEL GUILTY BECAUSE YOU DO IT FOR MONEY?
JUST DROP IT.
I'VE MANAGED TO CATCH UP WITH THE TARGET VEHICLE.
WE COULD HAVE USED HIS HELP IS ALL I'M SAYING.
I DON'T NEED HELP.
BOLD WORDS FOR A MAN IN PURPLE NEOPRENE.

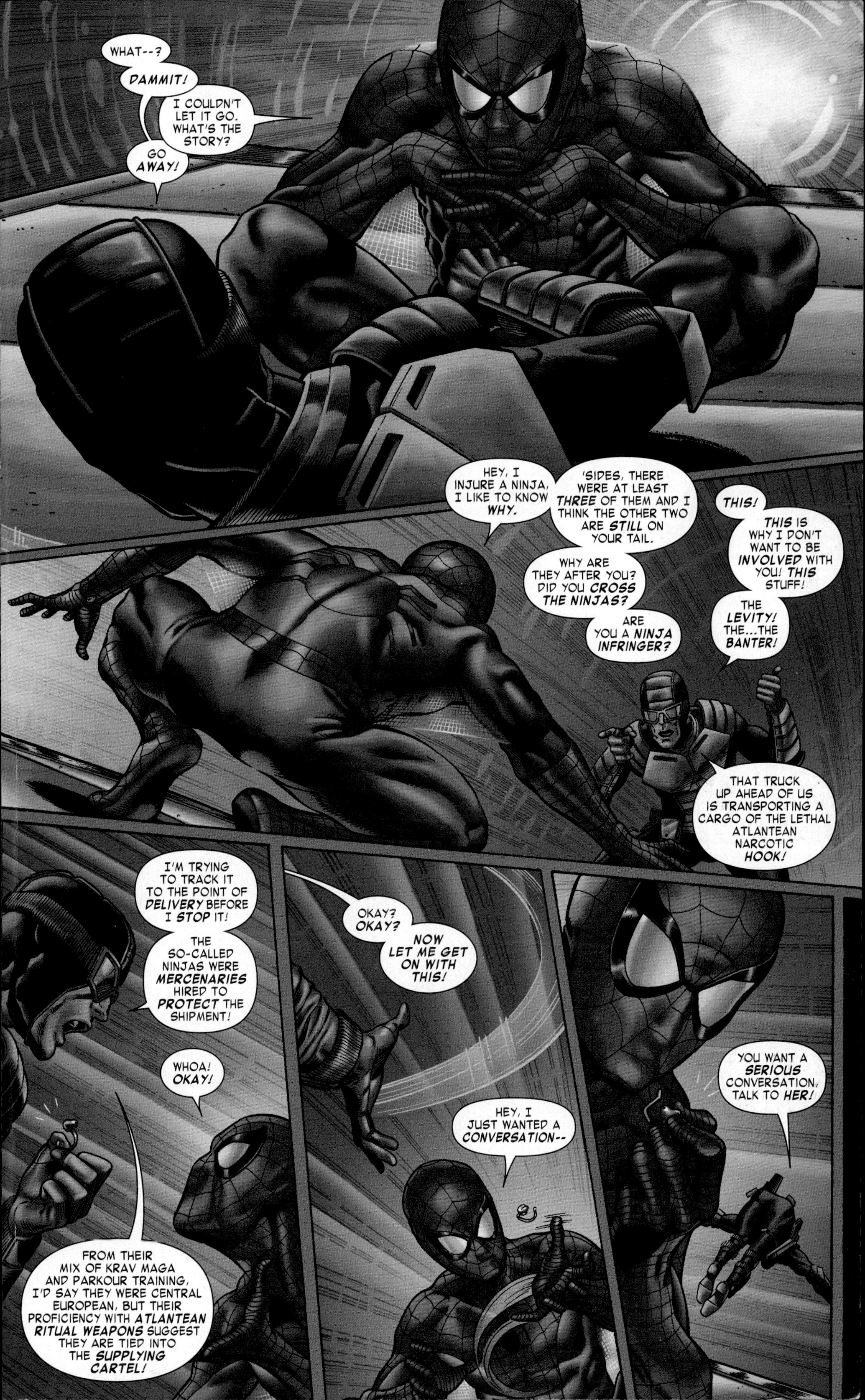
WHAT--?
DAMMIT!
I COULDN'T LET IT GO. WHAT'S THE STORY?
GO AWAY!
HEY, I INJURE A NINJA, I LIKE TO KNOW WHY.
'SIDES, THERE WERE AT LEAST THREE OF THEM AND I THINK THE OTHER TWO ARE STILL ON YOUR TAIL.
WHY ARE THEY AFTER YOU? DID YOU CROSS THE NINJAS?
ARE YOU A NINJA INFRINGER?
THIS!
THIS IS WHY I DON'T WANT TO BE INVOLVED WITH YOU! THIS STUFF!
THE LEVITY! THE...THE BANTER!
THAT TRUCK UP AHEAD OF US IS TRANSPORTING A CARGO OF THE LETHAL ATLANTEAN NARCOTIC HOOK!
I'M TRYING TO TRACK IT TO THE POINT OF DELIVERY BEFORE I STOP IT!
THE SO-CALLED NINJAS WERE MERCENARIES HIRED TO PROTECT THE SHIPMENT!
WHOA! OKAY!
FROM THEIR MIX OF KRAV MAGA AND PARKOUR TRAINING, I'D SAY THEY WERE CENTRAL EUROPEAN, BUT THEIR PROFICIENCY WITH ATLANTEAN RITUAL WEAPONS SUGGEST THEY ARE TIED INTO THE SUPPLYING CARTEL!
OKAY? OKAY?
NOW LET ME GET ON WITH THIS!
HEY, I JUST WANTED A CONVERSATION--
YOU WANT A SERIOUS CONVERSATION, TALK TO HER!

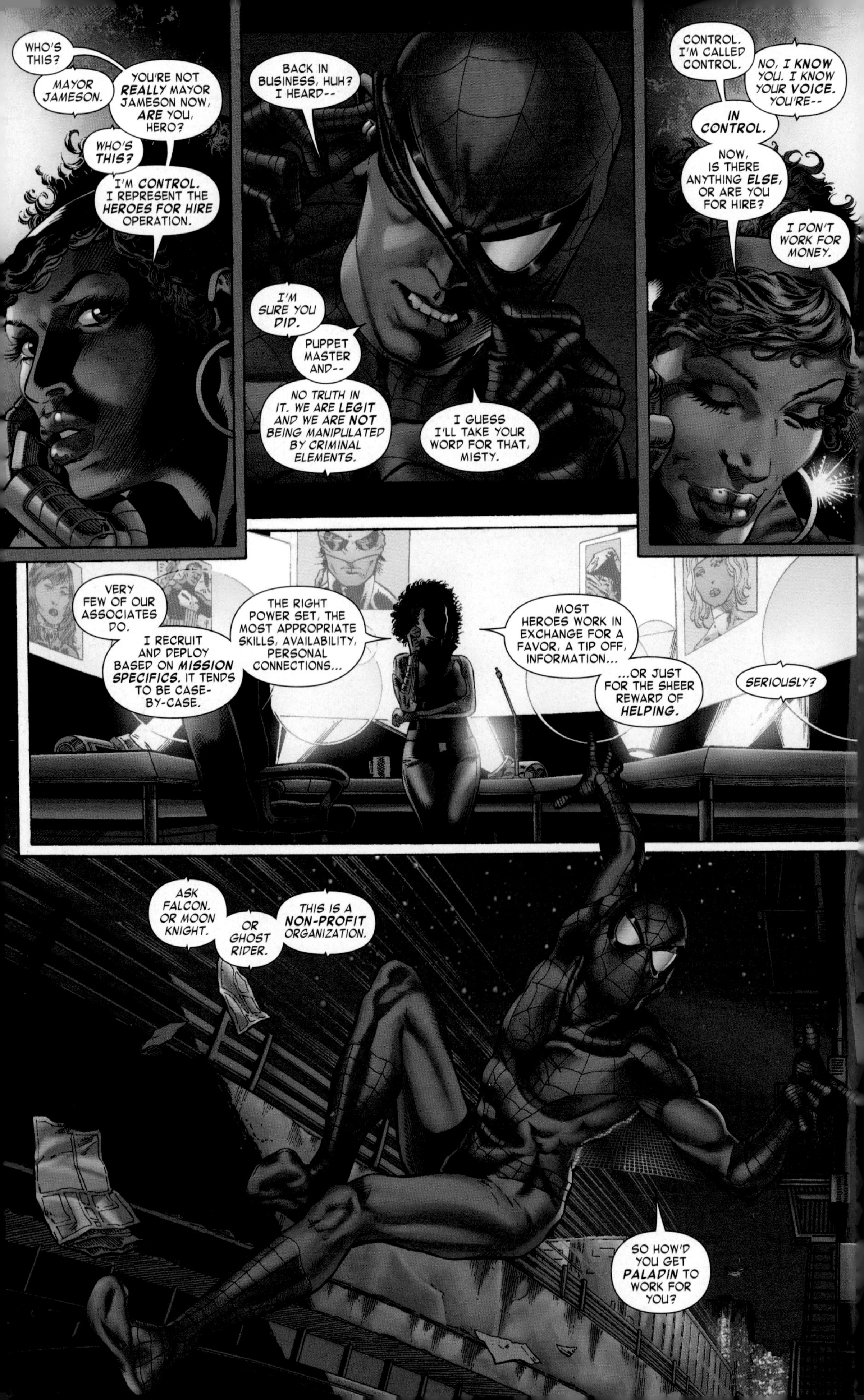
WHO'S THIS?
MAYOR JAMESON.
YOU'RE NOT REALLY MAYOR JAMESON NOW, ARE YOU, HERO?
WHO'S THIS?
I'M CONTROL. I REPRESENT THE HEROES FOR HIRE OPERATION.
BACK IN BUSINESS, HUH? I HEARD--
I'M SURE YOU DID.
PUPPET MASTER AND--
NO TRUTH IN IT. WE ARE LEGIT AND WE ARE NOT BEING MANIPULATED BY CRIMINAL ELEMENTS.
I GUESS I'LL TAKE YOUR WORD FOR THAT, MISTY.
CONTROL. I'M CALLED CONTROL.
NO, I KNOW YOU. I KNOW YOUR VOICE. YOU'RE--
IN CONTROL.
NOW, IS THERE ANYTHING ELSE, OR ARE YOU FOR HIRE?
I DON'T WORK FOR MONEY.
VERY FEW OF OUR ASSOCIATES DO.
I RECRUIT AND DEPLOY BASED ON MISSION SPECIFICS. IT TENDS TO BE CASE-BY-CASE.
THE RIGHT POWER SET, THE MOST APPROPRIATE SKILLS, AVAILABILITY, PERSONAL CONNECTIONS...
MOST HEROES WORK IN EXCHANGE FOR A FAVOR, A TIP OFF, INFORMATION...
...OR JUST FOR THE SHEER REWARD OF HELPING.
SERIOUSLY?
ASK FALCON. OR MOON KNIGHT.
OR GHOST RIDER.
THIS IS A NON-PROFIT ORGANIZATION.
SO HOW'D YOU GET PALADIN TO WORK FOR YOU?

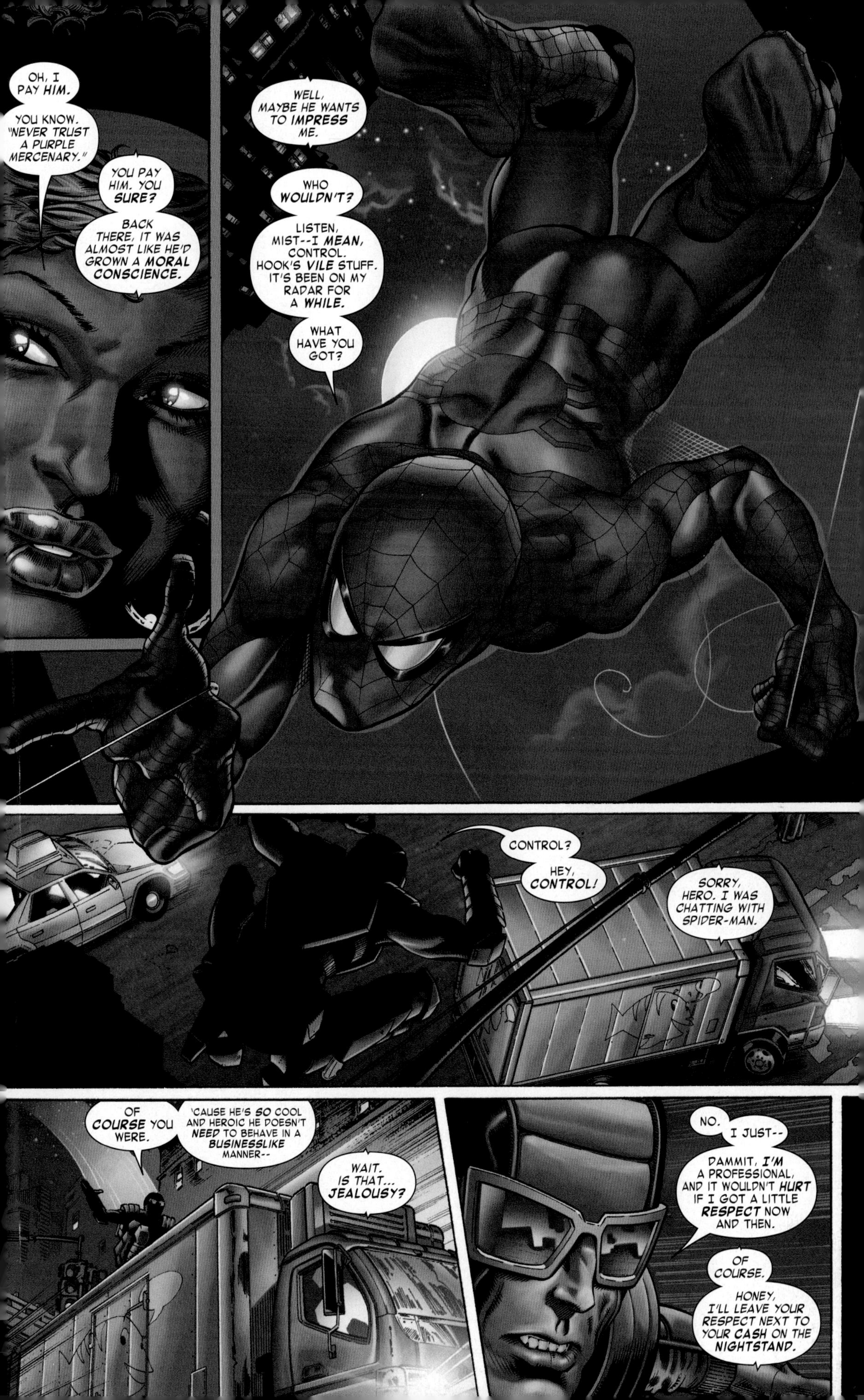

OH, I PAY HIM.
YOU KNOW. "NEVER TRUST A PURPLE MERCENARY."
YOU PAY HIM. YOU SURE?
BACK THERE, IT WAS ALMOST LIKE HE'D GROWN A MORAL CONSCIENCE.
WELL, MAYBE HE WANTS TO IMPRESS ME.
WHO WOULDN'T?
LISTEN, MIST--I MEAN, CONTROL. HOOK'S VILE STUFF. IT'S BEEN ON MY RADAR FOR A WHILE.
WHAT HAVE YOU GOT?
CONTROL?
HEY, CONTROL!
SORRY, HERO. I WAS CHATTING WITH SPIDER-MAN.
OF COURSE YOU WERE.
'CAUSE HE'S SO COOL AND HEROIC HE DOESN'T NEED TO BEHAVE IN A BUSINESSLIKE MANNER--
WAIT. IS THAT... JEALOUSY?
NO.
I JUST--
DAMMIT, I'M A PROFESSIONAL, AND IT WOULDN'T HURT IF I GOT A LITTLE RESPECT NOW AND THEN.
OF COURSE.
HONEY, I'LL LEAVE YOUR RESPECT NEXT TO YOUR CASH ON THE NIGHTSTAND.

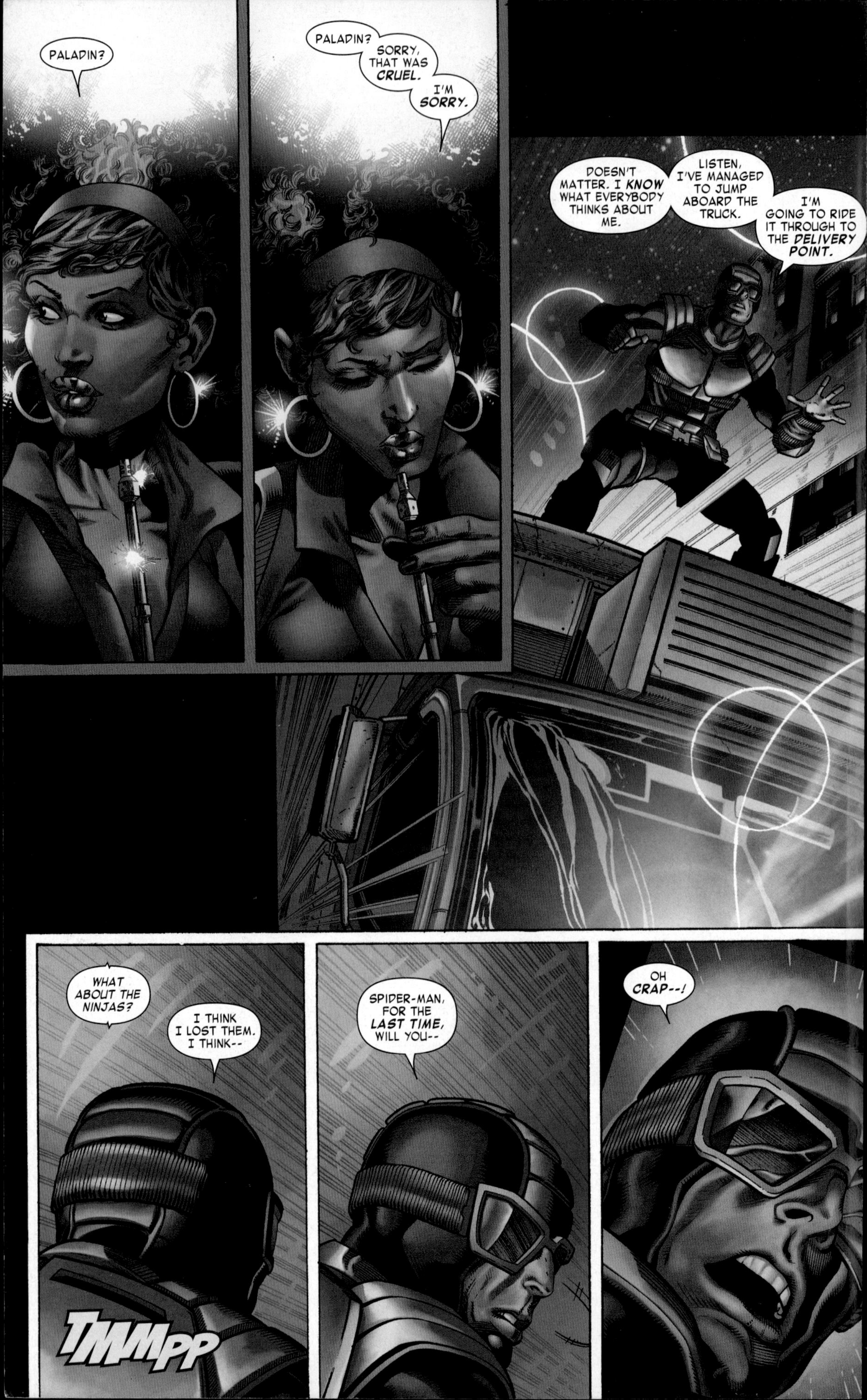
PALADIN?
PALADIN?
SORRY, THAT WAS CRUEL.
I'M SORRY.
DOESN'T MATTER. I KNOW WHAT EVERYBODY THINKS ABOUT ME.
LISTEN, I'VE MANAGED TO JUMP ABOARD THE TRUCK.
I'M GOING TO RIDE IT THROUGH TO THE DELIVERY POINT.
WHAT ABOUT THE NINJAS?
I THINK I LOST THEM. I THINK--
TMMPP
SPIDER-MAN, FOR THE LAST TIME, WILL YOU--
OH CRAP--!

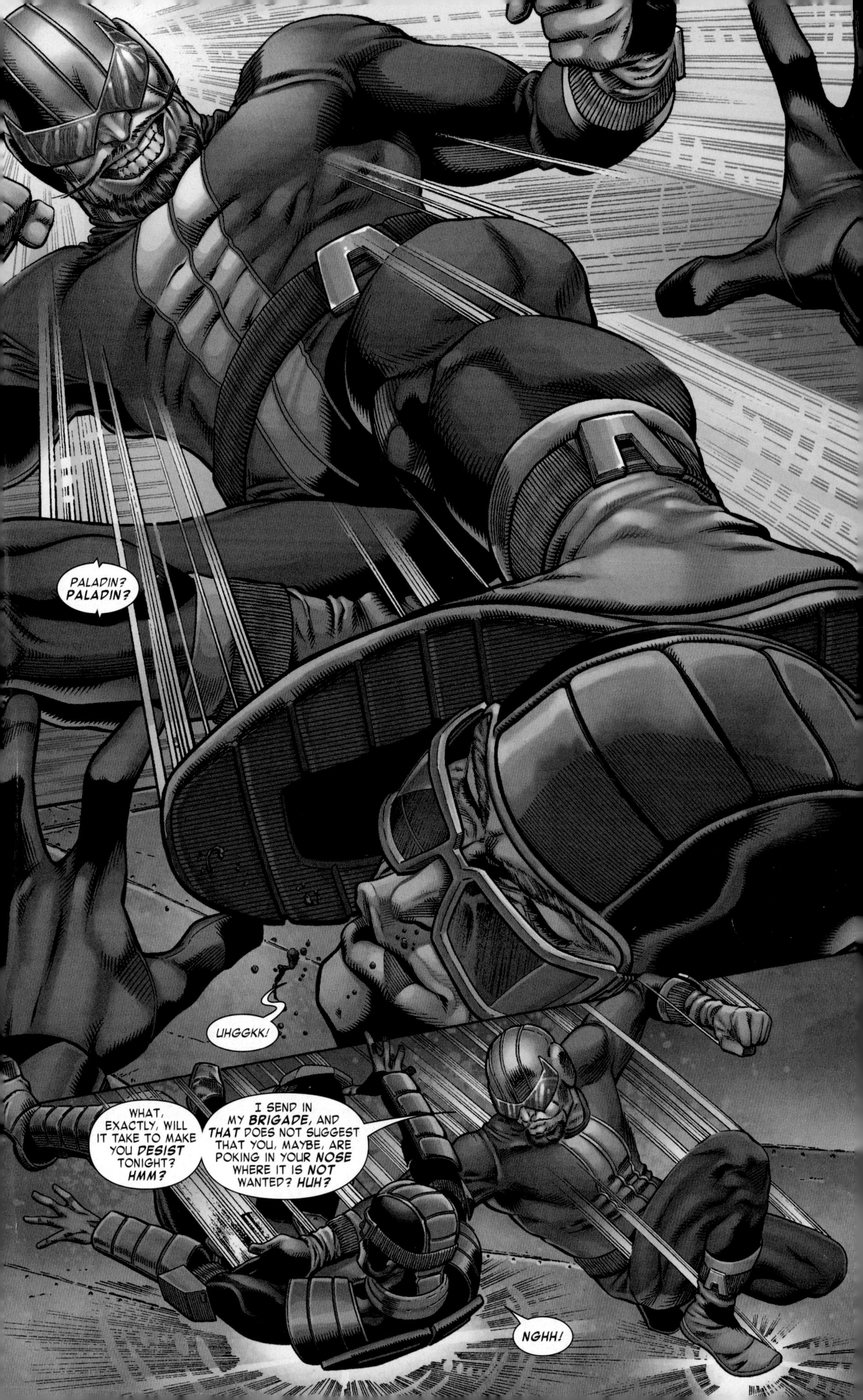
PALADIN? PALADIN?
UHGGKK!
WHAT, EXACTLY, WILL IT TAKE TO MAKE YOU DESIST TONIGHT? HMM?
I SEND IN MY BRIGADE, AND THAT DOES NOT SUGGEST THAT YOU, MAYBE, ARE POKING IN YOUR NOSE WHERE IT IS NOT WANTED? HUH?
NGHH!

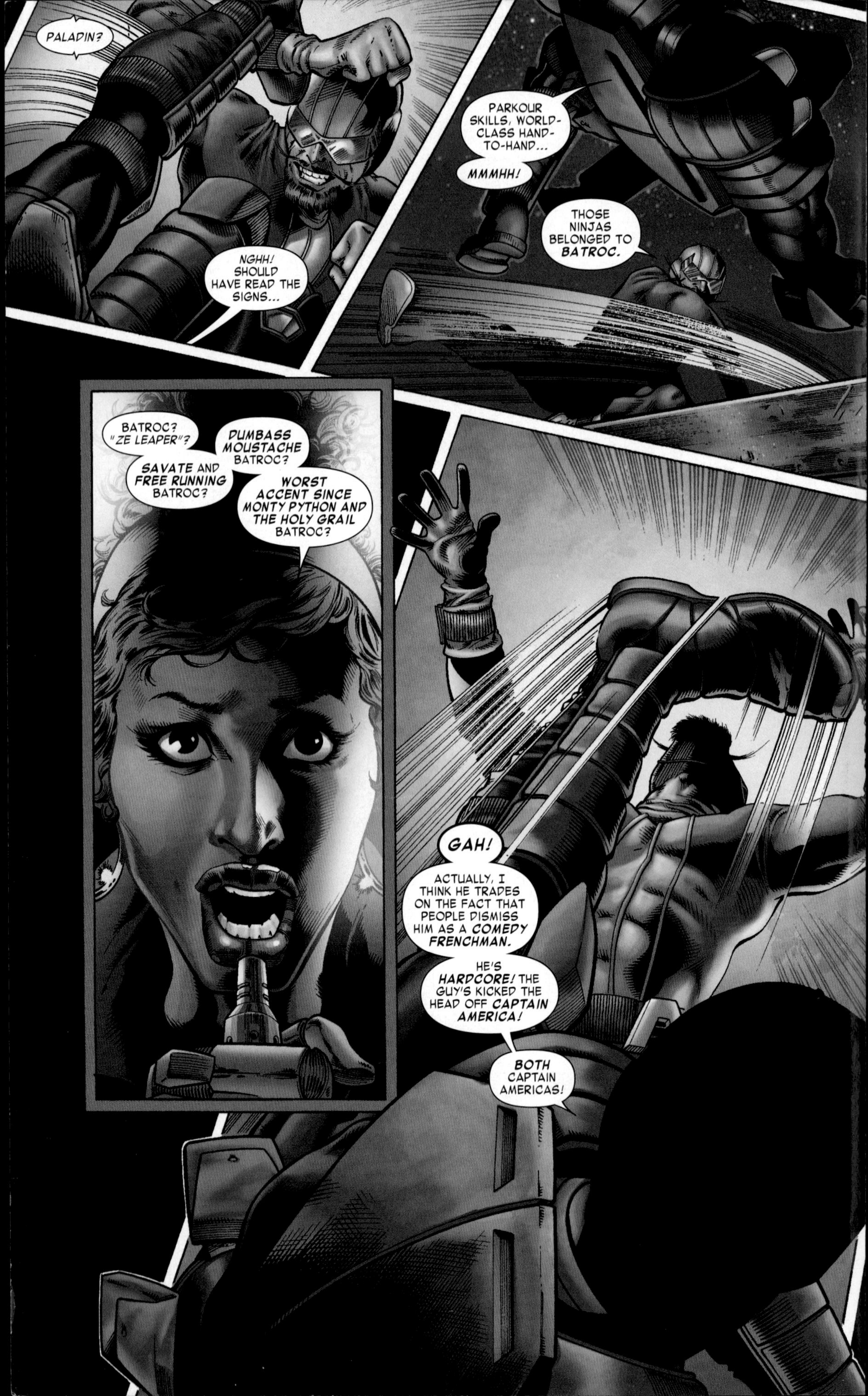
PALADIN?
NGHH! SHOULD HAVE READ THE SIGNS...
PARKOUR SKILLS, WORLD-CLASS HAND-TO-HAND...
MMMHH!
THOSE NINJAS BELONGED TO BATROC.
BATROC? "ZE LEAPER"?
SAVATE AND FREE RUNNING BATROC?
DUMBASS MOUSTACHE BATROC?
WORST ACCENT SINCE MONTY PYTHON AND THE HOLY GRAIL BATROC?
GAH!
ACTUALLY, I THINK HE TRADES ON THE FACT THAT PEOPLE DISMISS HIM AS A COMEDY FRENCHMAN.
HE'S HARDCORE! THE GUY'S KICKED THE HEAD OFF CAPTAIN AMERICA!
BOTH CAPTAIN AMERICAS!

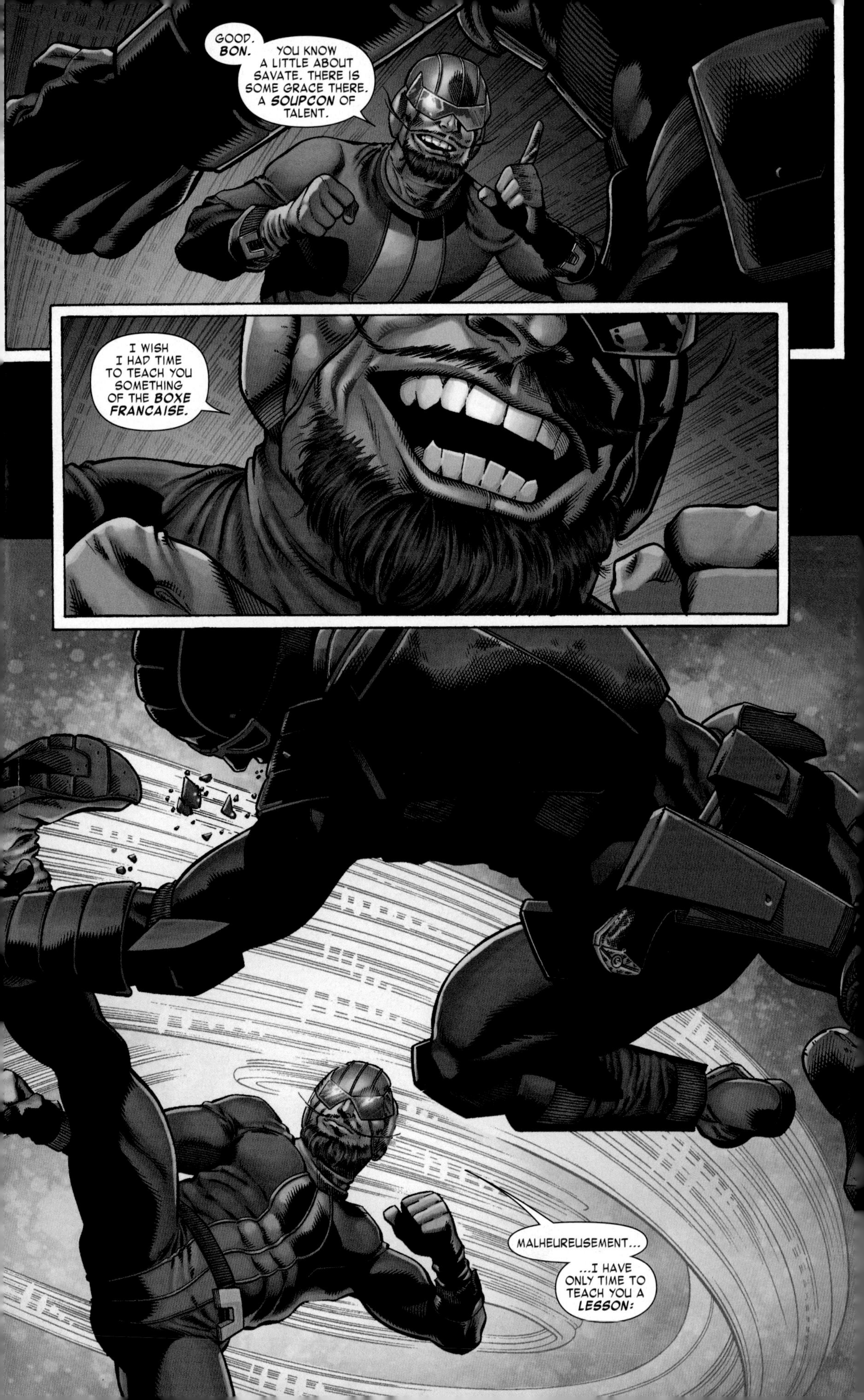
GOOD. BON.
YOU KNOW A LITTLE ABOUT SAVATE. THERE IS SOME GRACE THERE. A SOUPCON OF TALENT.
I WISH I HAD TIME TO TEACH YOU SOMETHING OF THE BOXE FRANCAISE.
MALHEUREUSEMENT...
...I HAVE ONLY TIME TO TEACH YOU A LESSON:

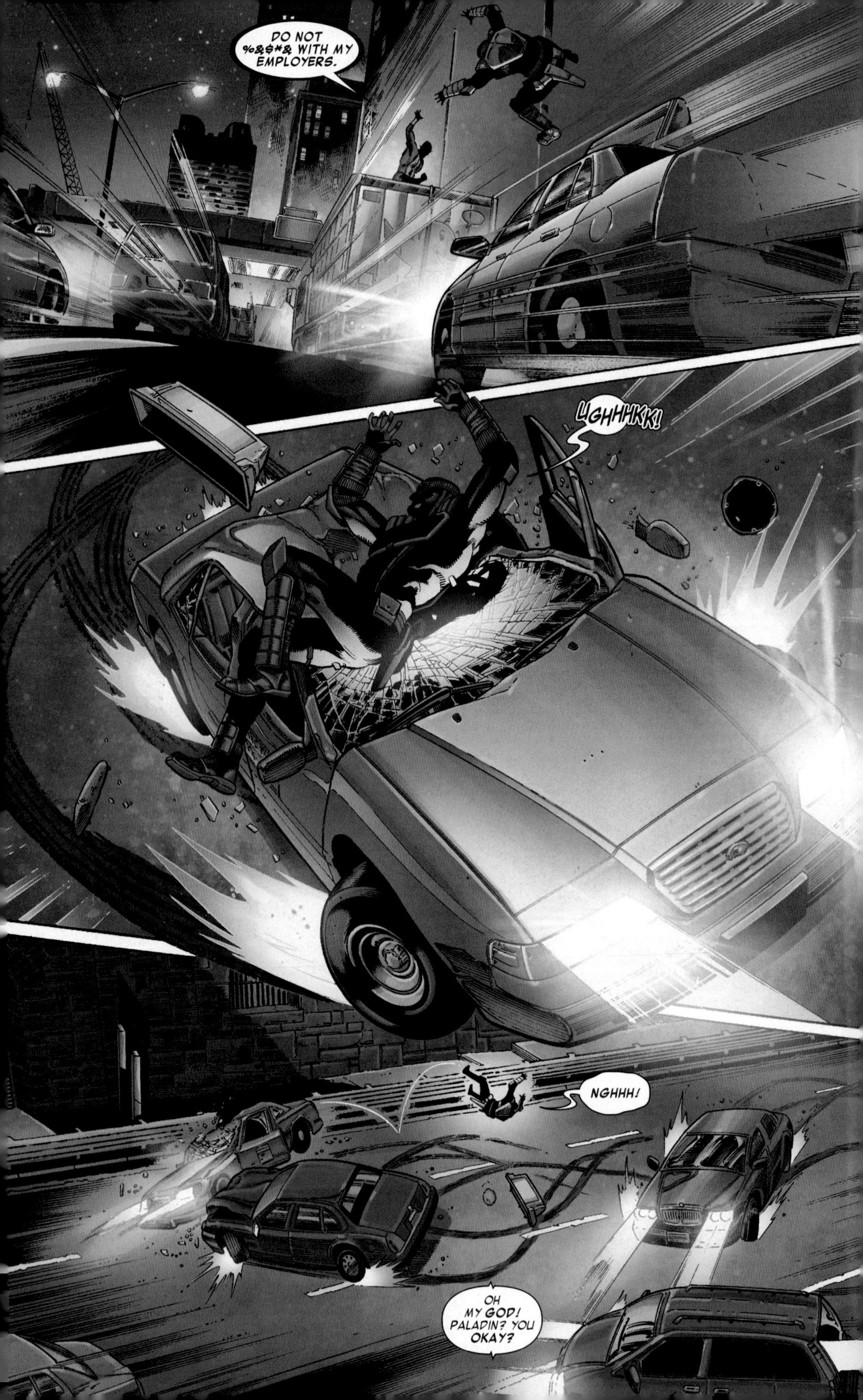
DO NOT %&$*& WITH MY EMPLOYERS.
UGHHHKK!
NGHHH!
OH MY GOD! PALADIN? YOU OKAY?

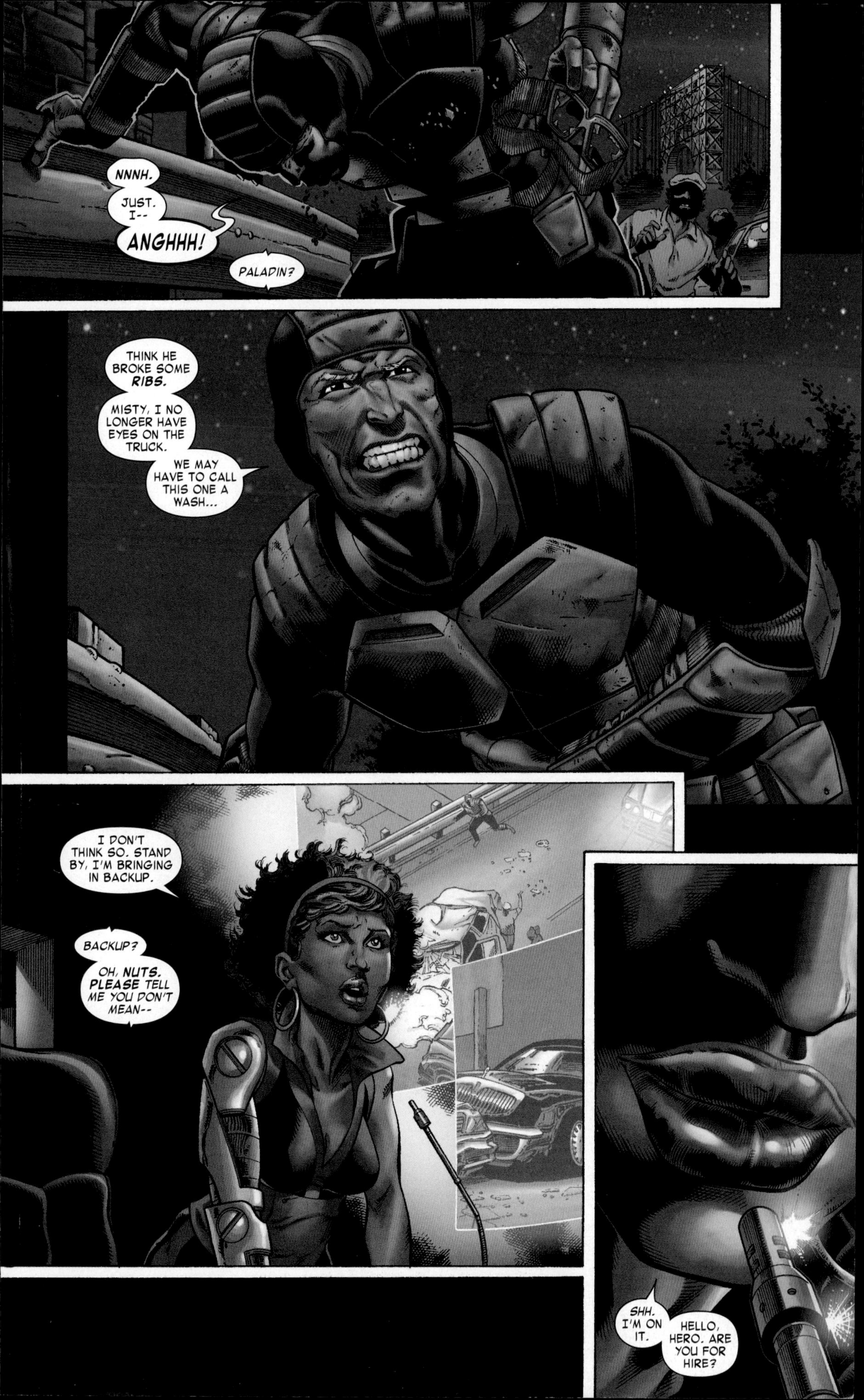
NNNH.
JUST. I--
ANGHHH!
PALADIN?
THINK HE BROKE SOME RIBS.
MISTY, I NO LONGER HAVE EYES ON THE TRUCK.
WE MAY HAVE TO CALL THIS ONE A WASH...
I DON'T THINK SO. STAND BY, I'M BRINGING IN BACKUP.
BACKUP?
OH, NUTS. PLEASE TELL ME YOU DON'T MEAN--
SHH. I'M ON IT.
HELLO, HERO. ARE YOU FOR HIRE?

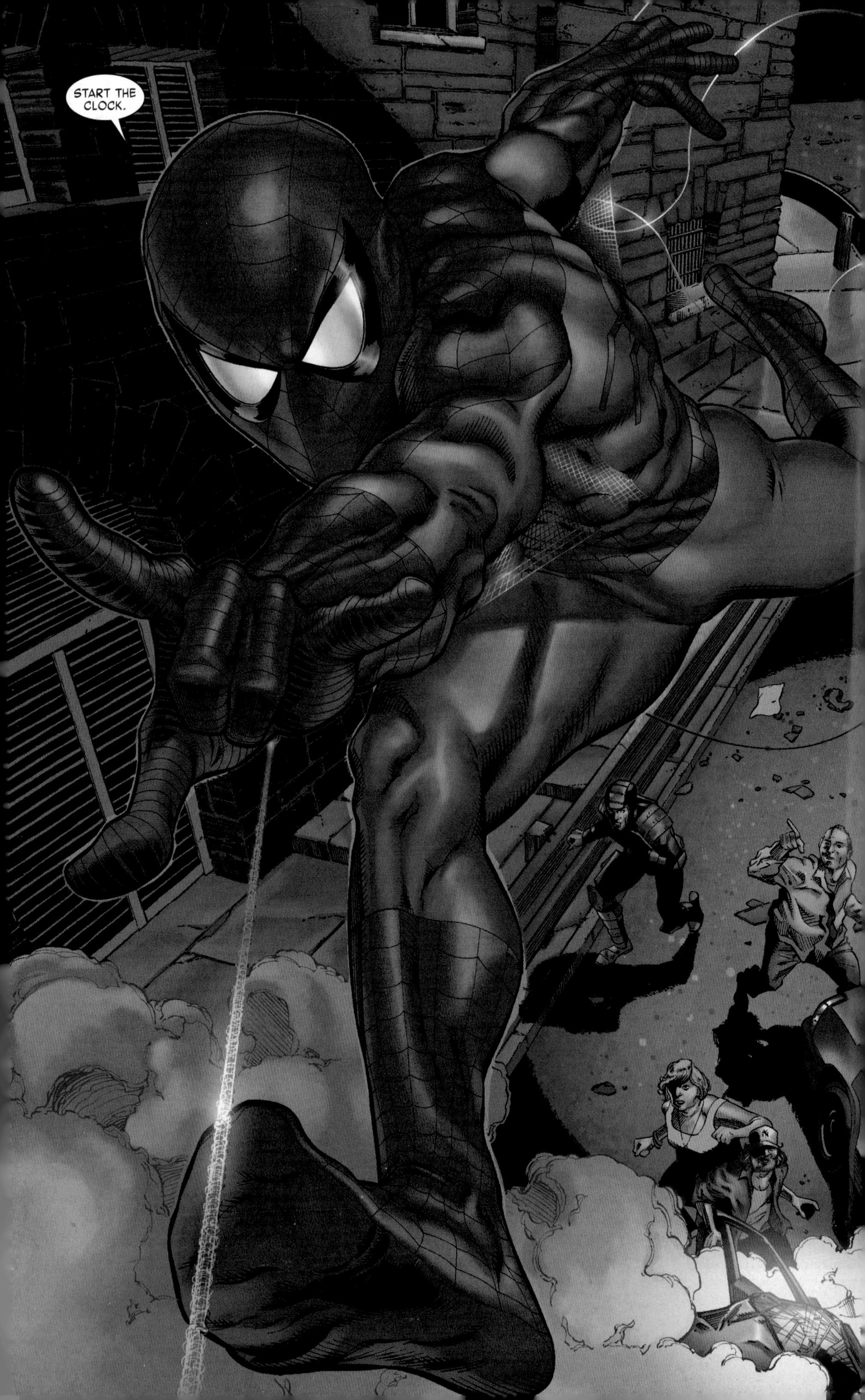
START THE CLOCK.

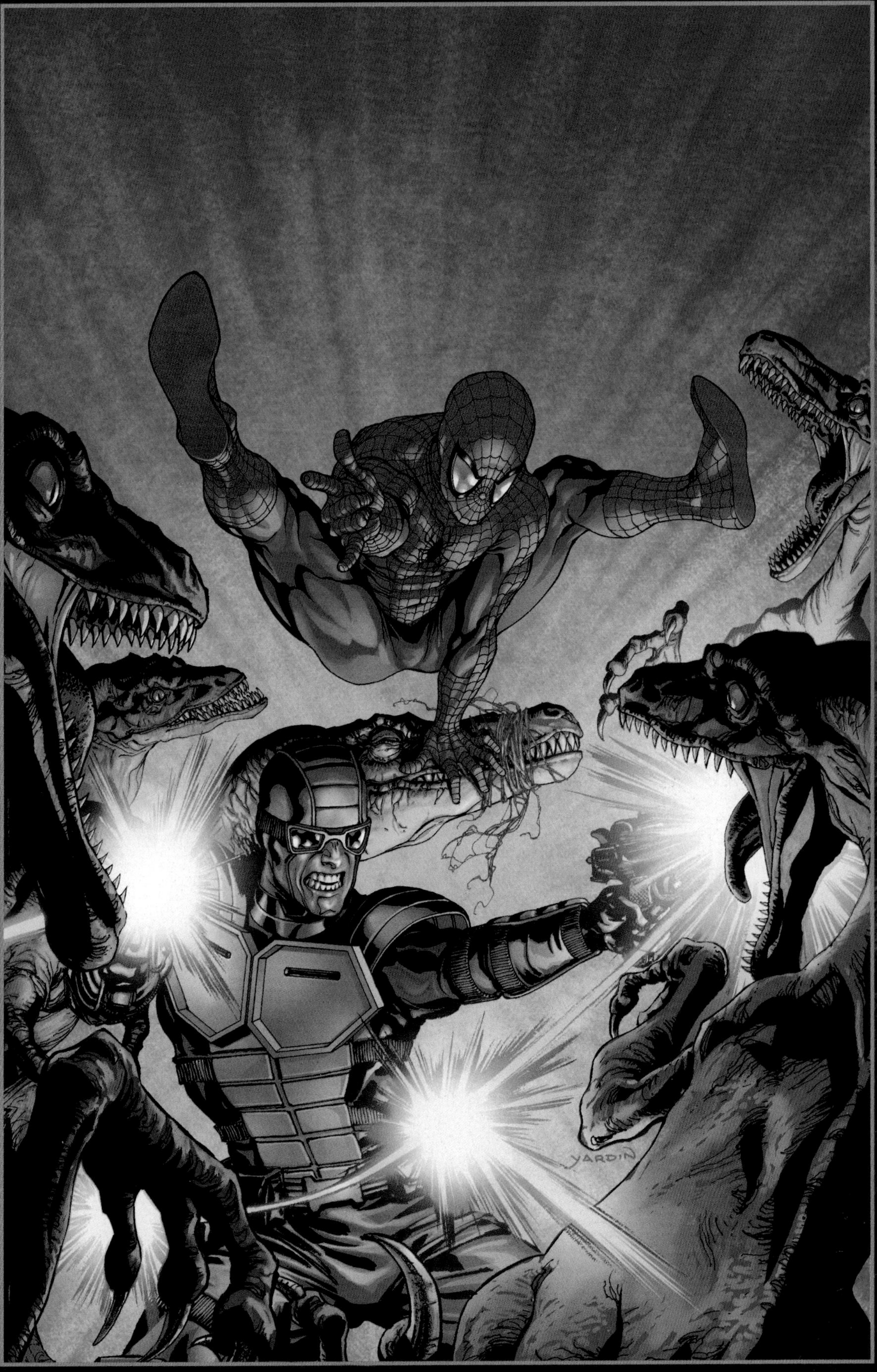
YARDIN

HEROES FOR HIRE #7

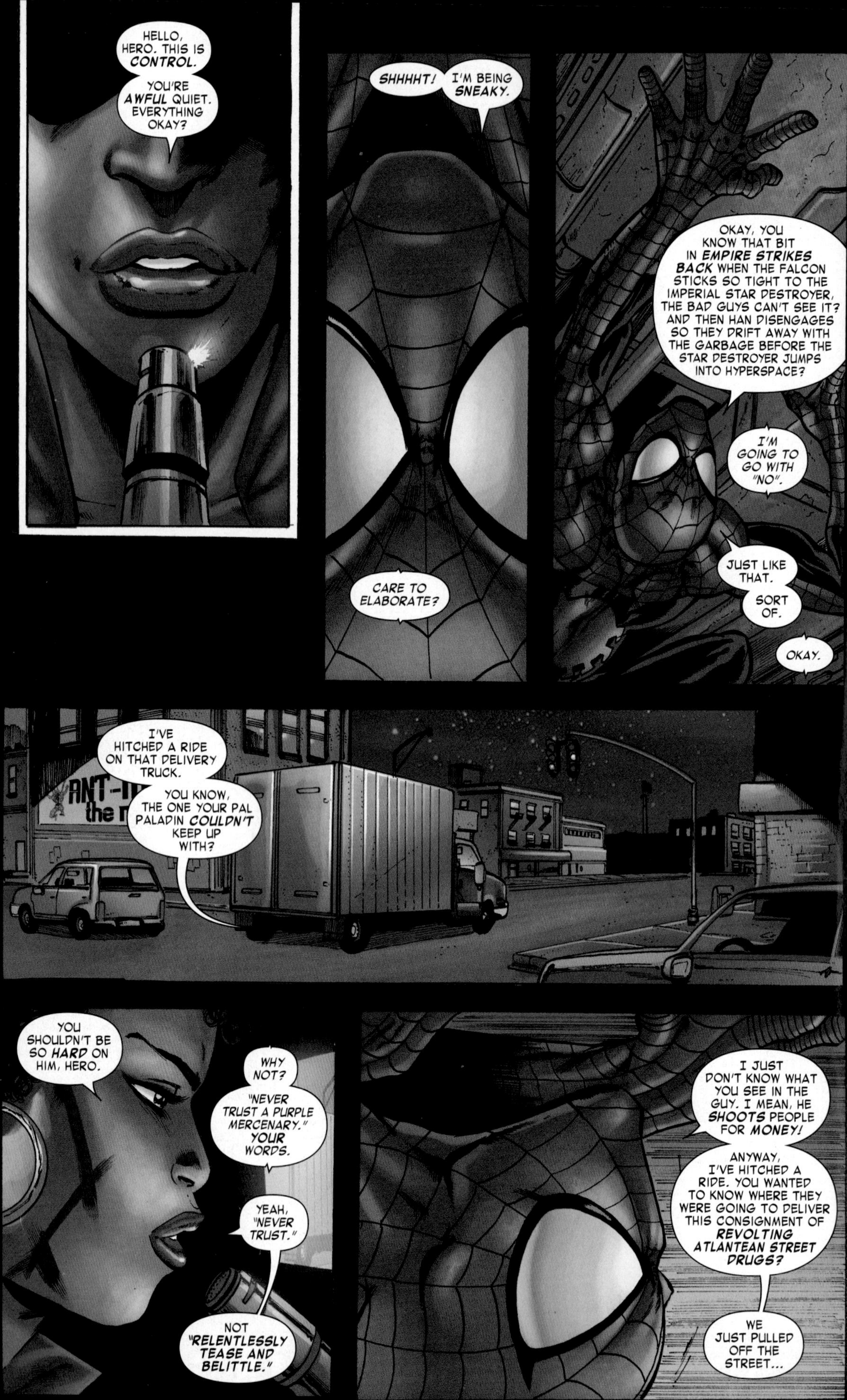
HELLO, HERO. THIS IS CONTROL.
YOU'RE AWFUL QUIET. EVERYTHING OKAY?
SHHHHT!
I'M BEING SNEAKY.
CARE TO ELABORATE?
OKAY, YOU KNOW THAT BIT IN EMPIRE STRIKES BACK WHEN THE FALCON STICKS SO TIGHT TO THE IMPERIAL STAR DESTROYER, THE BAD GUYS CAN'T SEE IT? AND THEN HAN DISENGAGES SO THEY DRIFT AWAY WITH THE GARBAGE BEFORE THE STAR DESTROYER JUMPS INTO HYPERSPACE?
I'M GOING TO GO WITH "NO".
JUST LIKE THAT.
SORT OF.
OKAY.
I'VE HITCHED A RIDE ON THAT DELIVERY TRUCK.
YOU KNOW, THE ONE YOUR PAL PALADIN COULDN'T KEEP UP WITH?
YOU SHOULDN'T BE SO HARD ON HIM, HERO.
WHY NOT?
"NEVER TRUST A PURPLE MERCENARY." YOUR WORDS.
YEAH, "NEVER TRUST."
NOT "RELENTLESSLY TEASE AND BELITTLE."
I JUST DON'T KNOW WHAT YOU SEE IN THE GUY. I MEAN, HE SHOOTS PEOPLE FOR MONEY!
ANYWAY, I'VE HITCHED A RIDE. YOU WANTED TO KNOW WHERE THEY WERE GOING TO DELIVER THIS CONSIGNMENT OF REVOLTING ATLANTEAN STREET DRUGS?
WE JUST PULLED OFF THE STREET...

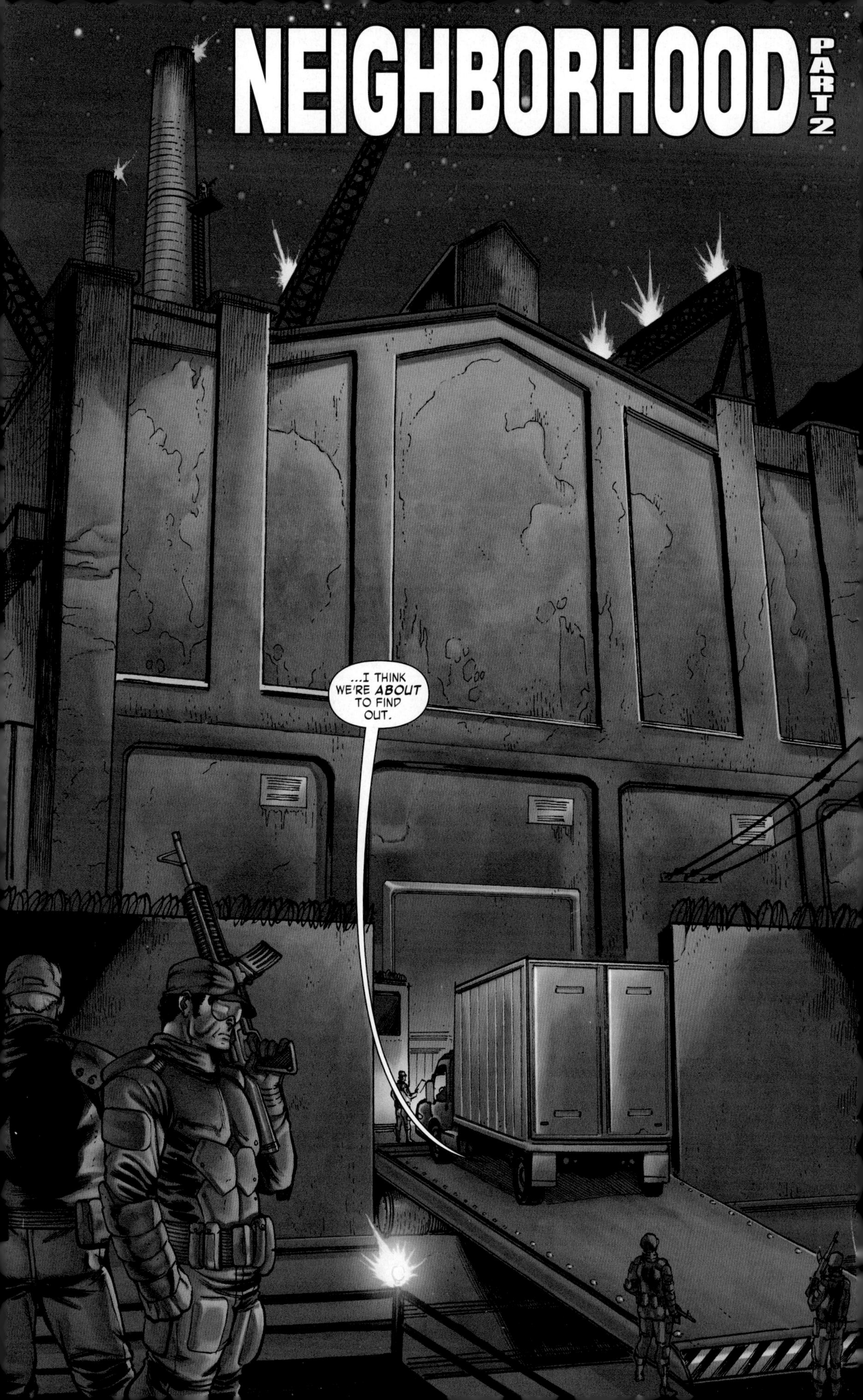
NEIGHBORHOOD PART 2
...I THINK WE'RE ABOUT TO FIND OUT.

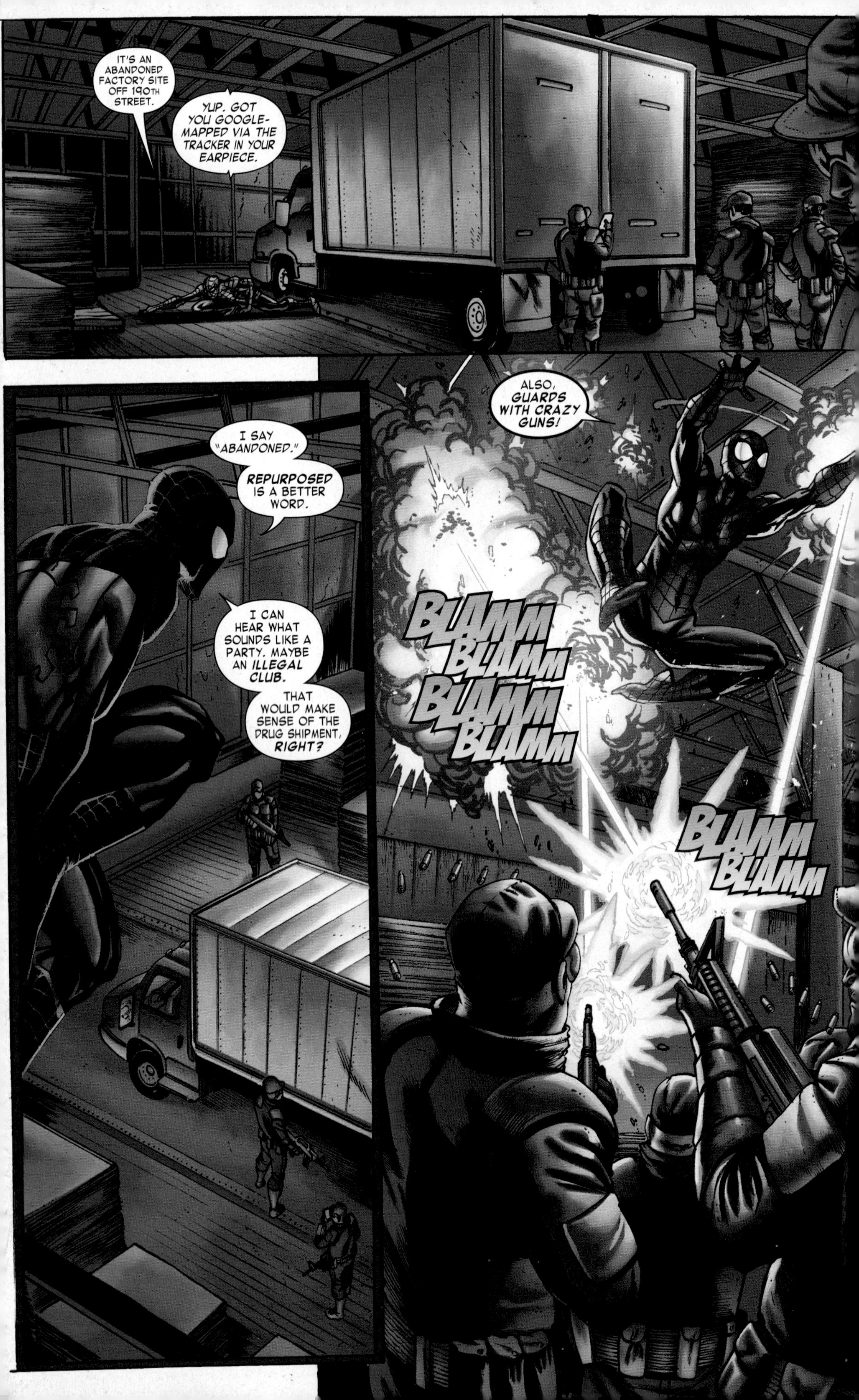
IT'S AN ABANDONED FACTORY SITE OFF 190TH STREET.
YUP. GOT YOU GOOGLE-MAPPED VIA THE TRACKER IN YOUR EARPIECE.
I SAY "ABANDONED."
REPURPOSED IS A BETTER WORD.
I CAN HEAR WHAT SOUNDS LIKE A PARTY. MAYBE AN ILLEGAL CLUB.
THAT WOULD MAKE SENSE OF THE DRUG SHIPMENT, RIGHT?
ALSO, GUARDS WITH CRAZY GUNS!
BLAMM BLAMM BLAMM BLAMM
BLAMM BLAMM

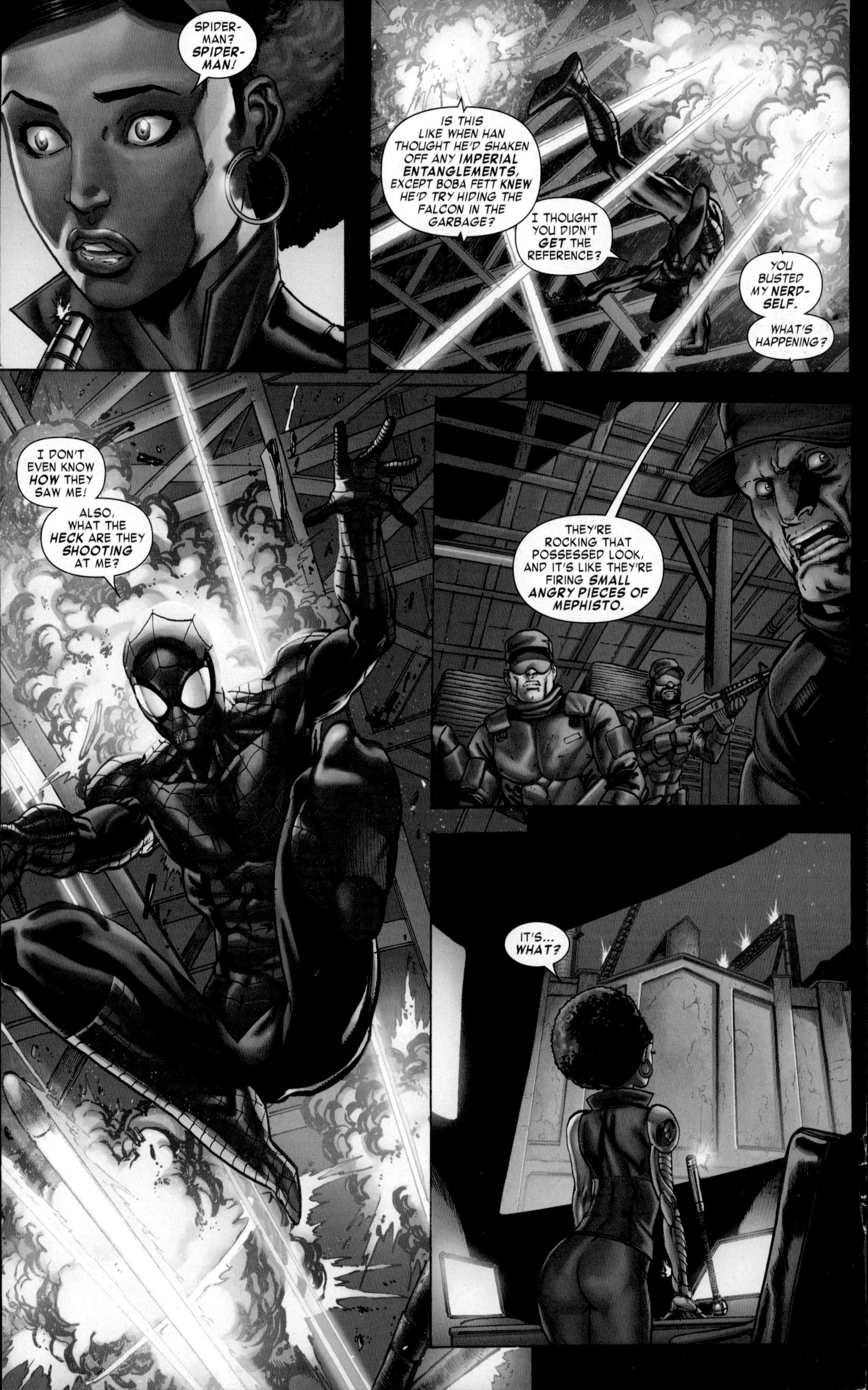
SPIDER-MAN? SPIDER-MAN!
IS THIS LIKE WHEN HAN THOUGHT HE'D SHAKEN OFF ANY IMPERIAL ENTANGLEMENTS, EXCEPT BOBA FETT KNEW HE'D TRY HIDING THE FALCON IN THE GARBAGE?
I THOUGHT YOU DIDN'T GET THE REFERENCE?
YOU BUSTED MY NERD-SELF.
WHAT'S HAPPENING?
I DON'T EVEN KNOW HOW THEY SAW ME!
ALSO, WHAT THE HECK ARE THEY SHOOTING AT ME?
THEY'RE ROCKING THAT POSSESSED LOOK, AND IT'S LIKE THEY'RE FIRING SMALL ANGRY PIECES OF MEPHISTO.
IT'S... WHAT?

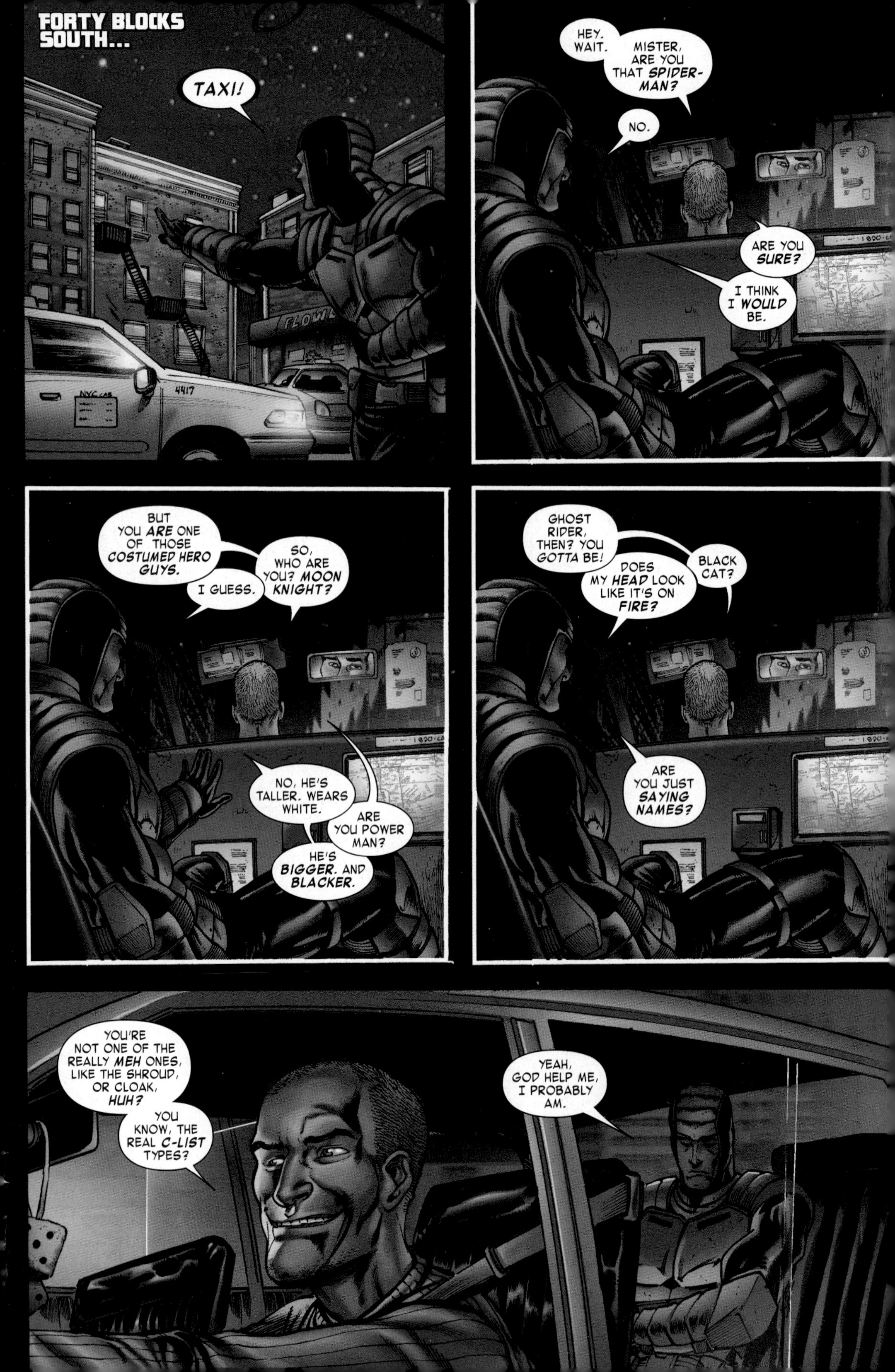
FORTY BLOCKS SOUTH...
TAXI!
HEY. WAIT.
MISTER, ARE YOU THAT SPIDER-MAN?
NO.
ARE YOU SURE?
I THINK I WOULD BE.
BUT YOU ARE ONE OF THOSE COSTUMED HERO GUYS.
I GUESS.
SO, WHO ARE YOU? MOON KNIGHT?
NO, HE'S TALLER. WEARS WHITE.
ARE YOU POWER MAN?
HE'S BIGGER. AND BLACKER.
GHOST RIDER, THEN? YOU GOTTA BE!
DOES MY HEAD LOOK LIKE IT'S ON FIRE?
BLACK CAT?
ARE YOU JUST SAYING NAMES?
YOU'RE NOT ONE OF THE REALLY MEH ONES, LIKE THE SHROUD, OR CLOAK, HUH?
YOU KNOW, THE REAL C-LIST TYPES?
YEAH, GOD HELP ME, I PROBABLY AM.

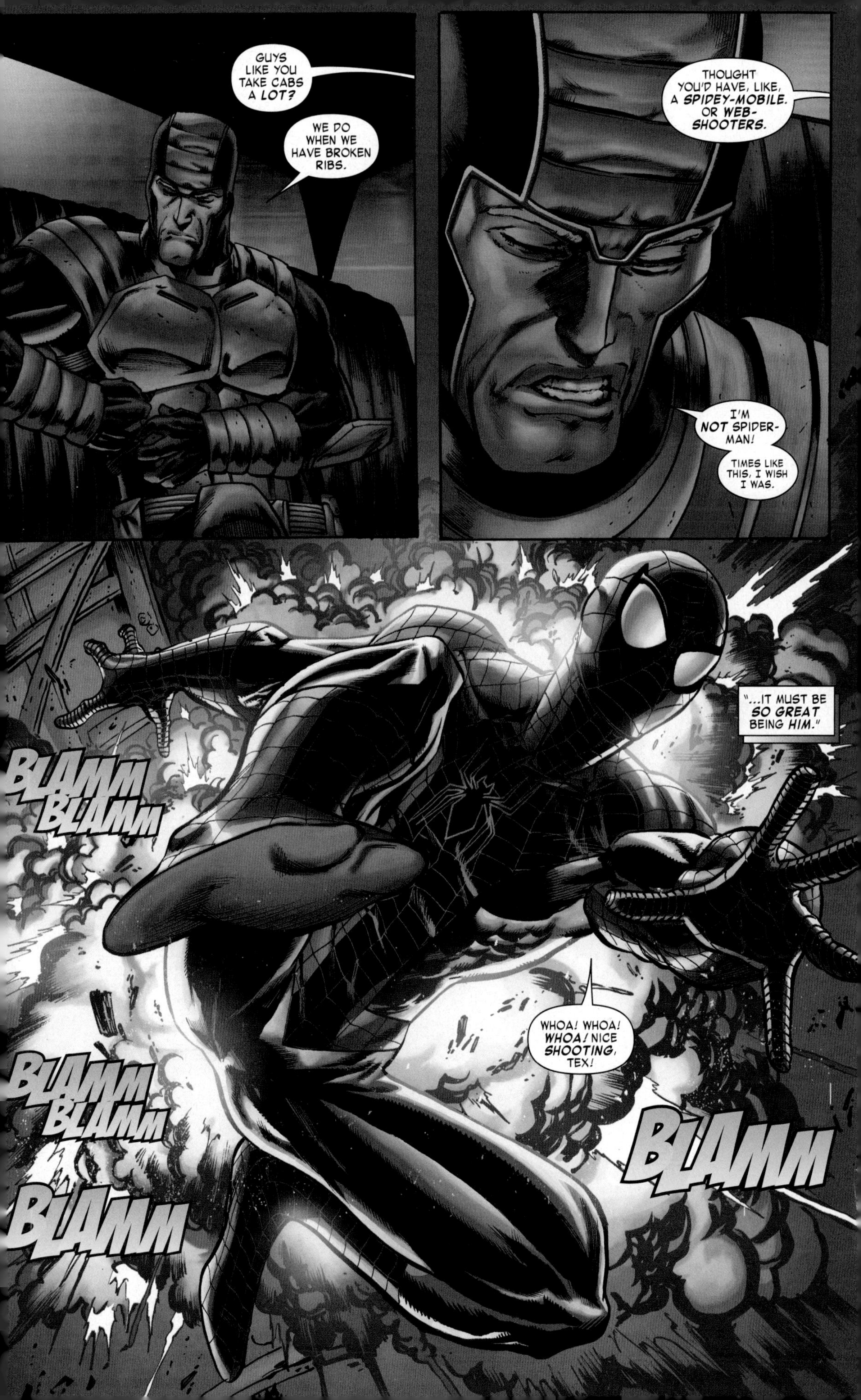
GUYS LIKE YOU TAKE CABS A *LOT?*
WE DO WHEN WE HAVE BROKEN RIBS.
THOUGHT YOU'D HAVE, LIKE, A *SPIDEY-MOBILE.* OR *WEB-SHOOTERS.*
I'M *NOT* SPIDER-MAN!
TIMES LIKE THIS, I WISH I WAS.
"...IT MUST BE *SO GREAT* BEING *HIM.*"
BLAMM BLAMM
WHOA! WHOA! *WHOA!* NICE *SHOOTING,* TEX!
BLAMM BLAMM
BLAMM
BLAMM

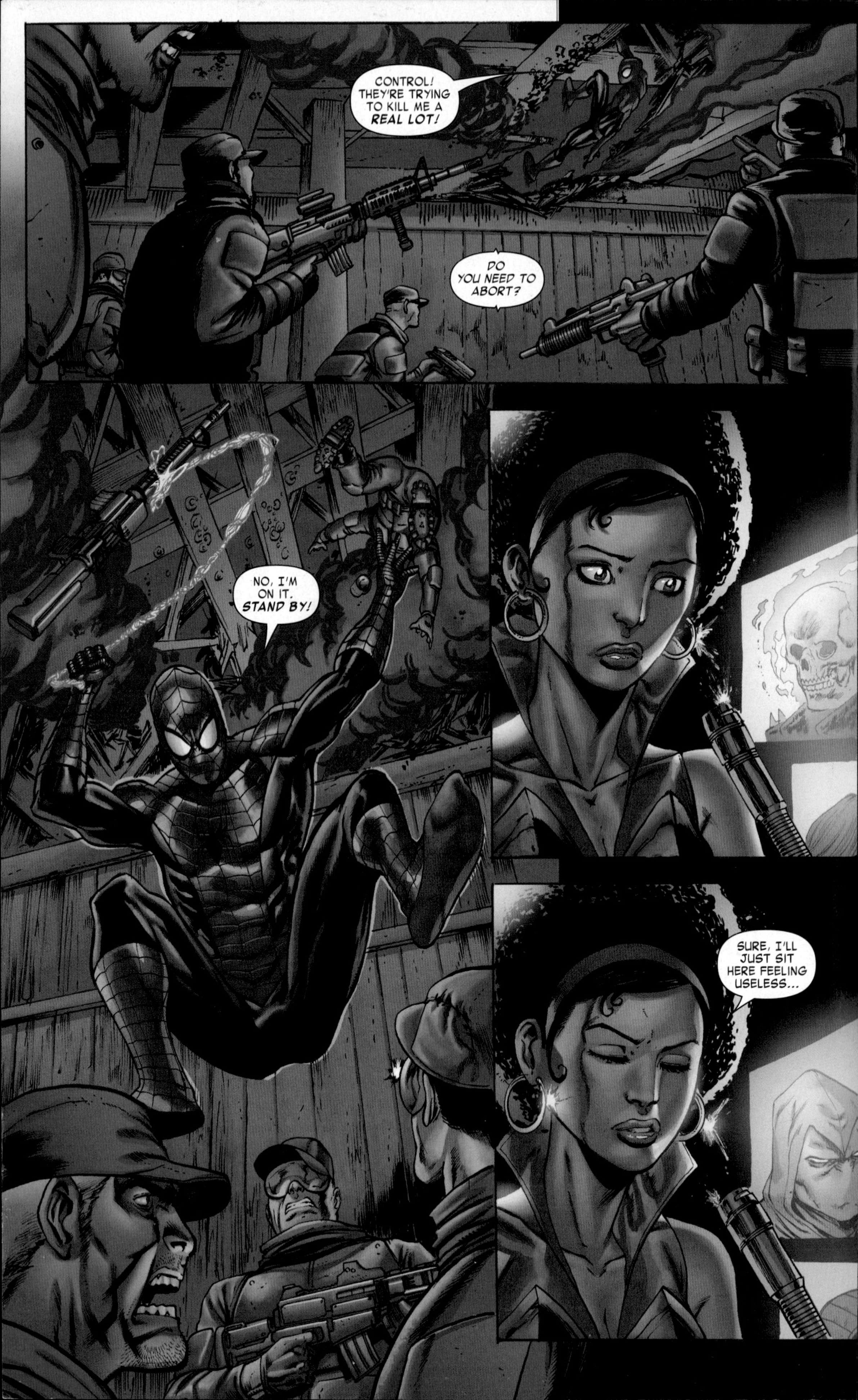
CONTROL! THEY'RE TRYING TO KILL ME A REAL LOT!
DO YOU NEED TO ABORT?
NO, I'M ON IT. STAND BY!
SURE, I'LL JUST SIT HERE FEELING USELESS...

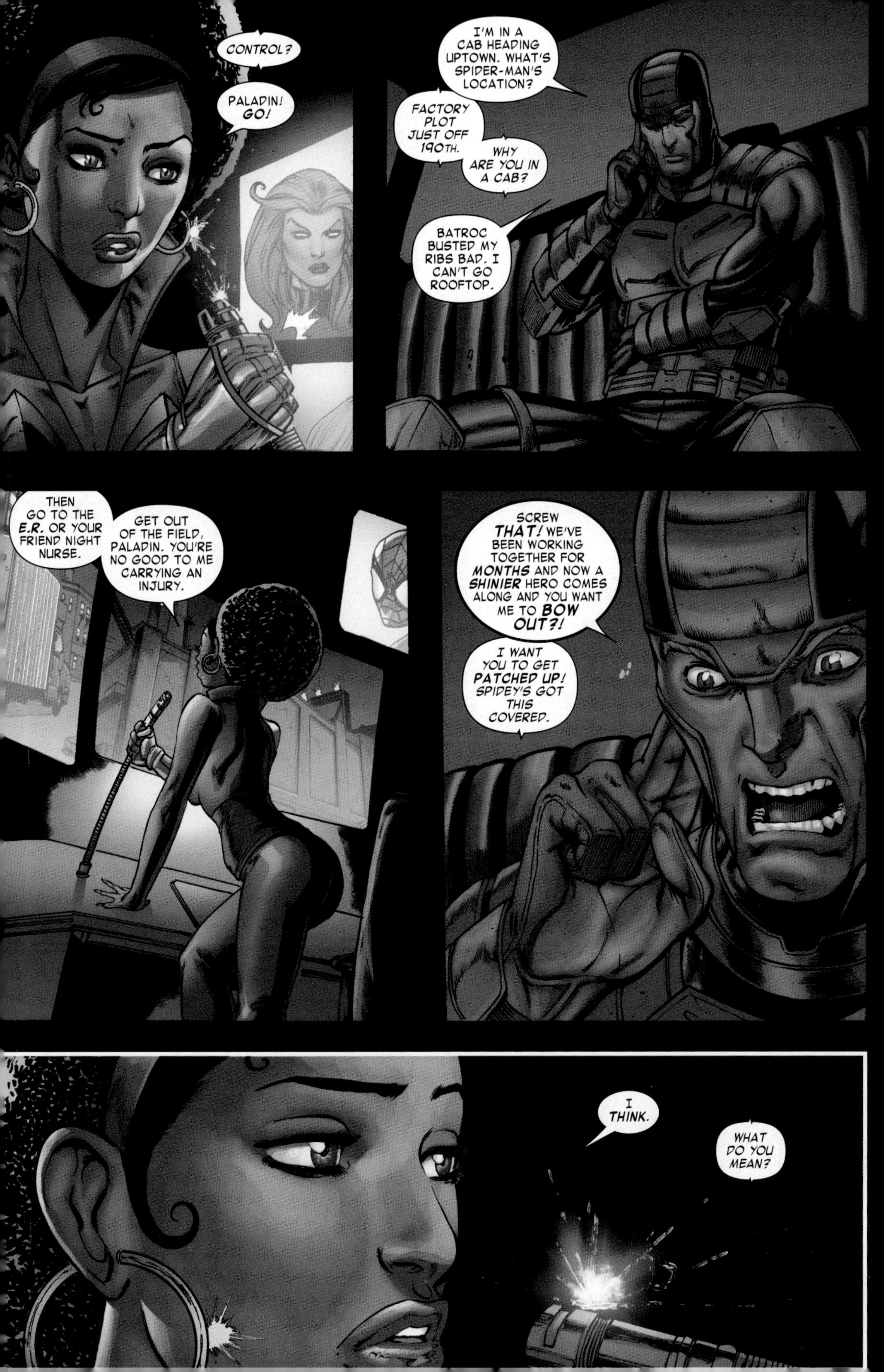
CONTROL?
PALADIN! GO!
I'M IN A CAB HEADING UPTOWN. WHAT'S SPIDER-MAN'S LOCATION?
FACTORY PLOT JUST OFF 190TH.
WHY ARE YOU IN A CAB?
BATROC BUSTED MY RIBS BAD. I CAN'T GO ROOFTOP.
THEN GO TO THE E.R. OR YOUR FRIEND NIGHT NURSE.
GET OUT OF THE FIELD, PALADIN. YOU'RE NO GOOD TO ME CARRYING AN INJURY.
SCREW THAT! WE'VE BEEN WORKING TOGETHER FOR MONTHS AND NOW A SHINIER HERO COMES ALONG AND YOU WANT ME TO BOW OUT?!
I WANT YOU TO GET PATCHED UP! SPIDEY'S GOT THIS COVERED.
I THINK.
WHAT DO YOU MEAN?

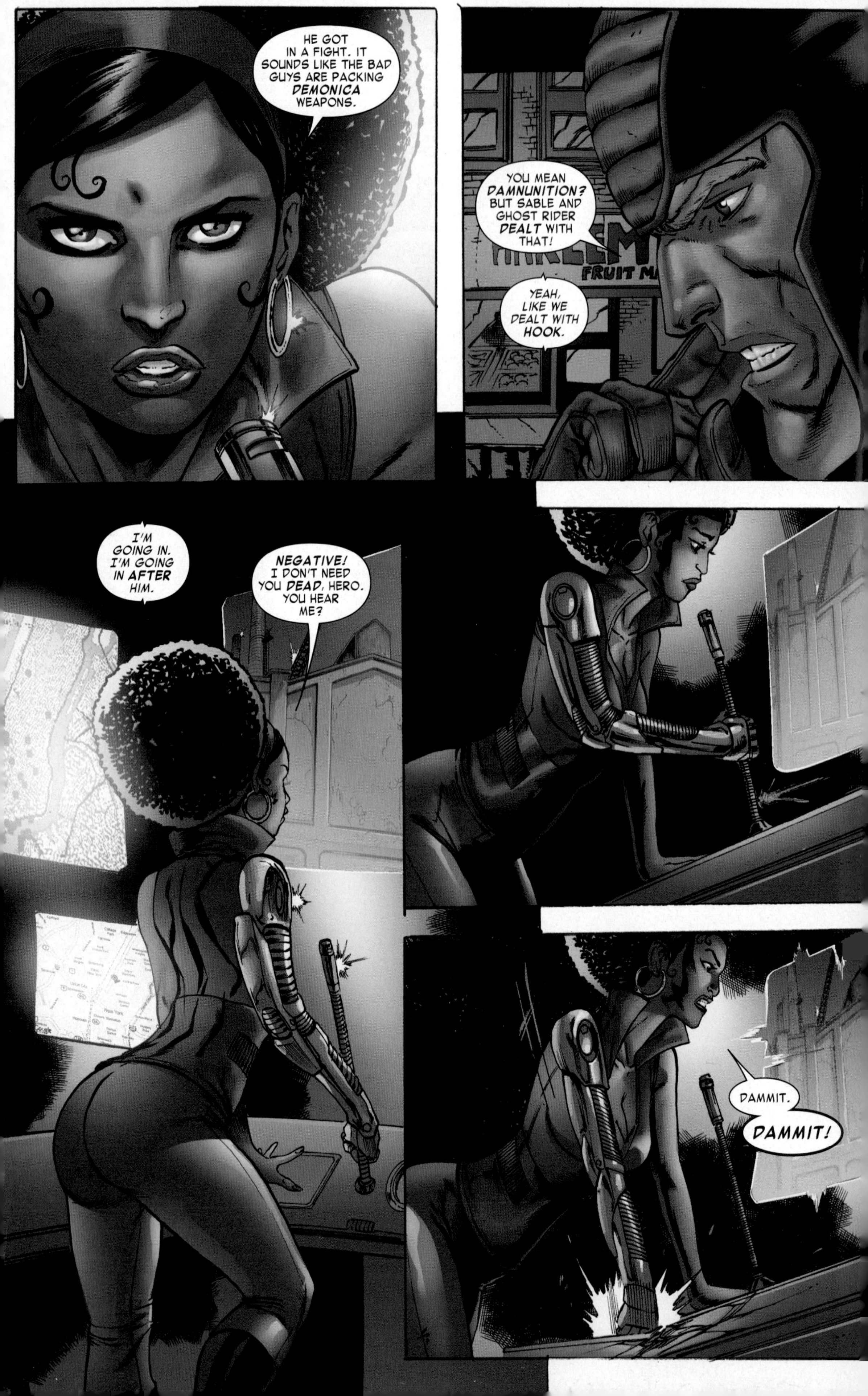
HE GOT IN A FIGHT. IT SOUNDS LIKE THE BAD GUYS ARE PACKING DEMONICA WEAPONS.
YOU MEAN DAMNUNITION? BUT SABLE AND GHOST RIDER DEALT WITH THAT!
FRUIT MA
YEAH, LIKE WE DEALT WITH HOOK.
I'M GOING IN. I'M GOING IN AFTER HIM.
NEGATIVE! I DON'T NEED YOU DEAD, HERO. YOU HEAR ME?
DAMMIT.
DAMMIT!

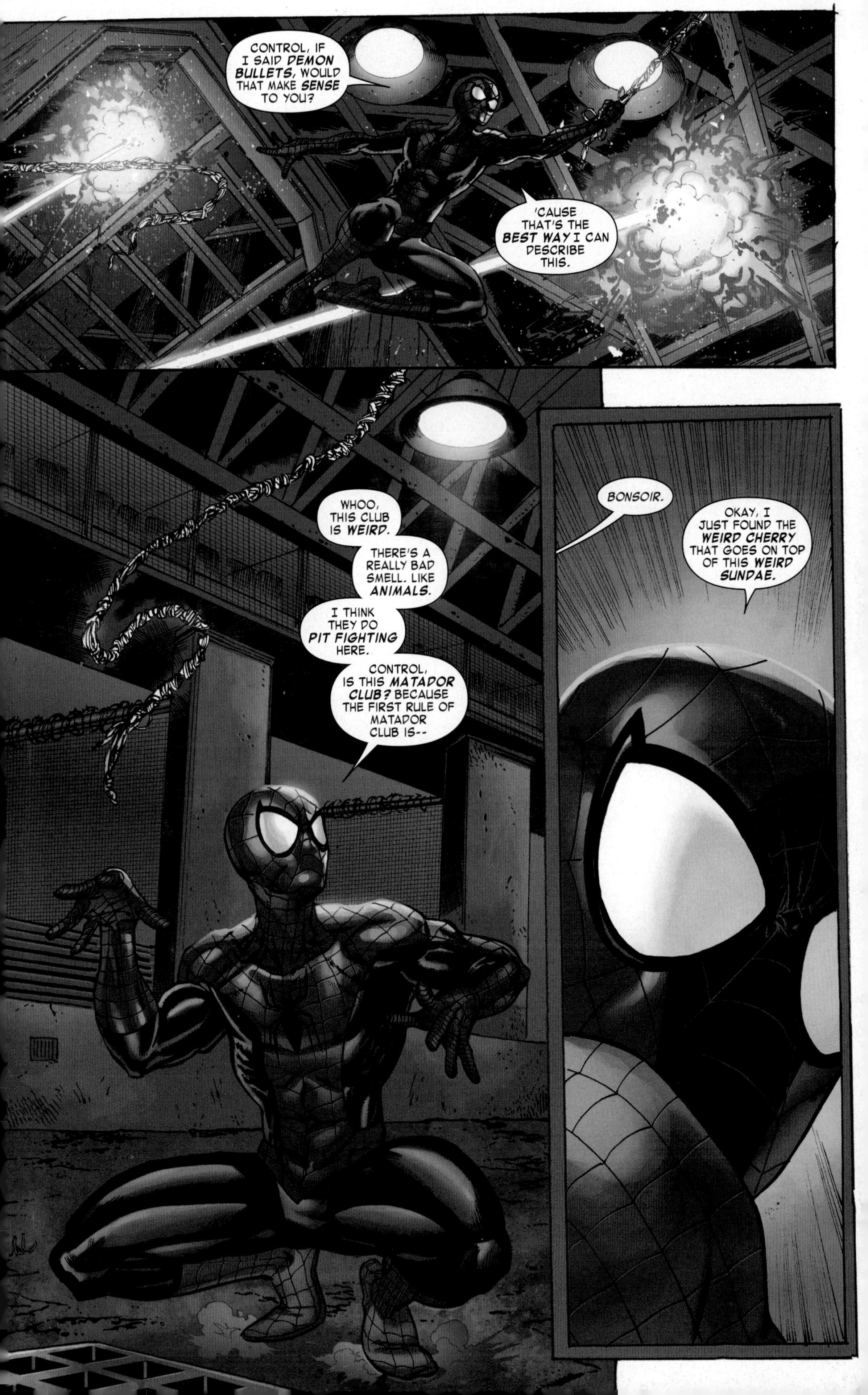

CONTROL, IF I SAID DEMON BULLETS, WOULD THAT MAKE SENSE TO YOU?
'CAUSE THAT'S THE BEST WAY I CAN DESCRIBE THIS.
WHOO, THIS CLUB IS WEIRD.
THERE'S A REALLY BAD SMELL. LIKE ANIMALS.
I THINK THEY DO PIT FIGHTING HERE.
CONTROL, IS THIS MATADOR CLUB? BECAUSE THE FIRST RULE OF MATADOR CLUB IS--
BONSOIR.
OKAY, I JUST FOUND THE WEIRD CHERRY THAT GOES ON TOP OF THIS WEIRD SUNDAE.

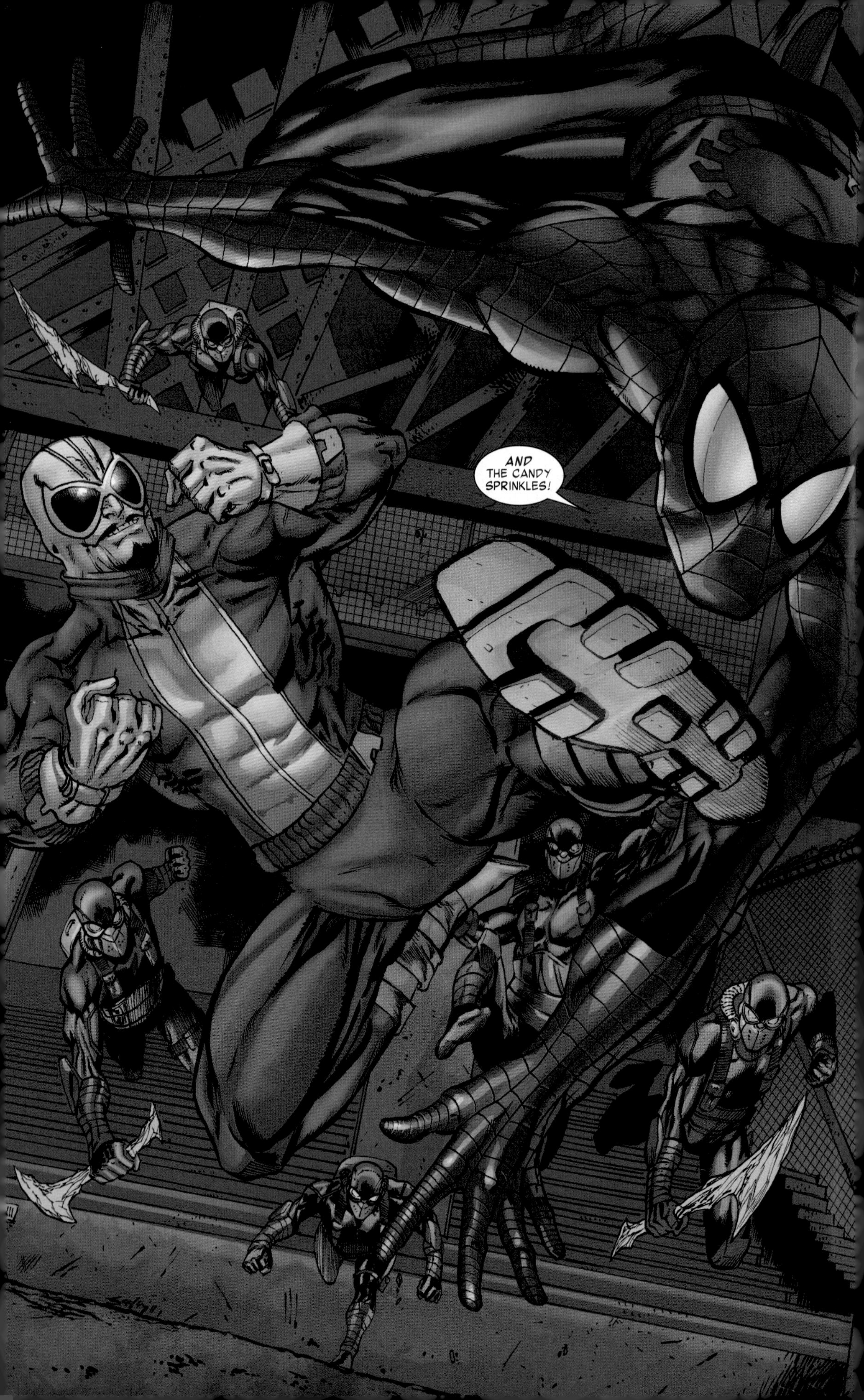
AND THE CANDY SPRINKLES!

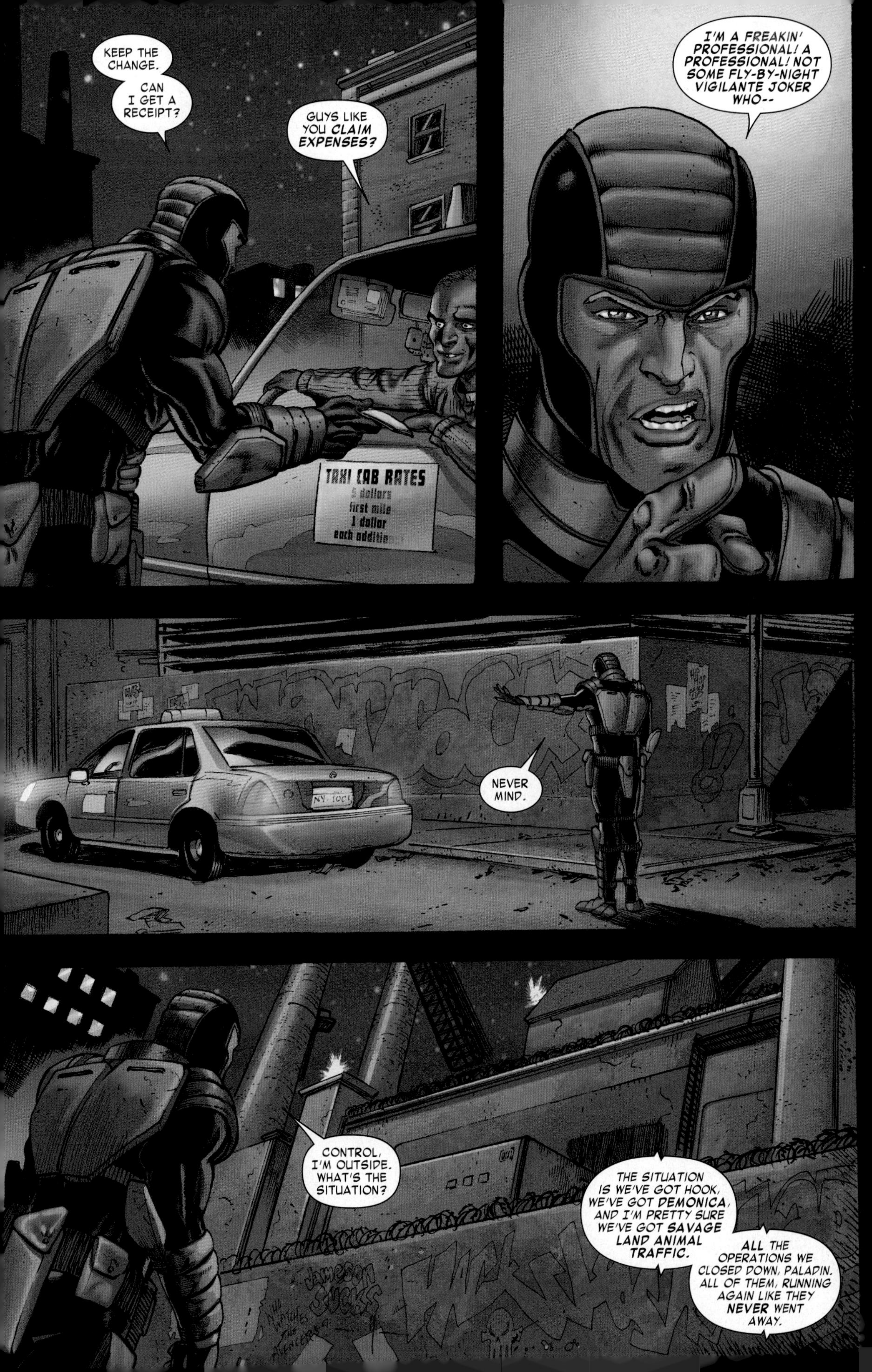
KEEP THE CHANGE.
CAN I GET A RECEIPT?
GUYS LIKE YOU CLAIM EXPENSES?
TAXI CAB RATES
5 dollars
first mile
1 dollar
I'M A FREAKIN' PROFESSIONAL! A PROFESSIONAL! NOT SOME FLY-BY-NIGHT VIGILANTE JOKER WHO--
NEVER MIND.
CONTROL, I'M OUTSIDE. WHAT'S THE SITUATION?
THE SITUATION IS WE'VE GOT HOOK, WE'VE GOT DEMONICA, AND I'M PRETTY SURE WE'VE GOT SAVAGE LAND ANIMAL TRAFFIC.
ALL THE OPERATIONS WE CLOSED DOWN, PALADIN. ALL OF THEM, RUNNING AGAIN LIKE THEY NEVER WENT AWAY.
JAMESON SUCKS

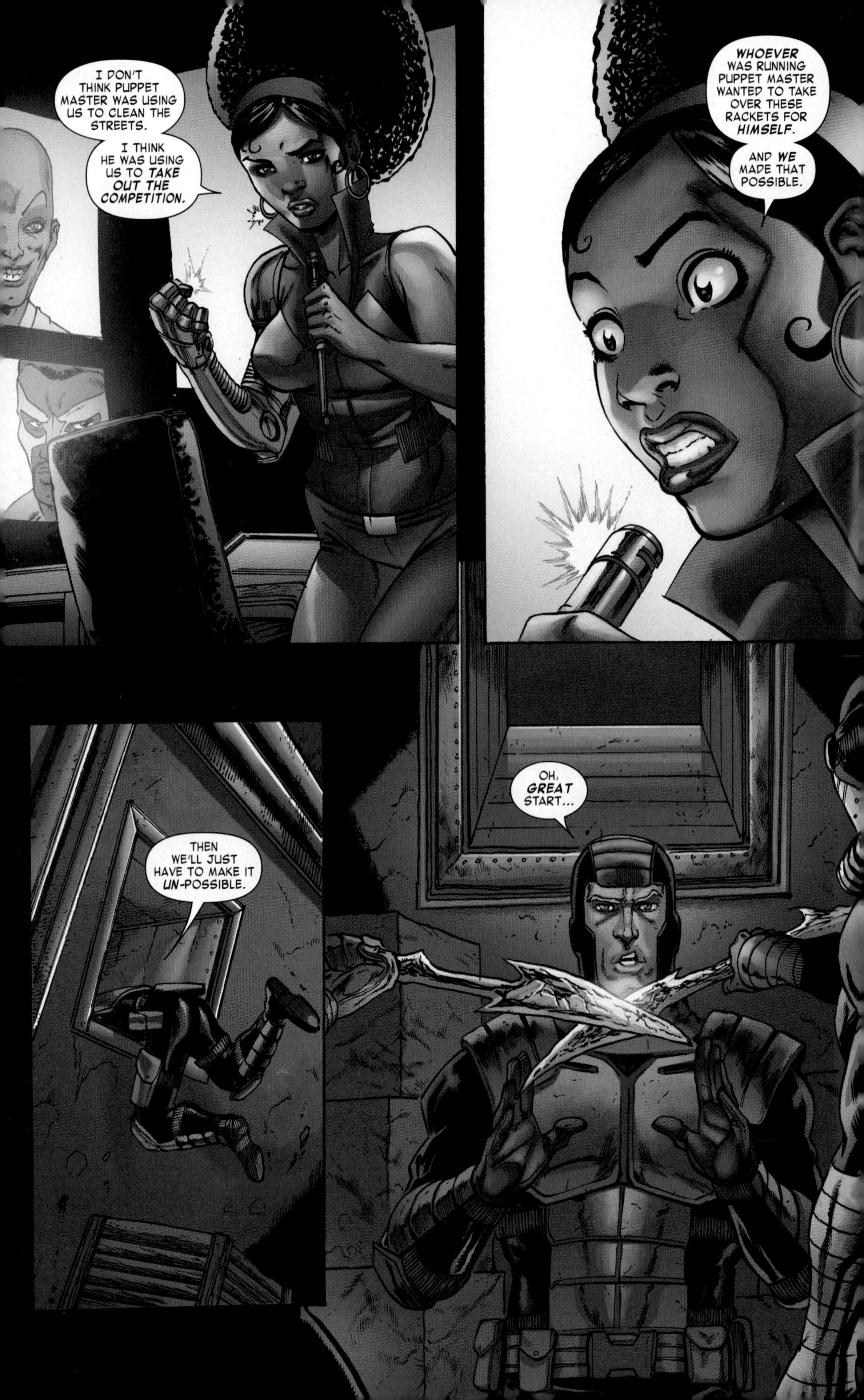
I DON'T THINK PUPPET MASTER WAS USING US TO CLEAN THE STREETS.
I THINK HE WAS USING US TO TAKE OUT THE COMPETITION.
WHOEVER WAS RUNNING PUPPET MASTER WANTED TO TAKE OVER THESE RACKETS FOR HIMSELF.
AND WE MADE THAT POSSIBLE.
THEN WE'LL JUST HAVE TO MAKE IT UN-POSSIBLE.
OH, GREAT START...

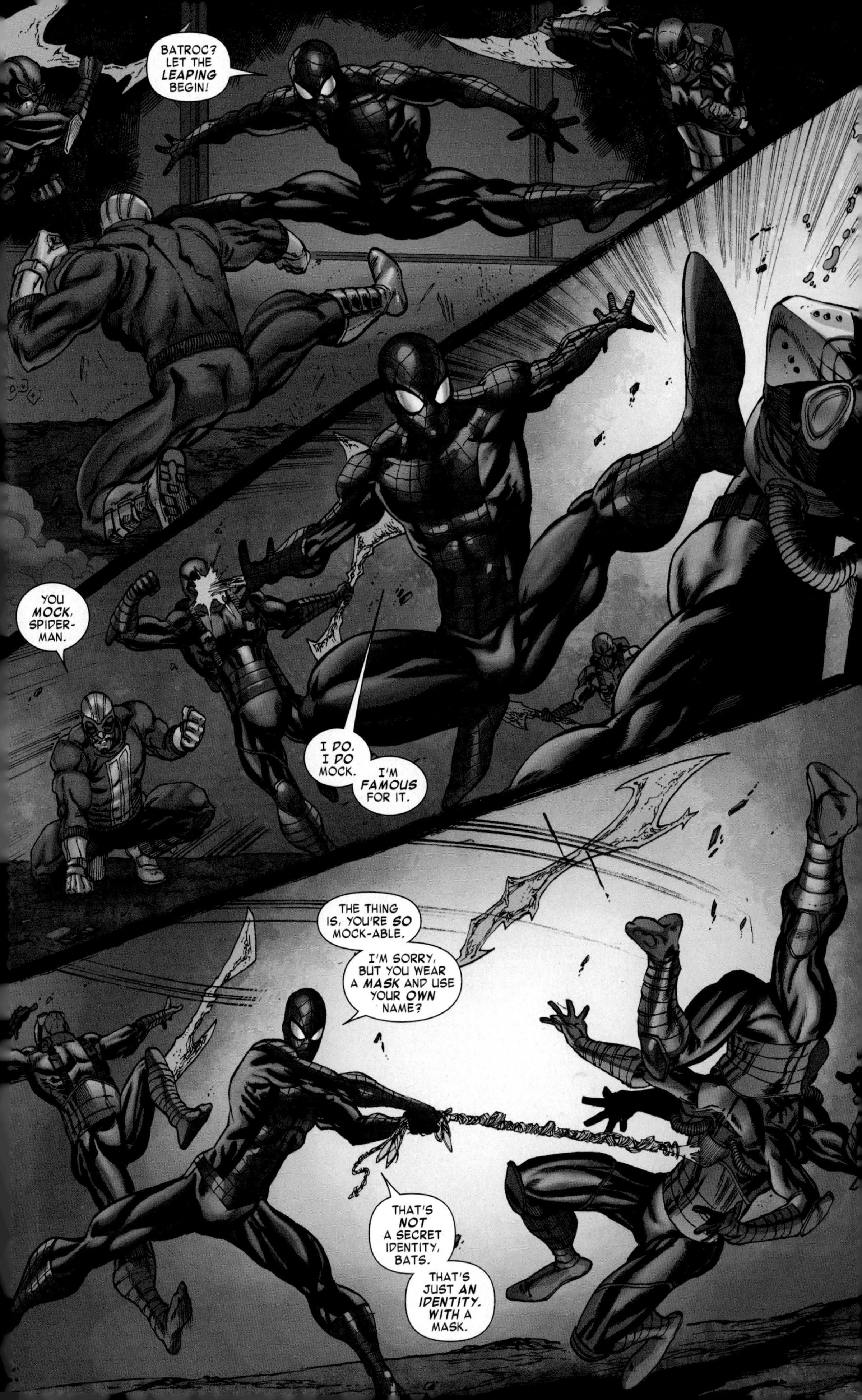
BATROC? LET THE LEAPING BEGIN!
YOU MOCK, SPIDER-MAN.
I DO. I DO MOCK.
I'M FAMOUS FOR IT.
THE THING IS, YOU'RE SO MOCK-ABLE.
I'M SORRY, BUT YOU WEAR A MASK AND USE YOUR OWN NAME?
THAT'S NOT A SECRET IDENTITY, BATS.
THAT'S JUST AN IDENTITY. WITH A MASK.

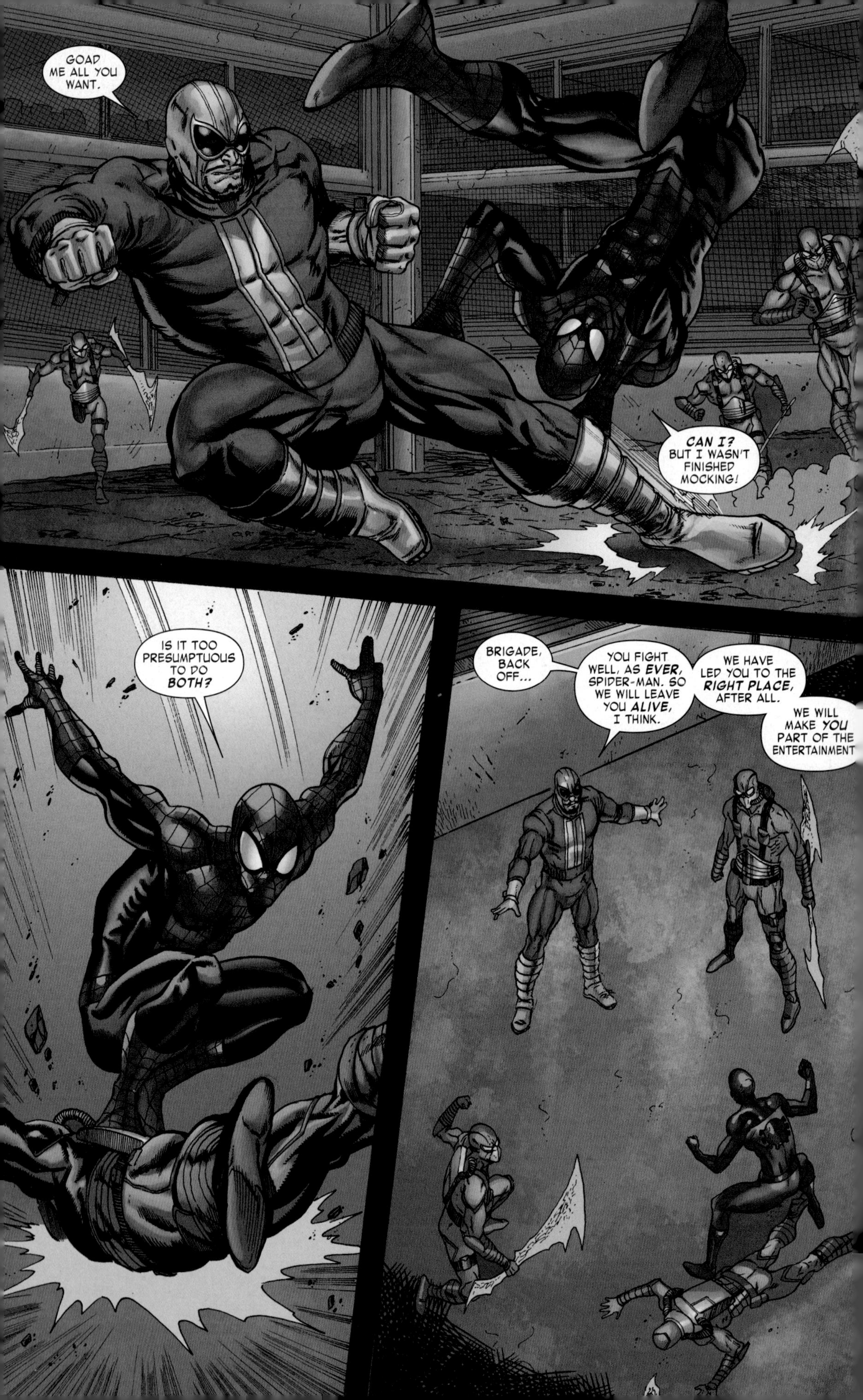
GOAD ME ALL YOU WANT.
CAN I? BUT I WASN'T FINISHED MOCKING!
IS IT TOO PRESUMPTUOUS TO DO BOTH?
BRIGADE, BACK OFF...
YOU FIGHT WELL, AS EVER, SPIDER-MAN. SO WE WILL LEAVE YOU ALIVE, I THINK.
WE HAVE LED YOU TO THE RIGHT PLACE, AFTER ALL.
WE WILL MAKE YOU PART OF THE ENTERTAINMENT

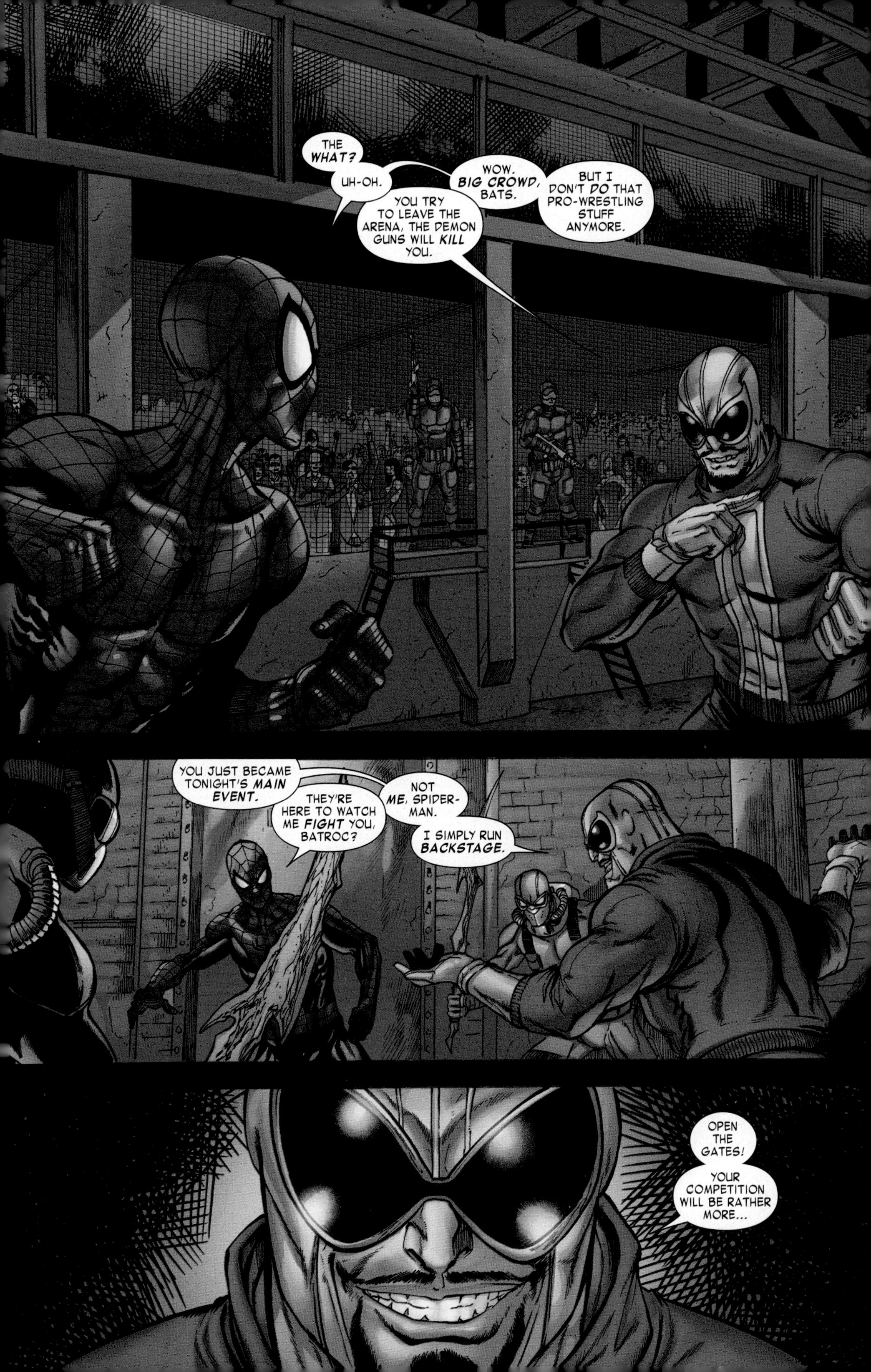
THE *WHAT?*
UH-OH.
YOU TRY TO LEAVE THE ARENA, THE DEMON GUNS WILL *KILL* YOU.
WOW. *BIG CROWD,* BATS.
BUT I DON'T *DO* THAT PRO-WRESTLING STUFF ANYMORE.
YOU JUST BECAME TONIGHT'S *MAIN EVENT.*
THEY'RE HERE TO WATCH ME *FIGHT* YOU, BATROC?
NOT *ME,* SPIDER-MAN.
I SIMPLY RUN *BACKSTAGE.*
OPEN THE GATES!
YOUR COMPETITION WILL BE RATHER MORE...

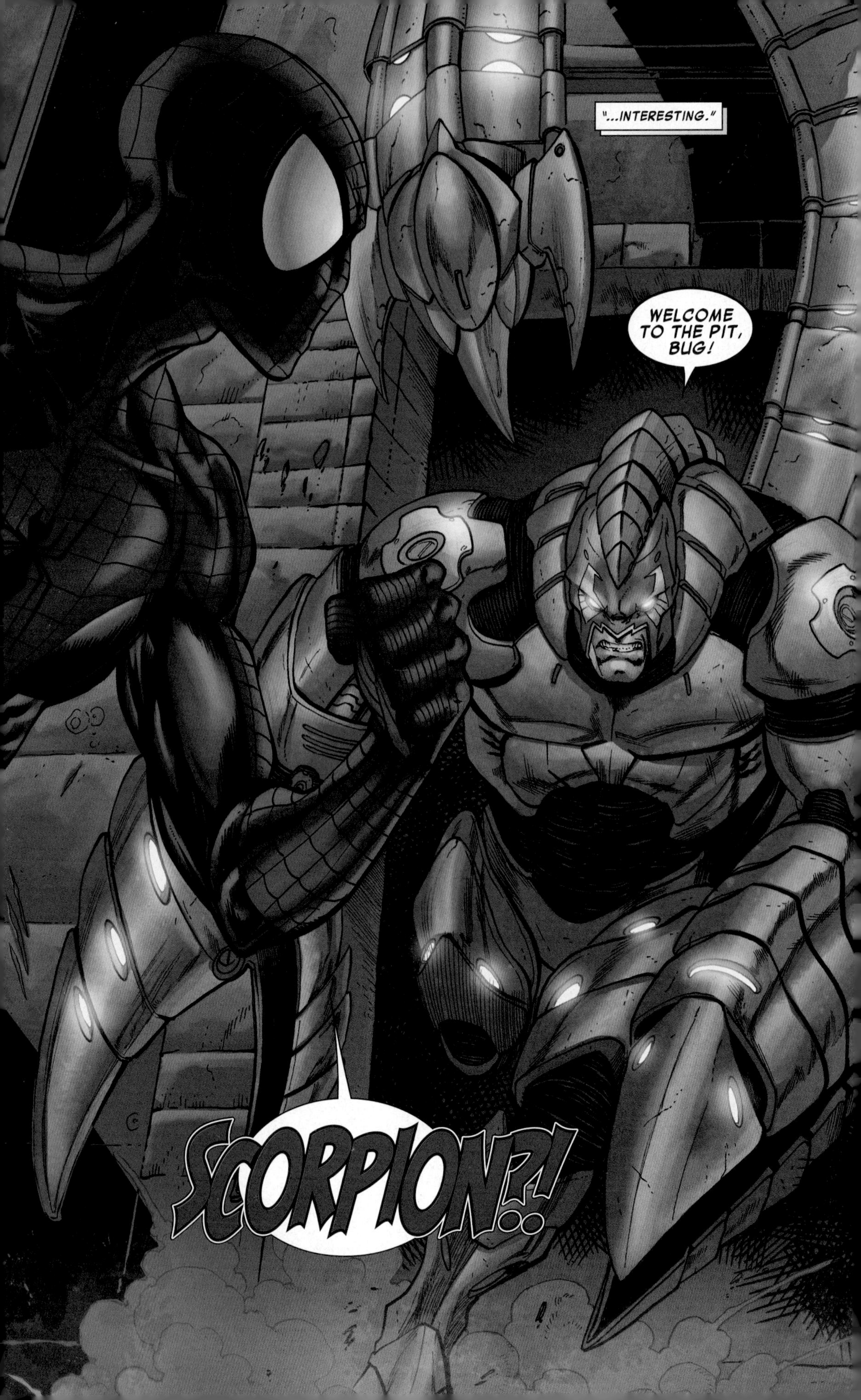
"...INTERESTING."
WELCOME TO THE PIT, BUG!
SCORPION?!

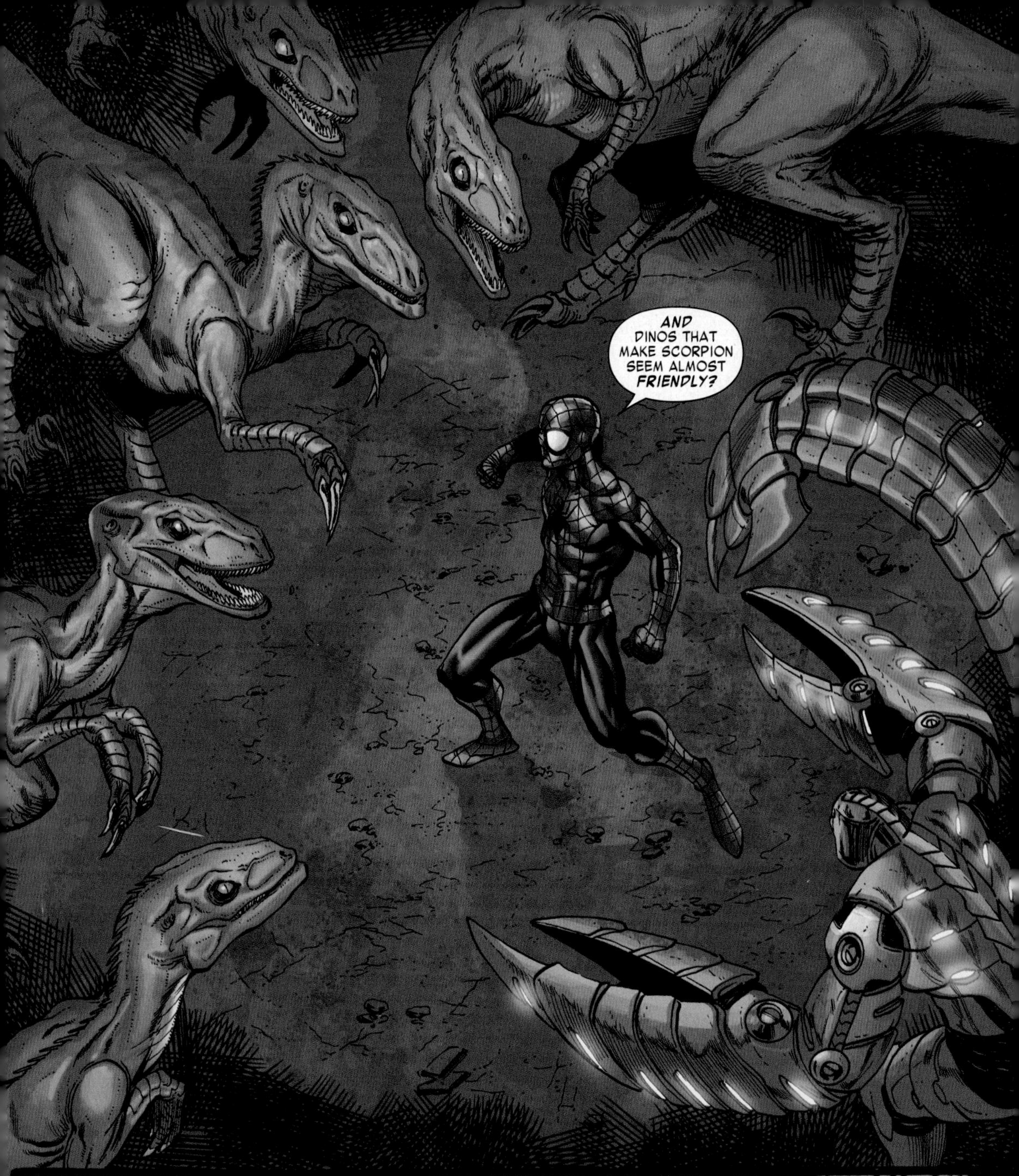
AND DINOS THAT MAKE SCORPION SEEM ALMOST FRIENDLY?

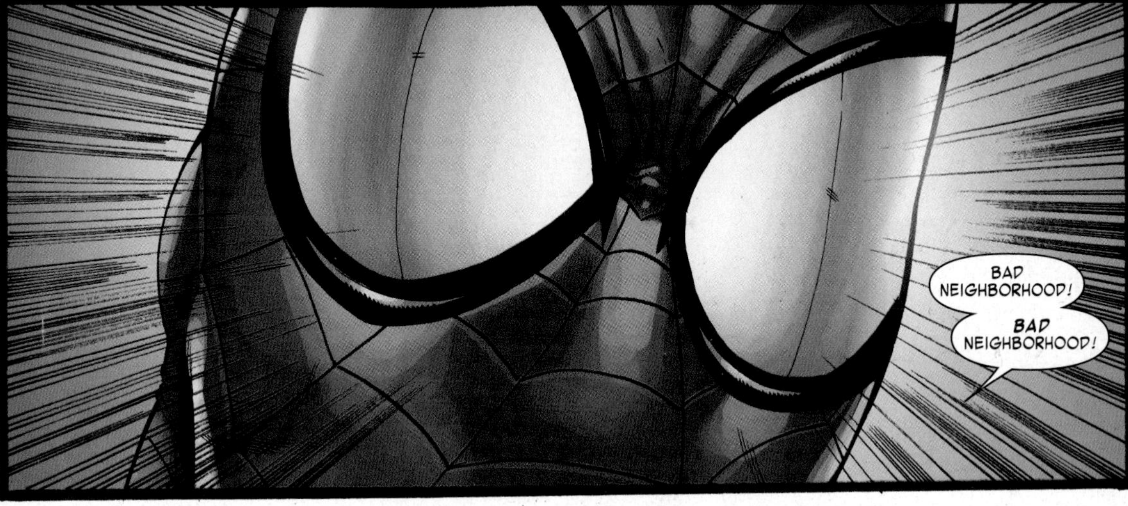
BAD NEIGHBORHOOD!
BAD NEIGHBORHOOD!

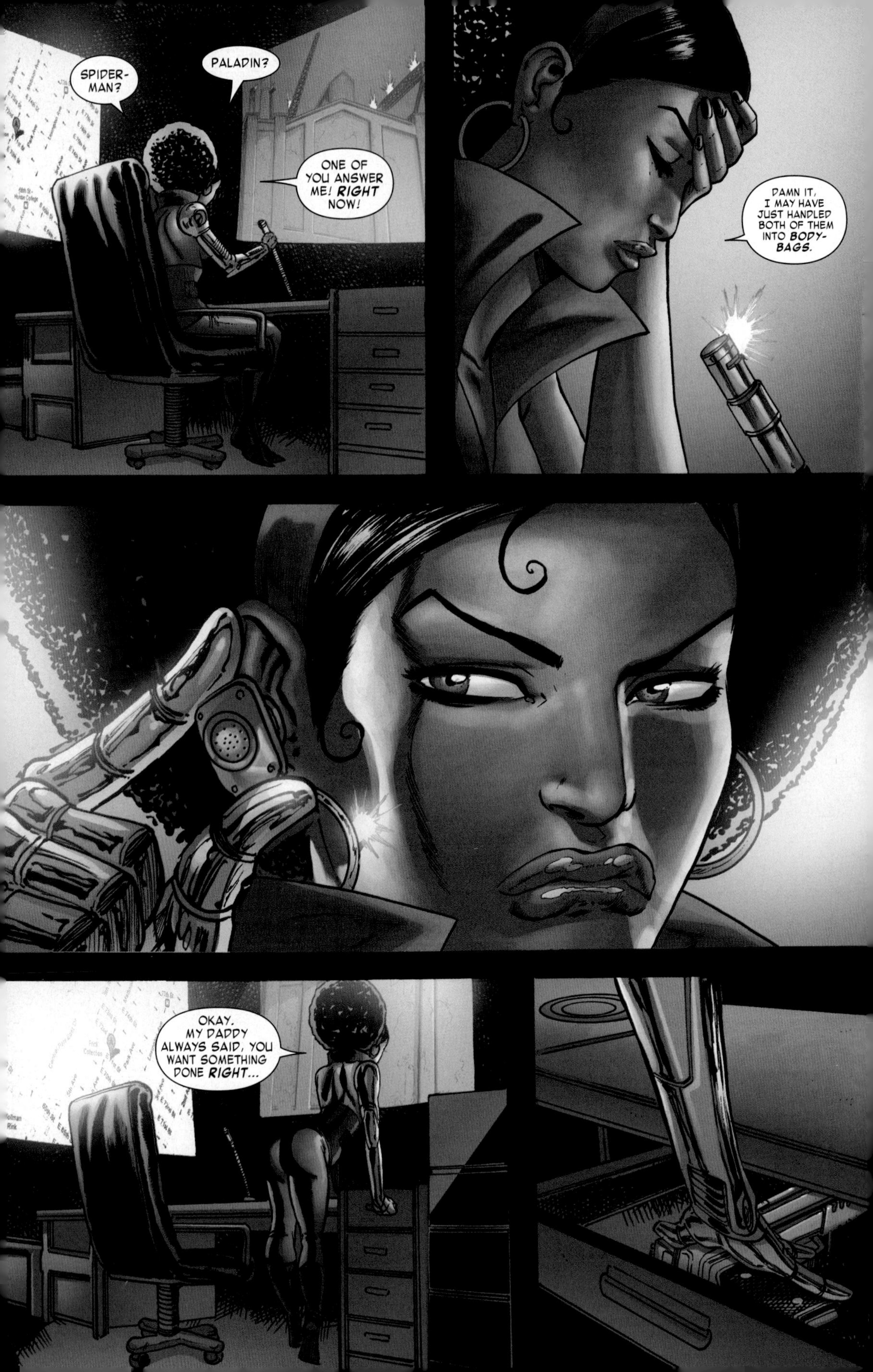

SPIDER-MAN?
PALADIN?
ONE OF YOU ANSWER ME! RIGHT NOW!
DAMN IT, I MAY HAVE JUST HANDLED BOTH OF THEM INTO BODY-BAGS.
OKAY. MY DADDY ALWAYS SAID, YOU WANT SOMETHING DONE RIGHT...

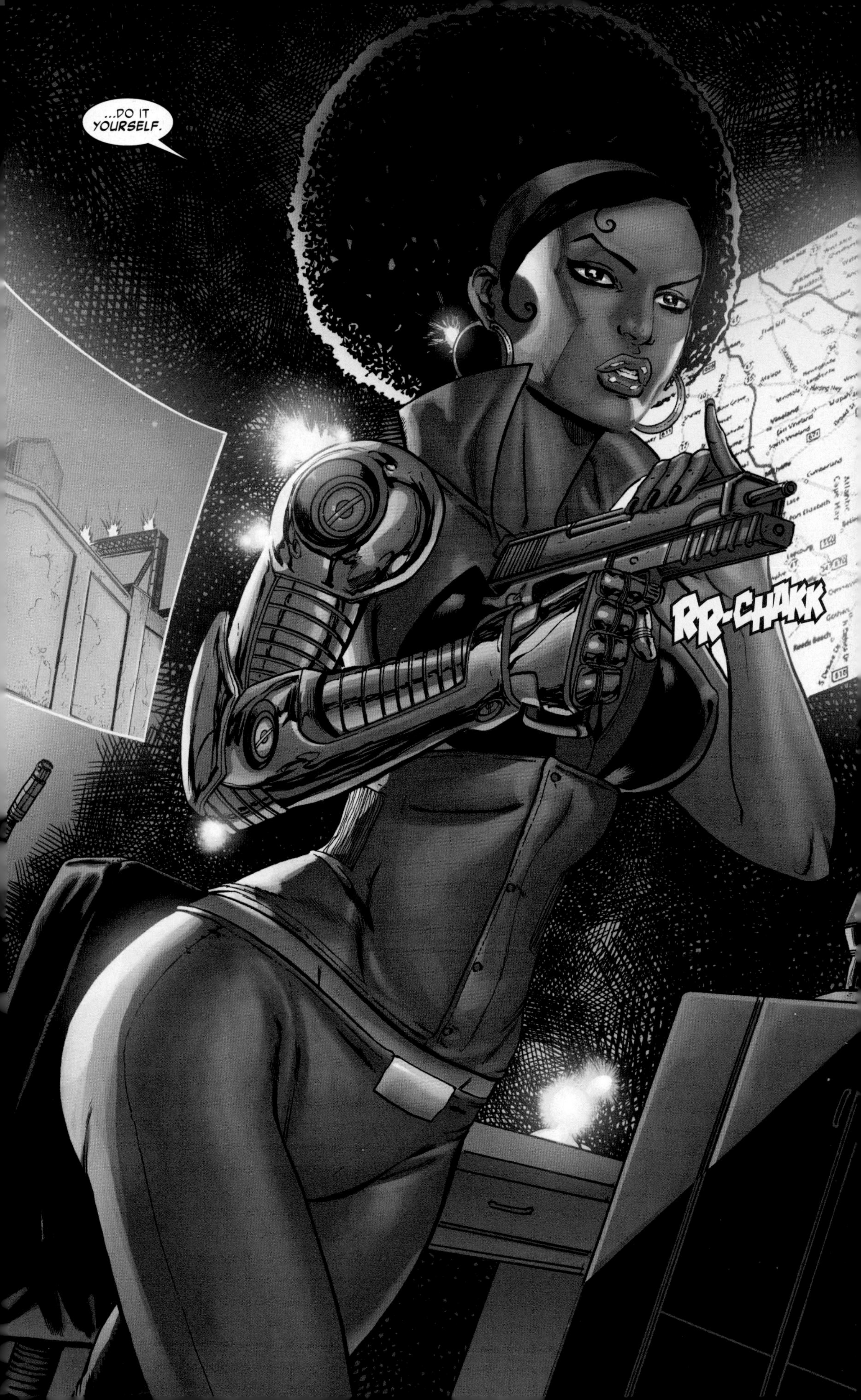
...DO IT YOURSELF.
RR-CHAKK

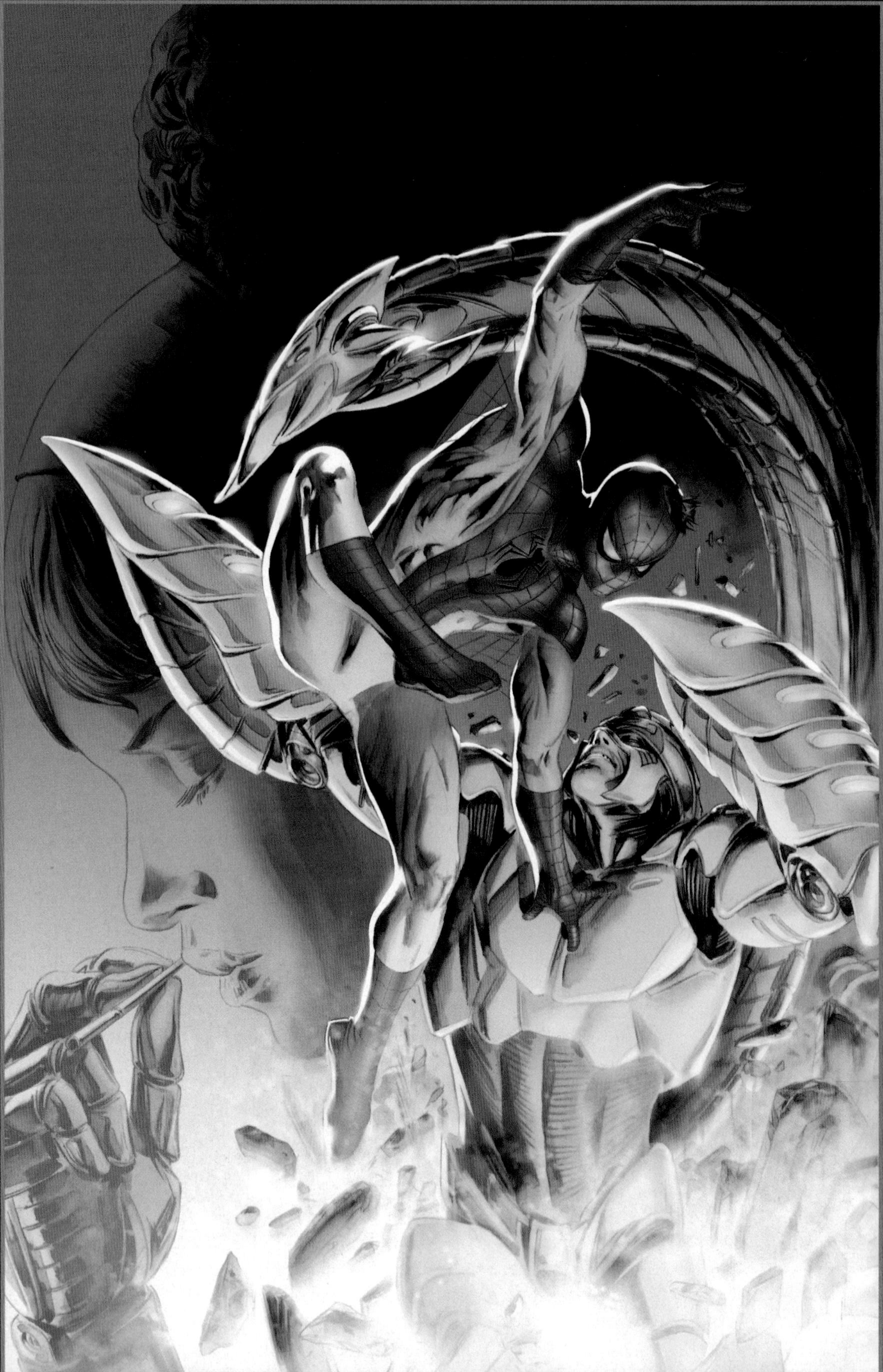

HEROES FOR HIRE #8

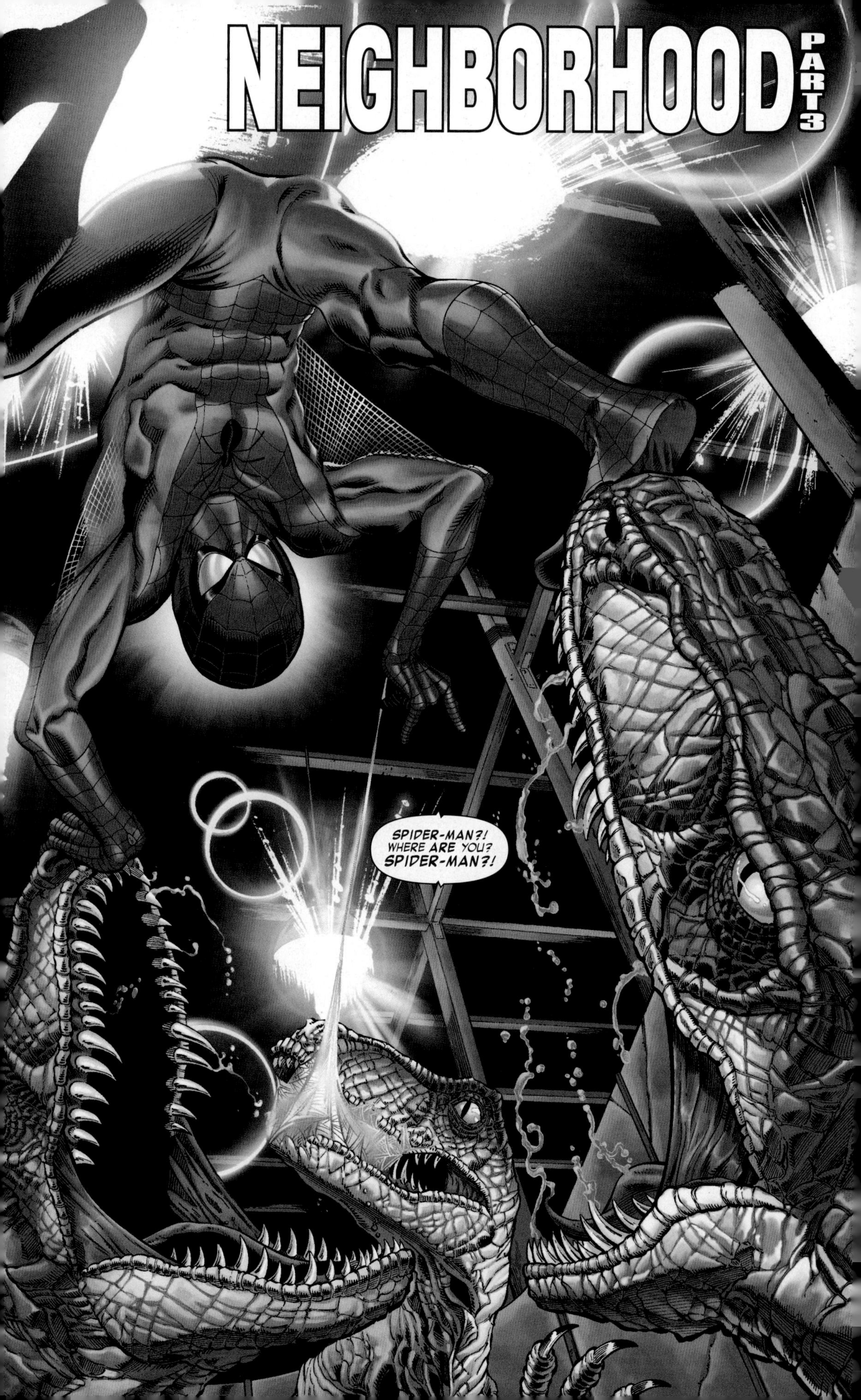
NEIGHBORHOOD PART 3
SPIDER-MAN?! WHERE ARE YOU? SPIDER-MAN?!

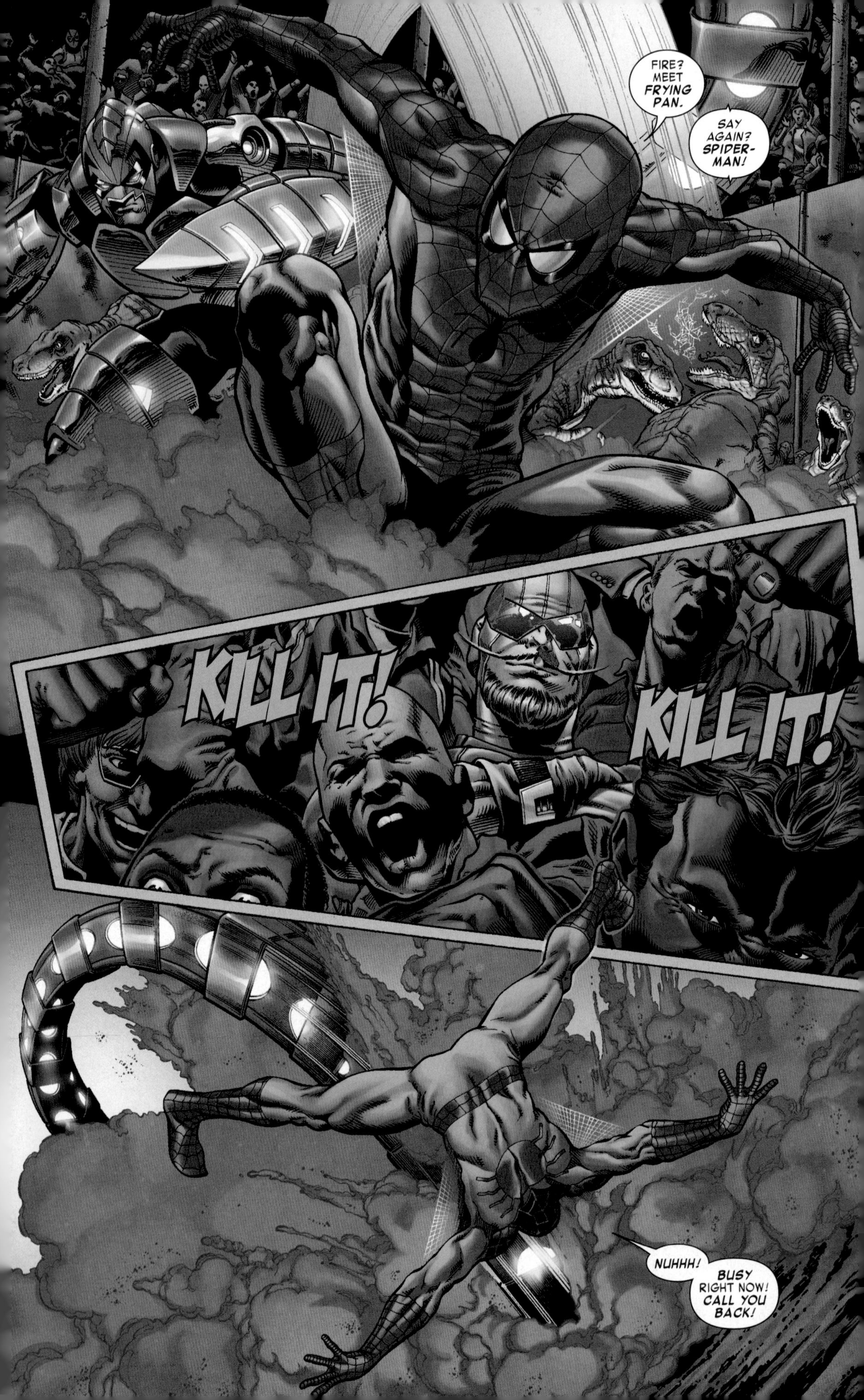
FIRE? MEET FRYING PAN.
SAY AGAIN? SPIDER-MAN!
KILL IT!
KILL IT!
NUHHH!
BUSY RIGHT NOW! CALL YOU BACK!

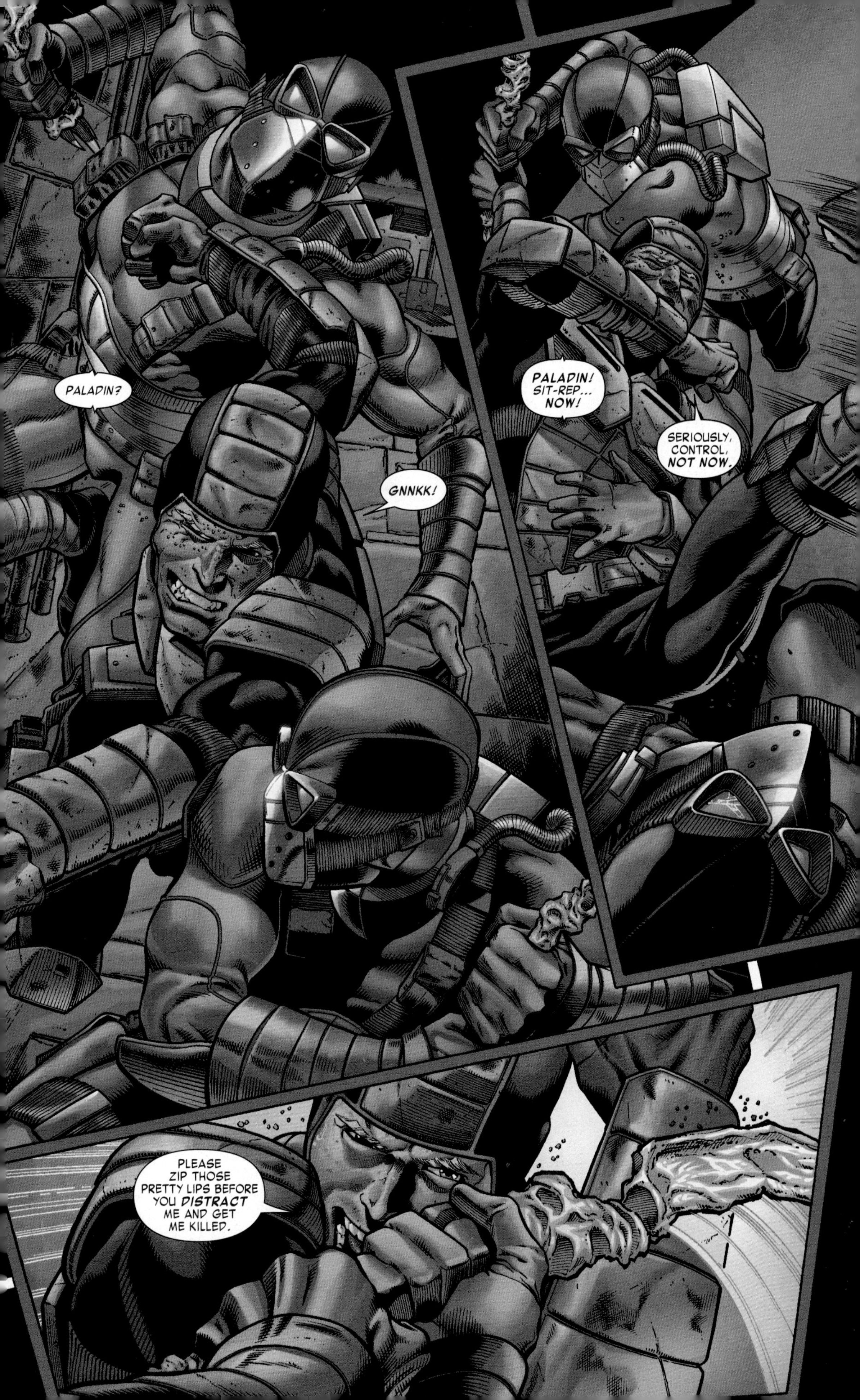
PALADIN?
GNNKK!
PALADIN! SIT-REP... NOW!
SERIOUSLY, CONTROL, NOT NOW.
PLEASE ZIP THOSE PRETTY LIPS BEFORE YOU DISTRACT ME AND GET ME KILLED.

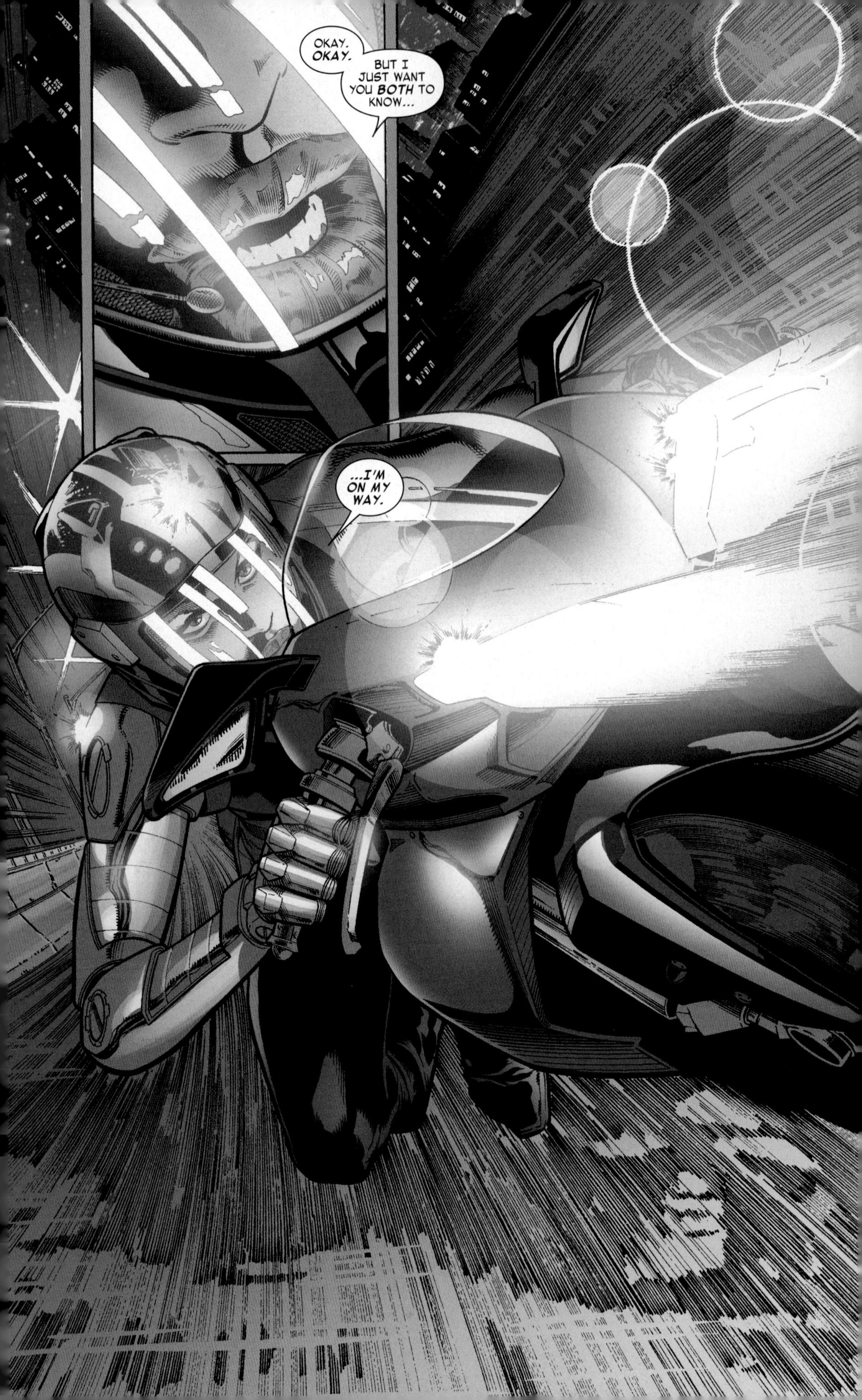
OKAY. OKAY.
BUT I JUST WANT YOU BOTH TO KNOW...
...I'M ON MY WAY.

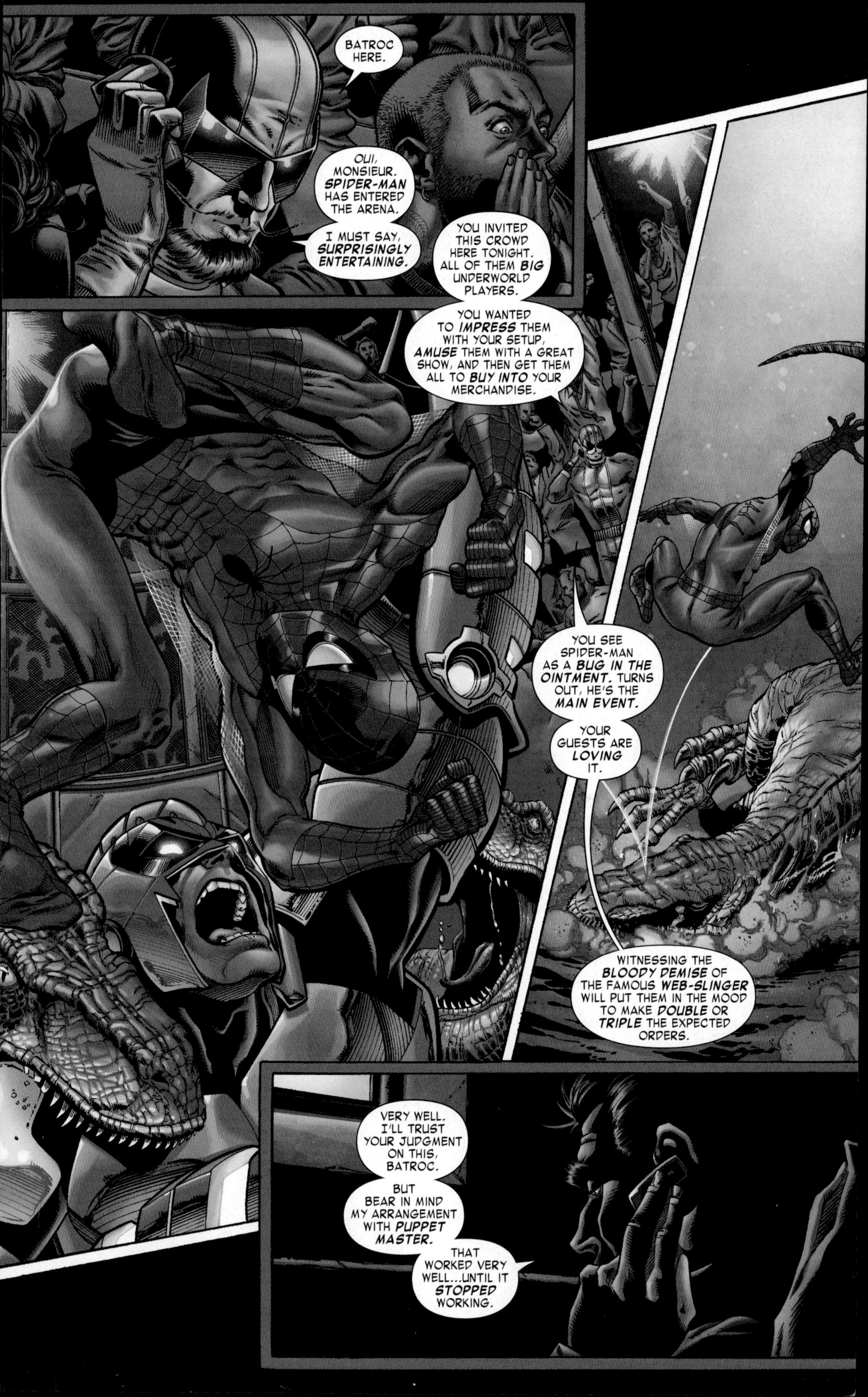

BATROC HERE.
OUI, MONSIEUR. SPIDER-MAN HAS ENTERED THE ARENA.
I MUST SAY, SURPRISINGLY ENTERTAINING.
YOU INVITED THIS CROWD HERE TONIGHT. ALL OF THEM BIG UNDERWORLD PLAYERS.
YOU WANTED TO IMPRESS THEM WITH YOUR SETUP, AMUSE THEM WITH A GREAT SHOW, AND THEN GET THEM ALL TO BUY INTO YOUR MERCHANDISE.
YOU SEE SPIDER-MAN AS A BUG IN THE OINTMENT. TURNS OUT, HE'S THE MAIN EVENT.
YOUR GUESTS ARE LOVING IT.
WITNESSING THE BLOODY DEMISE OF THE FAMOUS WEB-SLINGER WILL PUT THEM IN THE MOOD TO MAKE DOUBLE OR TRIPLE THE EXPECTED ORDERS.
VERY WELL. I'LL TRUST YOUR JUDGMENT ON THIS, BATROC.
BUT BEAR IN MIND MY ARRANGEMENT WITH PUPPET MASTER.
THAT WORKED VERY WELL...UNTIL IT STOPPED WORKING.

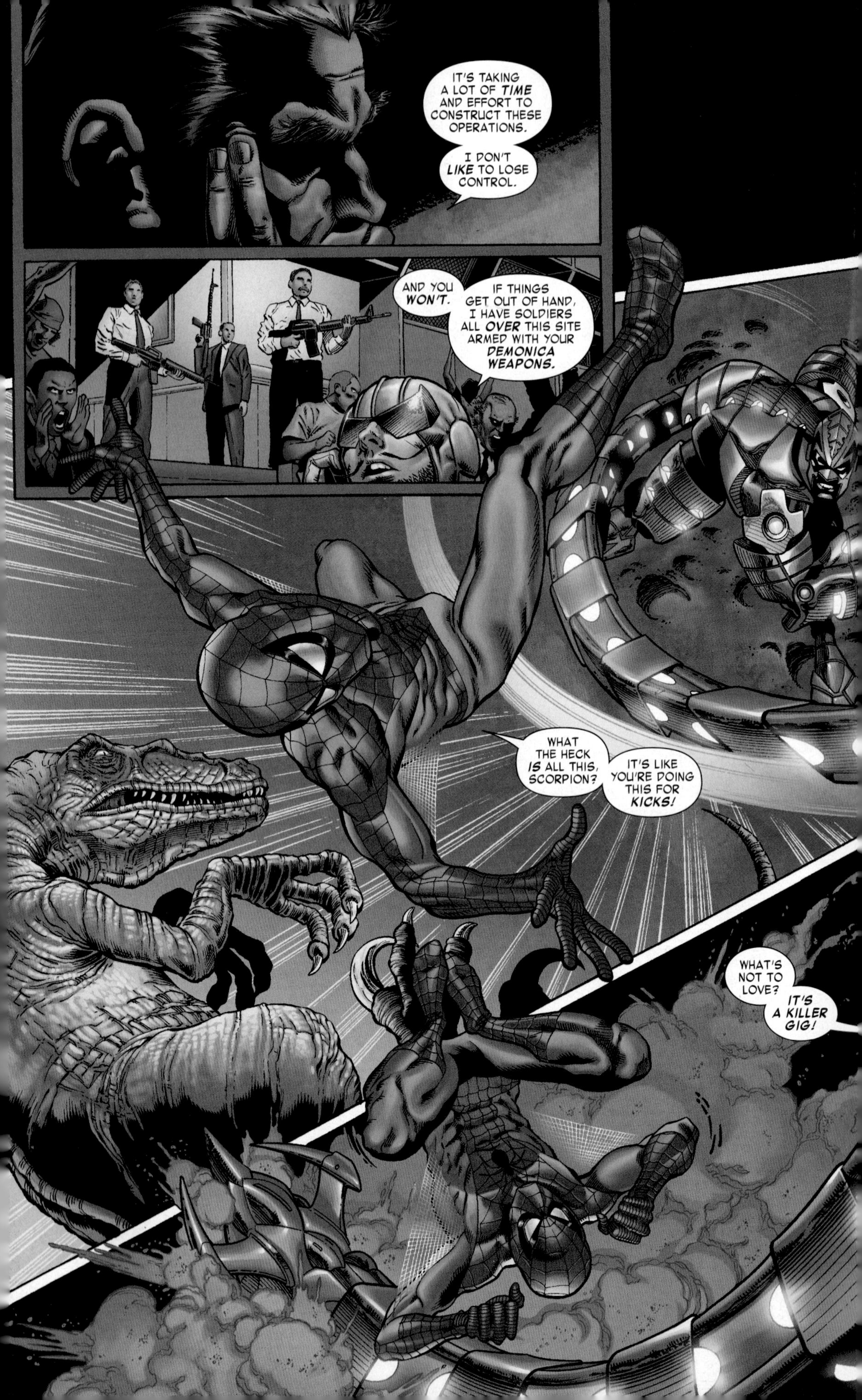
IT'S TAKING A LOT OF TIME AND EFFORT TO CONSTRUCT THESE OPERATIONS.
I DON'T LIKE TO LOSE CONTROL.
AND YOU WON'T.
IF THINGS GET OUT OF HAND, I HAVE SOLDIERS ALL OVER THIS SITE ARMED WITH YOUR DEMONICA WEAPONS.
WHAT THE HECK IS ALL THIS, SCORPION?
IT'S LIKE YOU'RE DOING THIS FOR KICKS!
WHAT'S NOT TO LOVE? IT'S A KILLER GIG!

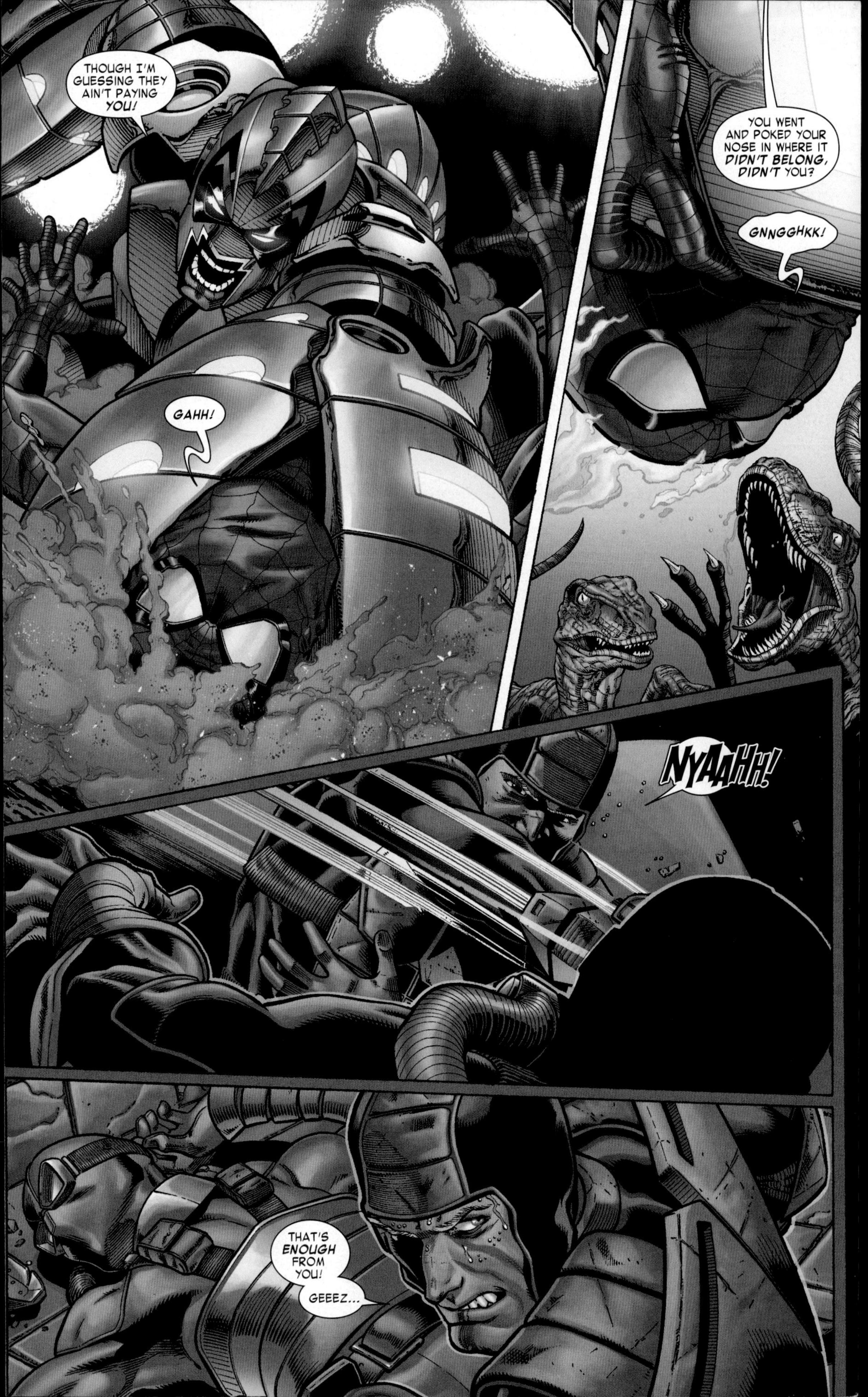
THOUGH I'M GUESSING THEY AIN'T PAYING YOU!
GAHH!
YOU WENT AND POKED YOUR NOSE IN WHERE IT DIDN'T BELONG, DIDN'T YOU?
GNNGGHKK!
NYAAHH!
THAT'S ENOUGH FROM YOU!
GEEEZ...

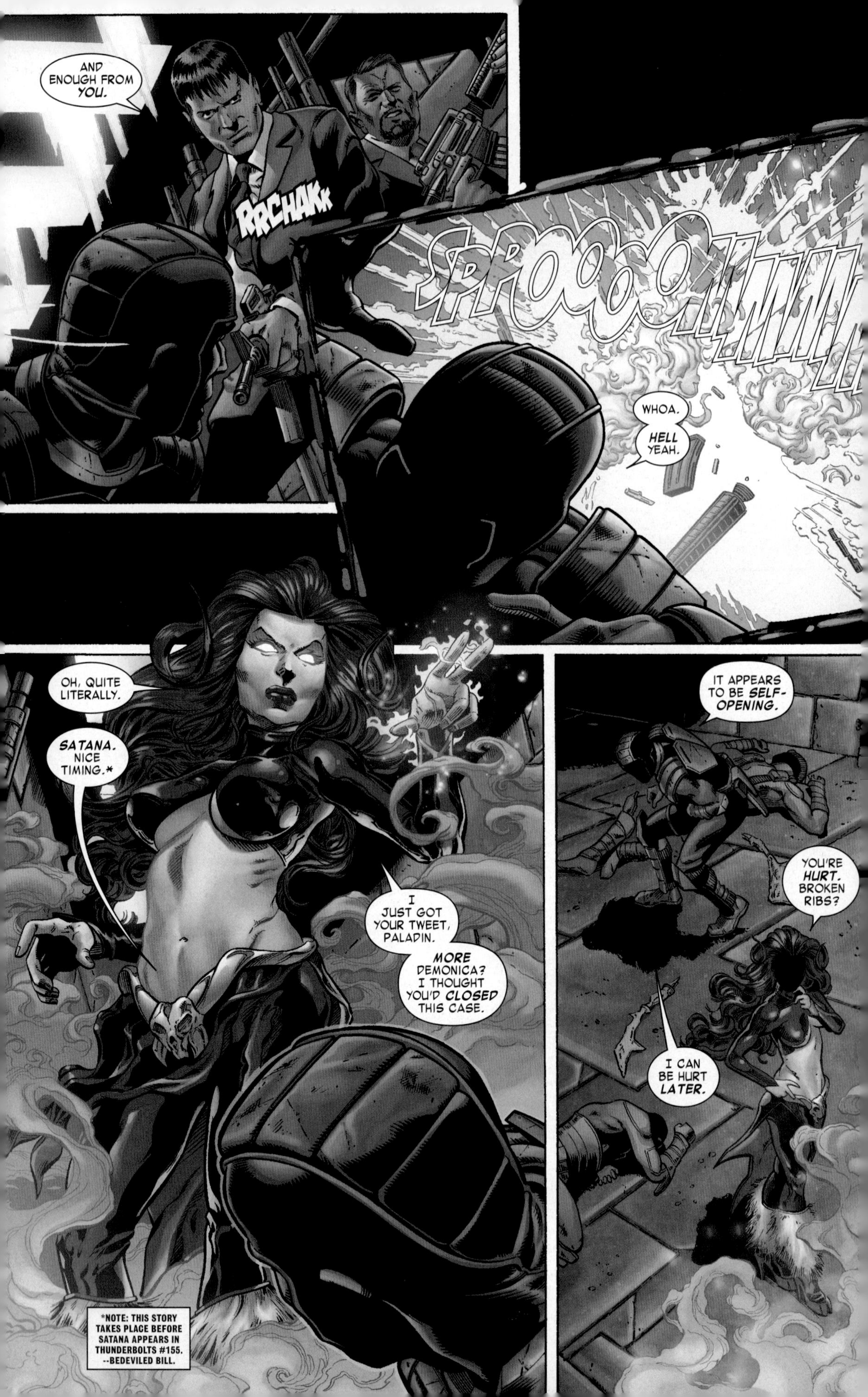
AND ENOUGH FROM YOU.
RRCHAKK
FROOOOOMMMM
WHOA. HELL YEAH.
OH, QUITE LITERALLY.
SATANA. NICE TIMING.*
I JUST GOT YOUR TWEET, PALADIN.
MORE DEMONICA? I THOUGHT YOU'D CLOSED THIS CASE.
IT APPEARS TO BE SELF-OPENING.
YOU'RE HURT. BROKEN RIBS?
I CAN BE HURT LATER.
*NOTE: THIS STORY TAKES PLACE BEFORE SATANA APPEARS IN THUNDERBOLTS #155. --BEDEVILED BILL.

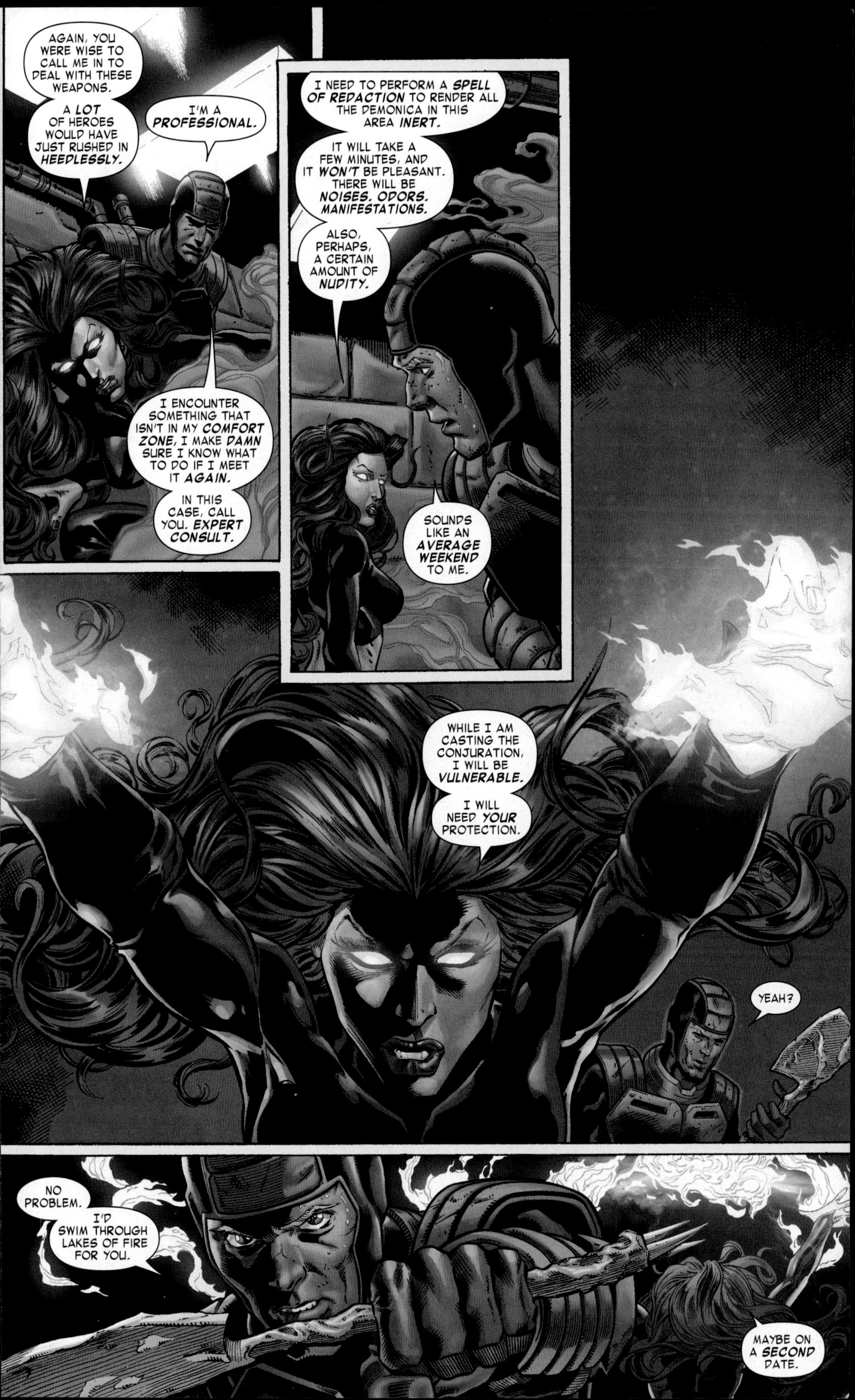

AGAIN, YOU WERE WISE TO CALL ME IN TO DEAL WITH THESE WEAPONS.
A LOT OF HEROES WOULD HAVE JUST RUSHED IN HEEDLESSLY.
I'M A PROFESSIONAL.
I ENCOUNTER SOMETHING THAT ISN'T IN MY COMFORT ZONE, I MAKE DAMN SURE I KNOW WHAT TO DO IF I MEET IT AGAIN.
IN THIS CASE, CALL YOU. EXPERT CONSULT.
I NEED TO PERFORM A SPELL OF REDACTION TO RENDER ALL THE DEMONICA IN THIS AREA INERT.
IT WILL TAKE A FEW MINUTES, AND IT WON'T BE PLEASANT. THERE WILL BE NOISES. ODORS. MANIFESTATIONS.
ALSO, PERHAPS, A CERTAIN AMOUNT OF NUDITY.
SOUNDS LIKE AN AVERAGE WEEKEND TO ME.
WHILE I AM CASTING THE CONJURATION, I WILL BE VULNERABLE.
I WILL NEED YOUR PROTECTION.
YEAH?
NO PROBLEM.
I'D SWIM THROUGH LAKES OF FIRE FOR YOU.
MAYBE ON A SECOND DATE.

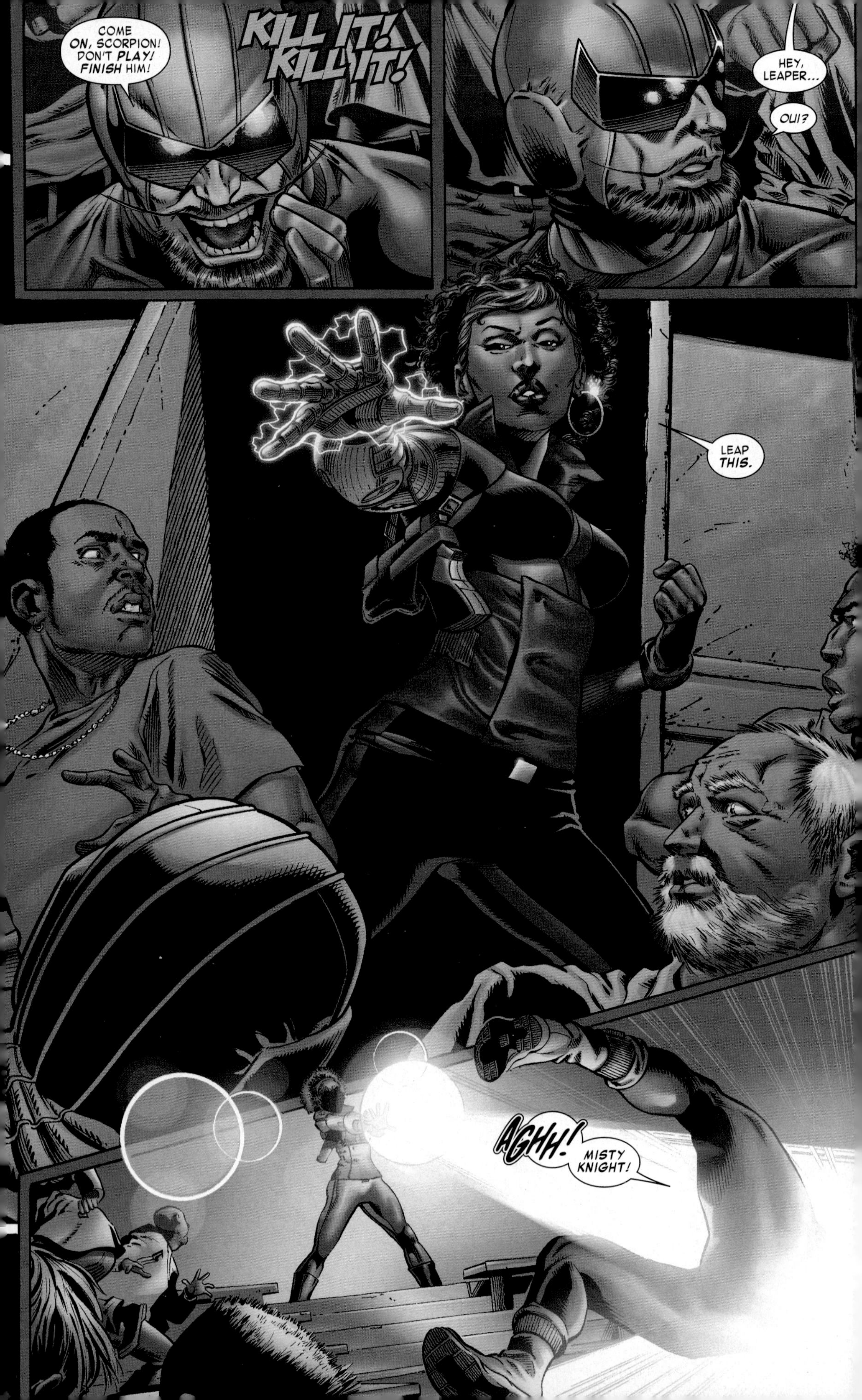
COME ON, SCORPION! DON'T PLAY! FINISH HIM!
KILL IT! KILL IT!
HEY, LEAPER...
OUI?
LEAP THIS.
AGHH!
MISTY KNIGHT!

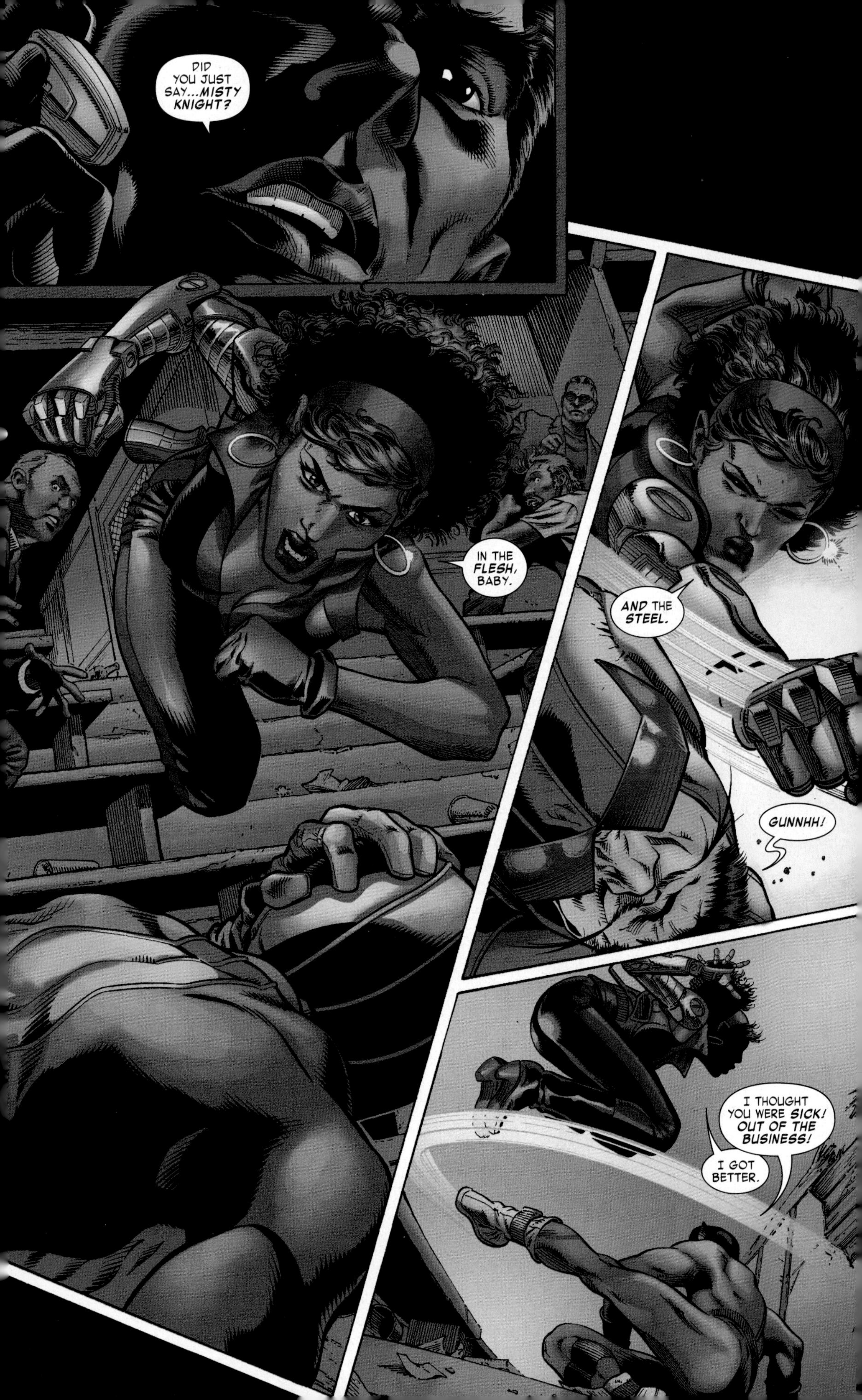
DID YOU JUST SAY...MISTY KNIGHT?
IN THE FLESH, BABY.
AND THE STEEL.
GUNNHH!
I THOUGHT YOU WERE SICK! OUT OF THE BUSINESS!
I GOT BETTER.

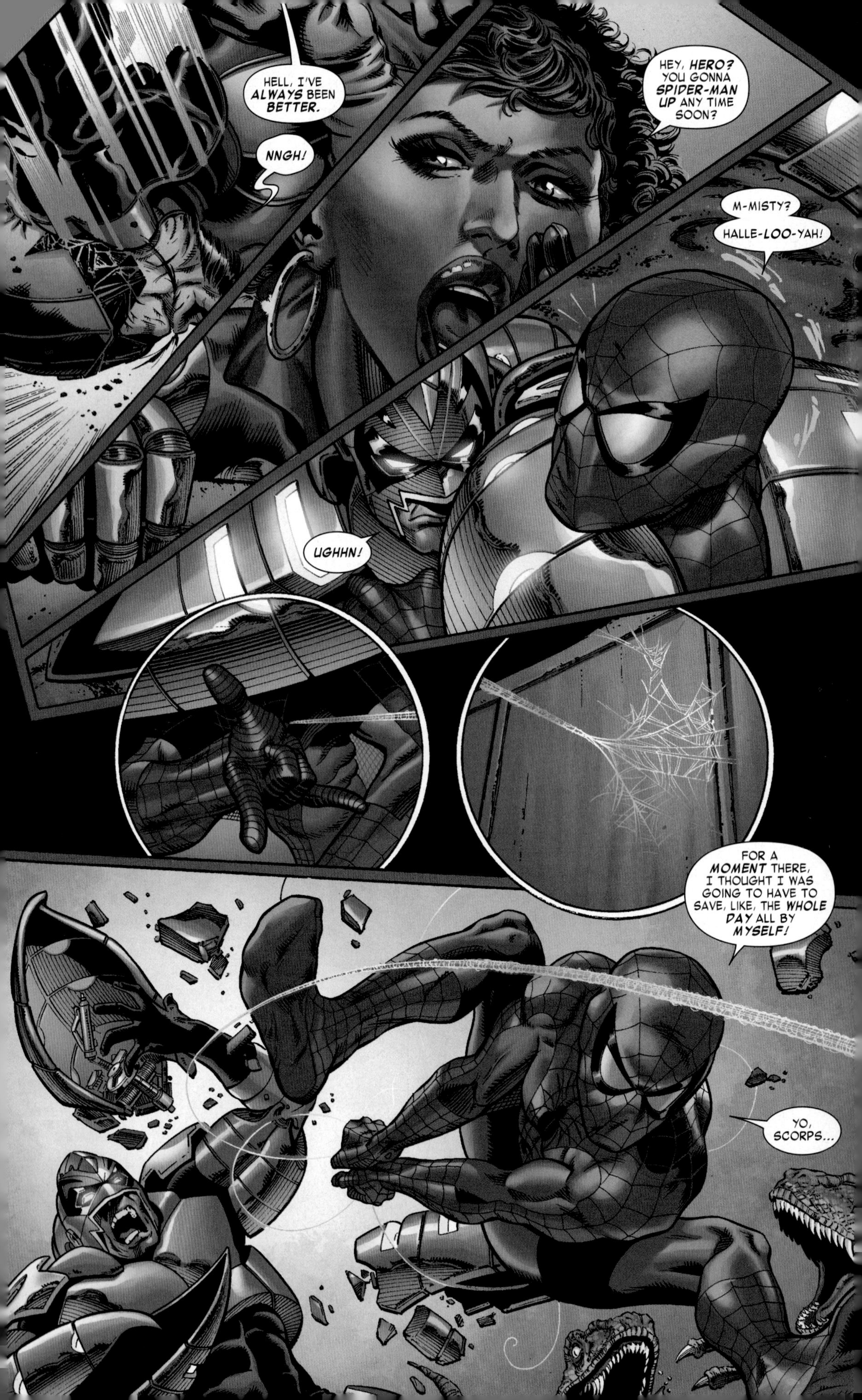
HELL, I'VE ALWAYS BEEN BETTER.
NNGH!
HEY, HERO? YOU GONNA SPIDER-MAN UP ANY TIME SOON?
M-MISTY?
HALLE-LOO-YAH!
UGHHN!
FOR A MOMENT THERE, I THOUGHT I WAS GOING TO HAVE TO SAVE, LIKE, THE WHOLE DAY ALL BY MYSELF!
YO, SCORPS...

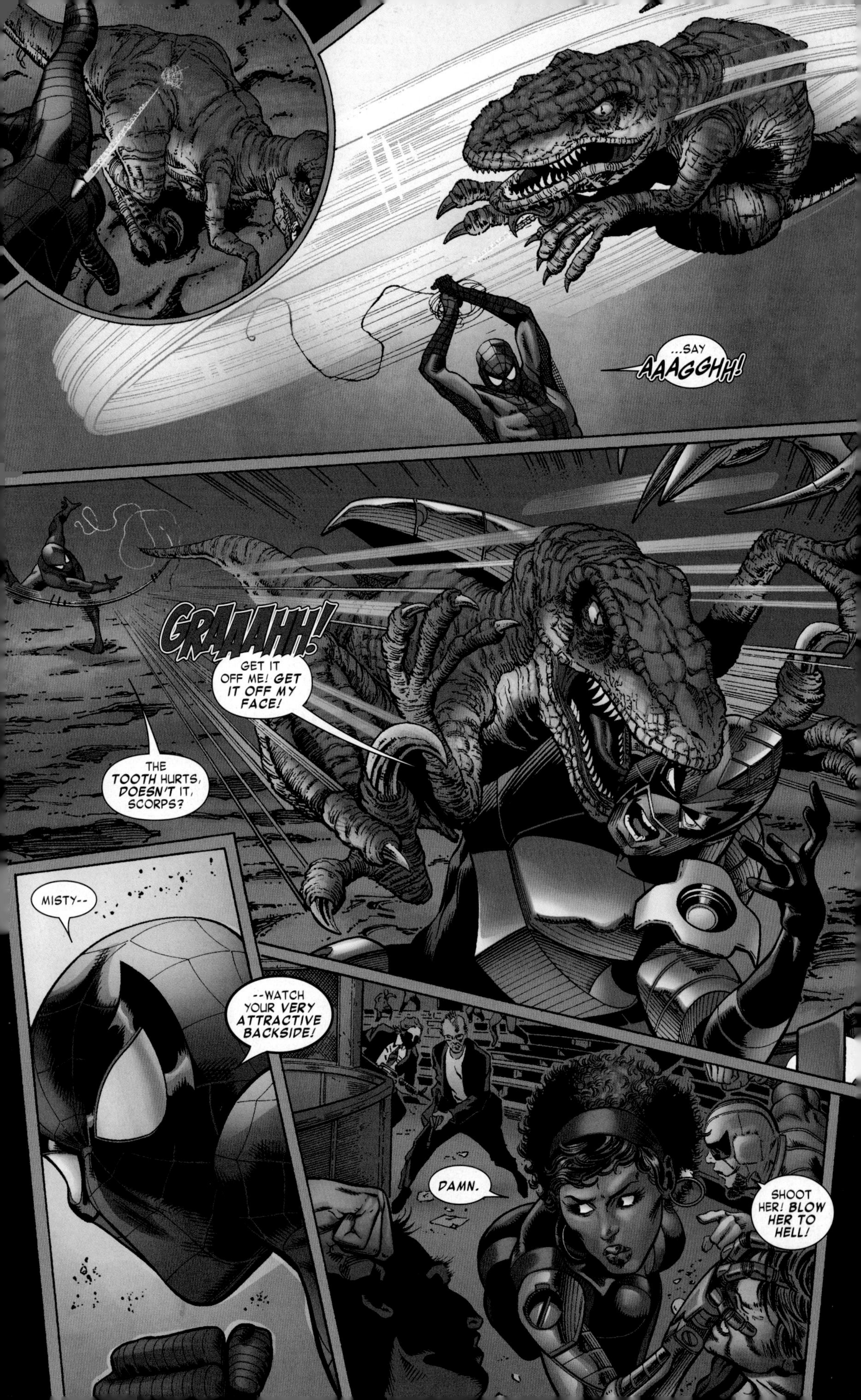
...SAY
AAAGGHH!
GRAAAHH!
GET IT OFF ME! GET IT OFF MY FACE!
THE TOOTH HURTS, DOESN'T IT, SCORPS?
MISTY--
--WATCH YOUR VERY ATTRACTIVE BACKSIDE!
DAMN.
SHOOT HER! BLOW HER TO HELL!

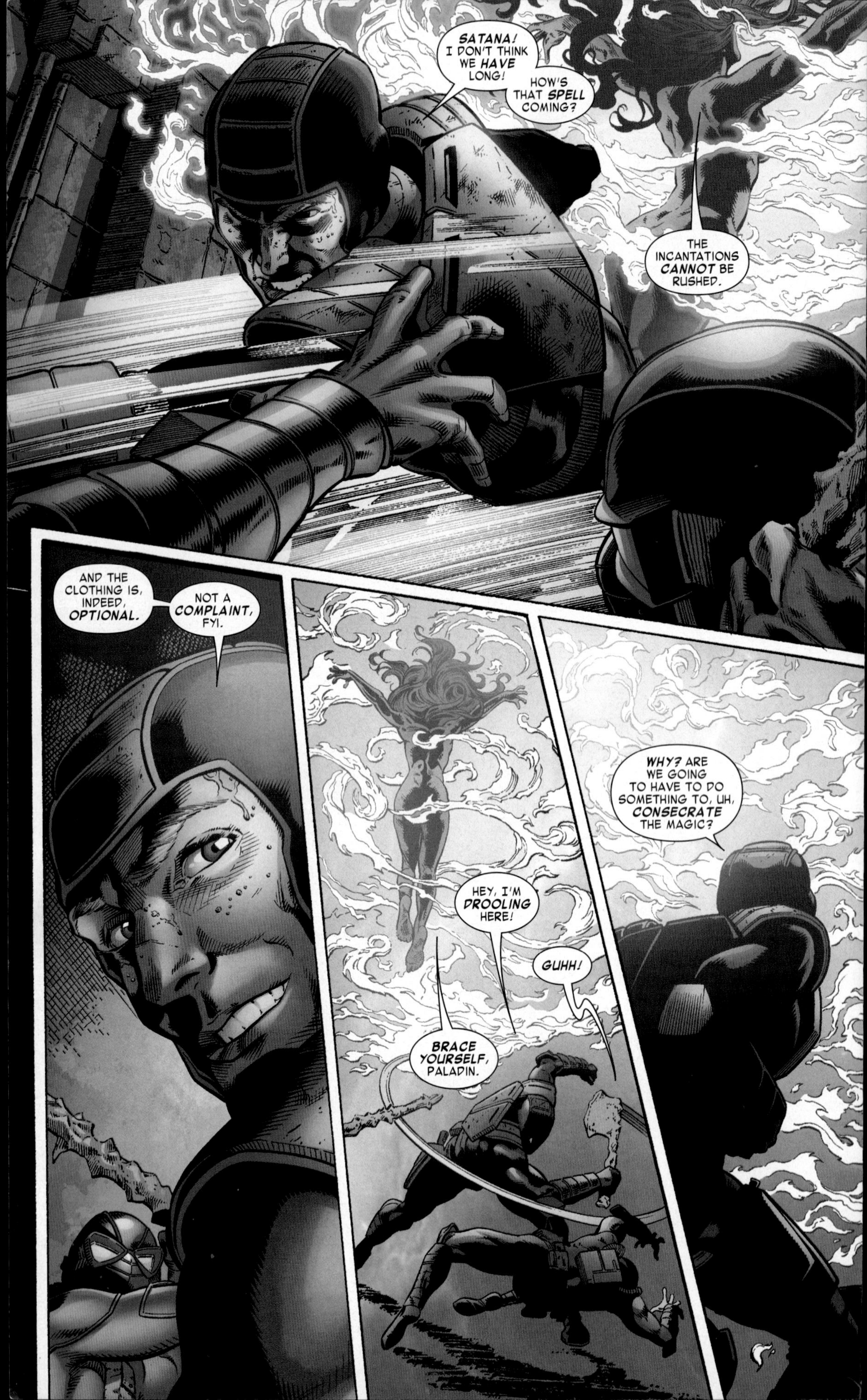
SATANA! I DON'T THINK WE HAVE LONG!
HOW'S THAT SPELL COMING?
THE INCANTATIONS CANNOT BE RUSHED.
AND THE CLOTHING IS, INDEED, OPTIONAL.
NOT A COMPLAINT, FYI.
HEY, I'M DROOLING HERE!
BRACE YOURSELF, PALADIN.
GUHH!
WHY? ARE WE GOING TO HAVE TO DO SOMETHING TO, UH, CONSECRATE THE MAGIC?

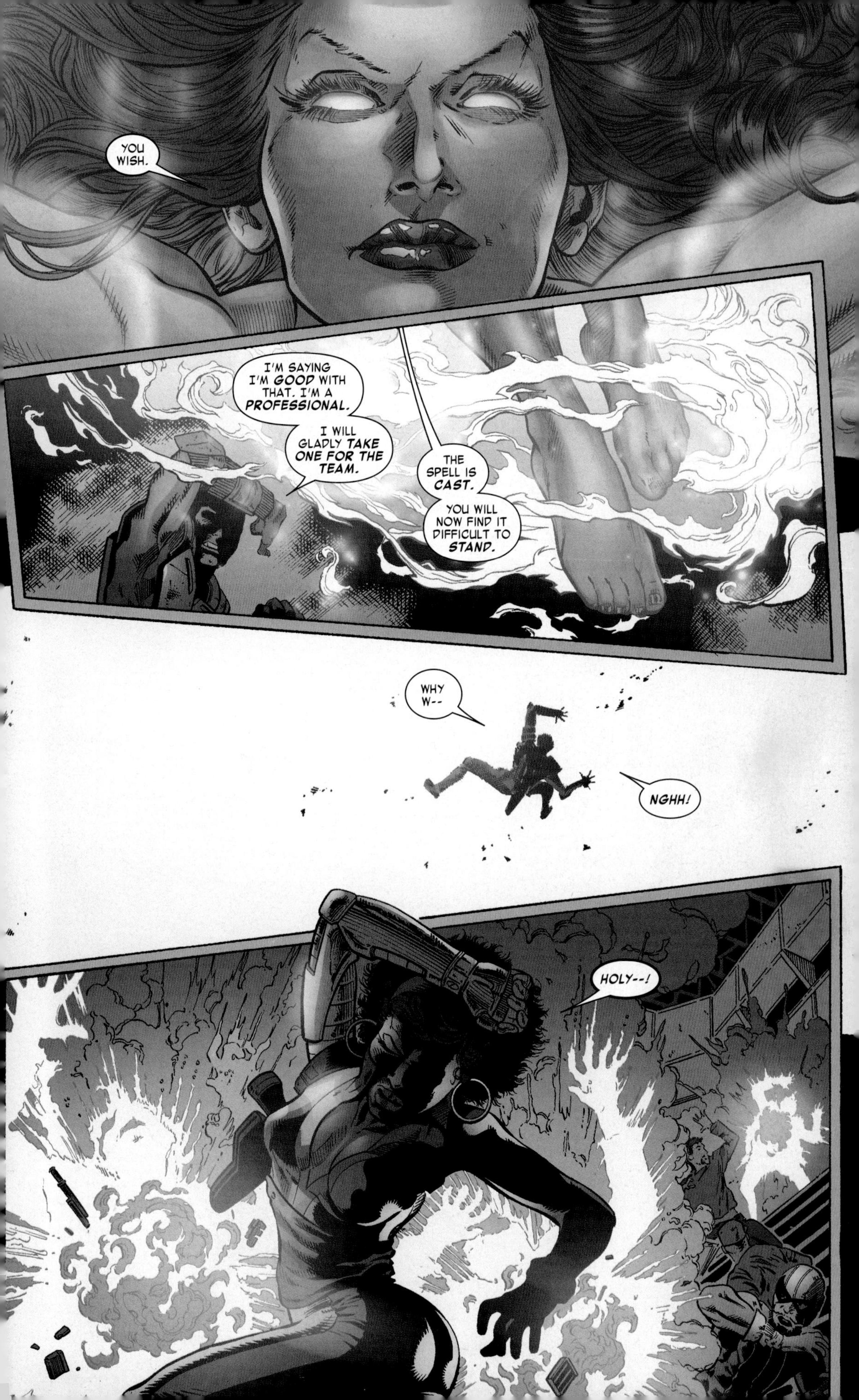
YOU WISH.
I'M SAYING I'M GOOD WITH THAT. I'M A PROFESSIONAL.
I WILL GLADLY TAKE ONE FOR THE TEAM.
THE SPELL IS CAST.
YOU WILL NOW FIND IT DIFFICULT TO STAND.
WHY W--
NGHH!
HOLY--!

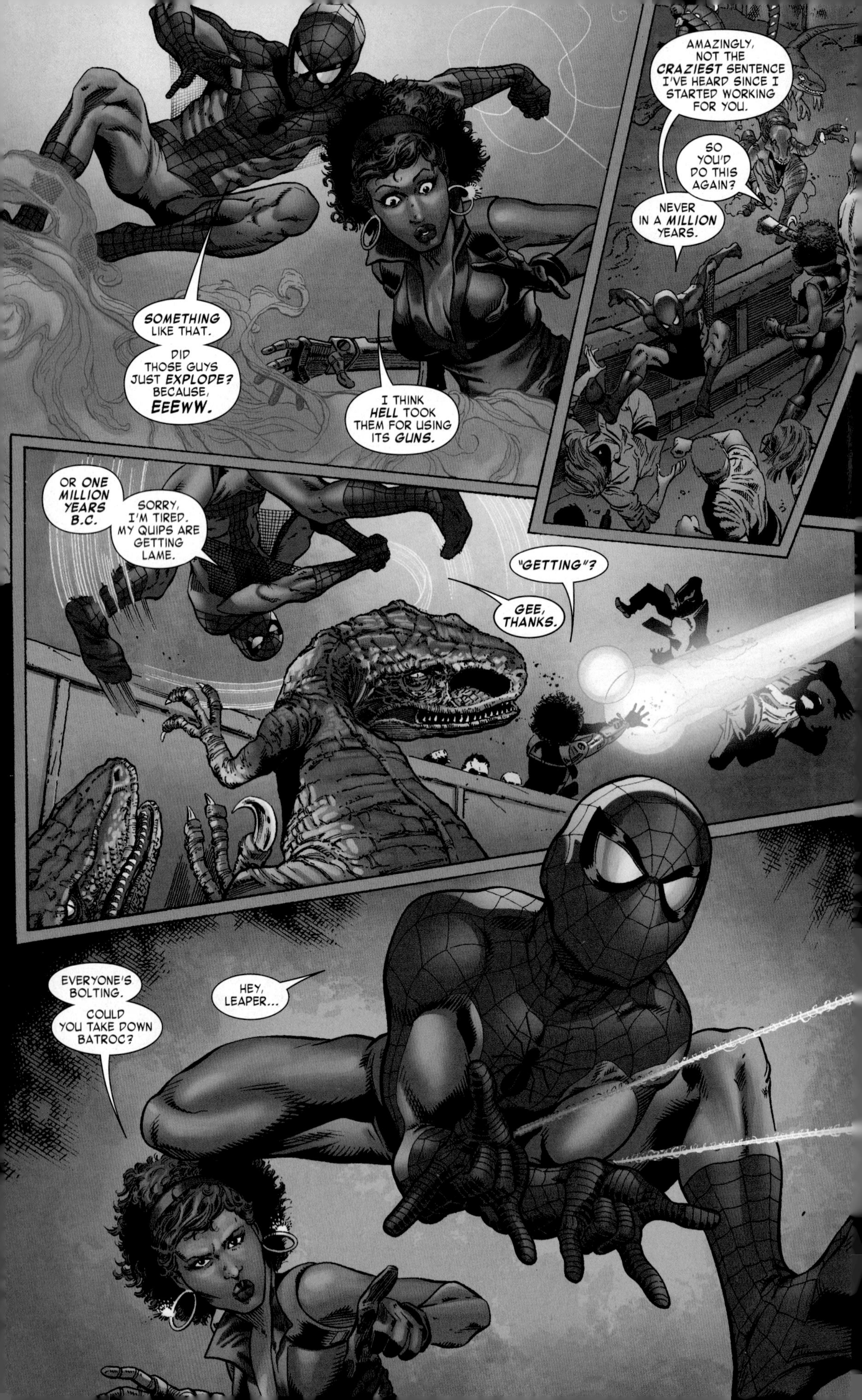
SOMETHING LIKE THAT.
DID THOSE GUYS JUST EXPLODE? BECAUSE, EEEWW.
I THINK HELL TOOK THEM FOR USING ITS GUNS.
AMAZINGLY, NOT THE CRAZIEST SENTENCE I'VE HEARD SINCE I STARTED WORKING FOR YOU.
SO YOU'D DO THIS AGAIN?
NEVER IN A MILLION YEARS.
OR ONE MILLION YEARS B.C.
SORRY, I'M TIRED. MY QUIPS ARE GETTING LAME.
"GETTING"?
GEE, THANKS.
EVERYONE'S BOLTING.
COULD YOU TAKE DOWN BATROC?
HEY, LEAPER...

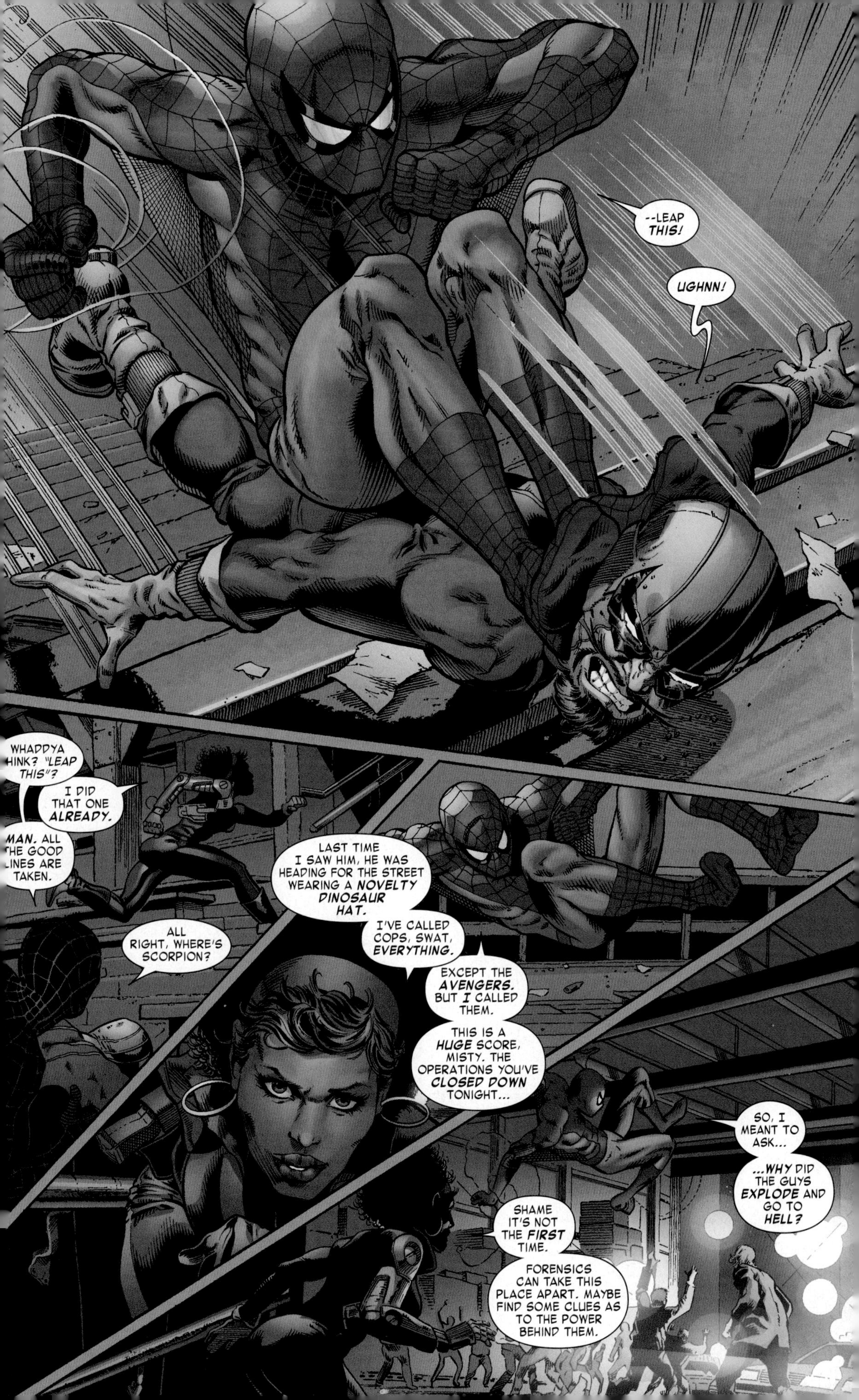
--LEAP THIS!
UGHNN!
WHADDYA HINK? "LEAP THIS"?
I DID THAT ONE ALREADY.
MAN. ALL THE GOOD LINES ARE TAKEN.
LAST TIME I SAW HIM, HE WAS HEADING FOR THE STREET WEARING A NOVELTY DINOSAUR HAT.
ALL RIGHT, WHERE'S SCORPION?
I'VE CALLED COPS, SWAT, EVERYTHING.
EXCEPT THE AVENGERS. BUT I CALLED THEM.
THIS IS A HUGE SCORE, MISTY. THE OPERATIONS YOU'VE CLOSED DOWN TONIGHT...
SO, I MEANT TO ASK...
...WHY DID THE GUYS EXPLODE AND GO TO HELL?
SHAME IT'S NOT THE FIRST TIME.
FORENSICS CAN TAKE THIS PLACE APART. MAYBE FIND SOME CLUES AS TO THE POWER BEHIND THEM.

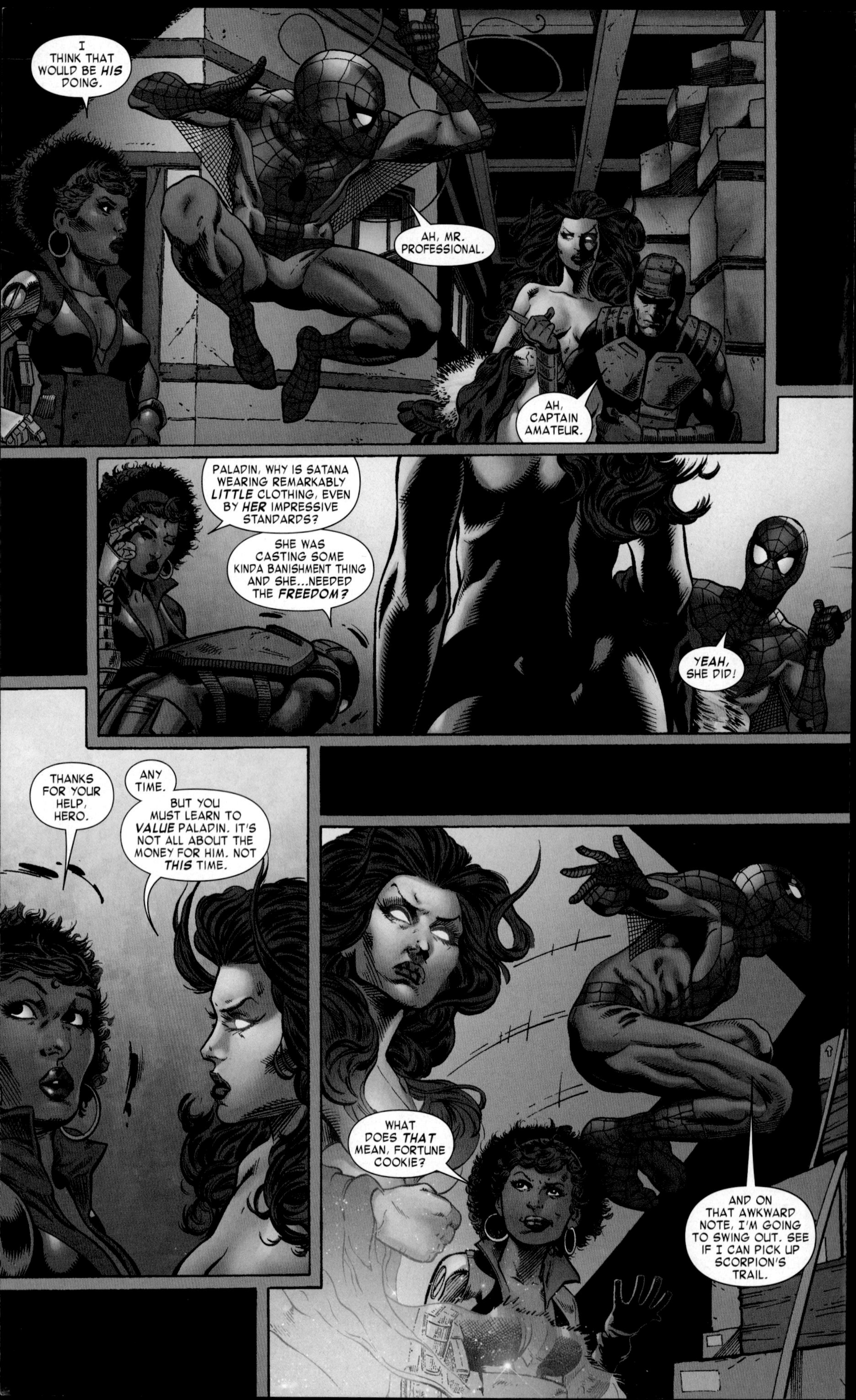
I THINK THAT WOULD BE HIS DOING.
AH, MR. PROFESSIONAL.
AH, CAPTAIN AMATEUR.
PALADIN, WHY IS SATANA WEARING REMARKABLY LITTLE CLOTHING, EVEN BY HER IMPRESSIVE STANDARDS?
SHE WAS CASTING SOME KINDA BANISHMENT THING AND SHE...NEEDED THE FREEDOM?
YEAH, SHE DID!
THANKS FOR YOUR HELP, HERO.
ANY TIME.
BUT YOU MUST LEARN TO VALUE PALADIN. IT'S NOT ALL ABOUT THE MONEY FOR HIM. NOT THIS TIME.
WHAT DOES THAT MEAN, FORTUNE COOKIE?
AND ON THAT AWKWARD NOTE, I'M GOING TO SWING OUT. SEE IF I CAN PICK UP SCORPION'S TRAIL.

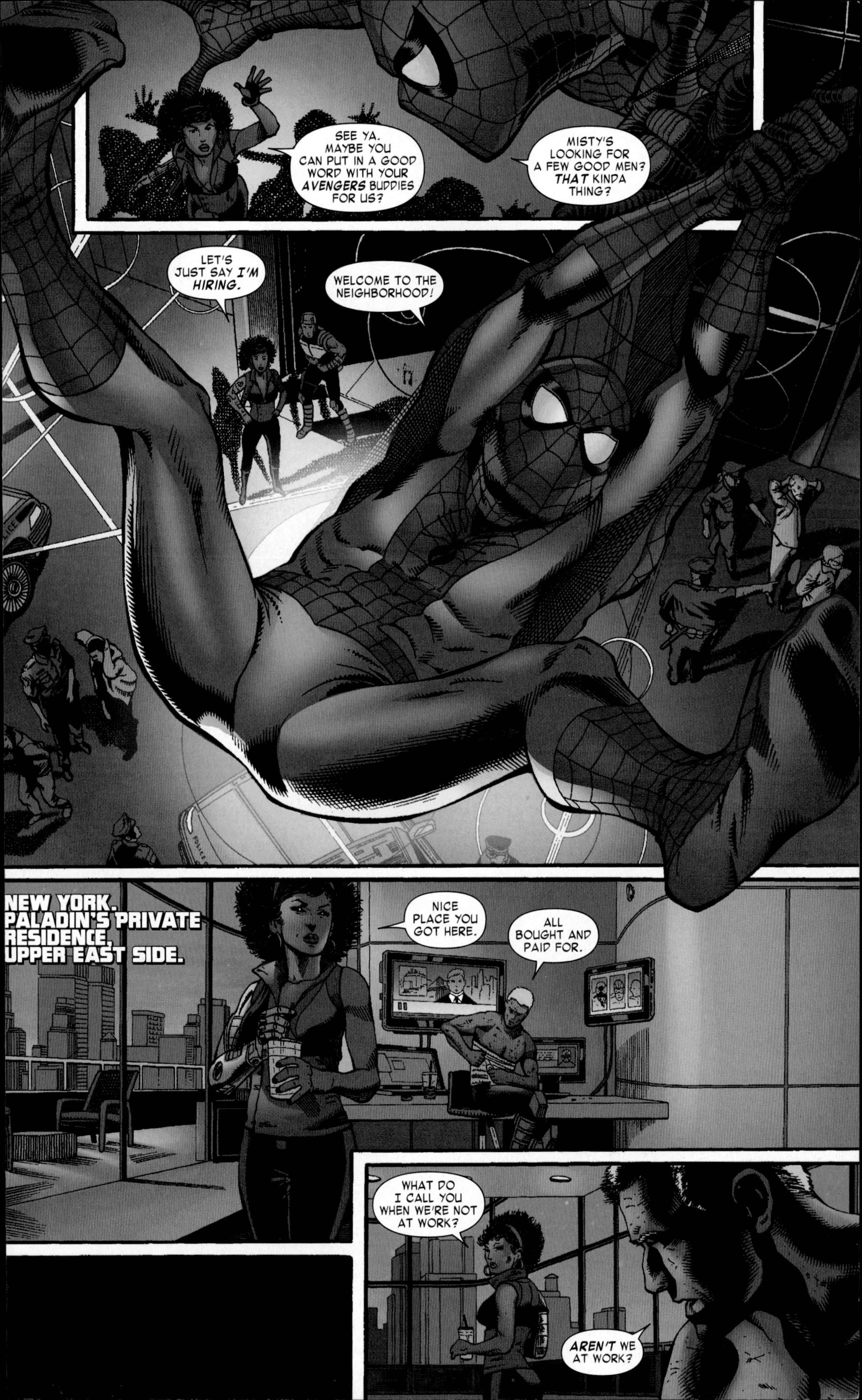
SEE YA. MAYBE YOU CAN PUT IN A GOOD WORD WITH YOUR AVENGERS BUDDIES FOR US?
MISTY'S LOOKING FOR A FEW GOOD MEN? THAT KINDA THING?
LET'S JUST SAY I'M HIRING.
WELCOME TO THE NEIGHBORHOOD!
NEW YORK. PALADIN'S PRIVATE RESIDENCE, UPPER EAST SIDE.
NICE PLACE YOU GOT HERE.
ALL BOUGHT AND PAID FOR.
WHAT DO I CALL YOU WHEN WE'RE NOT AT WORK?
AREN'T WE AT WORK?

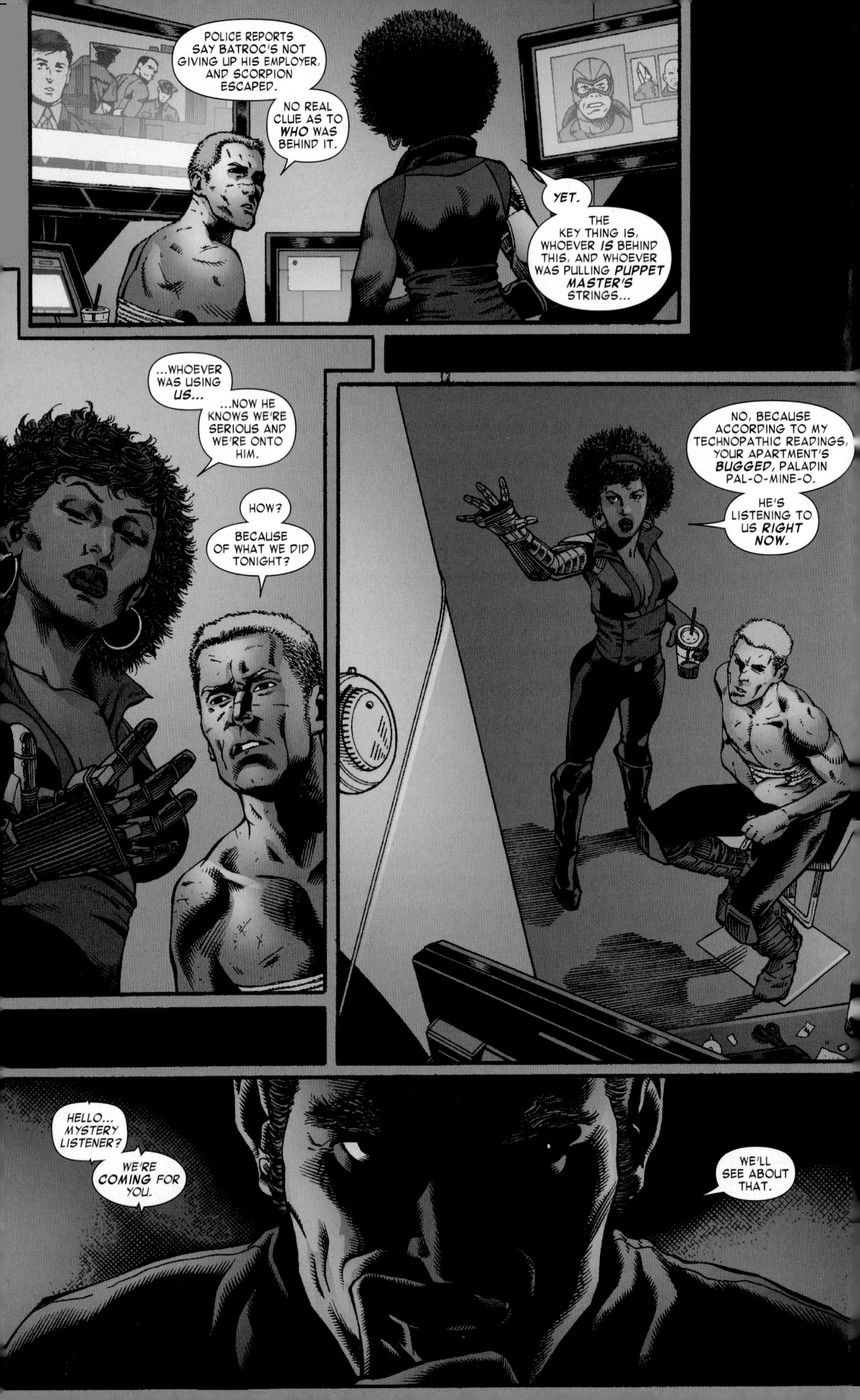
POLICE REPORTS SAY BATROC'S NOT GIVING UP HIS EMPLOYER, AND SCORPION ESCAPED.
NO REAL CLUE AS TO WHO WAS BEHIND IT.
YET.
THE KEY THING IS, WHOEVER IS BEHIND THIS, AND WHOEVER WAS PULLING PUPPET MASTER'S STRINGS...
...WHOEVER WAS USING US...
...NOW HE KNOWS WE'RE SERIOUS AND WE'RE ONTO HIM.
HOW?
BECAUSE OF WHAT WE DID TONIGHT?
NO, BECAUSE ACCORDING TO MY TECHNOPATHIC READINGS, YOUR APARTMENT'S BUGGED, PALADIN PAL-O-MINE-O.
HE'S LISTENING TO US RIGHT NOW.
HELLO... MYSTERY LISTENER?
WE'RE COMING FOR YOU.
WE'LL SEE ABOUT THAT.

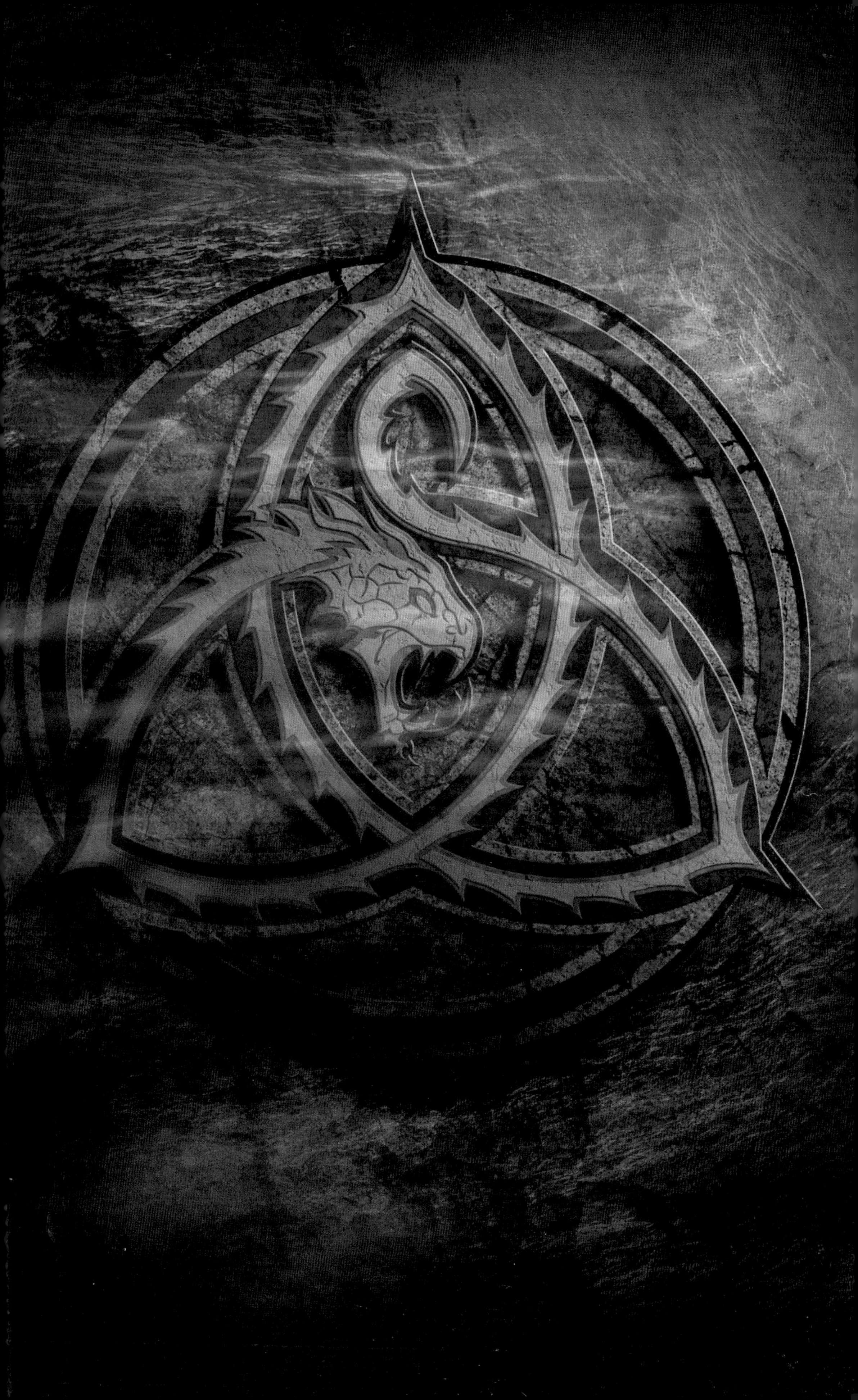

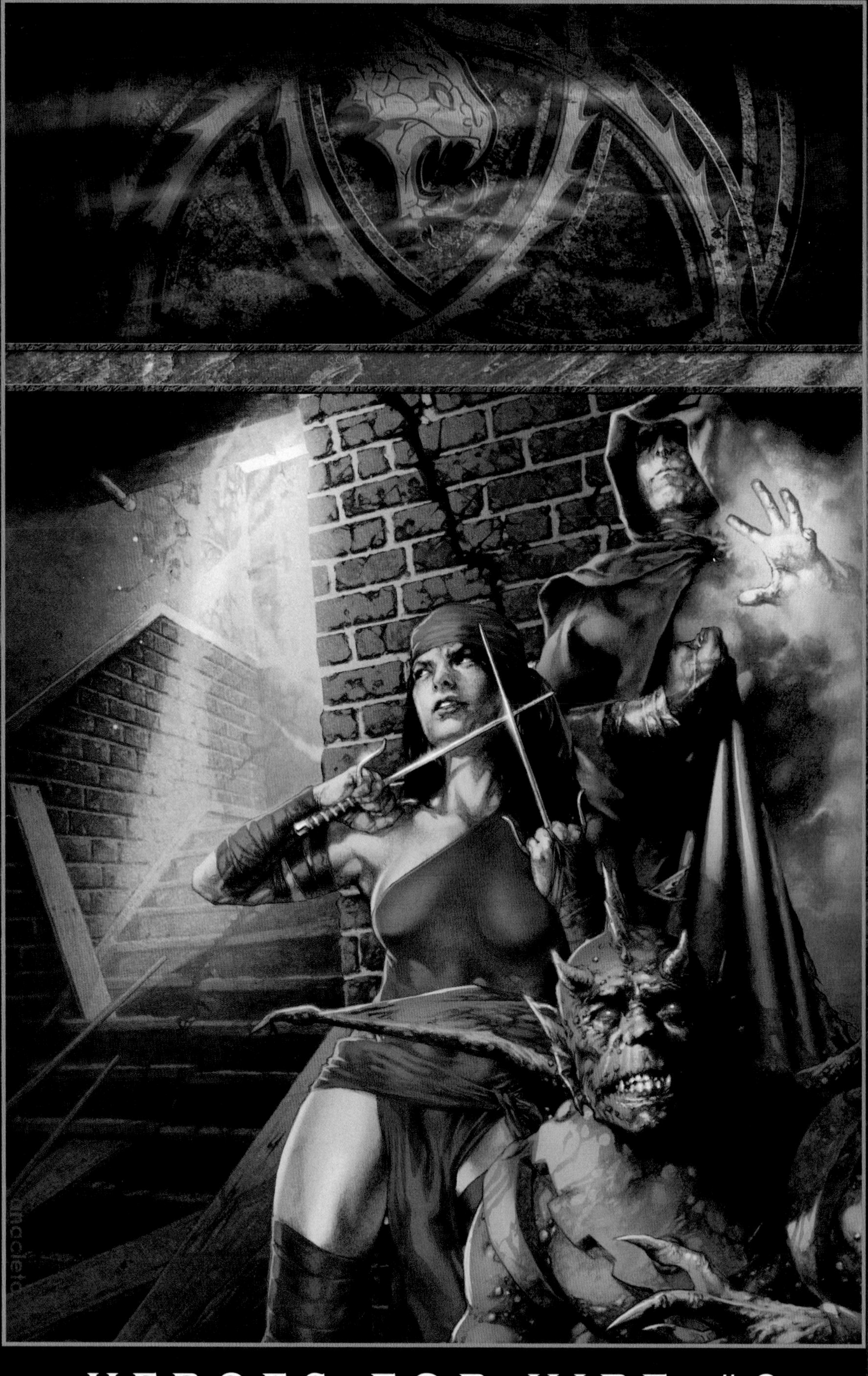

HEROES FOR HIRE #9

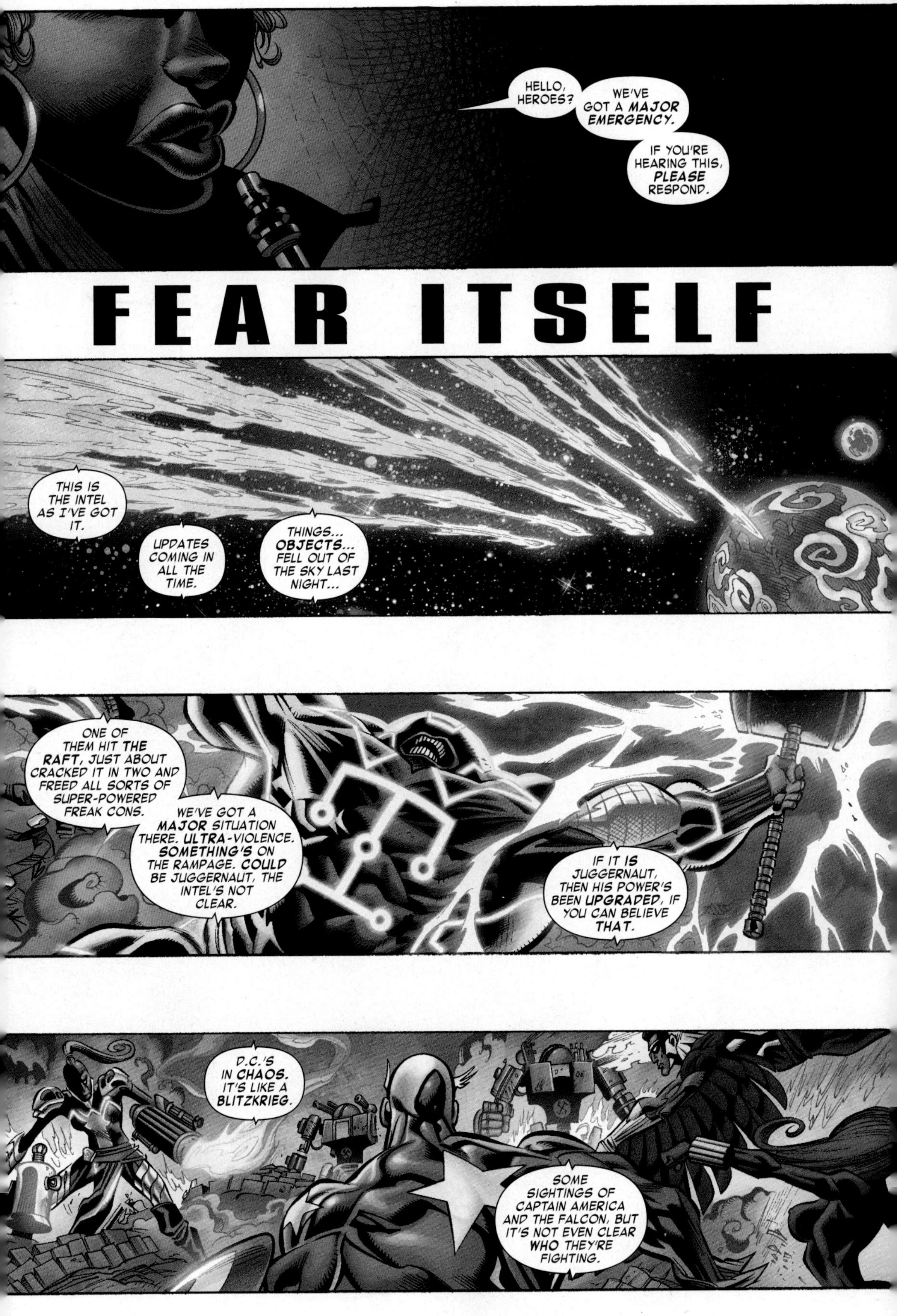
HELLO, HEROES?
WE'VE GOT A MAJOR EMERGENCY.
IF YOU'RE HEARING THIS, PLEASE RESPOND.
FEAR ITSELF
THIS IS THE INTEL AS I'VE GOT IT.
UPDATES COMING IN ALL THE TIME.
THINGS... OBJECTS... FELL OUT OF THE SKY LAST NIGHT...
ONE OF THEM HIT THE RAFT, JUST ABOUT CRACKED IT IN TWO AND FREED ALL SORTS OF SUPER-POWERED FREAK CONS.
WE'VE GOT A MAJOR SITUATION THERE. ULTRA-VIOLENCE. SOMETHING'S ON THE RAMPAGE. COULD BE JUGGERNAUT, THE INTEL'S NOT CLEAR.
IF IT IS JUGGERNAUT, THEN HIS POWER'S BEEN UPGRADED, IF YOU CAN BELIEVE THAT.
D.C.'S IN CHAOS. IT'S LIKE A BLITZKRIEG.
SOME SIGHTINGS OF CAPTAIN AMERICA AND THE FALCON, BUT IT'S NOT EVEN CLEAR WHO THEY'RE FIGHTING.

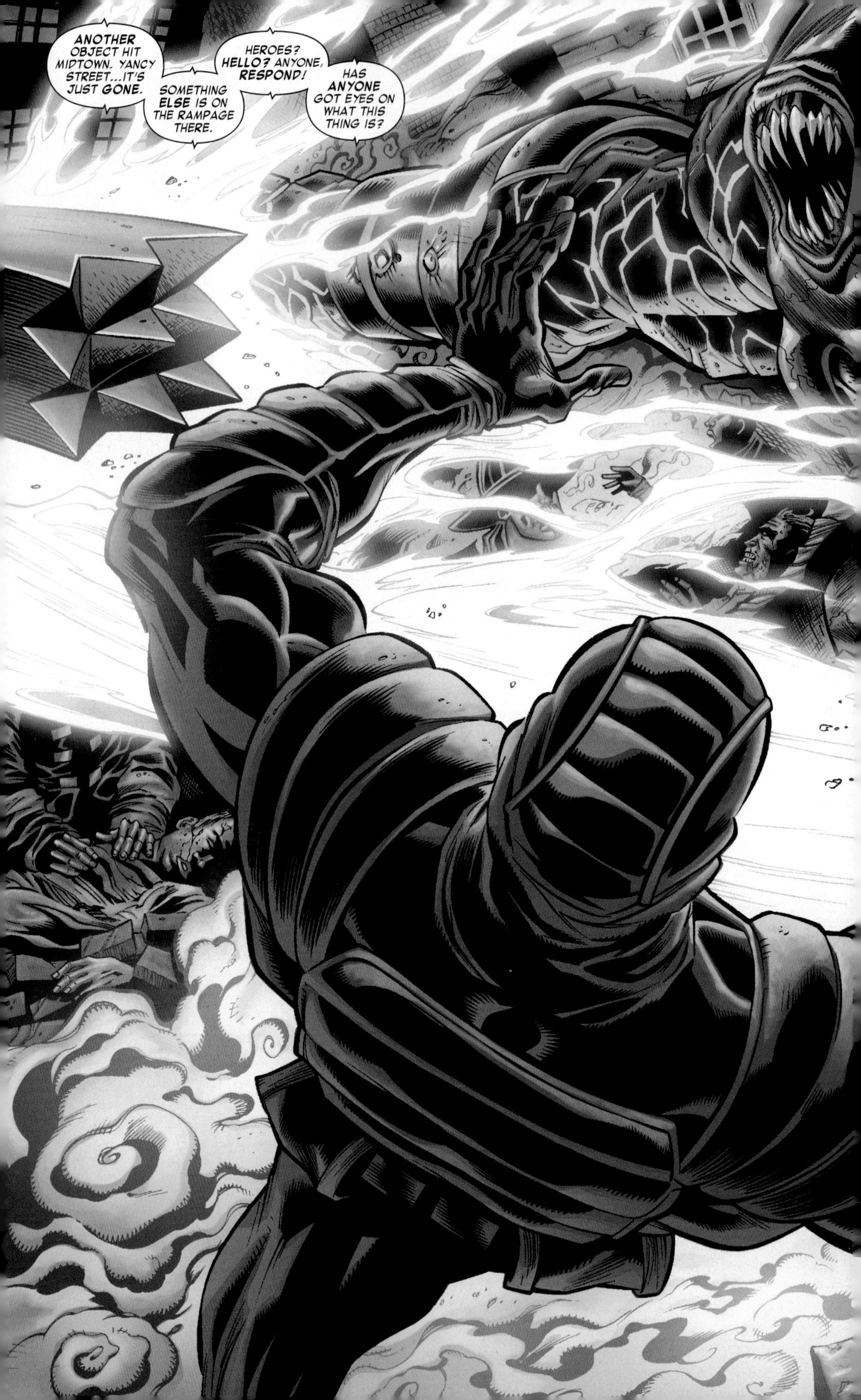
ANOTHER OBJECT HIT MIDTOWN. YANCY STREET...IT'S JUST GONE.
SOMETHING ELSE IS ON THE RAMPAGE THERE.
HEROES? HELLO? ANYONE, RESPOND!
HAS ANYONE GOT EYES ON WHAT THIS THING IS?

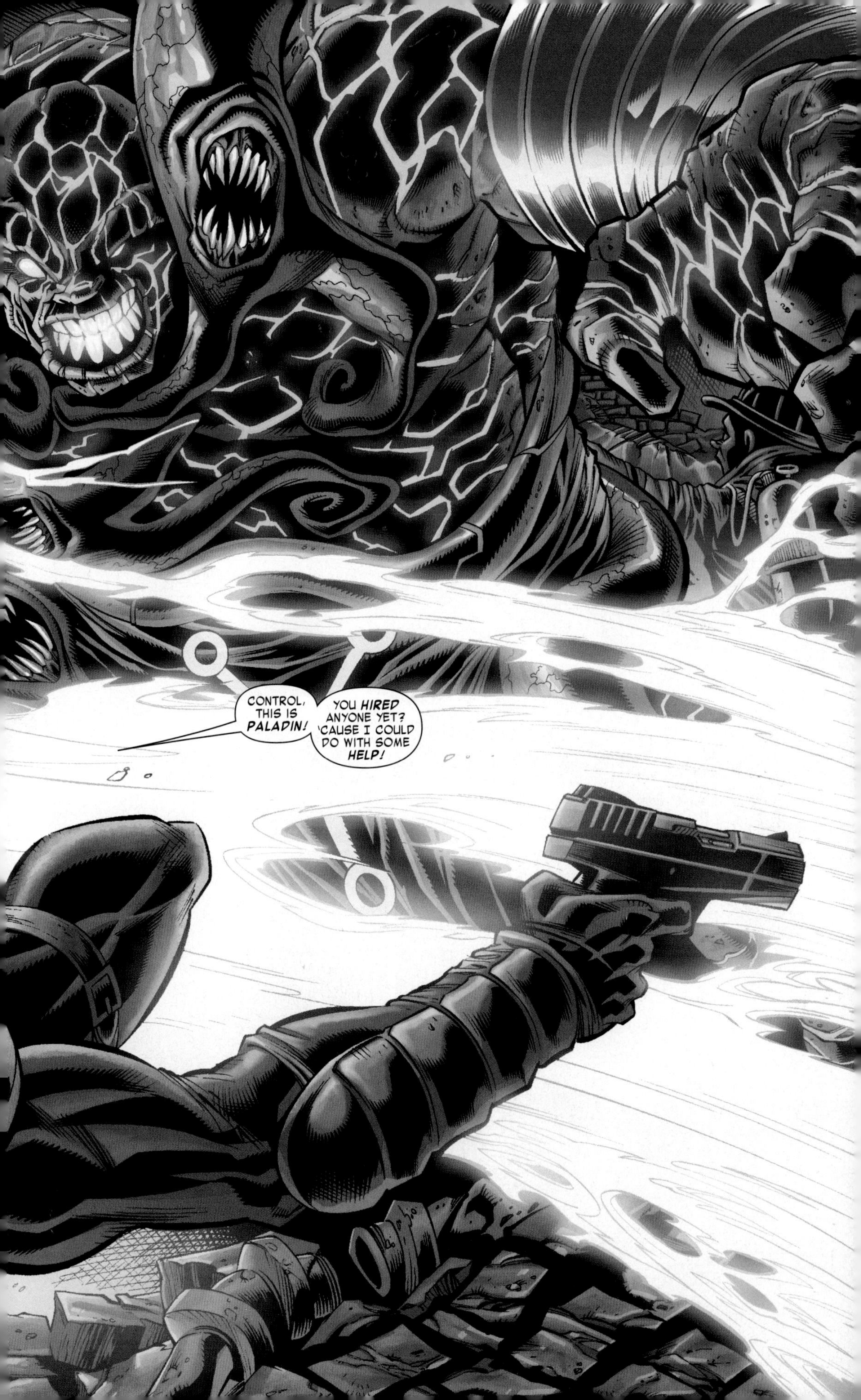
CONTROL, THIS IS PALADIN!
YOU HIRED ANYONE YET? 'CAUSE I COULD DO WITH SOME HELP!

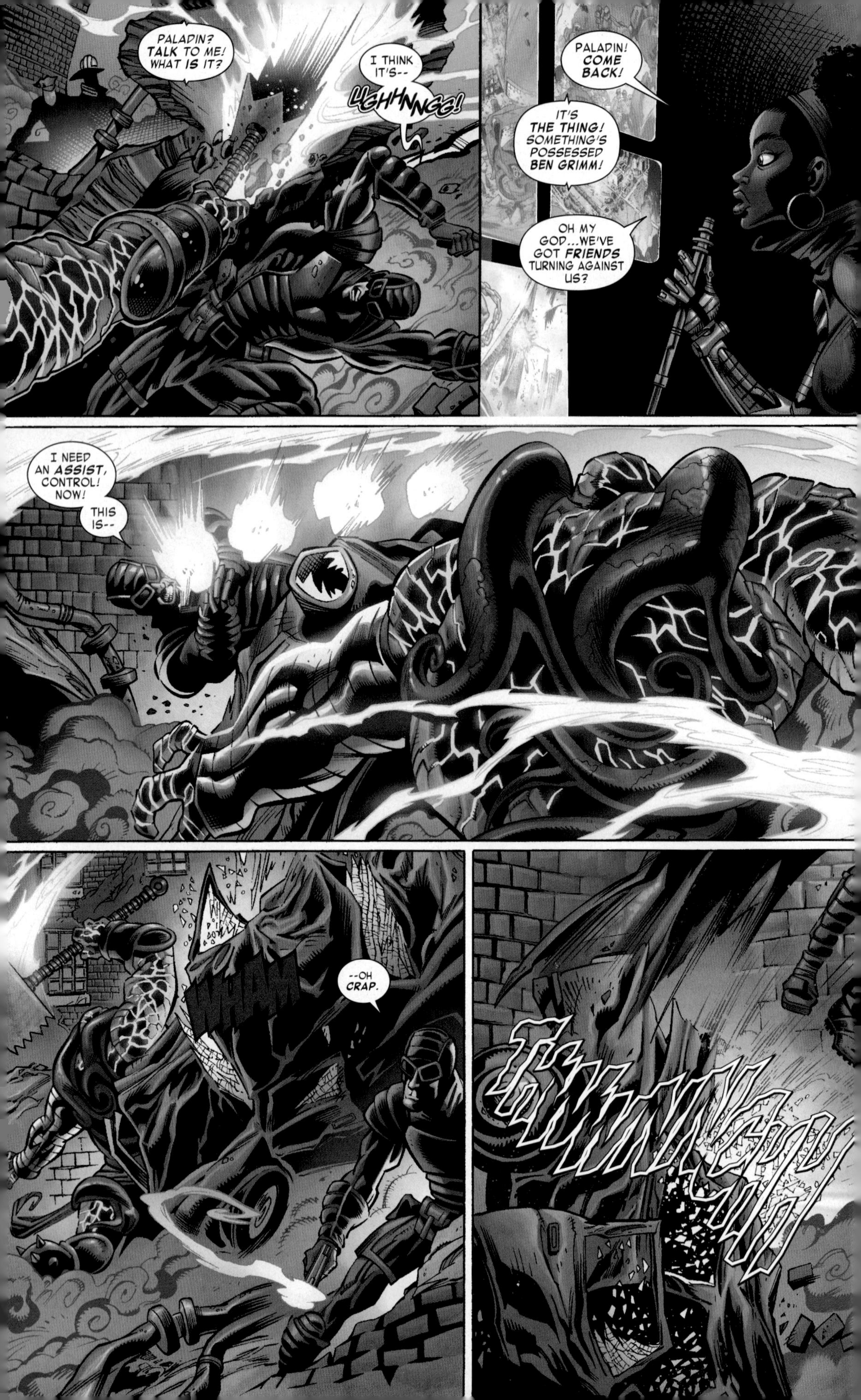
PALADIN? TALK TO ME! WHAT IS IT?
I THINK IT'S--
UGHHNNGG!
PALADIN! COME BACK!
IT'S THE THING! SOMETHING'S POSSESSED BEN GRIMM!
OH MY GOD...WE'VE GOT FRIENDS TURNING AGAINST US?
I NEED AN ASSIST, CONTROL! NOW!
THIS IS--
--OH CRAP.

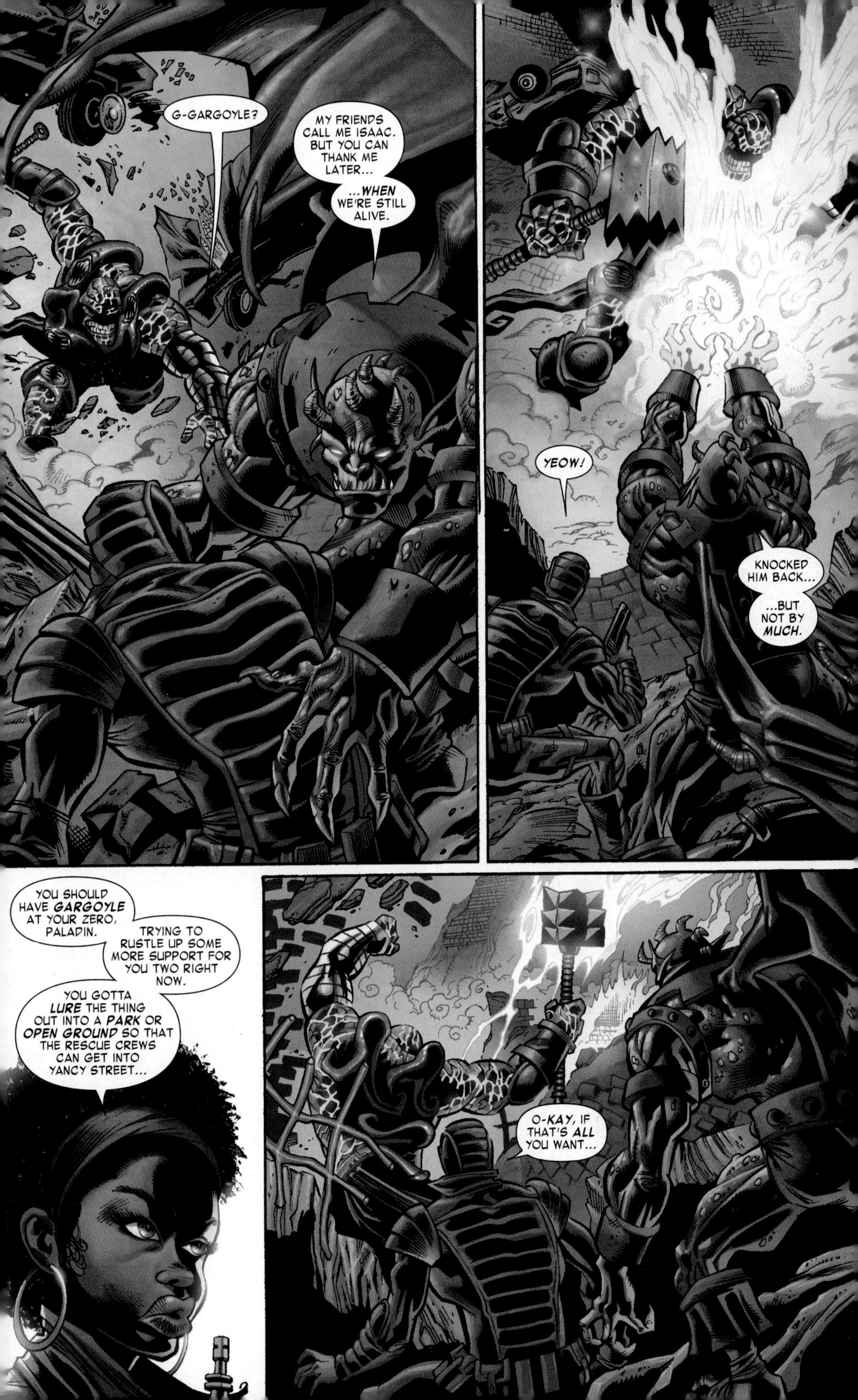
G-GARGOYLE?
MY FRIENDS CALL ME ISAAC. BUT YOU CAN THANK ME LATER...
...WHEN WE'RE STILL ALIVE.
YEOW!
KNOCKED HIM BACK...
...BUT NOT BY MUCH.
YOU SHOULD HAVE GARGOYLE AT YOUR ZERO, PALADIN.
TRYING TO RUSTLE UP SOME MORE SUPPORT FOR YOU TWO RIGHT NOW.
YOU GOTTA LURE THE THING OUT INTO A PARK OR OPEN GROUND SO THAT THE RESCUE CREWS CAN GET INTO YANCY STREET...
O-KAY, IF THAT'S ALL YOU WANT...

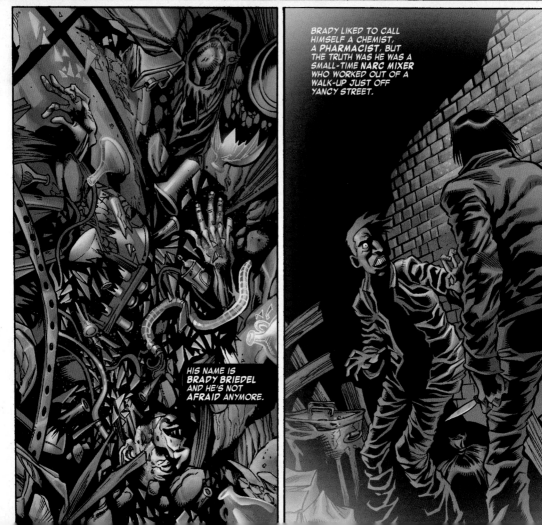

FIFTY METERS AWAY...

HE'S BEEN LYING IN THE RUBBLE FOR WHAT SEEMS LIKE HOURS.

PROBABLY ONLY BEEN A FEW MINUTES.

WHOLE PLACE CAME DOWN ON HIS HEAD.

HE FEELS WET. IT'S THE BLOOD FROM WHERE THE BROKEN GLASS CUT HIM.

IT'S THE SOLUTIONS FROM ALL THE SHATTERED BOTTLES.

HE CAN FEEL IT BURNING AS THE CHEMICALS SEEP INTO HIS WOUNDS AND HIS BLOODSTREAM.

HIS NAME IS BRADY BRIEDEL AND HE'S NOT AFRAID ANYMORE.

BRADY LIKED TO CALL HIMSELF A CHEMIST, A PHARMACIST, BUT THE TRUTH WAS HE WAS A SMALL-TIME NARC MIXER WHO WORKED OUT OF A WALK-UP JUST OFF YANCY STREET.

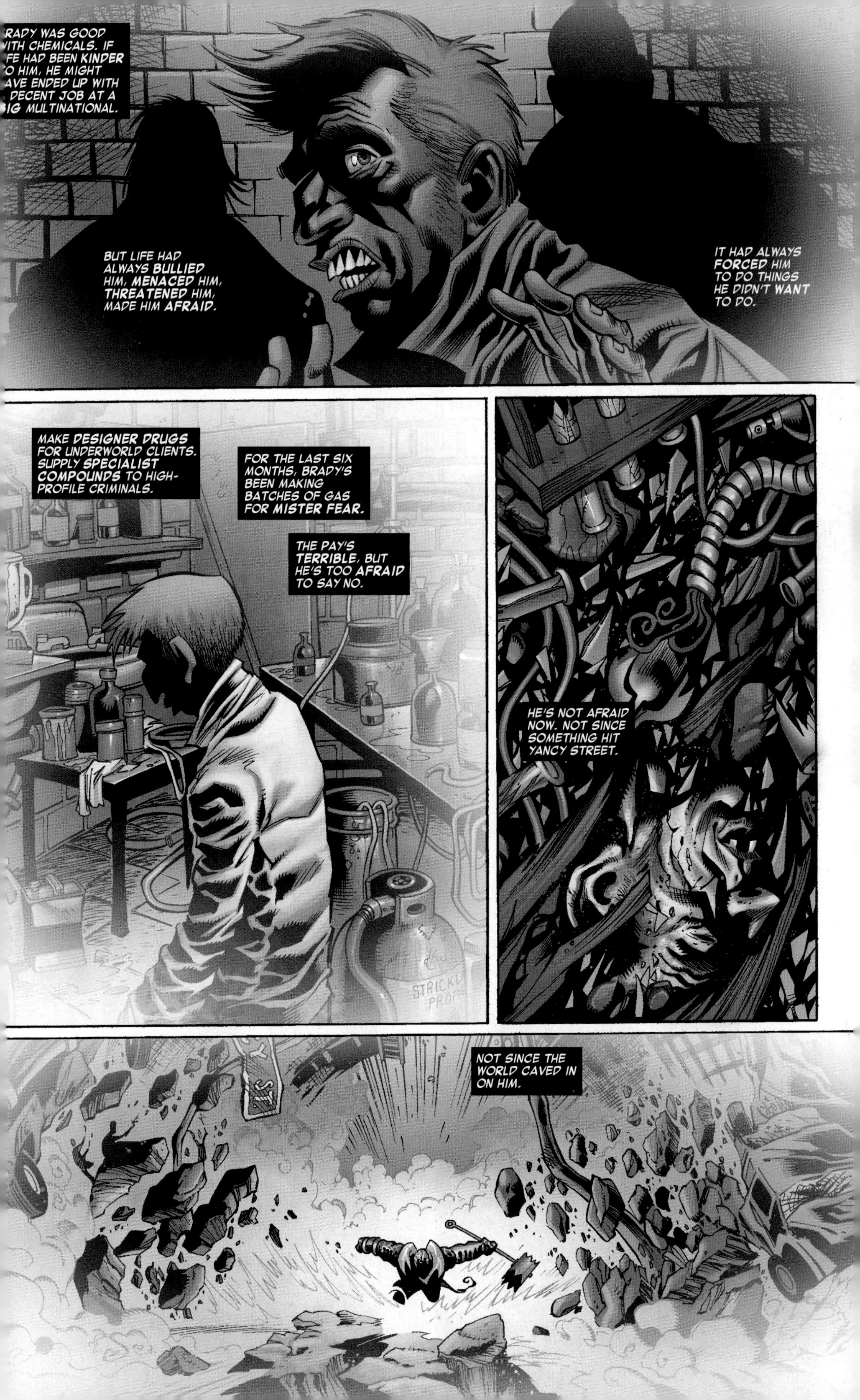
RADY WAS GOOD ITH CHEMICALS. IF FE HAD BEEN KINDER O HIM, HE MIGHT AVE ENDED UP WITH DECENT JOB AT A IG MULTINATIONAL.
BUT LIFE HAD ALWAYS BULLIED HIM, MENACED HIM, THREATENED HIM, MADE HIM AFRAID.
IT HAD ALWAYS FORCED HIM TO DO THINGS HE DIDN'T WANT TO DO.
MAKE DESIGNER DRUGS FOR UNDERWORLD CLIENTS. SUPPLY SPECIALIST COMPOUNDS TO HIGH-PROFILE CRIMINALS.
FOR THE LAST SIX MONTHS, BRADY'S BEEN MAKING BATCHES OF GAS FOR MISTER FEAR.
THE PAY'S TERRIBLE, BUT HE'S TOO AFRAID TO SAY NO.
STRICKL
PROP
HE'S NOT AFRAID NOW. NOT SINCE SOMETHING HIT YANCY STREET.
NOT SINCE THE WORLD CAVED IN ON HIM.

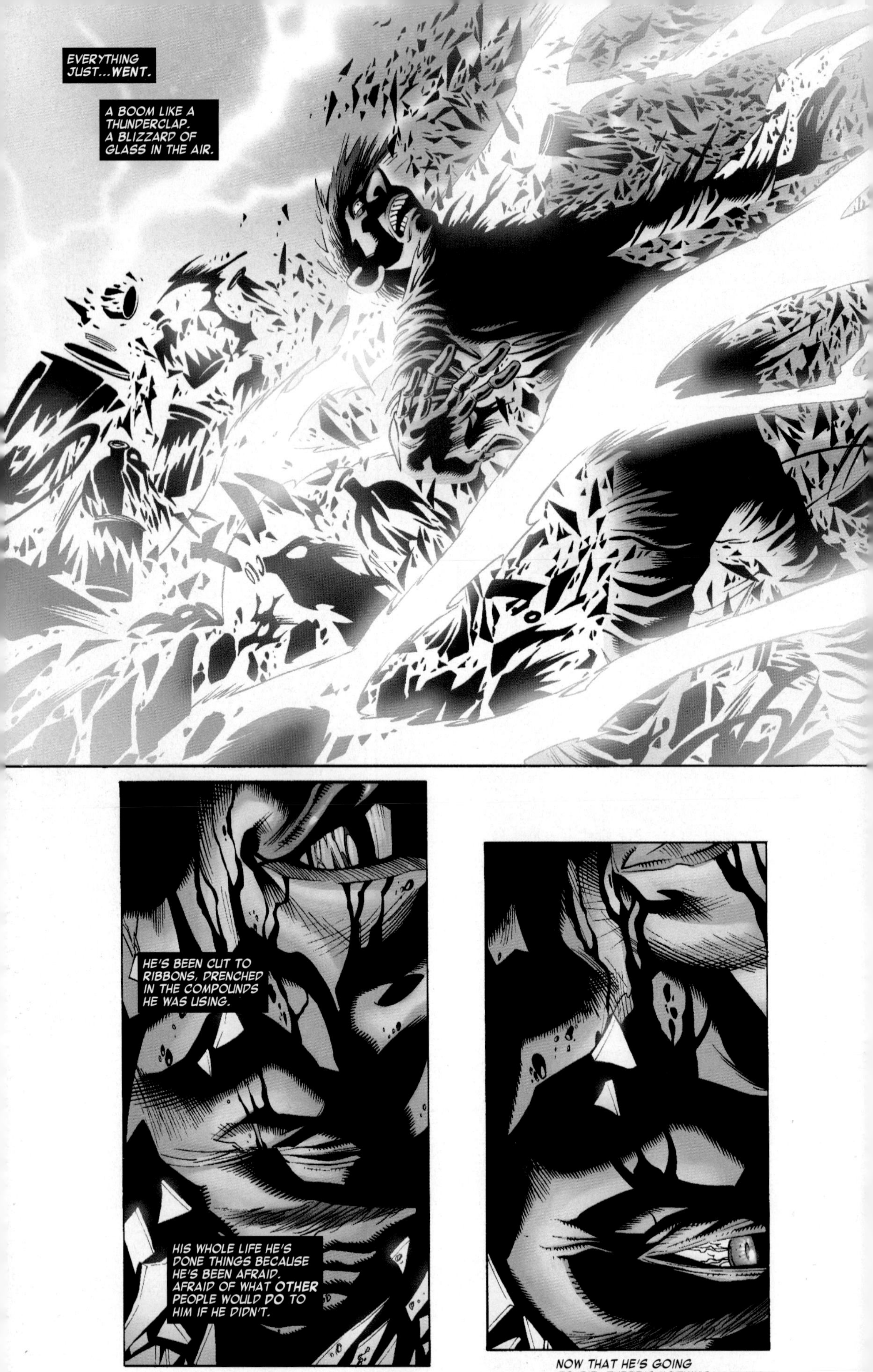
EVERYTHING JUST...WENT.
A BOOM LIKE A THUNDERCLAP. A BLIZZARD OF GLASS IN THE AIR.
HE'S BEEN CUT TO RIBBONS, DRENCHED IN THE COMPOUNDS HE WAS USING.
HIS WHOLE LIFE HE'S DONE THINGS BECAUSE HE'S BEEN AFRAID. AFRAID OF WHAT OTHER PEOPLE WOULD DO TO HIM IF HE DIDN'T.
NOW THAT HE'S GOING TO DIE, THERE'S NOTHING LEFT TO BE AFRAID OF.

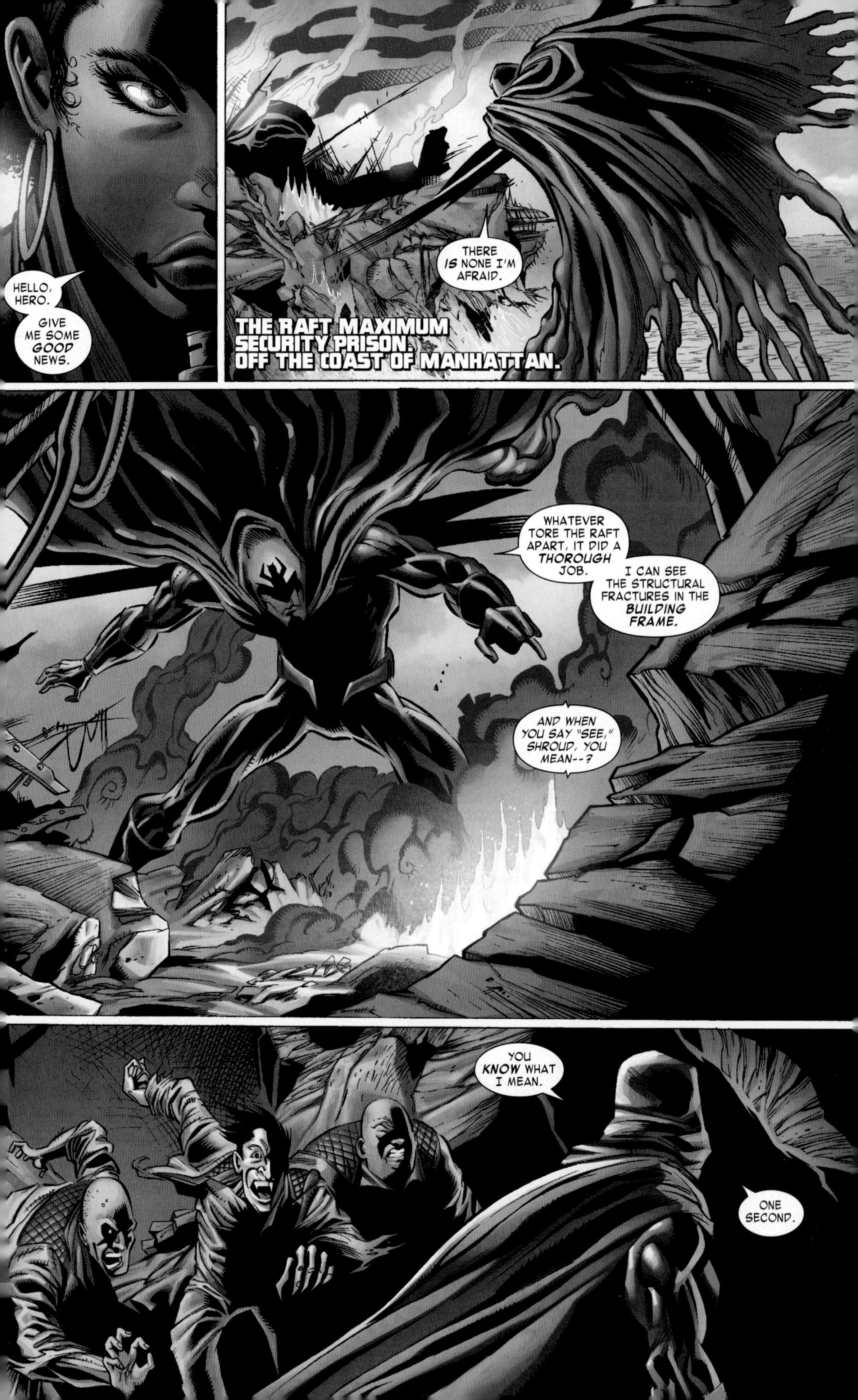
HELLO, HERO.
GIVE ME SOME GOOD NEWS.
THE RAFT MAXIMUM SECURITY PRISON. OFF THE COAST OF MANHATTAN.
THERE IS NONE I'M AFRAID.
WHATEVER TORE THE RAFT APART, IT DID A THOROUGH JOB.
I CAN SEE THE STRUCTURAL FRACTURES IN THE BUILDING FRAME.
AND WHEN YOU SAY "SEE," SHROUD, YOU MEAN--?
YOU KNOW WHAT I MEAN.
ONE SECOND.

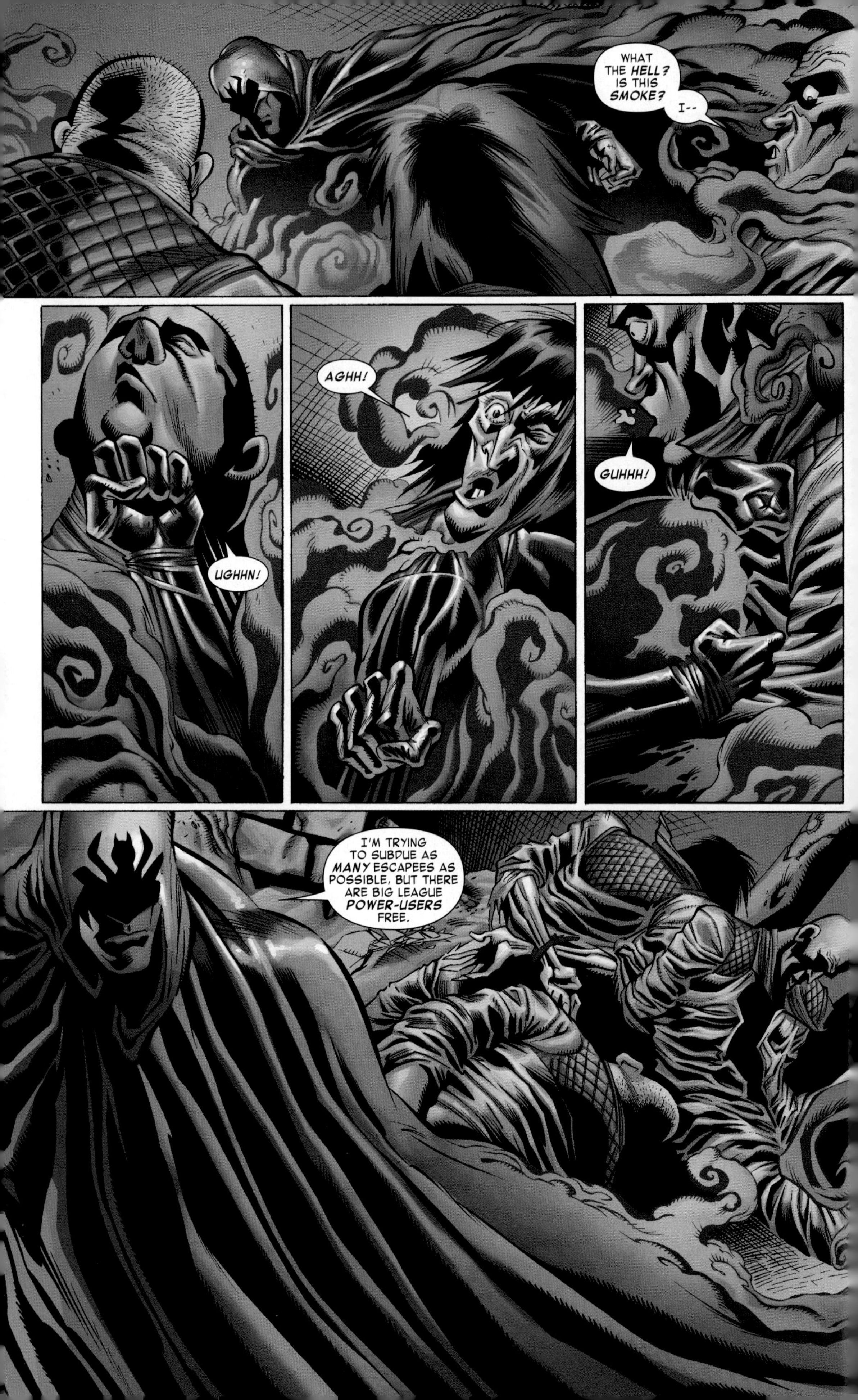
WHAT THE HELL? IS THIS SMOKE?
I--
UGHHN!
AGHH!
GUHHH!
I'M TRYING TO SUBDUE AS MANY ESCAPEES AS POSSIBLE, BUT THERE ARE BIG LEAGUE POWER-USERS FREE.

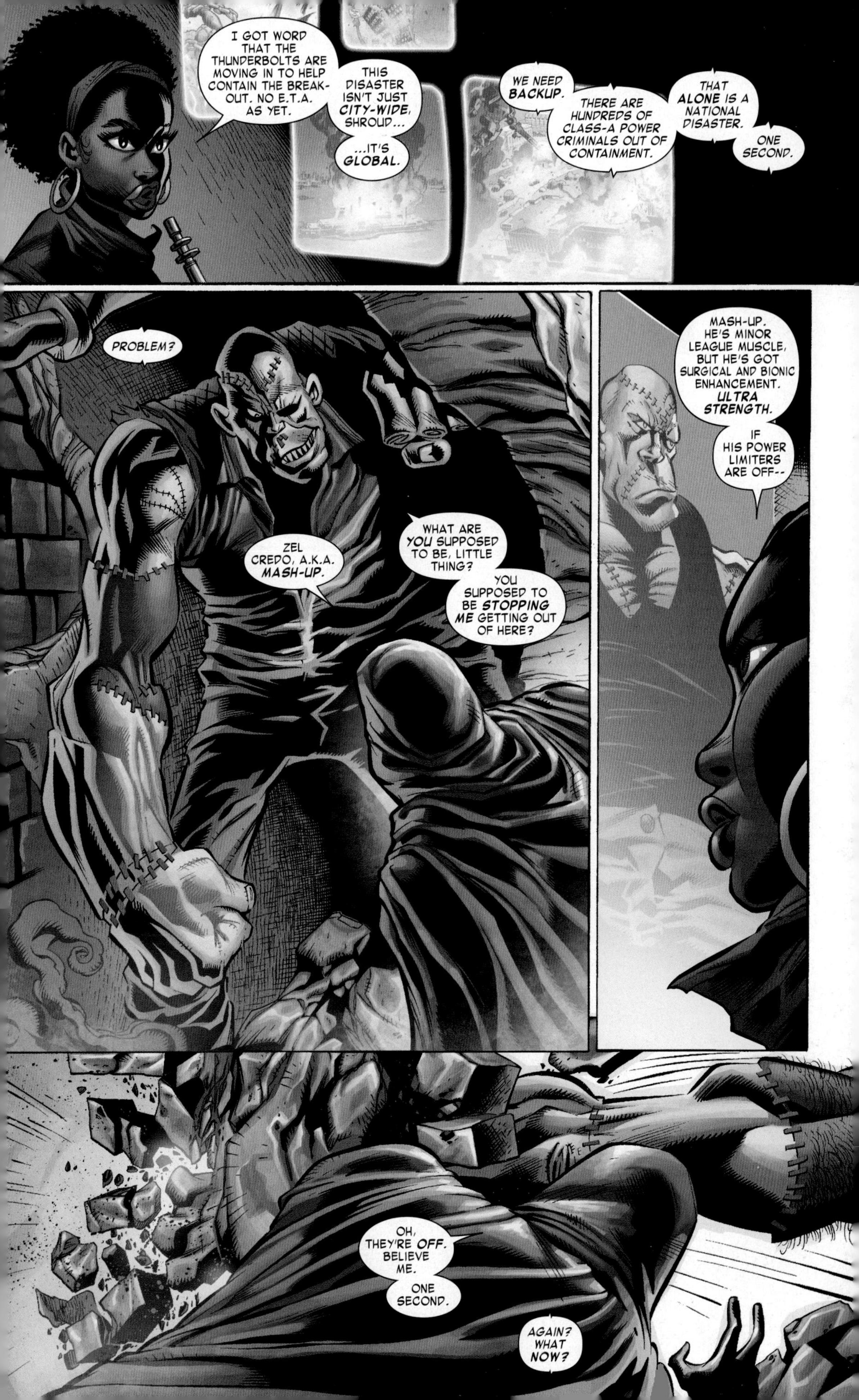
I GOT WORD THAT THE THUNDERBOLTS ARE MOVING IN TO HELP CONTAIN THE BREAK-OUT. NO E.T.A. AS YET.
THIS DISASTER ISN'T JUST CITY-WIDE, SHROUD...
...IT'S GLOBAL.
WE NEED BACKUP.
THERE ARE HUNDREDS OF CLASS-A POWER CRIMINALS OUT OF CONTAINMENT.
THAT ALONE IS A NATIONAL DISASTER.
ONE SECOND.
PROBLEM?
ZEL CREDO, A.K.A. MASH-UP.
WHAT ARE YOU SUPPOSED TO BE, LITTLE THING?
YOU SUPPOSED TO BE STOPPING ME GETTING OUT OF HERE?
MASH-UP. HE'S MINOR LEAGUE MUSCLE, BUT HE'S GOT SURGICAL AND BIONIC ENHANCEMENT. ULTRA STRENGTH.
IF HIS POWER LIMITERS ARE OFF--
OH, THEY'RE OFF. BELIEVE ME.
ONE SECOND.
AGAIN? WHAT NOW?

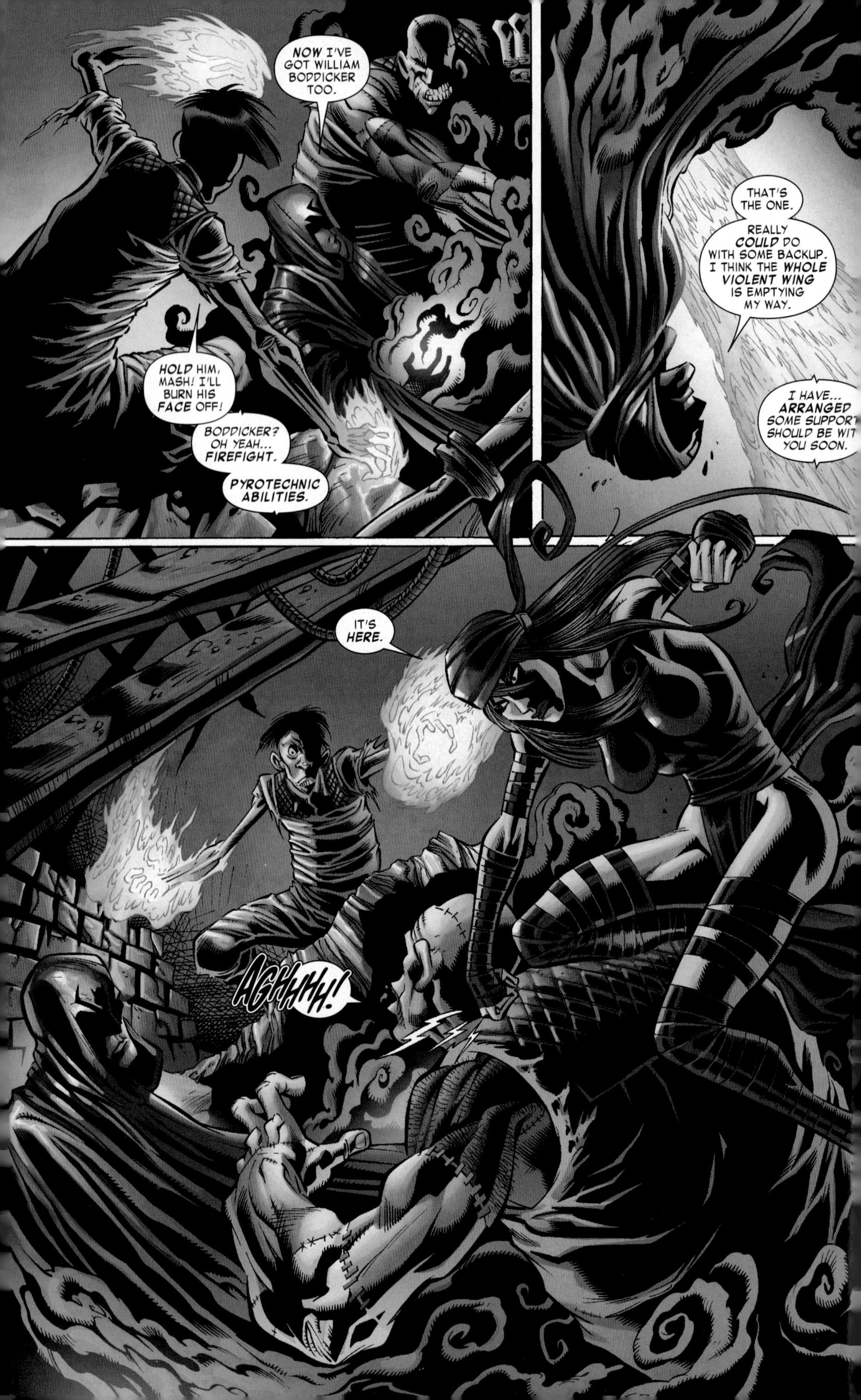
NOW I'VE GOT WILLIAM BODDICKER TOO.
HOLD HIM, MASH! I'LL BURN HIS FACE OFF!
BODDICKER? OH YEAH... FIREFIGHT.
PYROTECHNIC ABILITIES.
THAT'S THE ONE.
REALLY COULD DO WITH SOME BACKUP. I THINK THE WHOLE VIOLENT WING IS EMPTYING MY WAY.
I HAVE... ARRANGED SOME SUPPORT SHOULD BE WIT YOU SOON.
IT'S HERE.
AGHHHHH!

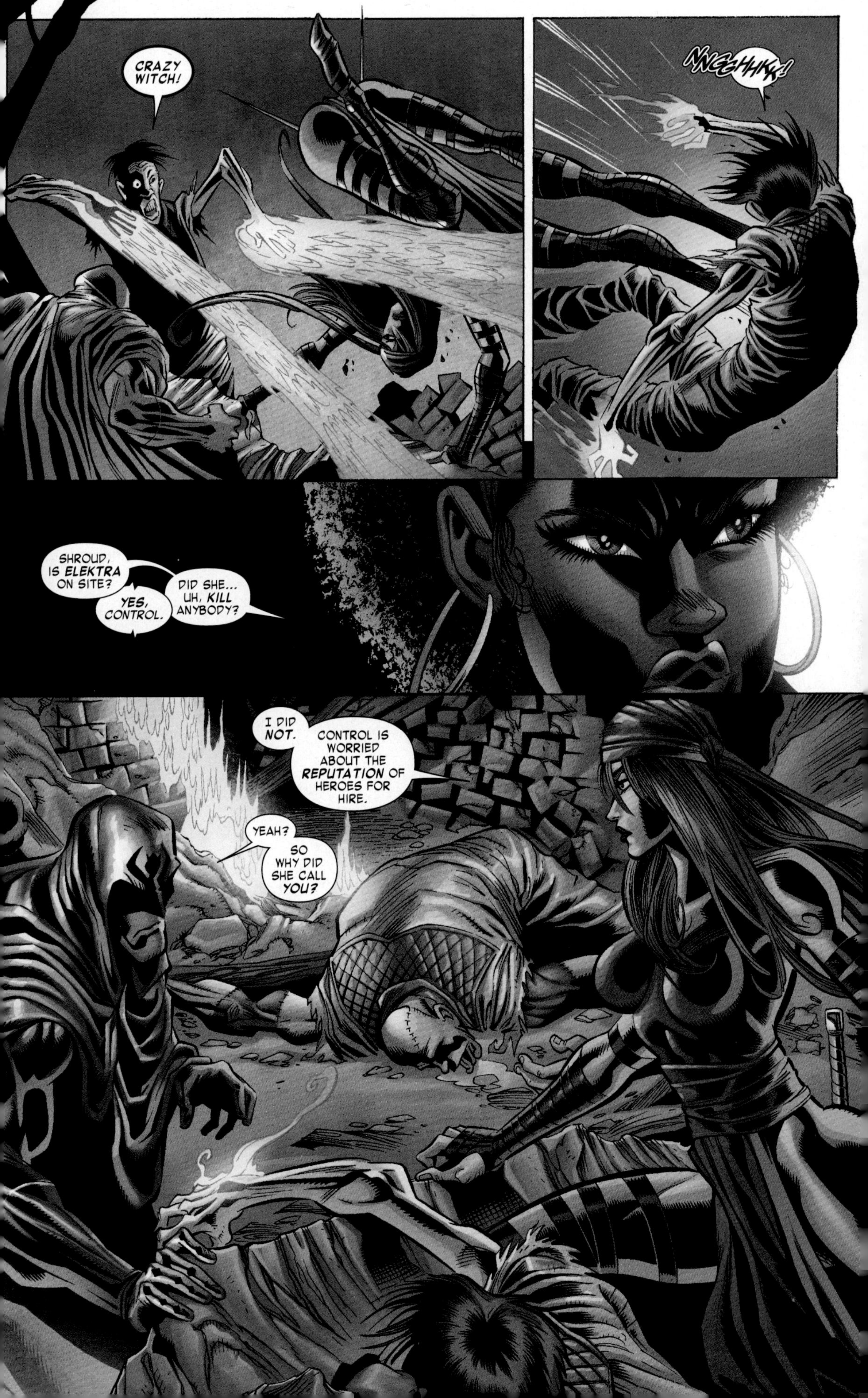
CRAZY WITCH!
NNGGHHKK!
SHROUD, IS ELEKTRA ON SITE?
YES, CONTROL.
DID SHE... UH, KILL ANYBODY?
I DID NOT.
CONTROL IS WORRIED ABOUT THE REPUTATION OF HEROES FOR HIRE.
YEAH? SO WHY DID SHE CALL YOU?

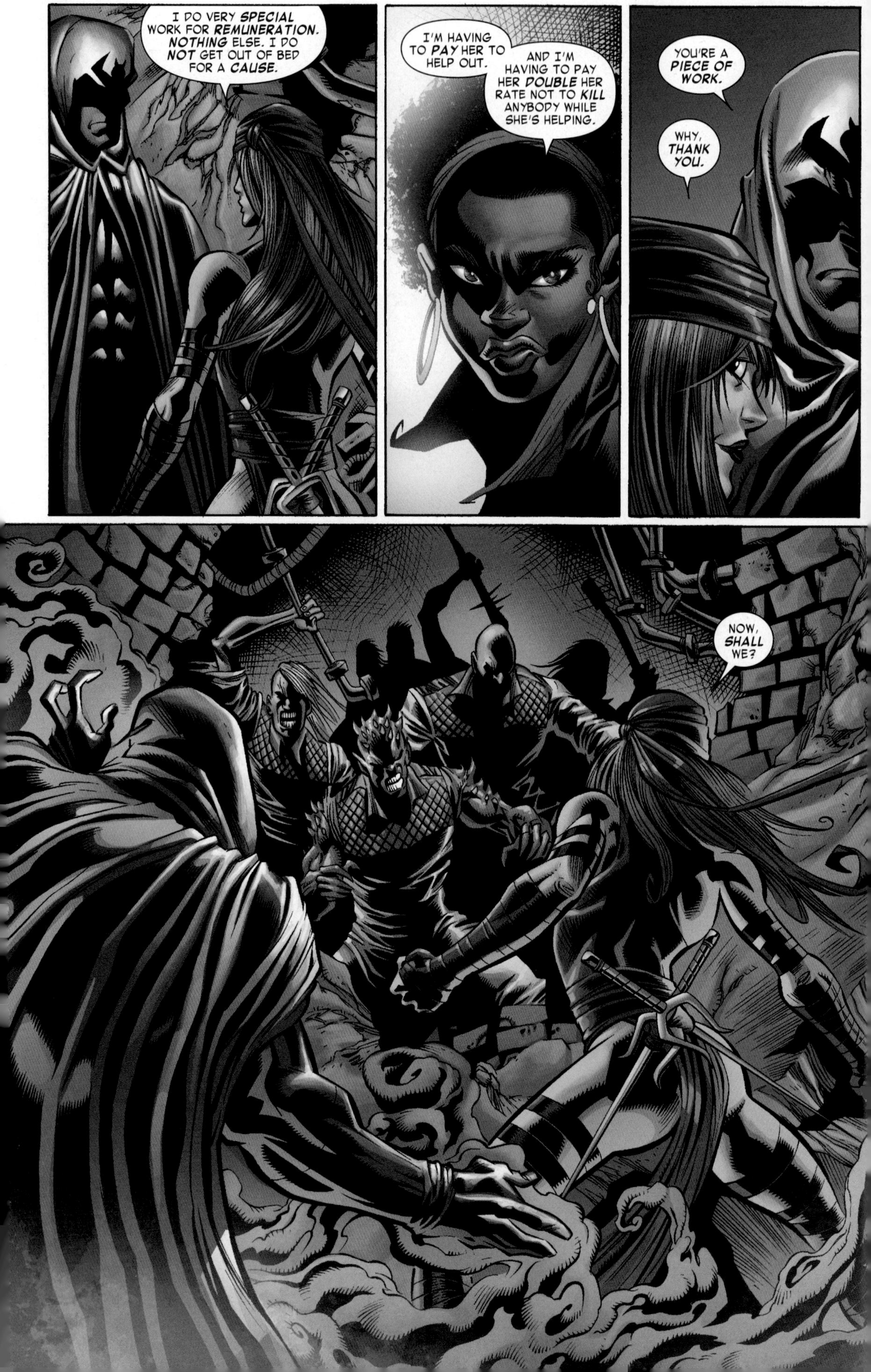
I DO VERY SPECIAL WORK FOR REMUNERATION. NOTHING ELSE. I DO NOT GET OUT OF BED FOR A CAUSE.
I'M HAVING TO PAY HER TO HELP OUT.
AND I'M HAVING TO PAY HER DOUBLE HER RATE NOT TO KILL ANYBODY WHILE SHE'S HELPING.
YOU'RE A PIECE OF WORK.
WHY, THANK YOU.
NOW, SHALL WE?

WHEN HE DOESN'T DIE, BRADY BRIEDEL DRAGS HIMSELF OUT OF THE RUBBLE.

P-PLEASE... PLEASE, I...

OH GOD! NOOOO!

PLEASE, GET AWAY FROM US! NOOOO!

AIIIEEEEEE!

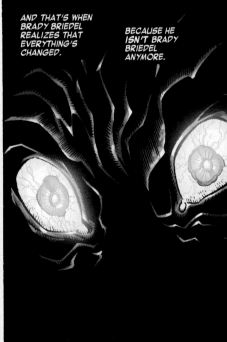

AND THAT'S WHEN BRADY BRIEDEL REALIZES THAT EVERYTHING'S CHANGED.

BECAUSE HE ISN'T BRADY BRIEDEL ANYMORE.

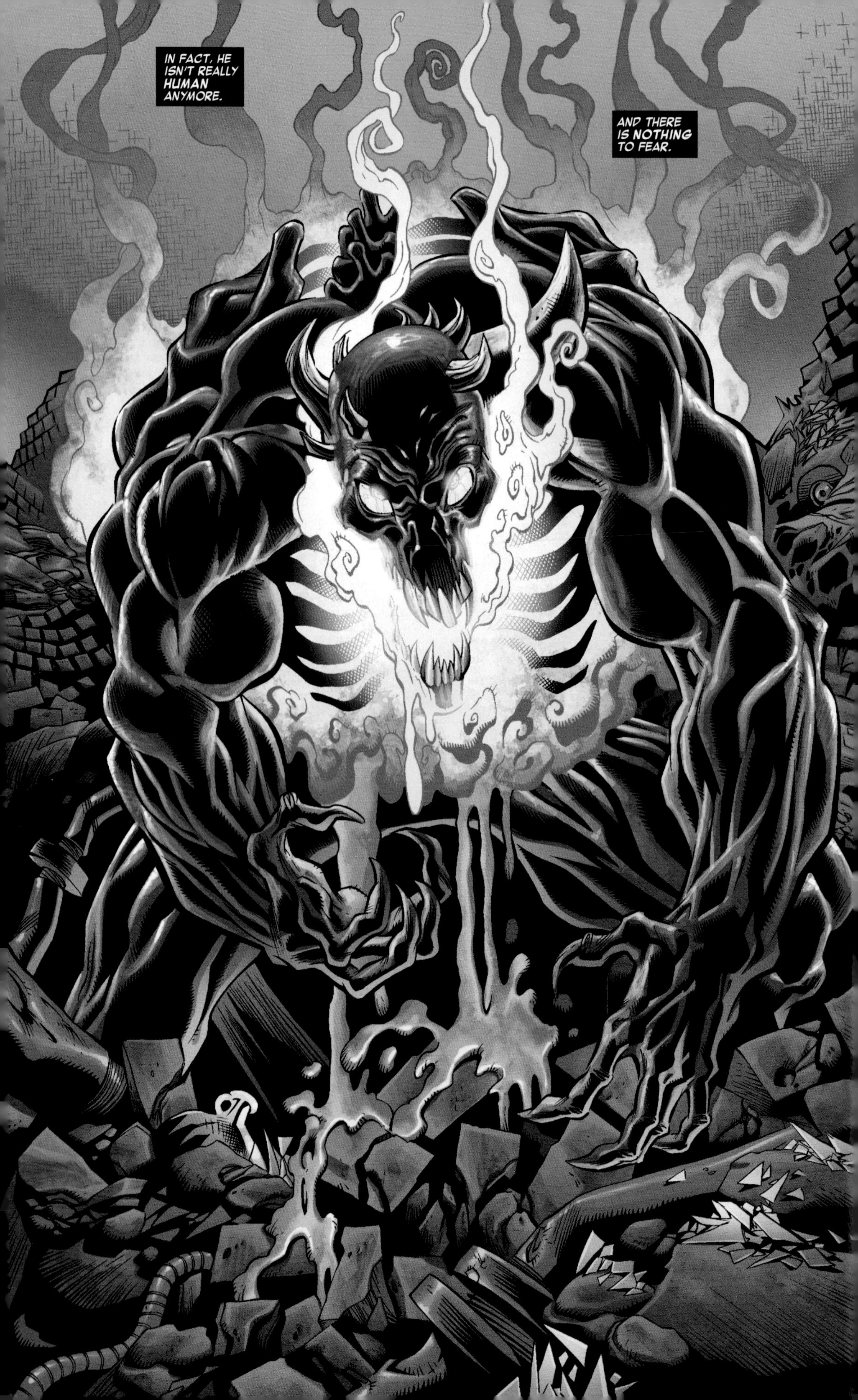
IN FACT, HE ISN'T REALLY HUMAN ANYMORE.
AND THERE IS NOTHING TO FEAR.

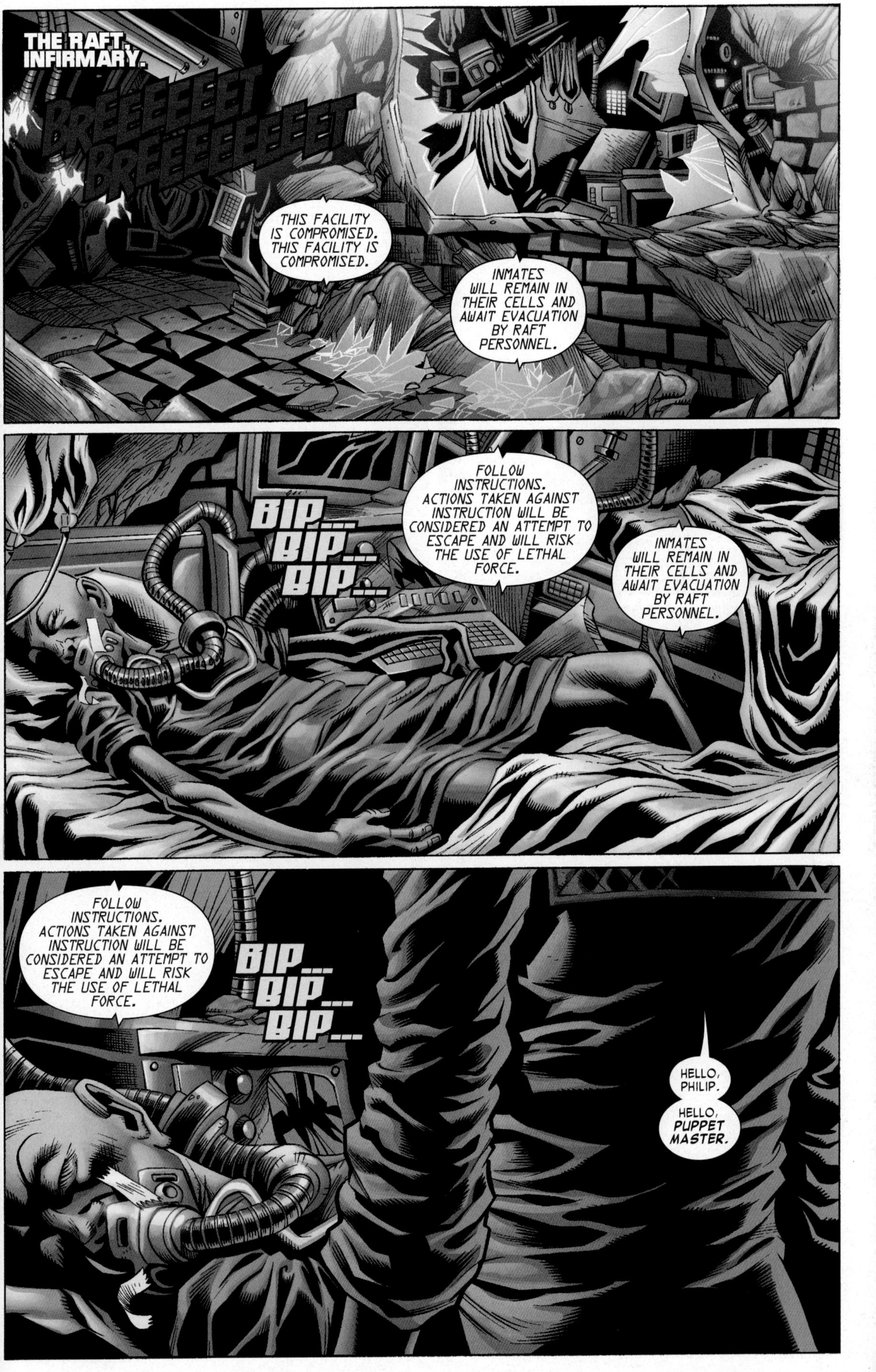
THE RAFT, INFIRMARY.
BREEEEEET BREEEEEEEET
THIS FACILITY IS COMPROMISED. THIS FACILITY IS COMPROMISED.
INMATES WILL REMAIN IN THEIR CELLS AND AWAIT EVACUATION BY RAFT PERSONNEL.
BIP... BIP... BIP...
FOLLOW INSTRUCTIONS. ACTIONS TAKEN AGAINST INSTRUCTION WILL BE CONSIDERED AN ATTEMPT TO ESCAPE AND WILL RISK THE USE OF LETHAL FORCE.
INMATES WILL REMAIN IN THEIR CELLS AND AWAIT EVACUATION BY RAFT PERSONNEL.
FOLLOW INSTRUCTIONS. ACTIONS TAKEN AGAINST INSTRUCTION WILL BE CONSIDERED AN ATTEMPT TO ESCAPE AND WILL RISK THE USE OF LETHAL FORCE.
BIP... BIP... BIP...
HELLO, PHILIP.
HELLO, PUPPET MASTER.

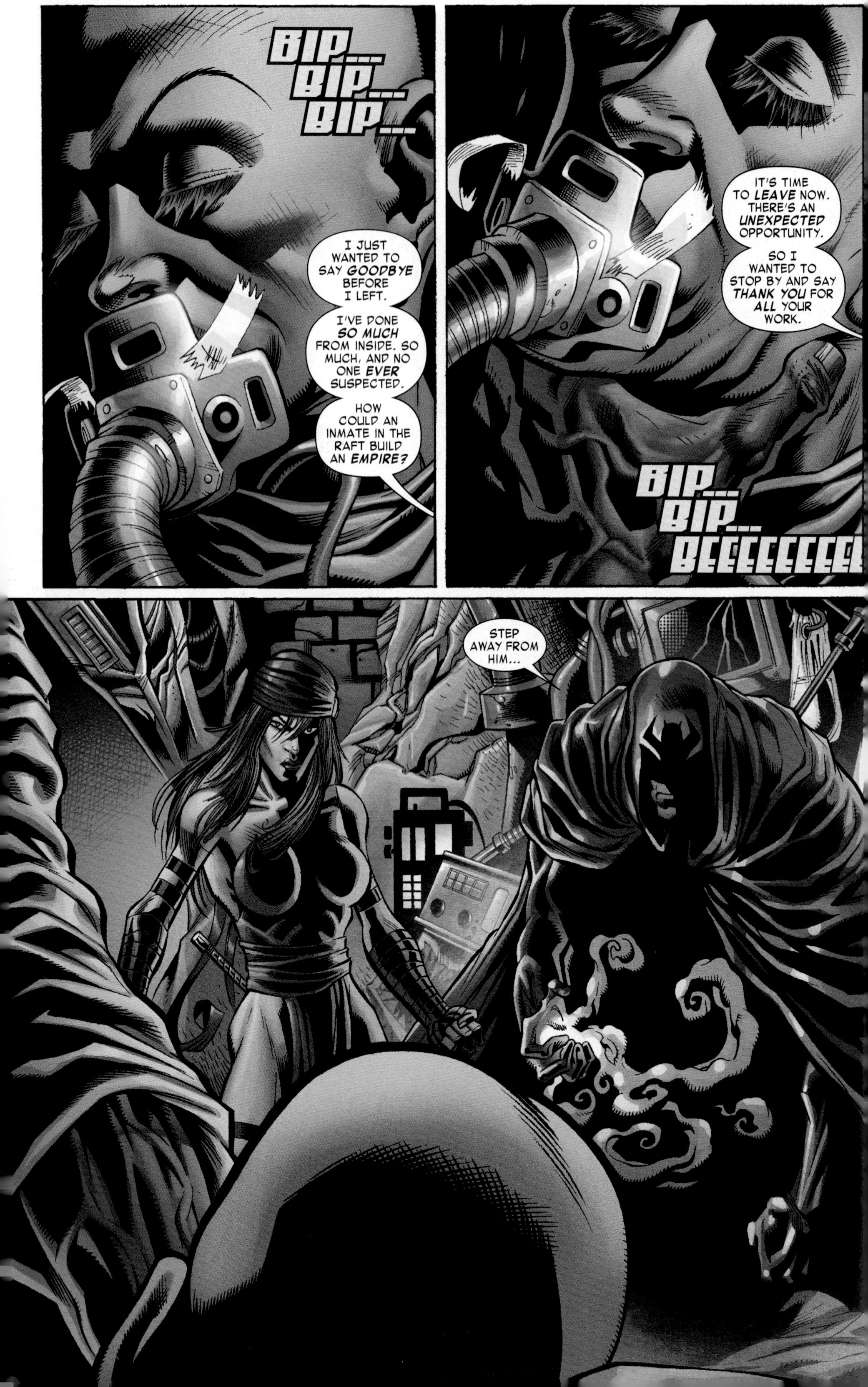
BIP... BIP... BIP...
I JUST WANTED TO SAY GOODBYE BEFORE I LEFT.
I'VE DONE SO MUCH FROM INSIDE. SO MUCH, AND NO ONE EVER SUSPECTED.
HOW COULD AN INMATE IN THE RAFT BUILD AN EMPIRE?
IT'S TIME TO LEAVE NOW. THERE'S AN UNEXPECTED OPPORTUNITY.
SO I WANTED TO STOP BY AND SAY THANK YOU FOR ALL YOUR WORK.
BIP... BIP... BEEEEEEEEE
STEP AWAY FROM HIM...

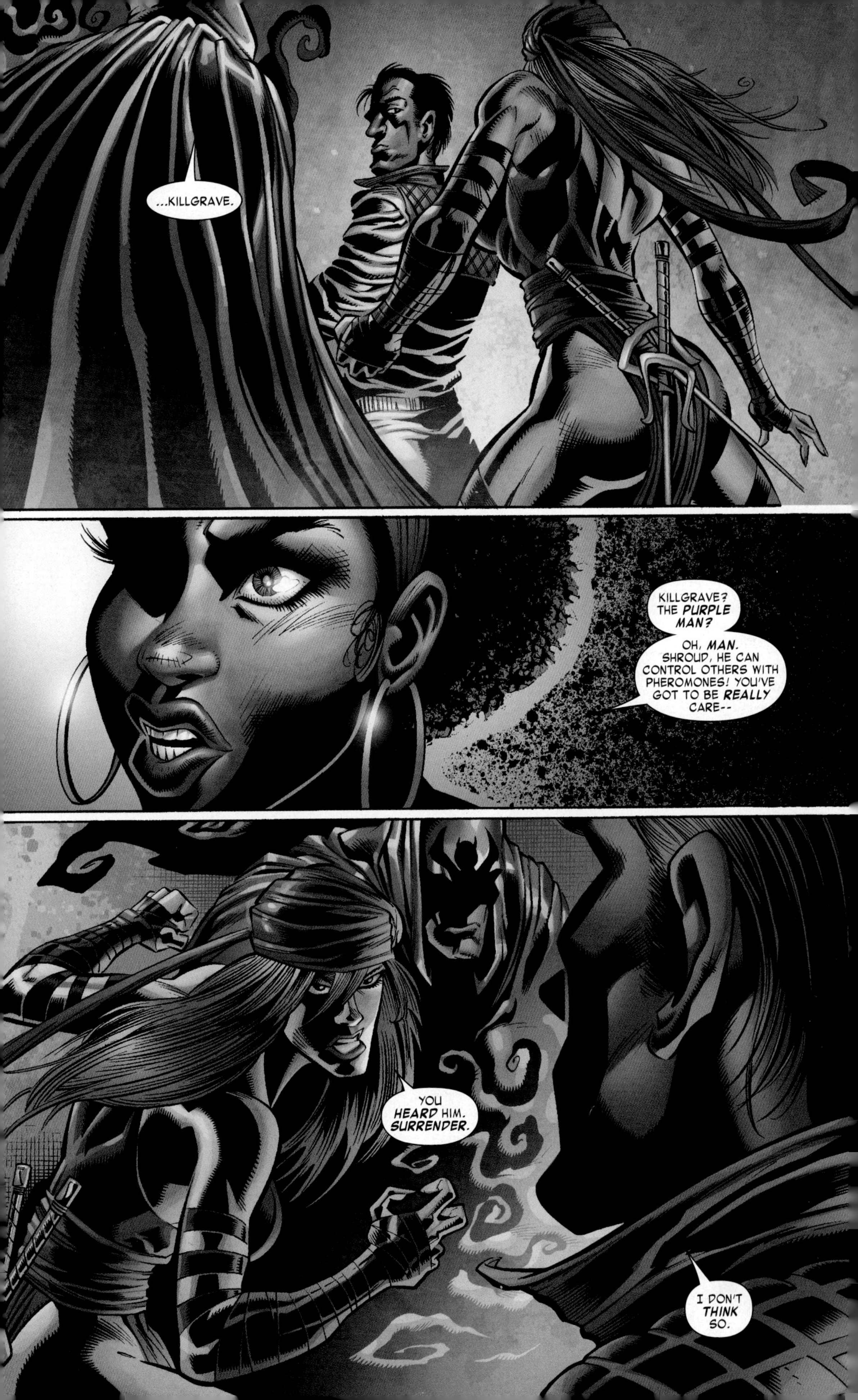
...KILLGRAVE.
KILLGRAVE? THE PURPLE MAN?
OH, MAN. SHROUD, HE CAN CONTROL OTHERS WITH PHEROMONES! YOU'VE GOT TO BE REALLY CARE--
YOU HEARD HIM. SURRENDER.
I DON'T THINK SO.

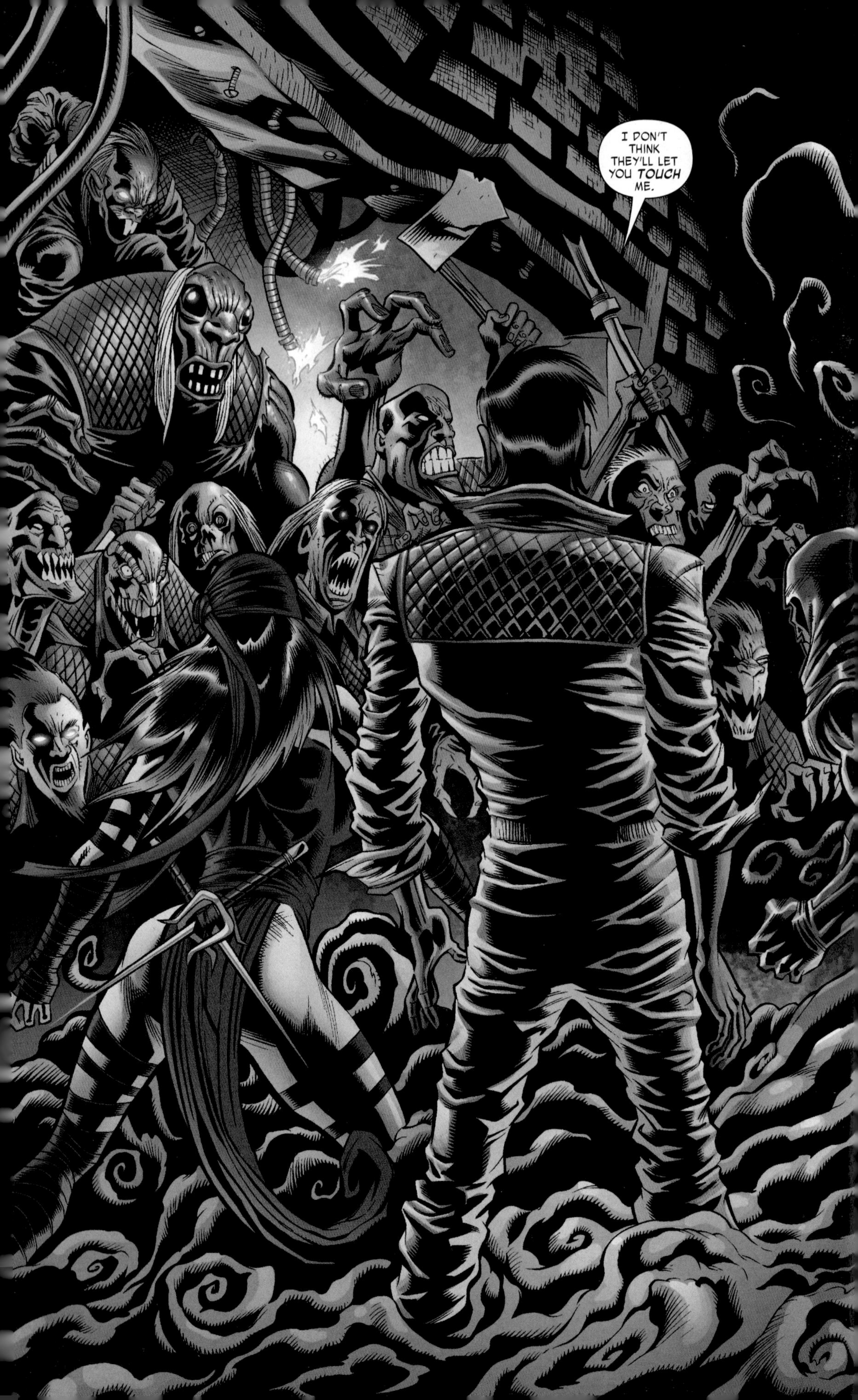
I DON'T THINK THEY'LL LET YOU *TOUCH* ME.

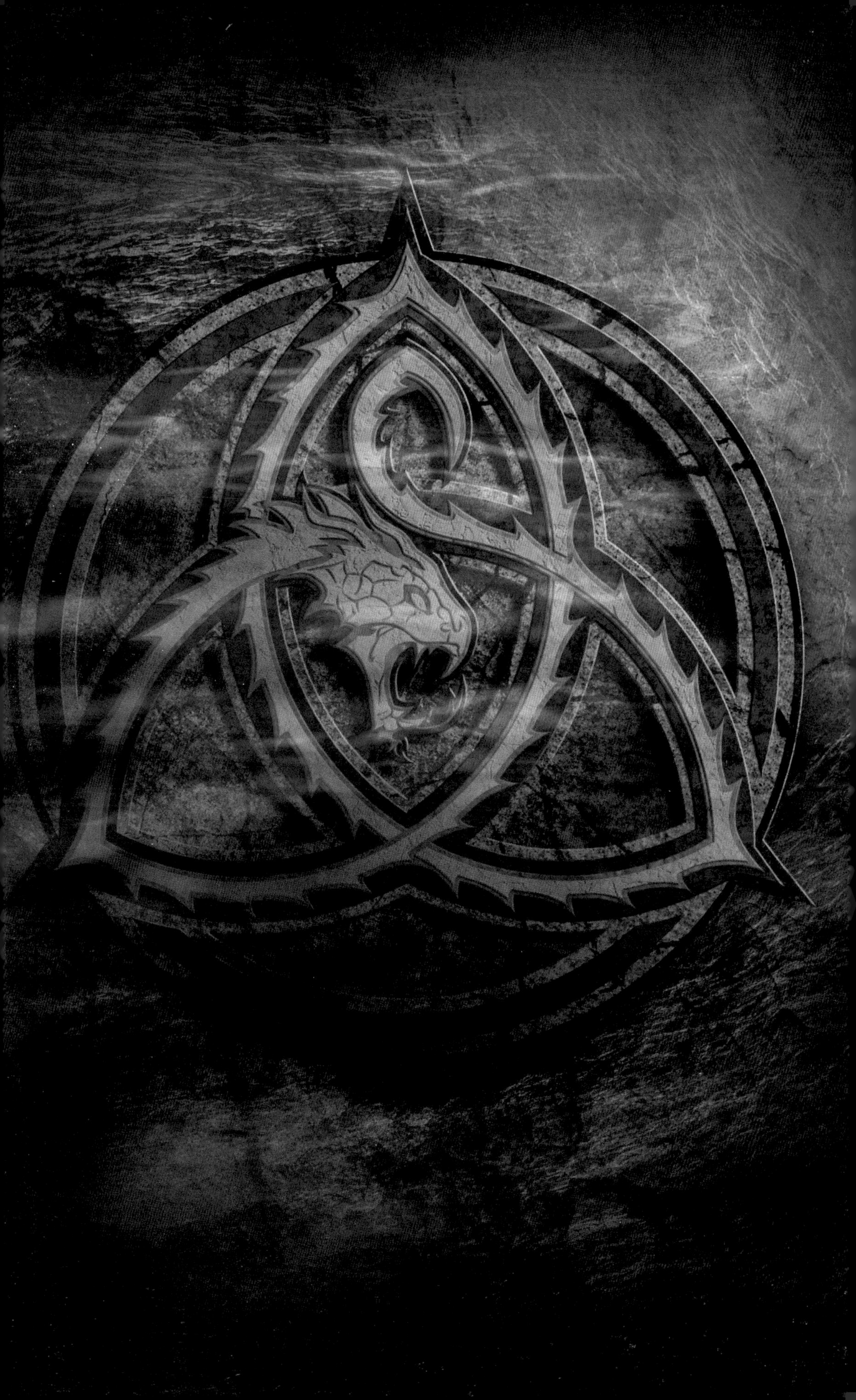

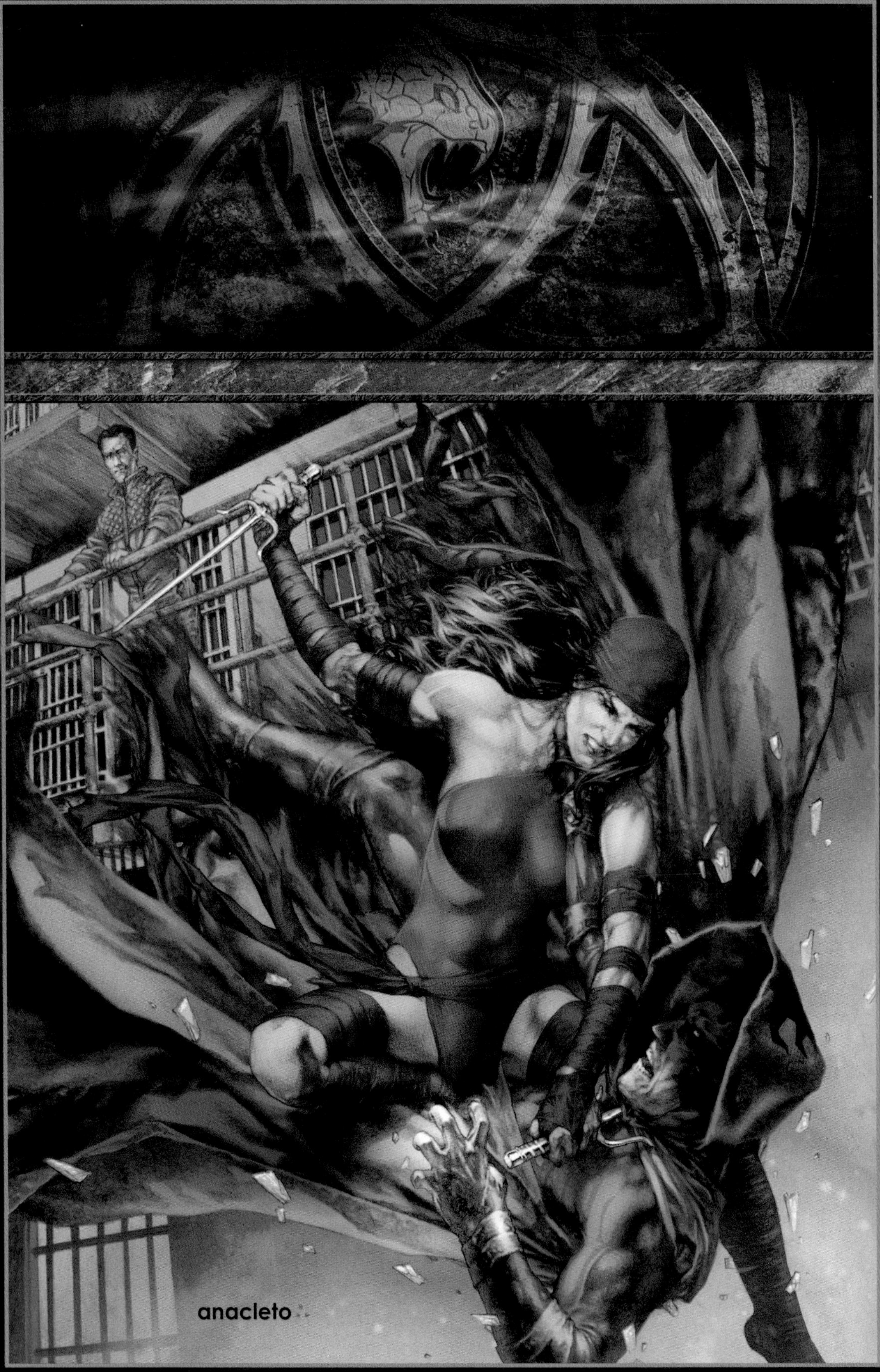
anacleto

HEROES FOR HIRE #10

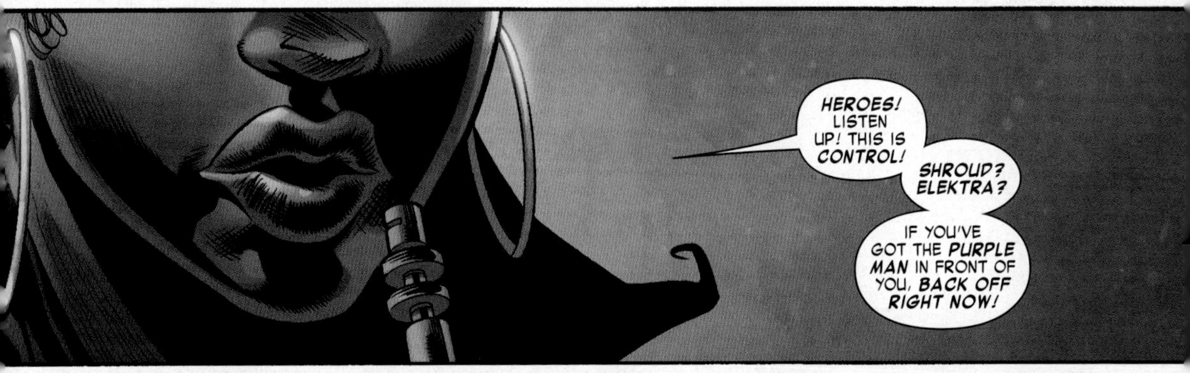
HEROES! LISTEN UP! THIS IS CONTROL!
SHROUD? ELEKTRA?
IF YOU'VE GOT THE PURPLE MAN IN FRONT OF YOU, BACK OFF RIGHT NOW!

EVERYTHING TO LOSE

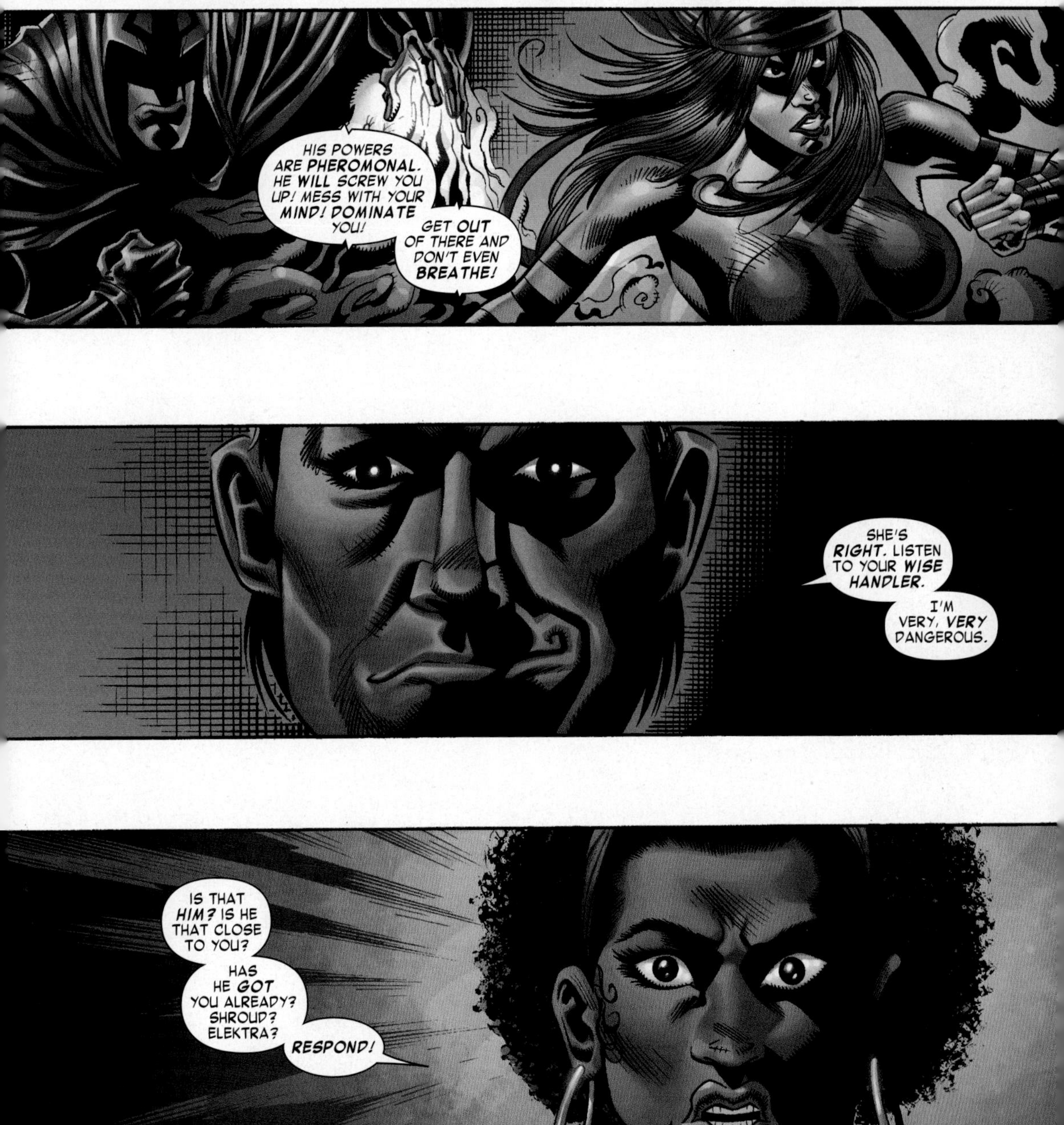
HIS POWERS ARE PHEROMONAL. HE WILL SCREW YOU UP! MESS WITH YOUR MIND! DOMINATE YOU!
GET OUT OF THERE AND DON'T EVEN BREATHE!
SHE'S RIGHT. LISTEN TO YOUR WISE HANDLER.
I'M VERY, VERY DANGEROUS.
IS THAT HIM? IS HE THAT CLOSE TO YOU?
HAS HE GOT YOU ALREADY? SHROUD? ELEKTRA?
RESPOND!

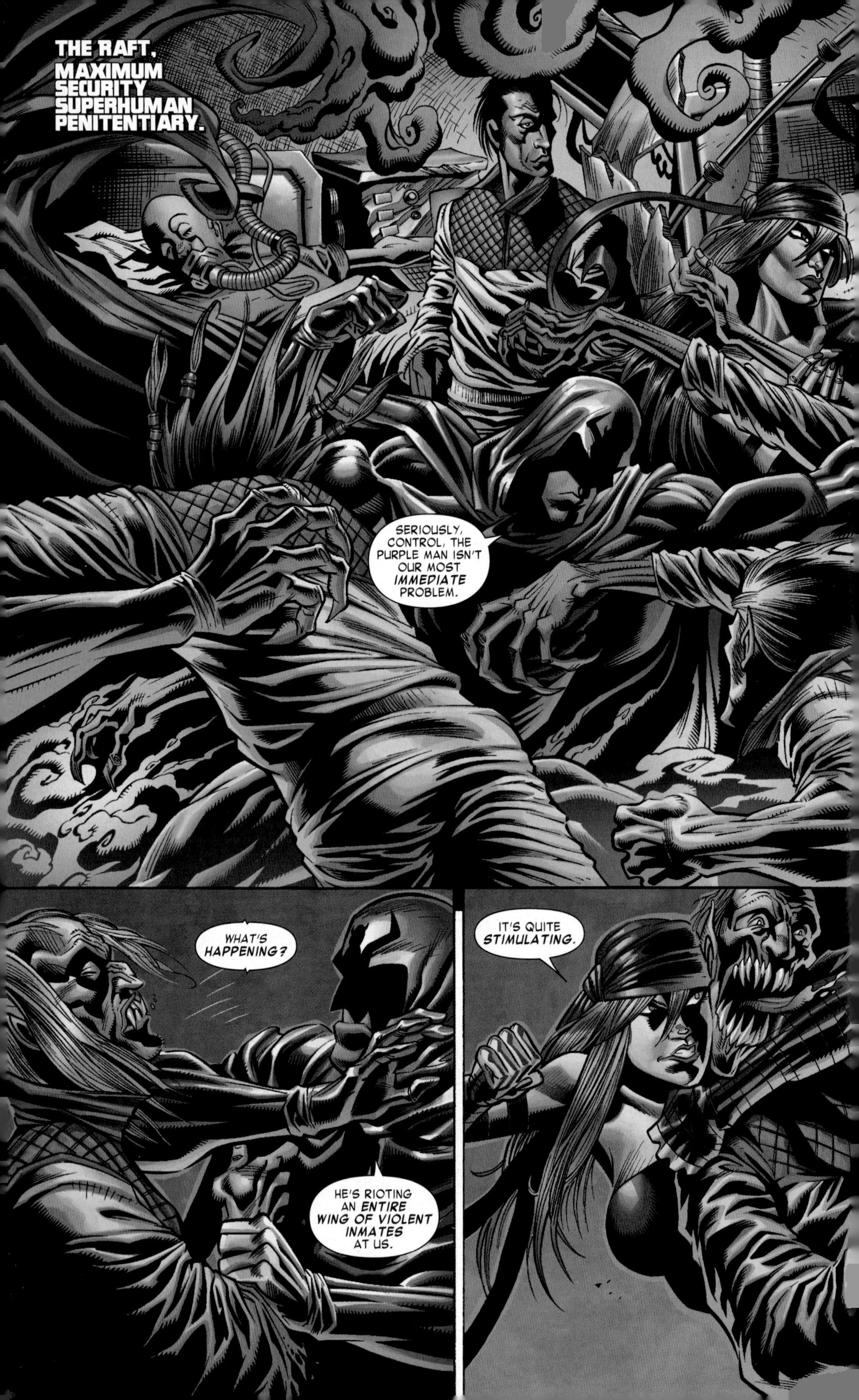
THE RAFT, MAXIMUM SECURITY SUPERHUMAN PENITENTIARY.
SERIOUSLY, CONTROL, THE PURPLE MAN ISN'T OUR MOST IMMEDIATE PROBLEM.
WHAT'S HAPPENING?
HE'S RIOTING AN ENTIRE WING OF VIOLENT INMATES AT US.
IT'S QUITE STIMULATING.

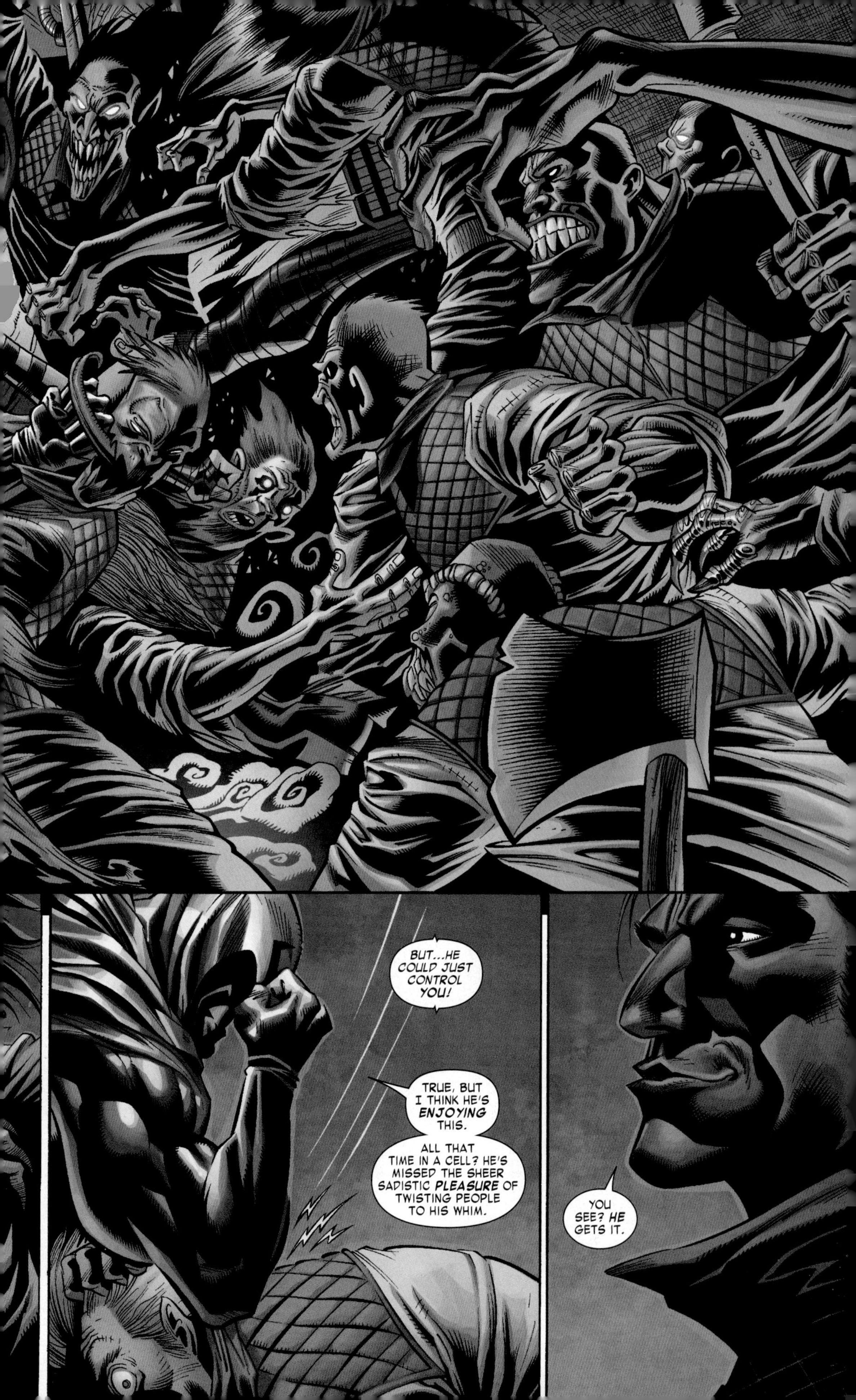
BUT...HE COULD JUST CONTROL YOU!
TRUE, BUT I THINK HE'S ENJOYING THIS.
ALL THAT TIME IN A CELL? HE'S MISSED THE SHEER SADISTIC PLEASURE OF TWISTING PEOPLE TO HIS WHIM.
YOU SEE? HE GETS IT.

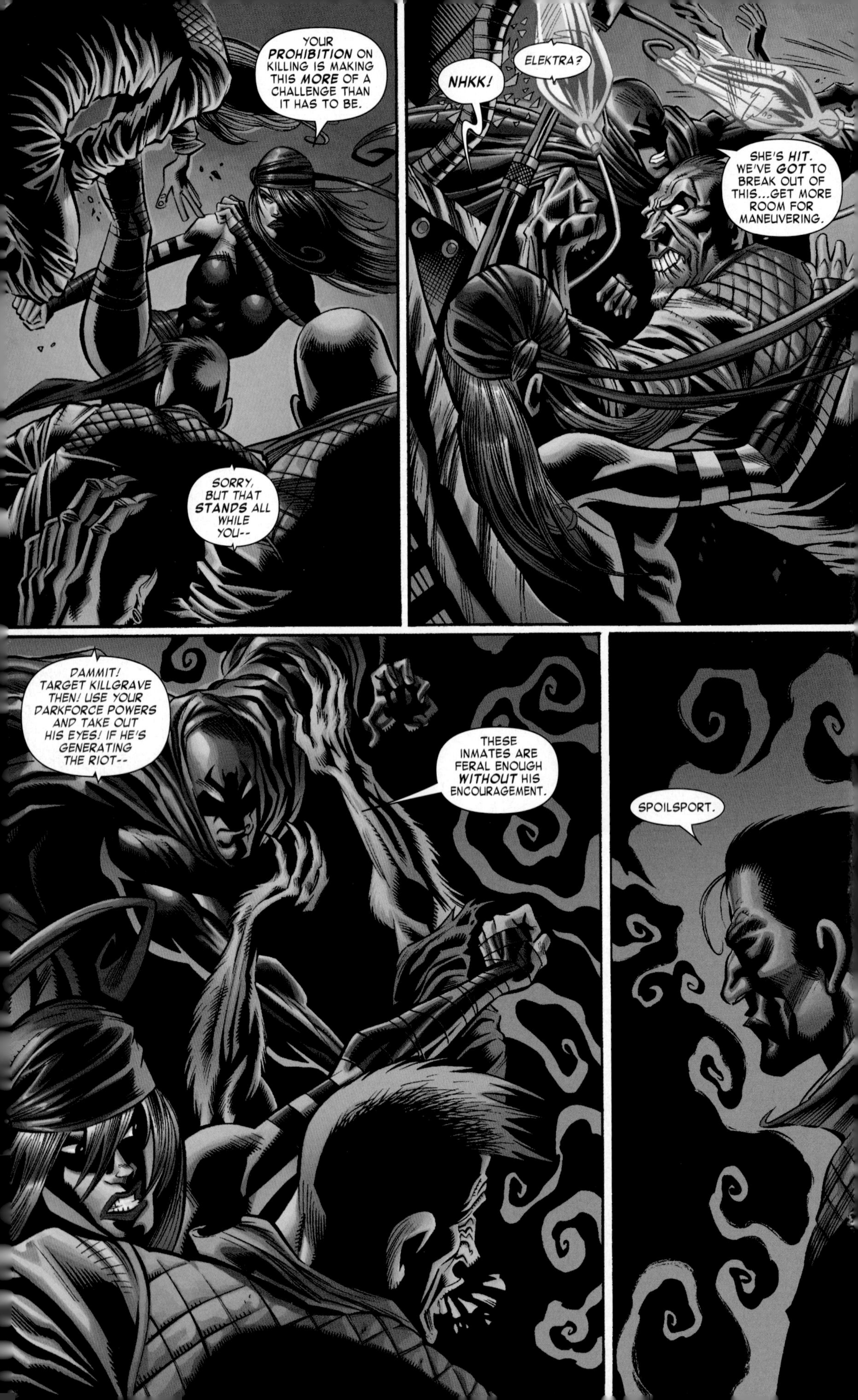
YOUR PROHIBITION ON KILLING IS MAKING THIS MORE OF A CHALLENGE THAN IT HAS TO BE.
SORRY, BUT THAT STANDS ALL WHILE YOU--
ELEKTRA?
NHKK!
SHE'S HIT. WE'VE GOT TO BREAK OUT OF THIS...GET MORE ROOM FOR MANEUVERING.
DAMMIT! TARGET KILLGRAVE THEN! USE YOUR DARKFORCE POWERS AND TAKE OUT HIS EYES! IF HE'S GENERATING THE RIOT--
THESE INMATES ARE FERAL ENOUGH WITHOUT HIS ENCOURAGEMENT.
SPOILSPORT.

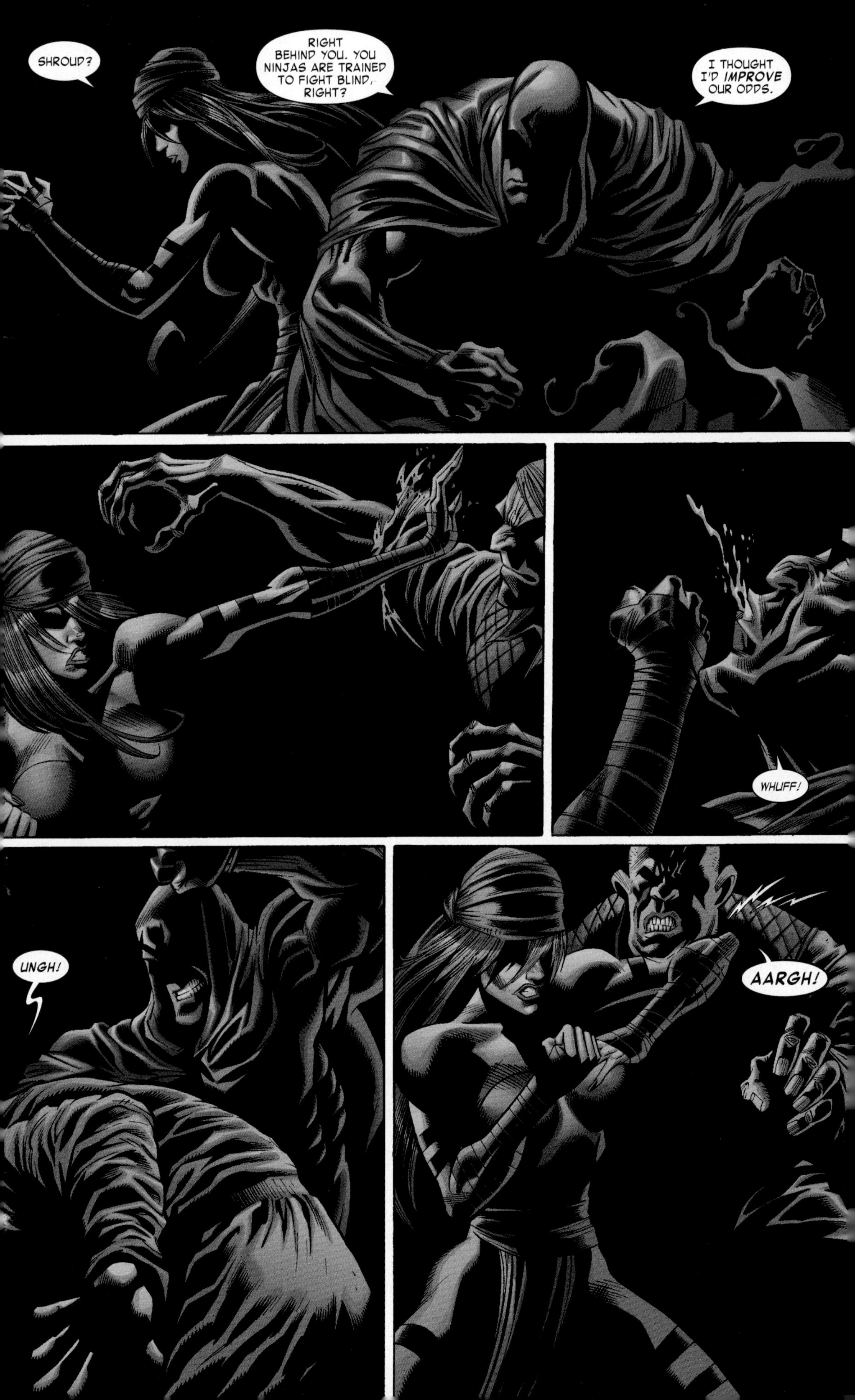
SHROUD?
RIGHT BEHIND YOU. YOU NINJAS ARE TRAINED TO FIGHT BLIND, RIGHT?
I THOUGHT I'D IMPROVE OUR ODDS.
WHUFF!
UNGH!
AARGH!

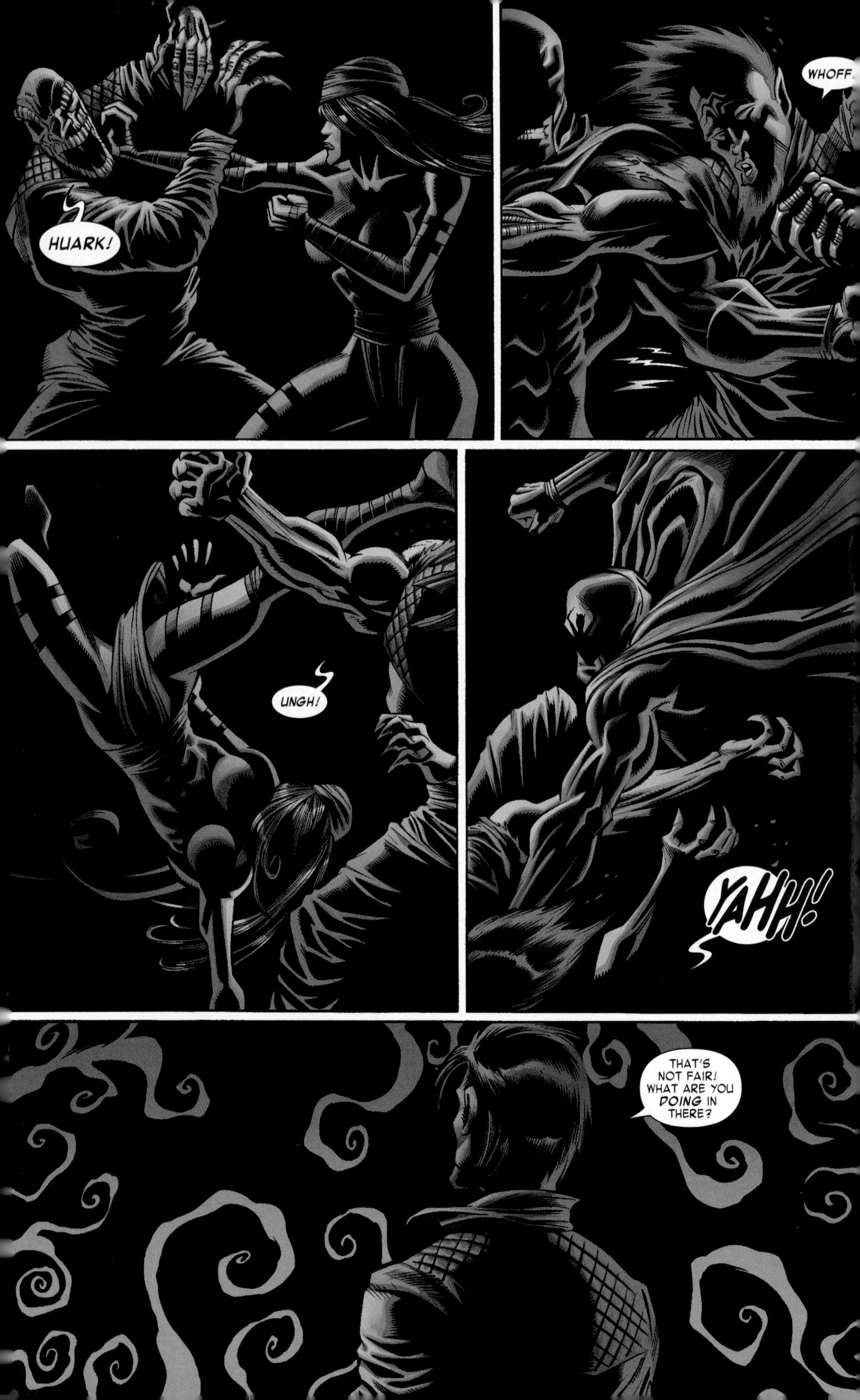
HUARK!
WHOFF.
UNGH!
YAHH!
THAT'S NOT FAIR! WHAT ARE YOU DOING IN THERE?

SHROUD?

ELEKTRA?

WE'RE GOING OFF LINK, CONTROL. YOUR AUDIO IS GIVING US AWAY.

BUT-- *KLLK*

DAMN...THE WORLD'S ENDING, AND I'M JUST *SITTING* HERE AGAIN...

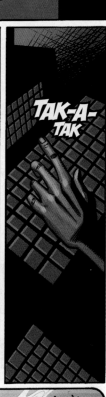

TAK-A-TAK

WASHINGTON, D.C.

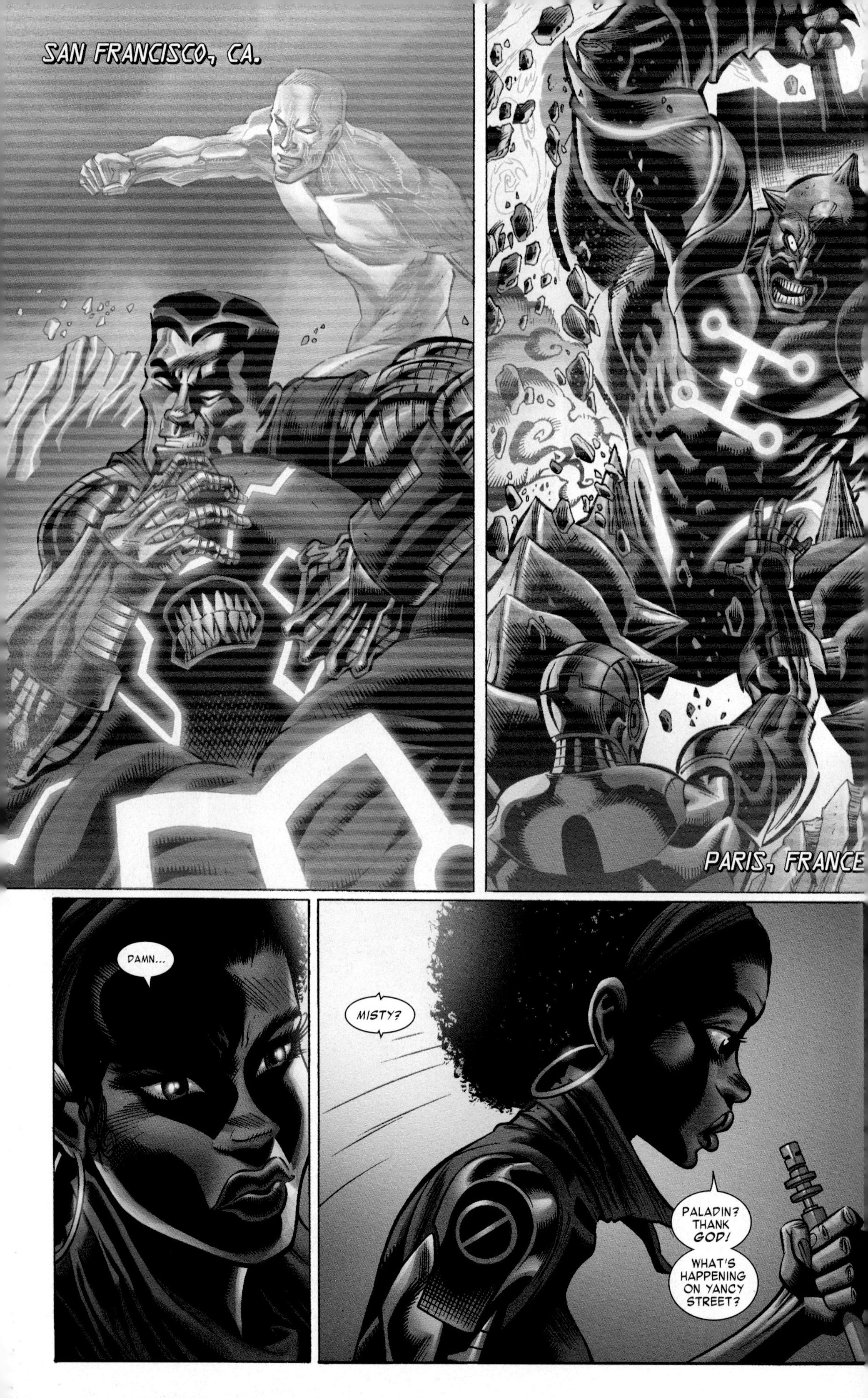
SAN FRANCISCO, CA.
PARIS, FRANCE
DAMN...
MISTY?
PALADIN? THANK GOD!
WHAT'S HAPPENING ON YANCY STREET?

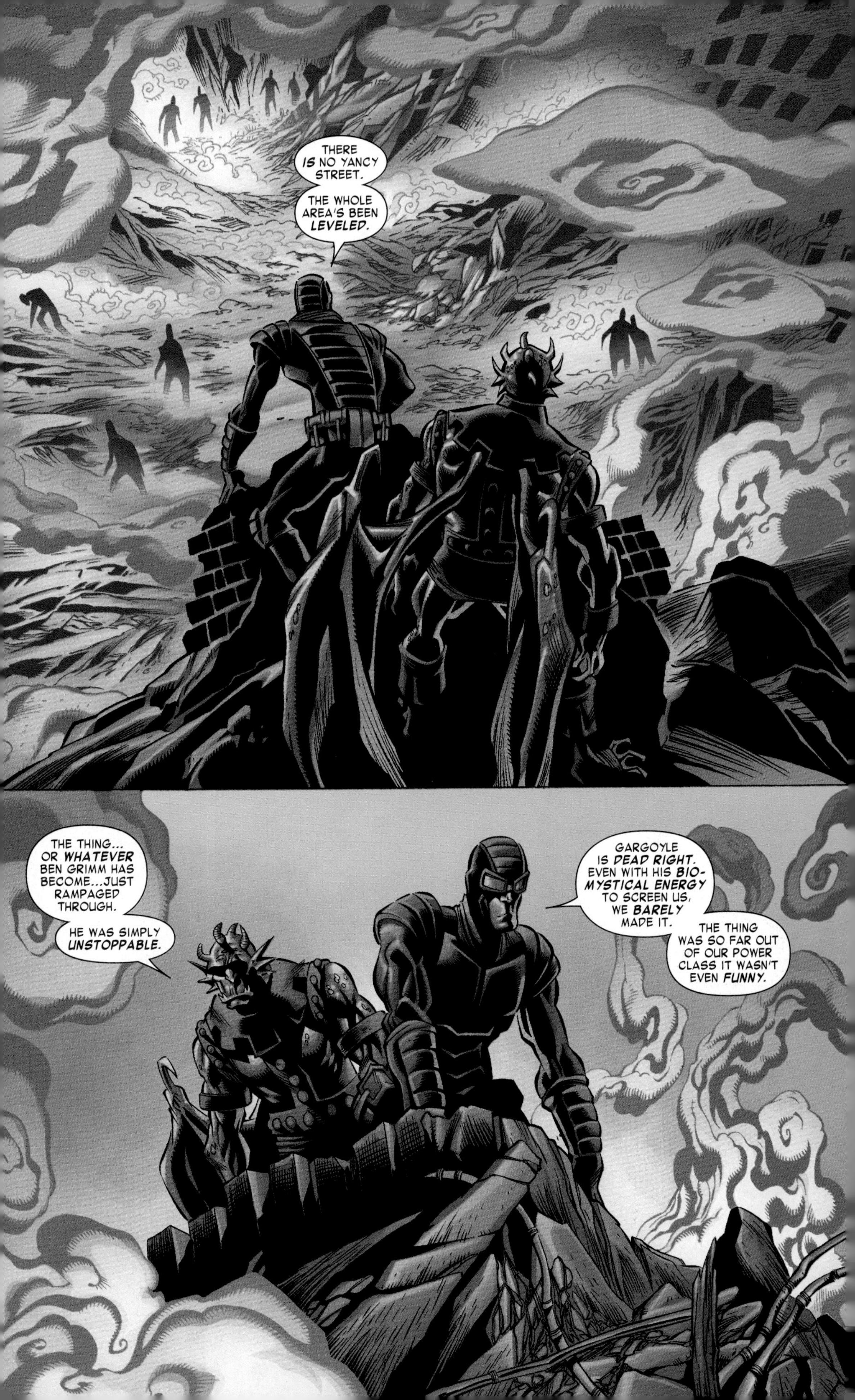
THERE IS NO YANCY STREET.
THE WHOLE AREA'S BEEN LEVELED.
THE THING... OR WHATEVER BEN GRIMM HAS BECOME...JUST RAMPAGED THROUGH.
HE WAS SIMPLY UNSTOPPABLE.
GARGOYLE IS DEAD RIGHT. EVEN WITH HIS BIO-MYSTICAL ENERGY TO SCREEN US, WE BARELY MADE IT.
THE THING WAS SO FAR OUT OF OUR POWER CLASS IT WASN'T EVEN FUNNY.

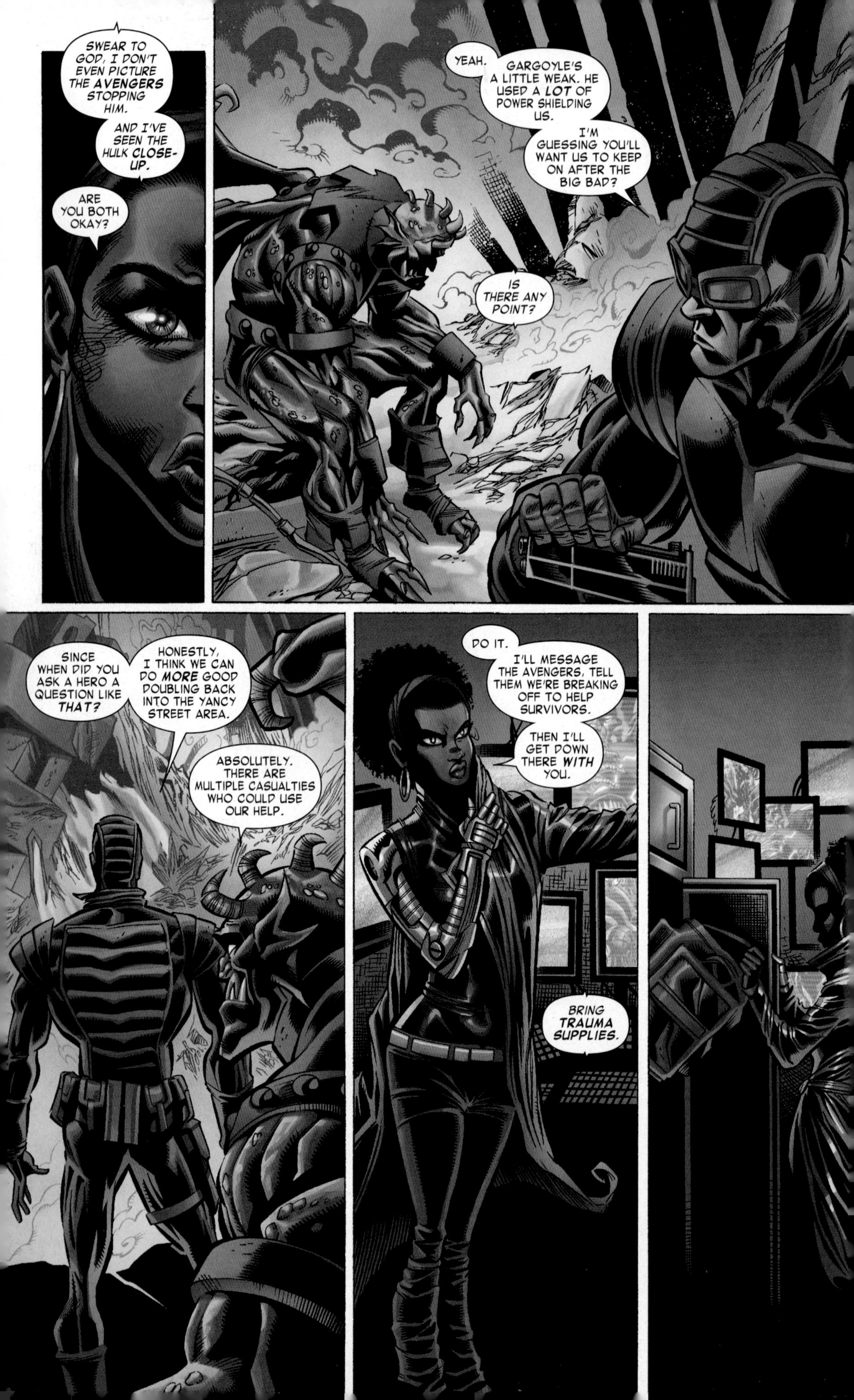
SWEAR TO GOD, I DON'T EVEN PICTURE THE AVENGERS STOPPING HIM.
AND I'VE SEEN THE HULK CLOSE-UP.
ARE YOU BOTH OKAY?
YEAH.
GARGOYLE'S A LITTLE WEAK. HE USED A LOT OF POWER SHIELDING US.
I'M GUESSING YOU'LL WANT US TO KEEP ON AFTER THE BIG BAD?
IS THERE ANY POINT?
SINCE WHEN DID YOU ASK A HERO A QUESTION LIKE THAT?
HONESTLY, I THINK WE CAN DO MORE GOOD DOUBLING BACK INTO THE YANCY STREET AREA.
ABSOLUTELY. THERE ARE MULTIPLE CASUALTIES WHO COULD USE OUR HELP.
DO IT.
I'LL MESSAGE THE AVENGERS, TELL THEM WE'RE BREAKING OFF TO HELP SURVIVORS.
THEN I'LL GET DOWN THERE WITH YOU.
BRING TRAUMA SUPPLIES.

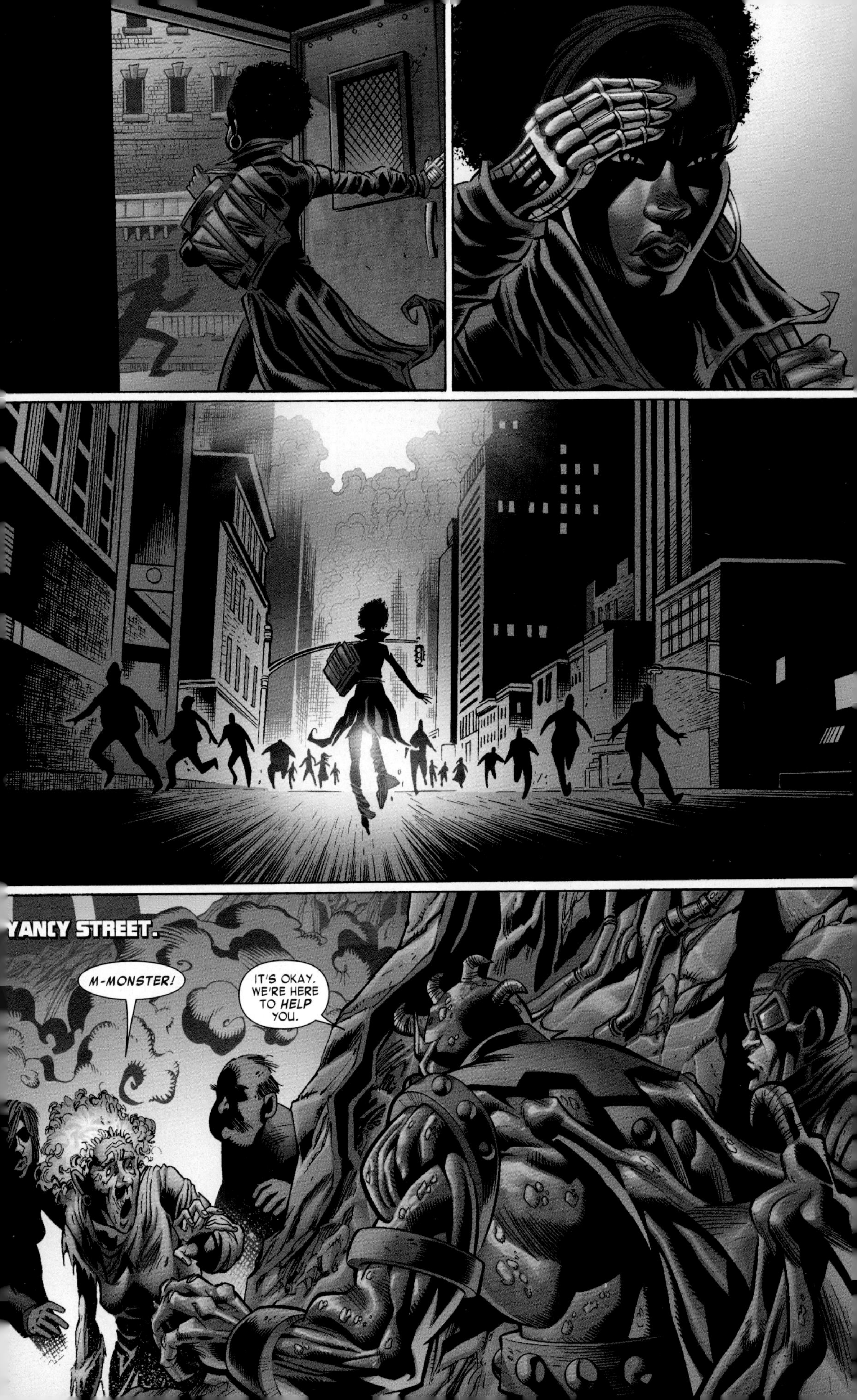
YANCY STREET.
M-MONSTER!
IT'S OKAY. WE'RE HERE TO HELP YOU.

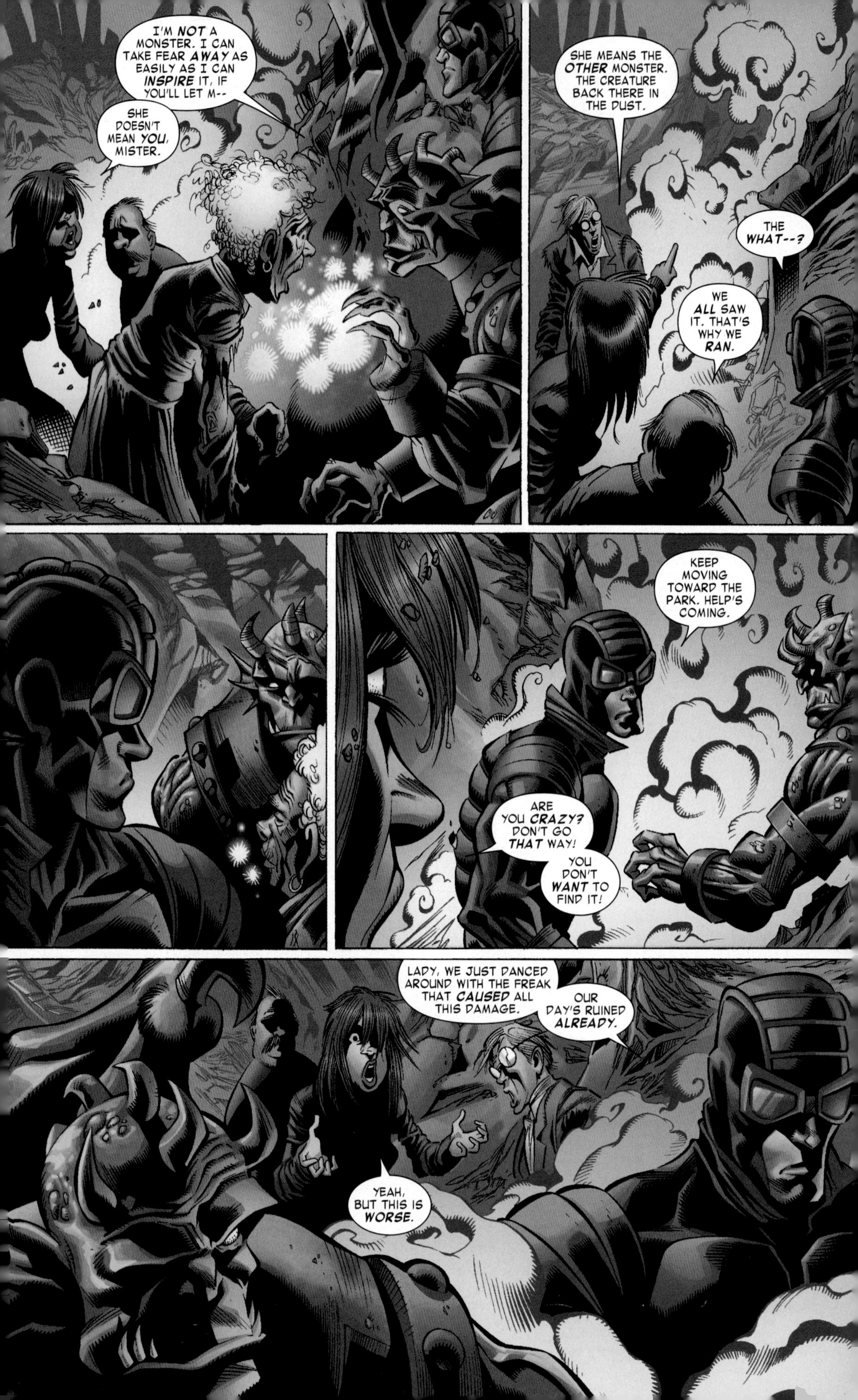
I'M NOT A MONSTER. I CAN TAKE FEAR AWAY AS EASILY AS I CAN INSPIRE IT, IF YOU'LL LET M--
SHE DOESN'T MEAN YOU, MISTER.
SHE MEANS THE OTHER MONSTER. THE CREATURE BACK THERE IN THE DUST.
THE WHAT--?
WE ALL SAW IT. THAT'S WHY WE RAN.
KEEP MOVING TOWARD THE PARK. HELP'S COMING.
ARE YOU CRAZY? DON'T GO THAT WAY!
YOU DON'T WANT TO FIND IT!
LADY, WE JUST DANCED AROUND WITH THE FREAK THAT CAUSED ALL THIS DAMAGE.
OUR DAY'S RUINED ALREADY.
YEAH, BUT THIS IS WORSE.

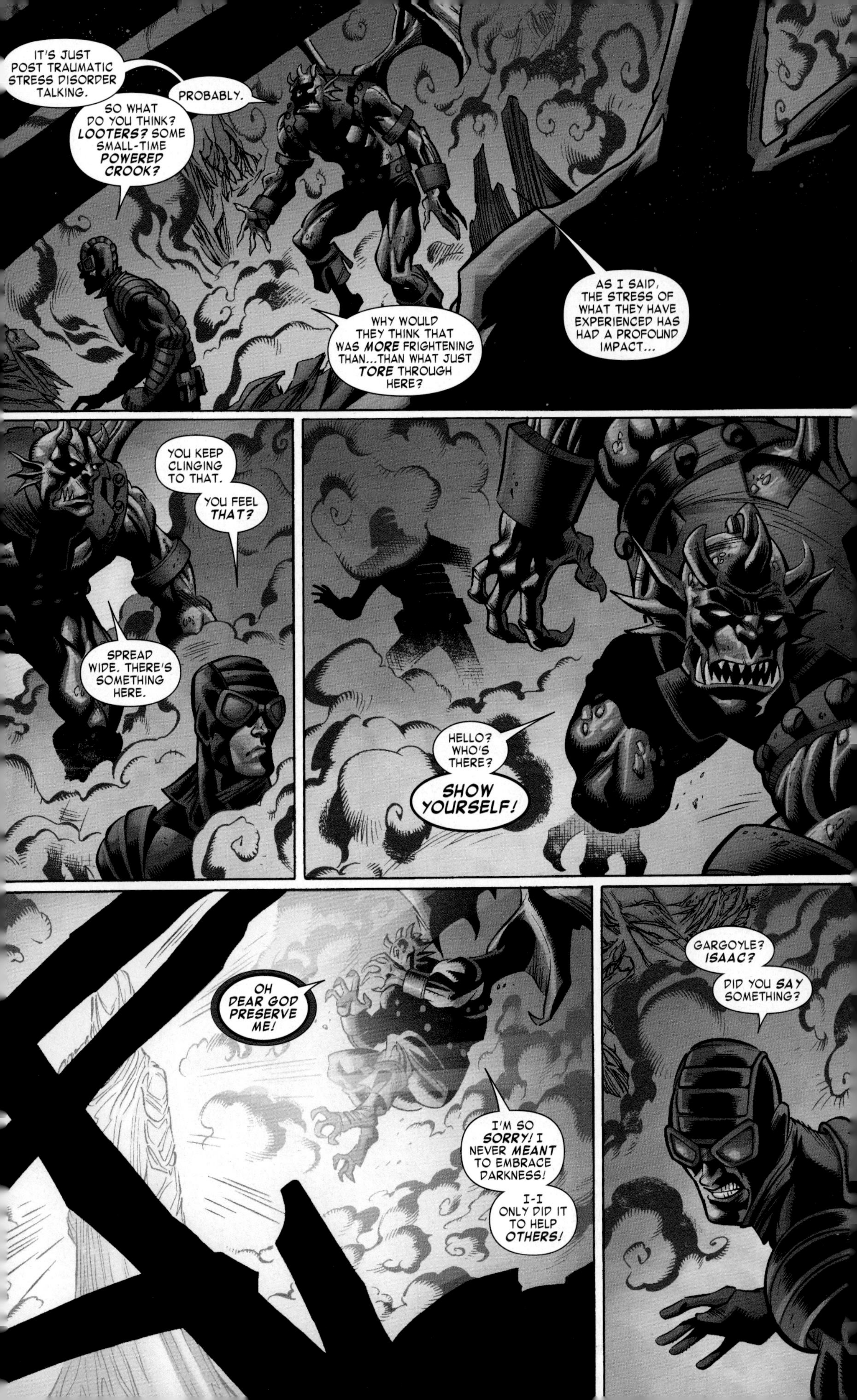
IT'S JUST POST TRAUMATIC STRESS DISORDER TALKING.
PROBABLY.
SO WHAT DO YOU THINK? LOOTERS? SOME SMALL-TIME POWERED CROOK?
WHY WOULD THEY THINK THAT WAS MORE FRIGHTENING THAN...THAN WHAT JUST TORE THROUGH HERE?
AS I SAID, THE STRESS OF WHAT THEY HAVE EXPERIENCED HAS HAD A PROFOUND IMPACT...
YOU KEEP CLINGING TO THAT.
YOU FEEL THAT?
SPREAD WIDE. THERE'S SOMETHING HERE.
HELLO? WHO'S THERE?
SHOW YOURSELF!
OH DEAR GOD PRESERVE ME!
I'M SO SORRY! I NEVER MEANT TO EMBRACE DARKNESS!
I-I ONLY DID IT TO HELP OTHERS!
GARGOYLE? ISAAC?
DID YOU SAY SOMETHING?

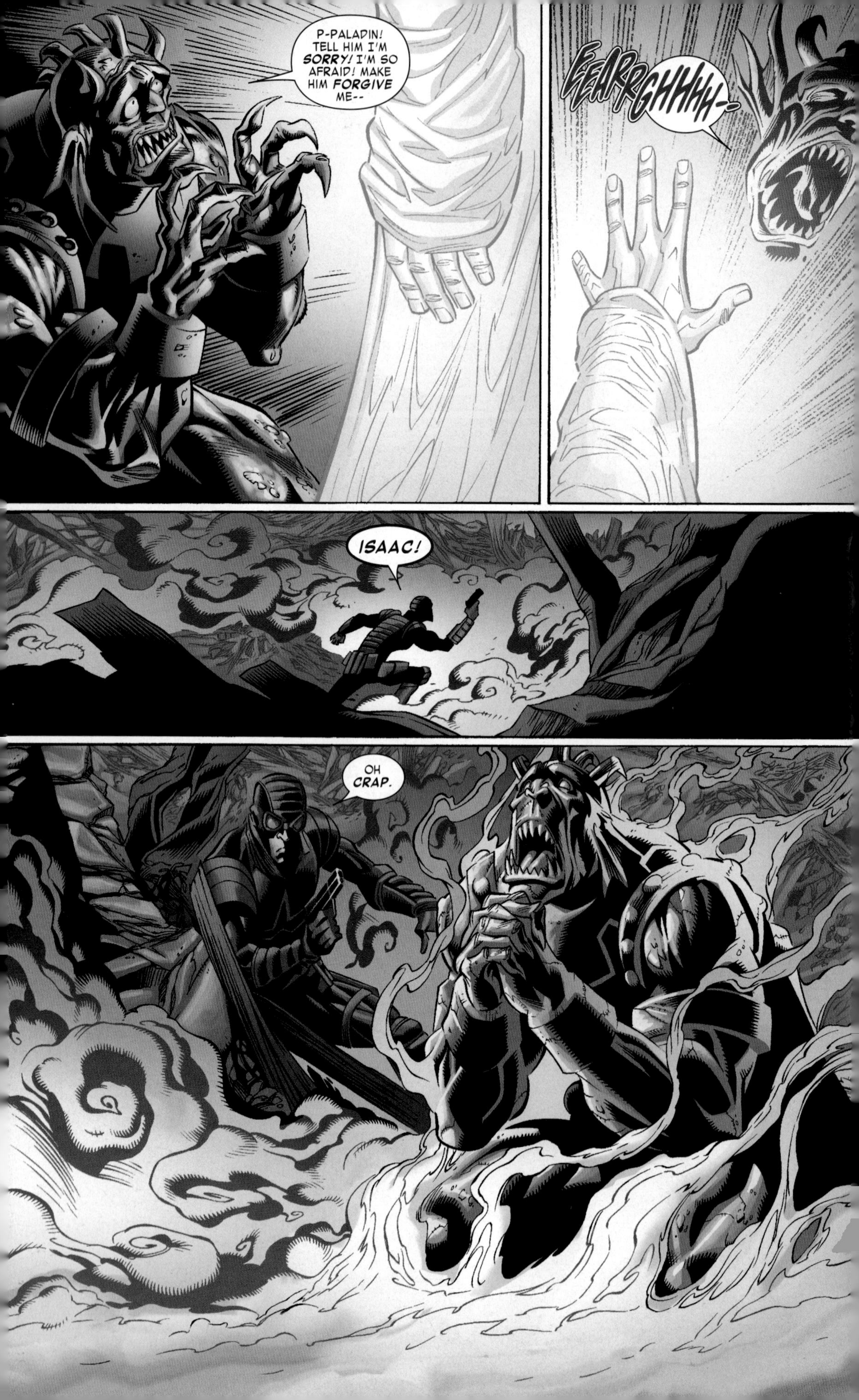
P-PALADIN! TELL HIM I'M SORRY! I'M SO AFRAID! MAKE HIM FORGIVE ME--
EEARRGHHHH--
ISAAC!
OH CRAP.

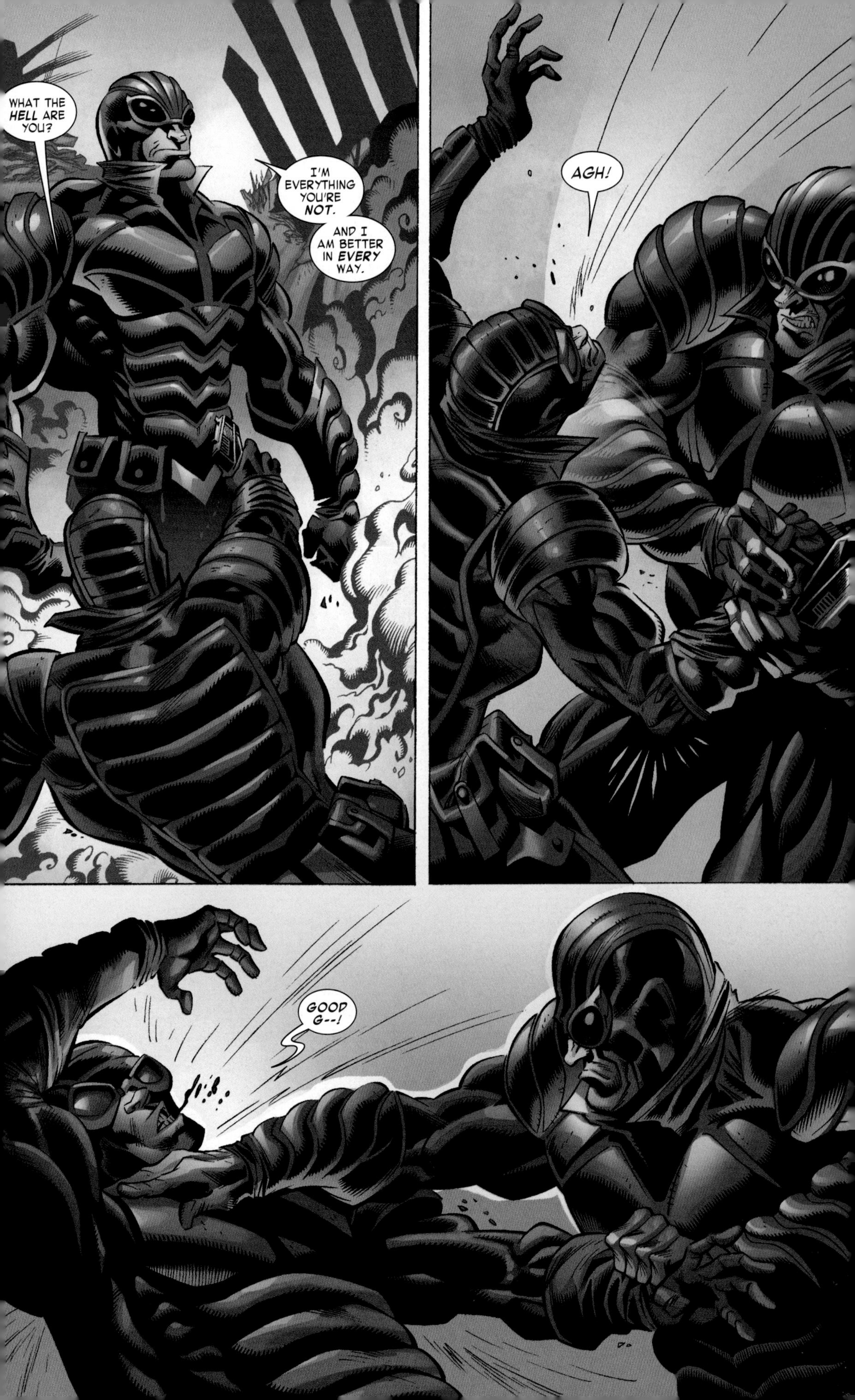
WHAT THE HELL ARE YOU?
I'M EVERYTHING YOU'RE NOT.
AND I AM BETTER IN EVERY WAY.
AGH!
GOOD G--!

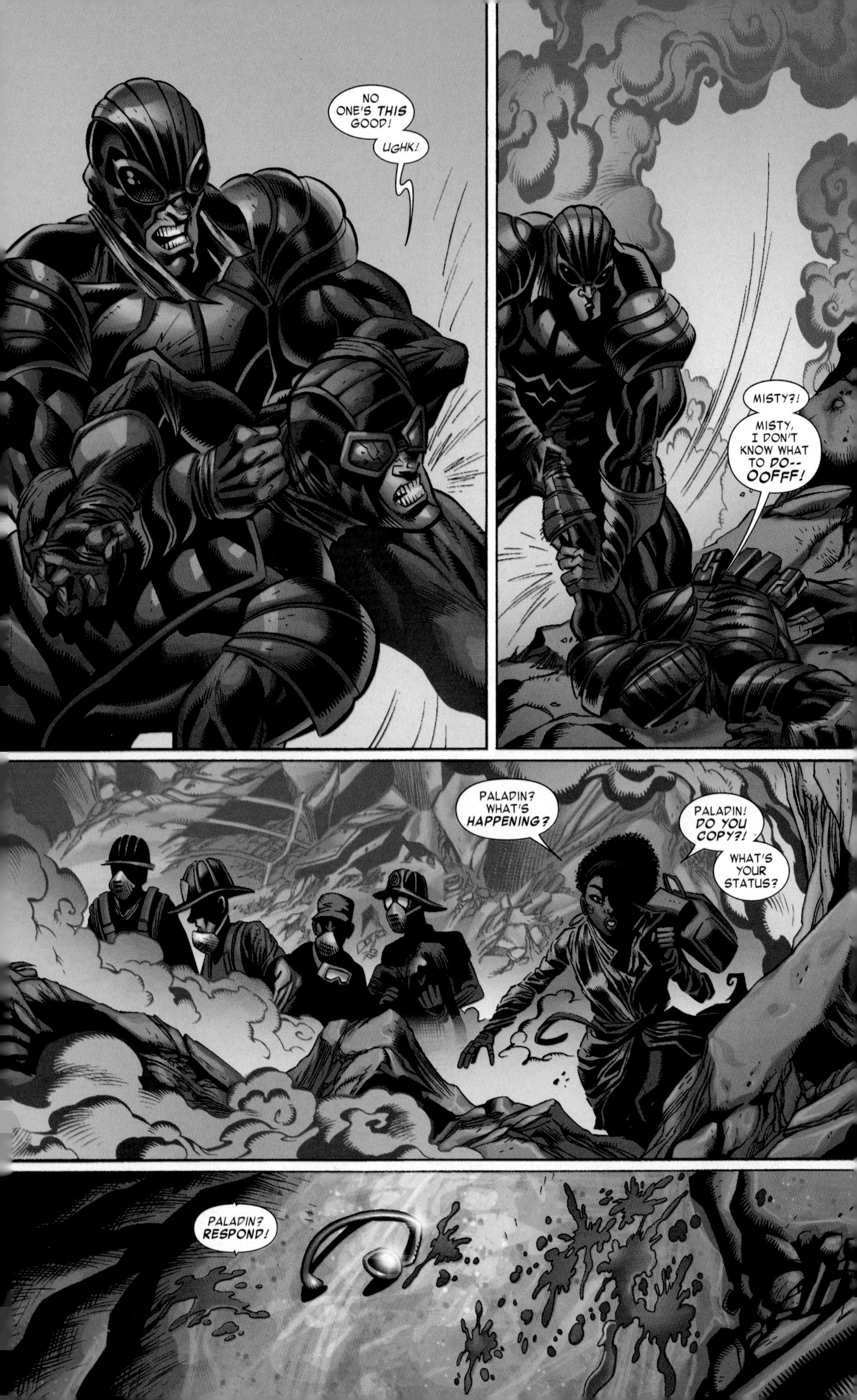
NO ONE'S THIS GOOD!
UGHK!
MISTY?!
MISTY, I DON'T KNOW WHAT TO DO--OOFFF!
PALADIN? WHAT'S HAPPENING?
PALADIN! DO YOU COPY?!
WHAT'S YOUR STATUS?
PALADIN? RESPOND!

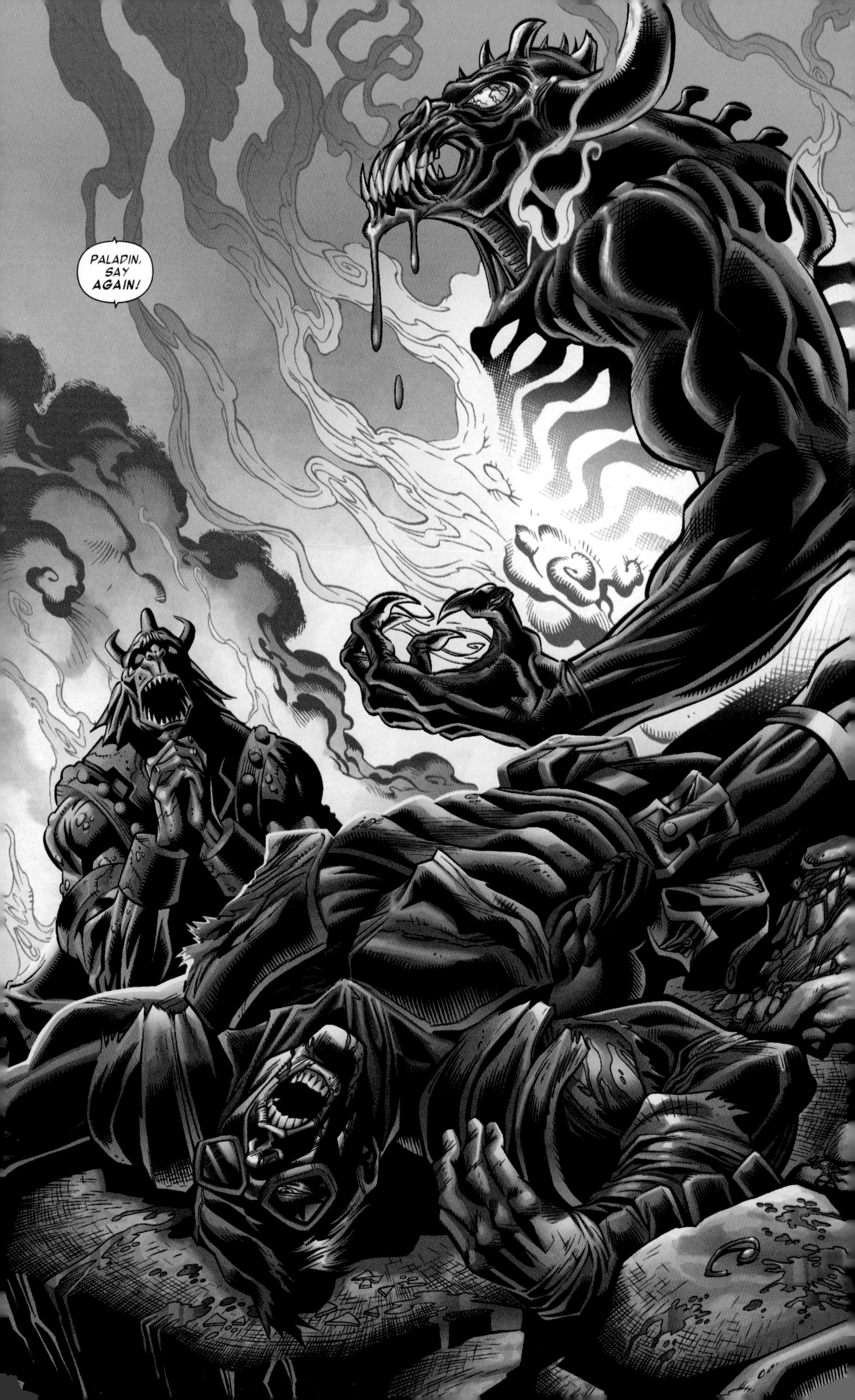
PALADIN, SAY AGAIN!

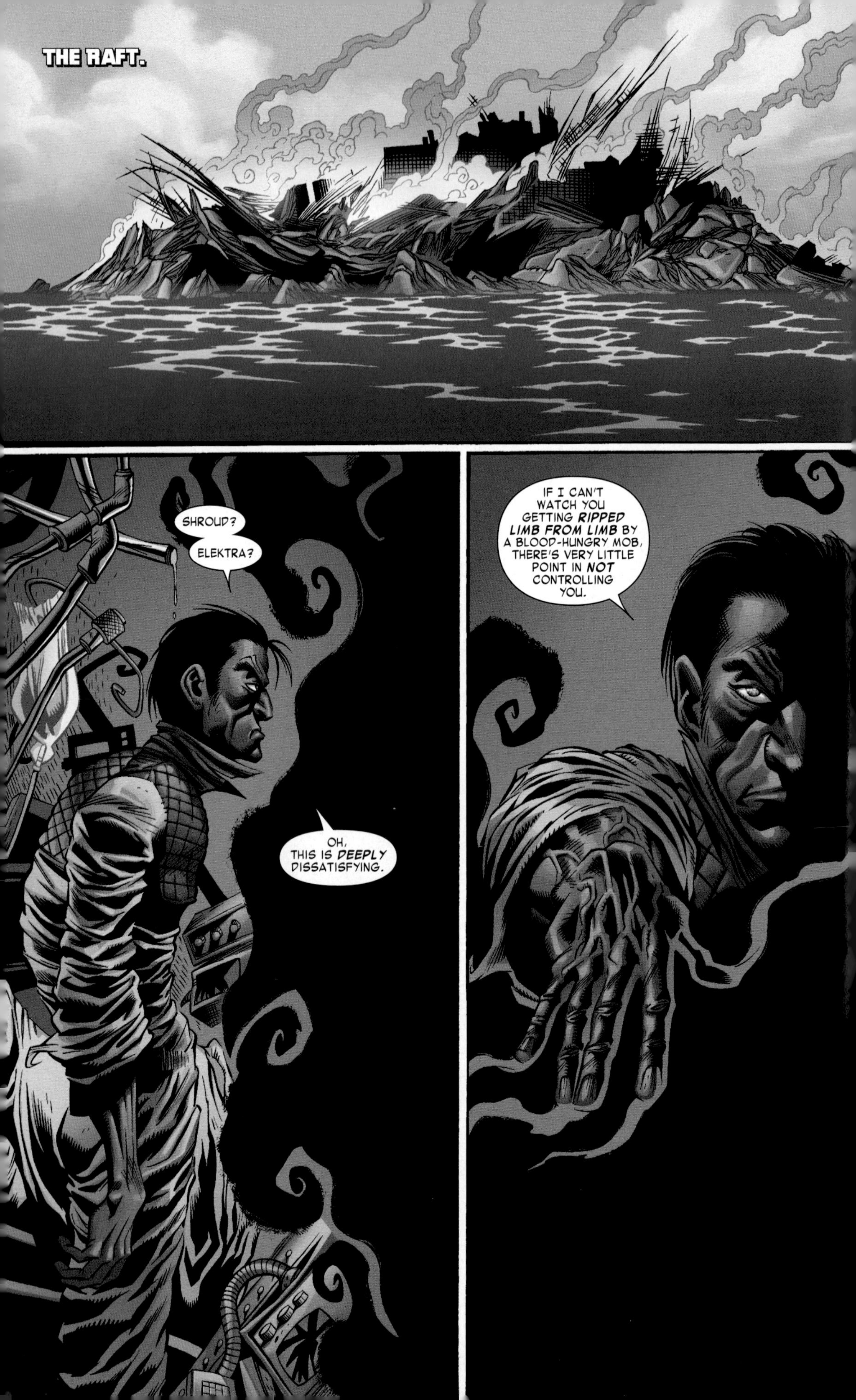
THE RAFT.
SHROUD?
ELEKTRA?
OH, THIS IS DEEPLY DISSATISFYING.
IF I CAN'T WATCH YOU GETTING RIPPED LIMB FROM LIMB BY A BLOOD-HUNGRY MOB, THERE'S VERY LITTLE POINT IN NOT CONTROLLING YOU.

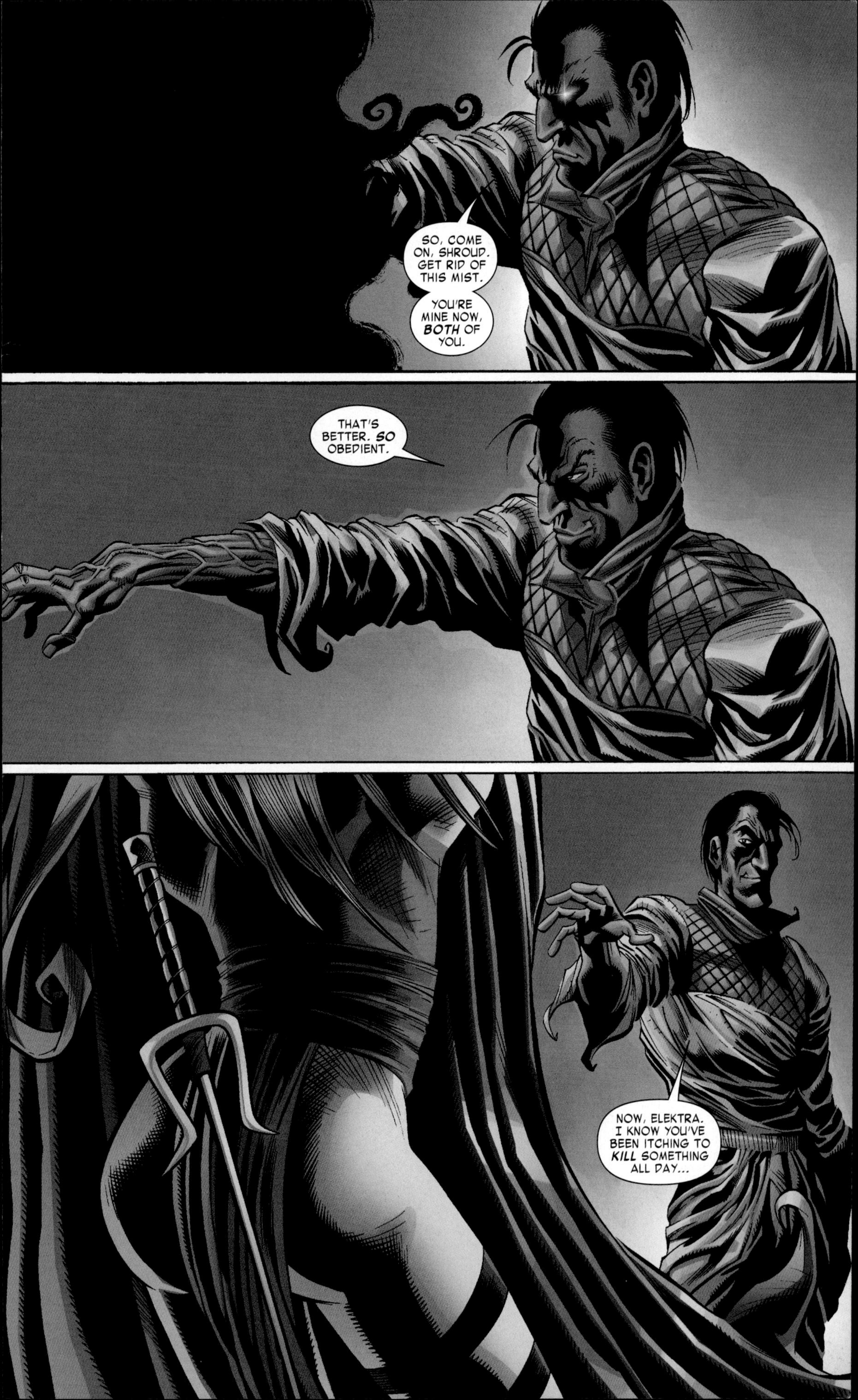
SO, COME ON, SHROUD. GET RID OF THIS MIST.
YOU'RE MINE NOW, *BOTH* OF YOU.
THAT'S BETTER. *SO* OBEDIENT.
NOW, ELEKTRA. I KNOW YOU'VE BEEN ITCHING TO *KILL* SOMETHING ALL DAY...

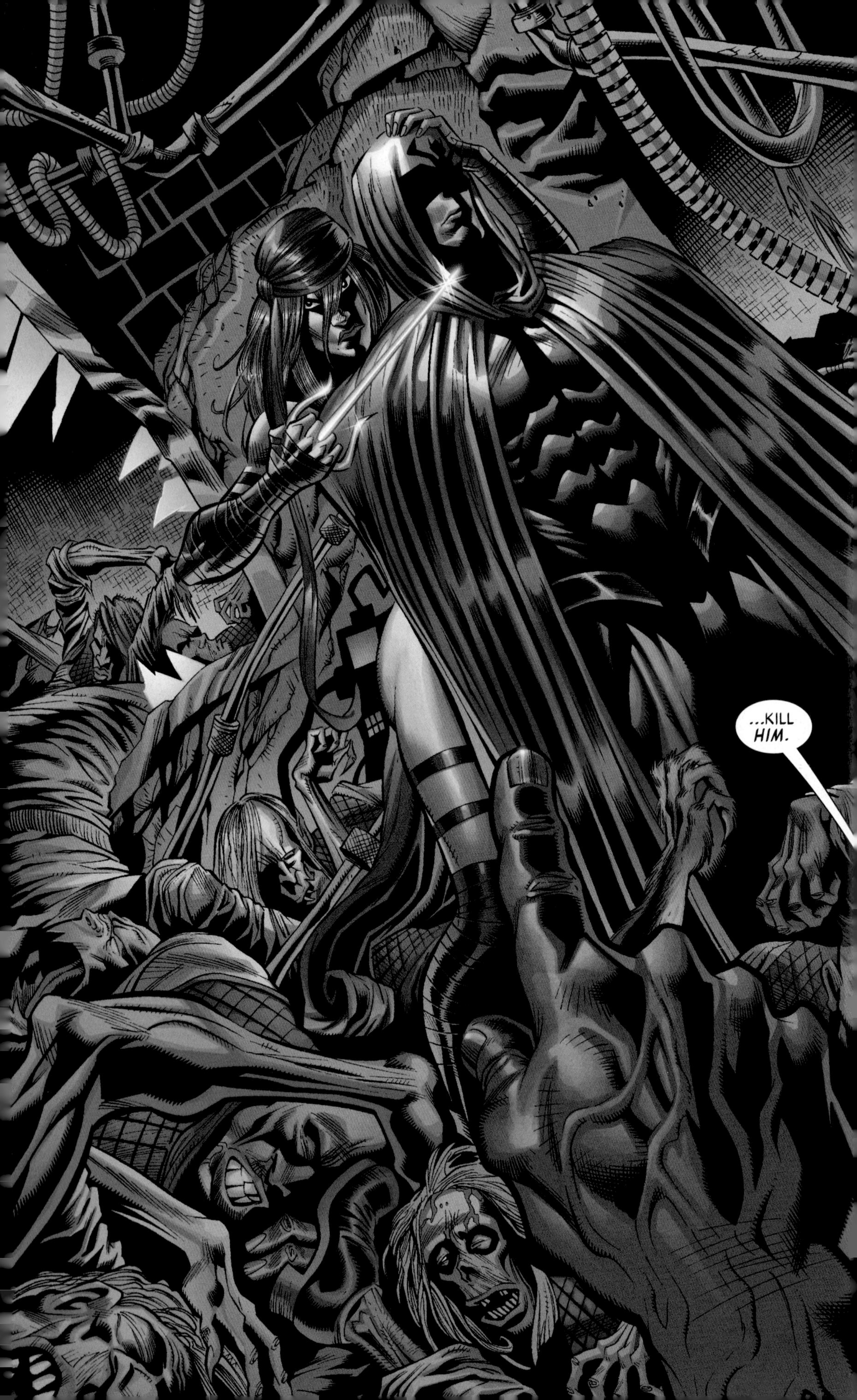
...KILL HIM.

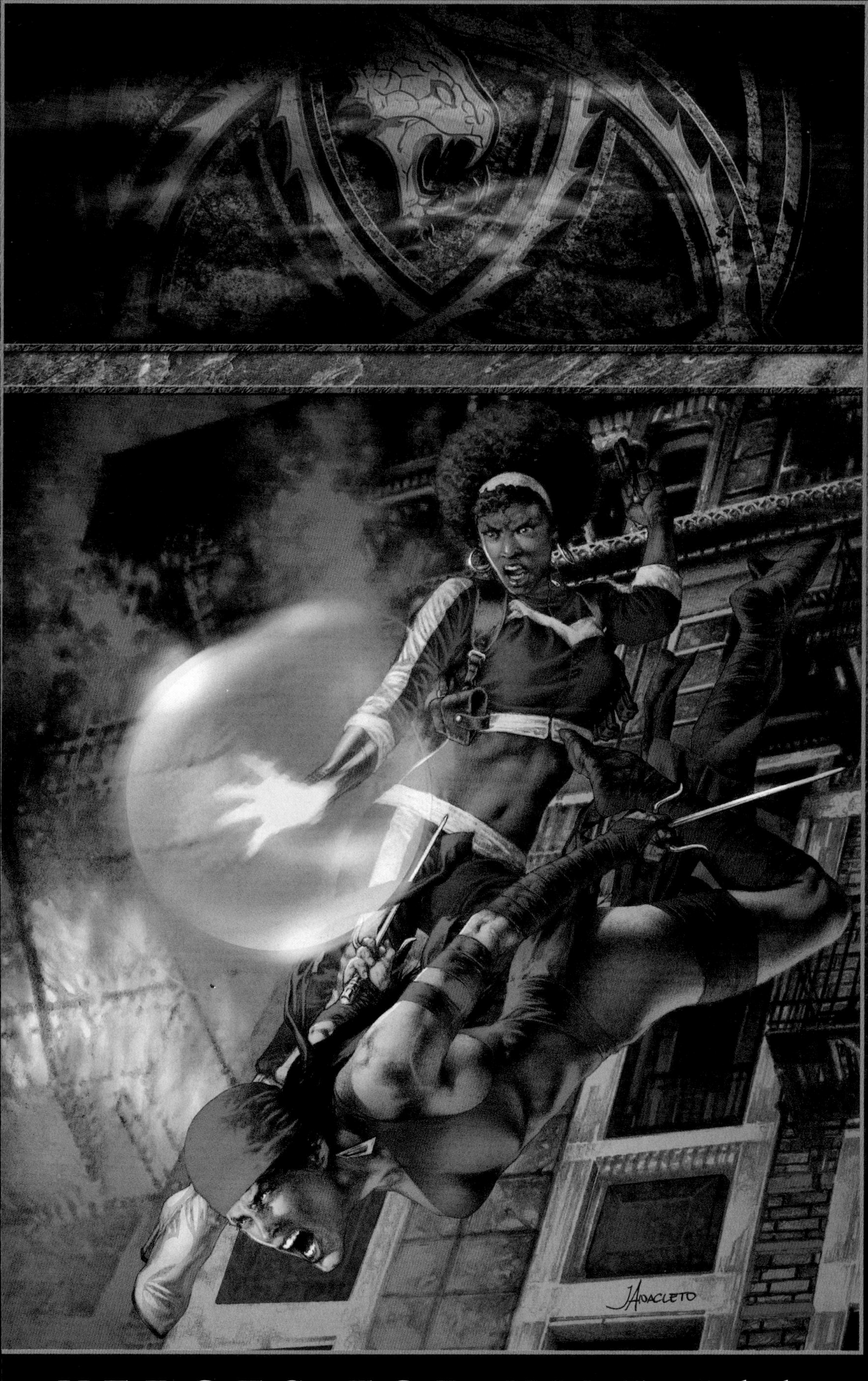

HEROES FOR HIRE #11

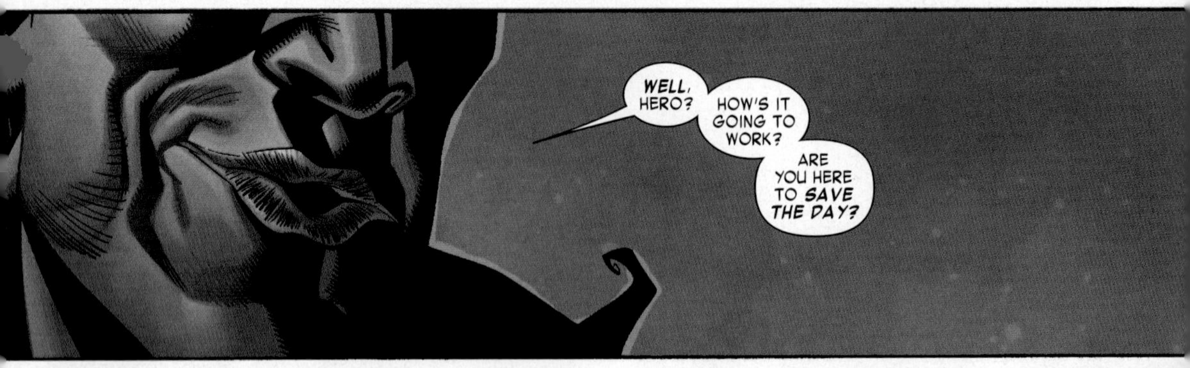
WELL, HERO?
HOW'S IT GOING TO WORK?
ARE YOU HERE TO SAVE THE DAY?

SOMETHING TO LIVE FOR

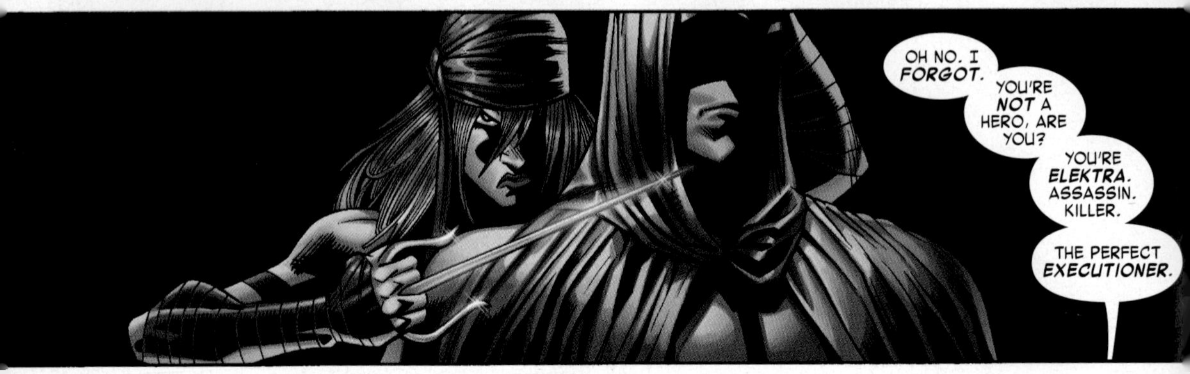
OH NO. I FORGOT.
YOU'RE NOT A HERO, ARE YOU?
YOU'RE ELEKTRA. ASSASSIN. KILLER.
THE PERFECT EXECUTIONER.

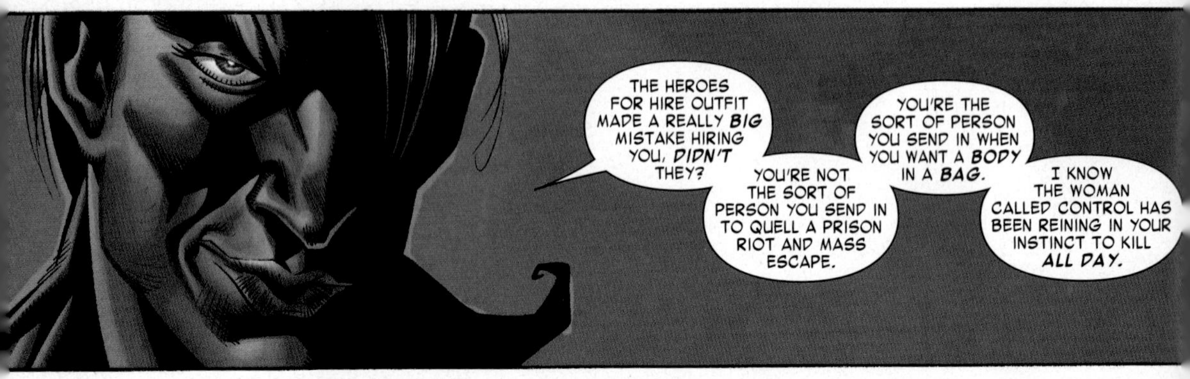
THE HEROES FOR HIRE OUTFIT MADE A REALLY BIG MISTAKE HIRING YOU, DIDN'T THEY?
YOU'RE NOT THE SORT OF PERSON YOU SEND IN TO QUELL A PRISON RIOT AND MASS ESCAPE.
YOU'RE THE SORT OF PERSON YOU SEND IN WHEN YOU WANT A BODY IN A BAG.
I KNOW THE WOMAN CALLED CONTROL HAS BEEN REINING IN YOUR INSTINCT TO KILL ALL DAY.

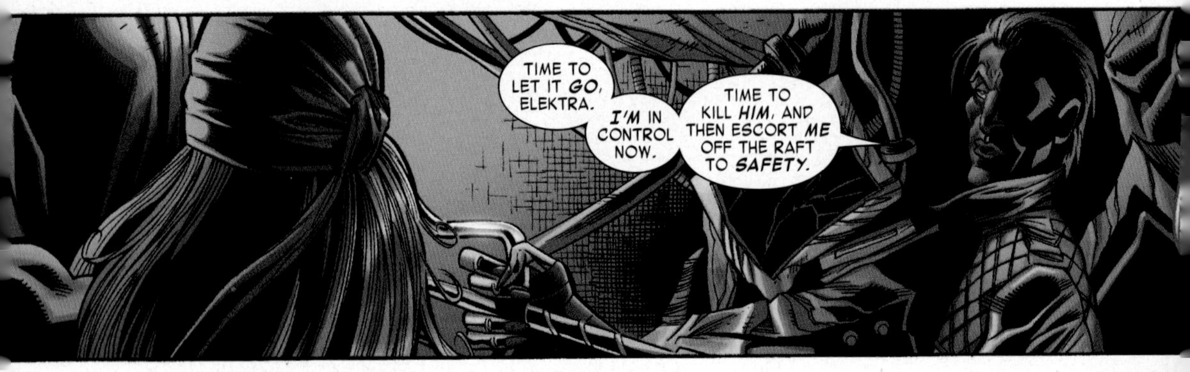
TIME TO LET IT GO, ELEKTRA.
I'M IN CONTROL NOW.
TIME TO KILL HIM, AND THEN ESCORT ME OFF THE RAFT TO SAFETY.

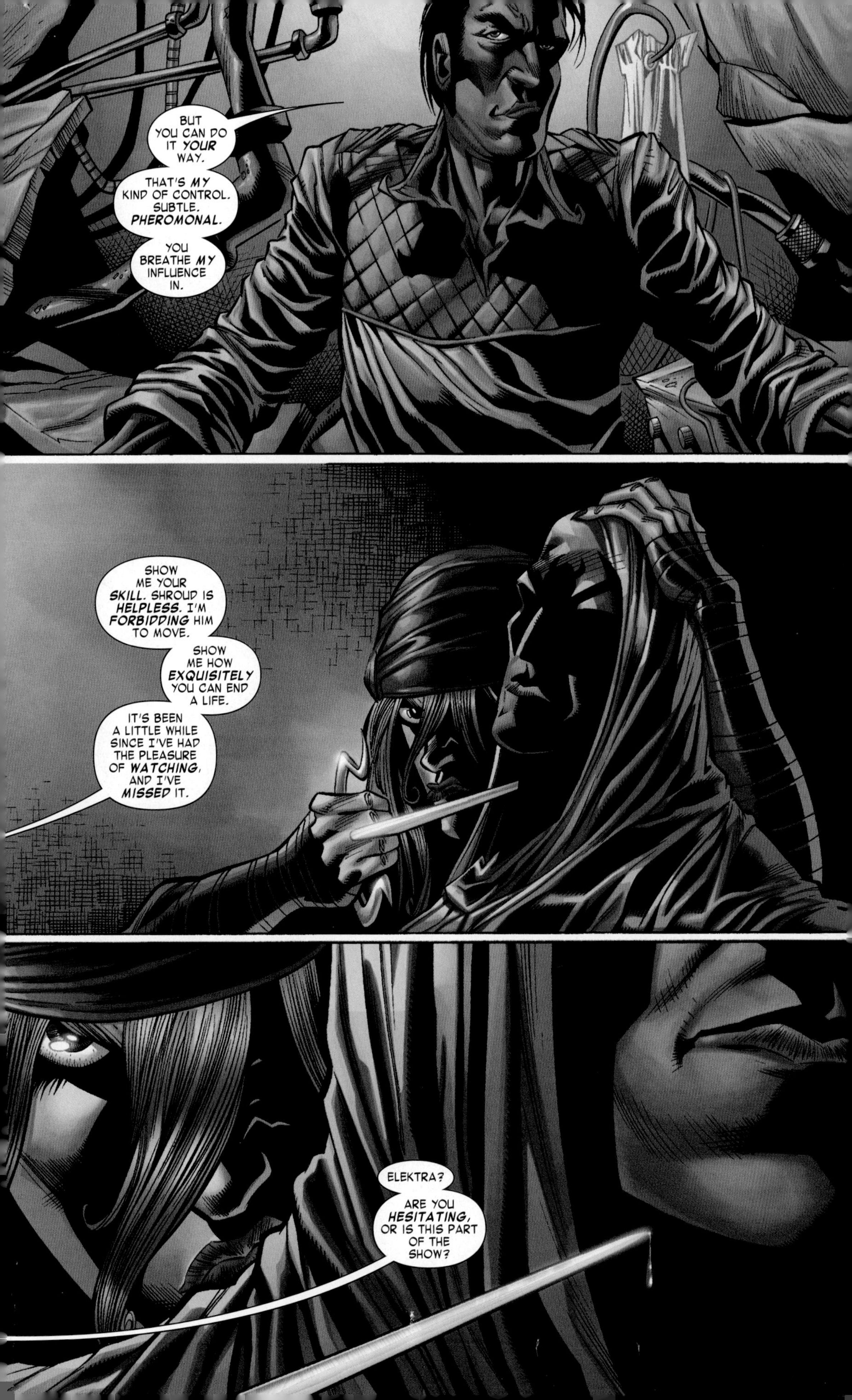
BUT YOU CAN DO IT YOUR WAY.
THAT'S MY KIND OF CONTROL. SUBTLE. PHEROMONAL.
YOU BREATHE MY INFLUENCE IN.
SHOW ME YOUR SKILL. SHROUD IS HELPLESS. I'M FORBIDDING HIM TO MOVE.
SHOW ME HOW EXQUISITELY YOU CAN END A LIFE.
IT'S BEEN A LITTLE WHILE SINCE I'VE HAD THE PLEASURE OF WATCHING, AND I'VE MISSED IT.
ELEKTRA?
ARE YOU HESITATING, OR IS THIS PART OF THE SHOW?

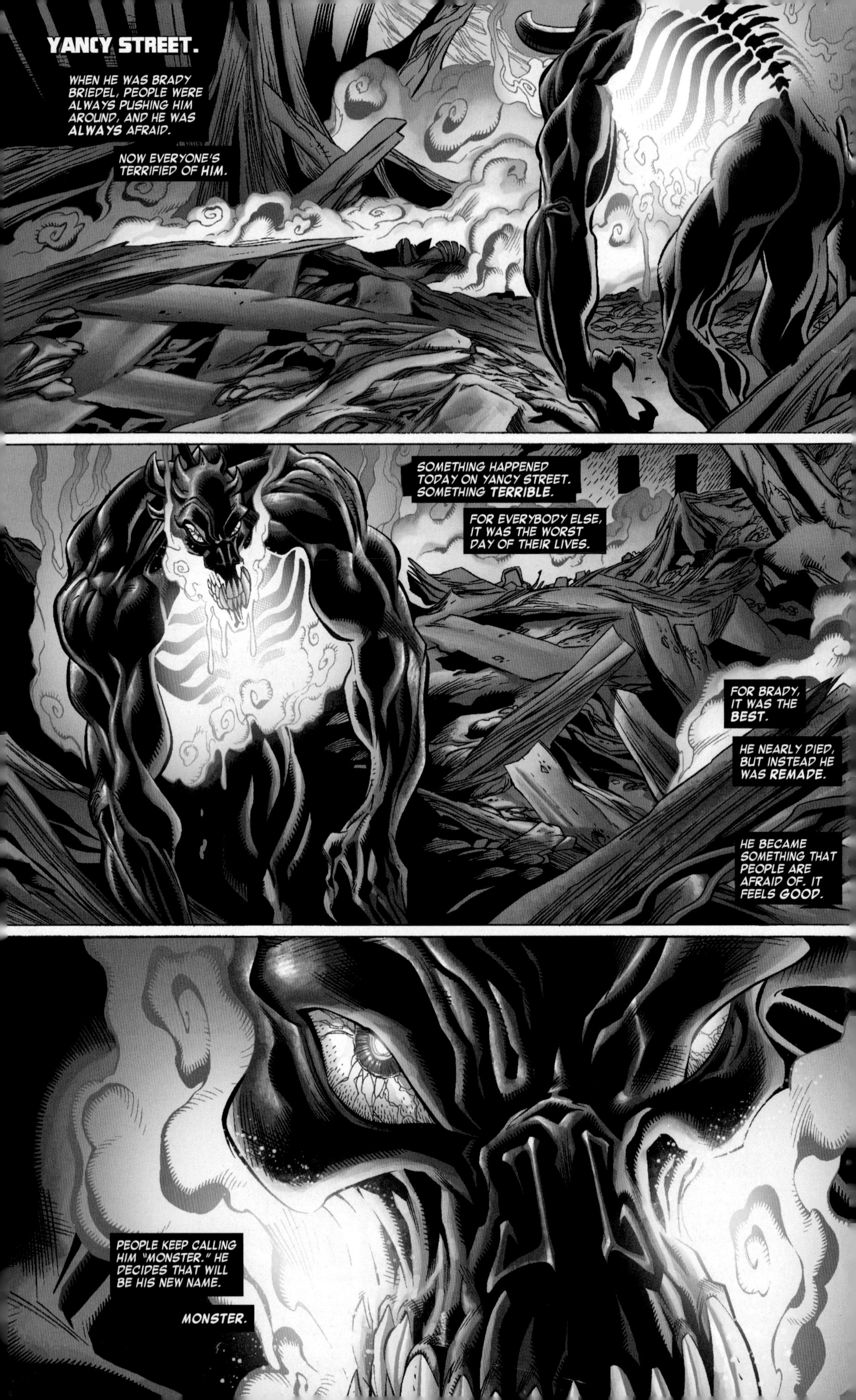
YANCY STREET.
WHEN HE WAS BRADY BRIEDEL, PEOPLE WERE ALWAYS PUSHING HIM AROUND, AND HE WAS ALWAYS AFRAID.
NOW EVERYONE'S TERRIFIED OF HIM.
SOMETHING HAPPENED TODAY ON YANCY STREET. SOMETHING TERRIBLE.
FOR EVERYBODY ELSE, IT WAS THE WORST DAY OF THEIR LIVES.
FOR BRADY, IT WAS THE BEST.
HE NEARLY DIED, BUT INSTEAD HE WAS REMADE.
HE BECAME SOMETHING THAT PEOPLE ARE AFRAID OF. IT FEELS GOOD.
PEOPLE KEEP CALLING HIM "MONSTER." HE DECIDES THAT WILL BE HIS NEW NAME.
MONSTER.

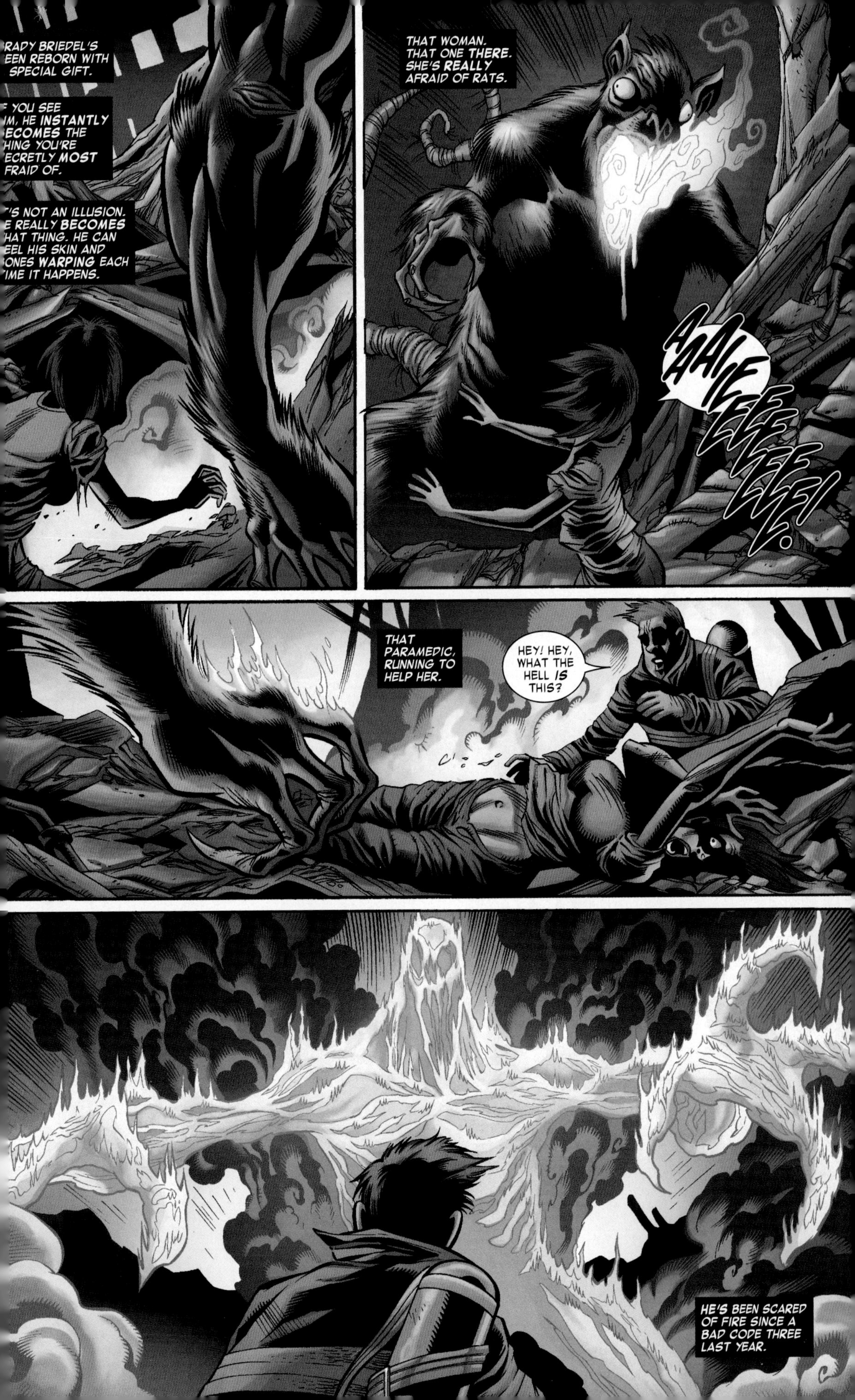
RADY BRIEDEL'S EEN REBORN WITH SPECIAL GIFT.
F YOU SEE IM, HE INSTANTLY ECOMES THE HING YOU'RE ECRETLY MOST FRAID OF.
'S NOT AN ILLUSION. E REALLY BECOMES HAT THING. HE CAN EEL HIS SKIN AND ONES WARPING EACH IME IT HAPPENS.
THAT WOMAN. THAT ONE THERE. SHE'S REALLY AFRAID OF RATS.
AAAIEEEEEEEEEEEEE!
THAT PARAMEDIC, RUNNING TO HELP HER.
HEY! HEY, WHAT THE HELL IS THIS?
HE'S BEEN SCARED OF FIRE SINCE A BAD CODE THREE LAST YEAR.

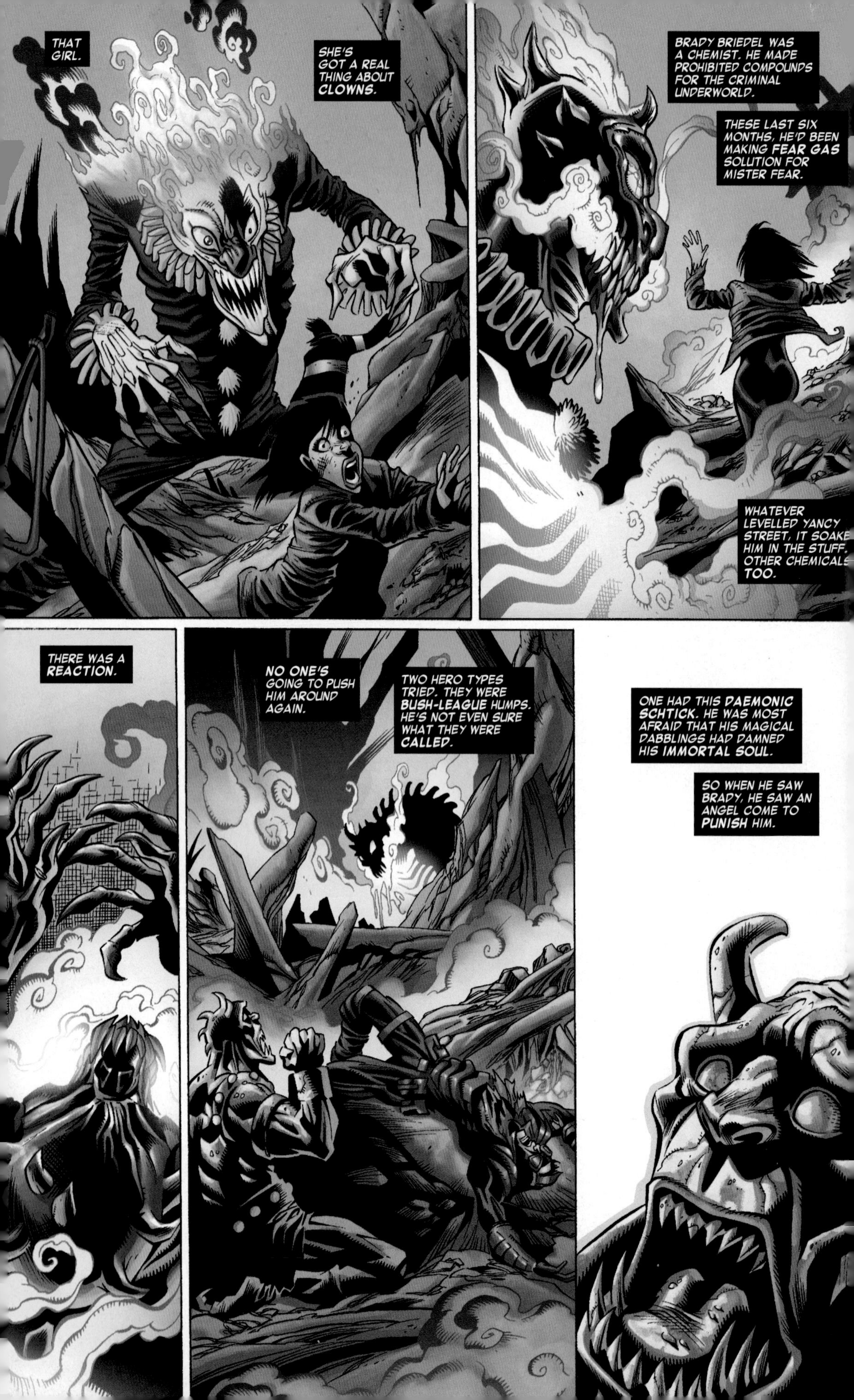
THAT GIRL.
SHE'S GOT A REAL THING ABOUT CLOWNS.
BRADY BRIEDEL WAS A CHEMIST. HE MADE PROHIBITED COMPOUNDS FOR THE CRIMINAL UNDERWORLD.
THESE LAST SIX MONTHS, HE'D BEEN MAKING FEAR GAS SOLUTION FOR MISTER FEAR.
WHATEVER LEVELLED YANCY STREET, IT SOAKE HIM IN THE STUFF. OTHER CHEMICALS TOO.
THERE WAS A REACTION.
NO ONE'S GOING TO PUSH HIM AROUND AGAIN.
TWO HERO TYPES TRIED. THEY WERE BUSH-LEAGUE HUMPS. HE'S NOT EVEN SURE WHAT THEY WERE CALLED.
ONE HAD THIS DAEMONIC SCHTICK. HE WAS MOST AFRAID THAT HIS MAGICAL DABBLINGS HAD DAMNED HIS IMMORTAL SOUL.
SO WHEN HE SAW BRADY, HE SAW AN ANGEL COME TO PUNISH HIM.

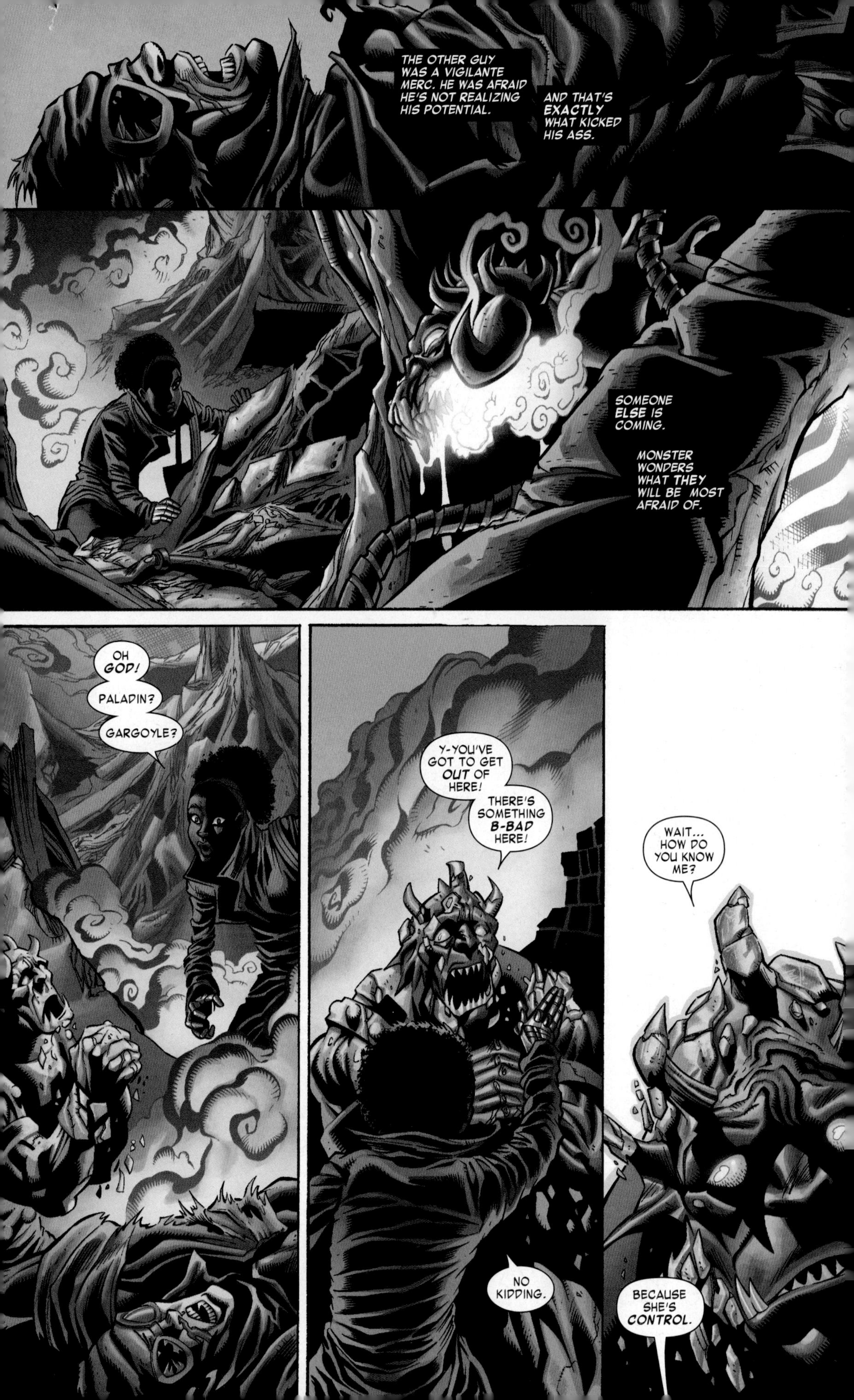
THE OTHER GUY WAS A VIGILANTE MERC. HE WAS AFRAID HE'S NOT REALIZING HIS POTENTIAL.
AND THAT'S EXACTLY WHAT KICKED HIS ASS.
SOMEONE ELSE IS COMING.
MONSTER WONDERS WHAT THEY WILL BE MOST AFRAID OF.
OH GOD!
PALADIN?
GARGOYLE?
Y-YOU'VE GOT TO GET OUT OF HERE!
THERE'S SOMETHING B-BAD HERE!
NO KIDDING.
WAIT... HOW DO YOU KNOW ME?
BECAUSE SHE'S CONTROL.

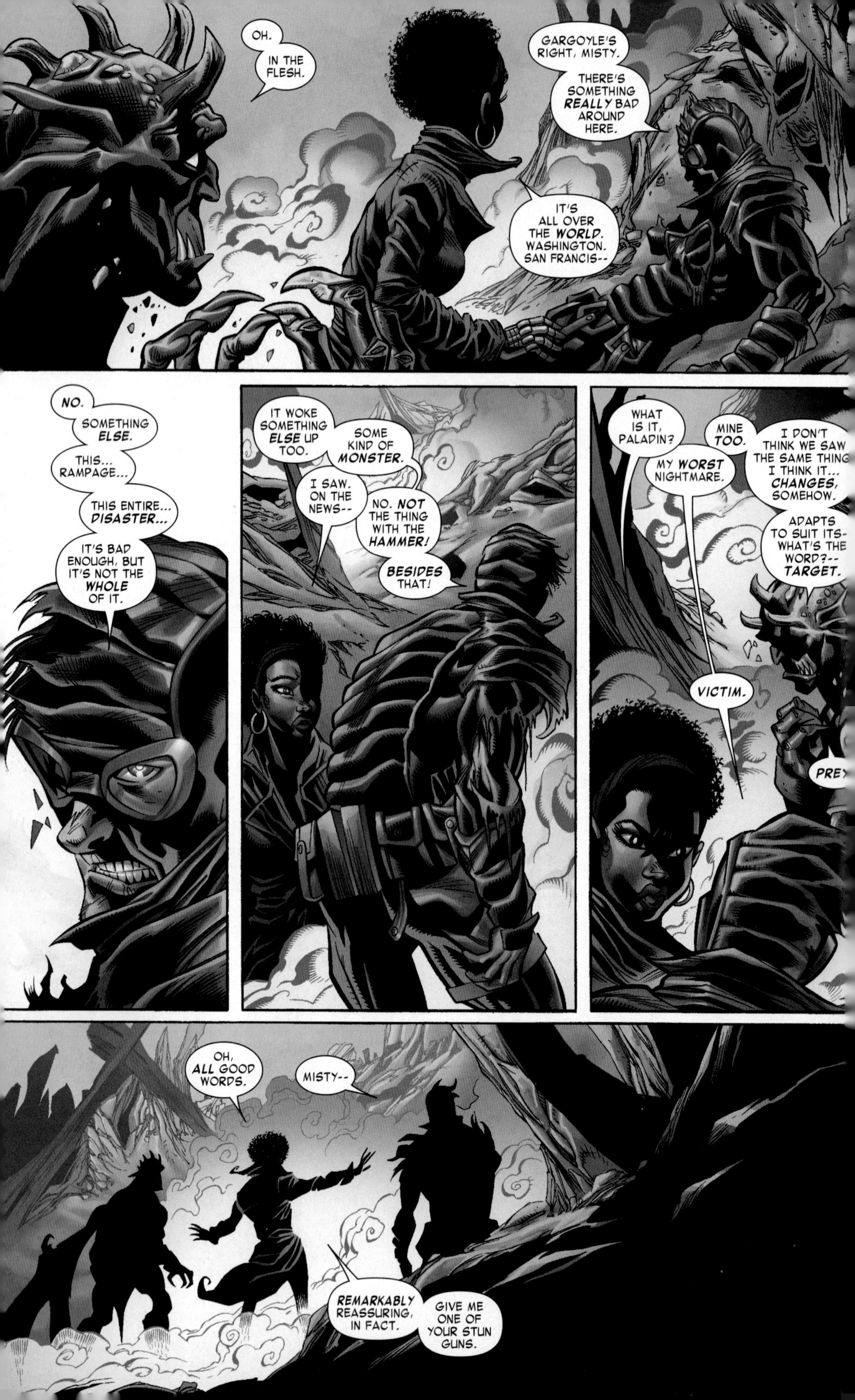
OH.
IN THE FLESH.
GARGOYLE'S RIGHT, MISTY.
THERE'S SOMETHING REALLY BAD AROUND HERE.
IT'S ALL OVER THE WORLD. WASHINGTON. SAN FRANCIS--
NO.
SOMETHING ELSE.
THIS... RAMPAGE...
THIS ENTIRE... DISASTER...
IT'S BAD ENOUGH, BUT IT'S NOT THE WHOLE OF IT.
IT WOKE SOMETHING ELSE UP TOO.
SOME KIND OF MONSTER.
I SAW. ON THE NEWS--
NO. NOT THE THING WITH THE HAMMER!
BESIDES THAT!
WHAT IS IT, PALADIN?
MY WORST NIGHTMARE.
MINE TOO.
I DON'T THINK WE SAW THE SAME THING. I THINK IT... CHANGES, SOMEHOW.
ADAPTS TO SUIT ITS-- WHAT'S THE WORD?-- TARGET.
VICTIM.
PREY
OH, ALL GOOD WORDS.
MISTY--
REMARKABLY REASSURING, IN FACT.
GIVE ME ONE OF YOUR STUN GUNS.

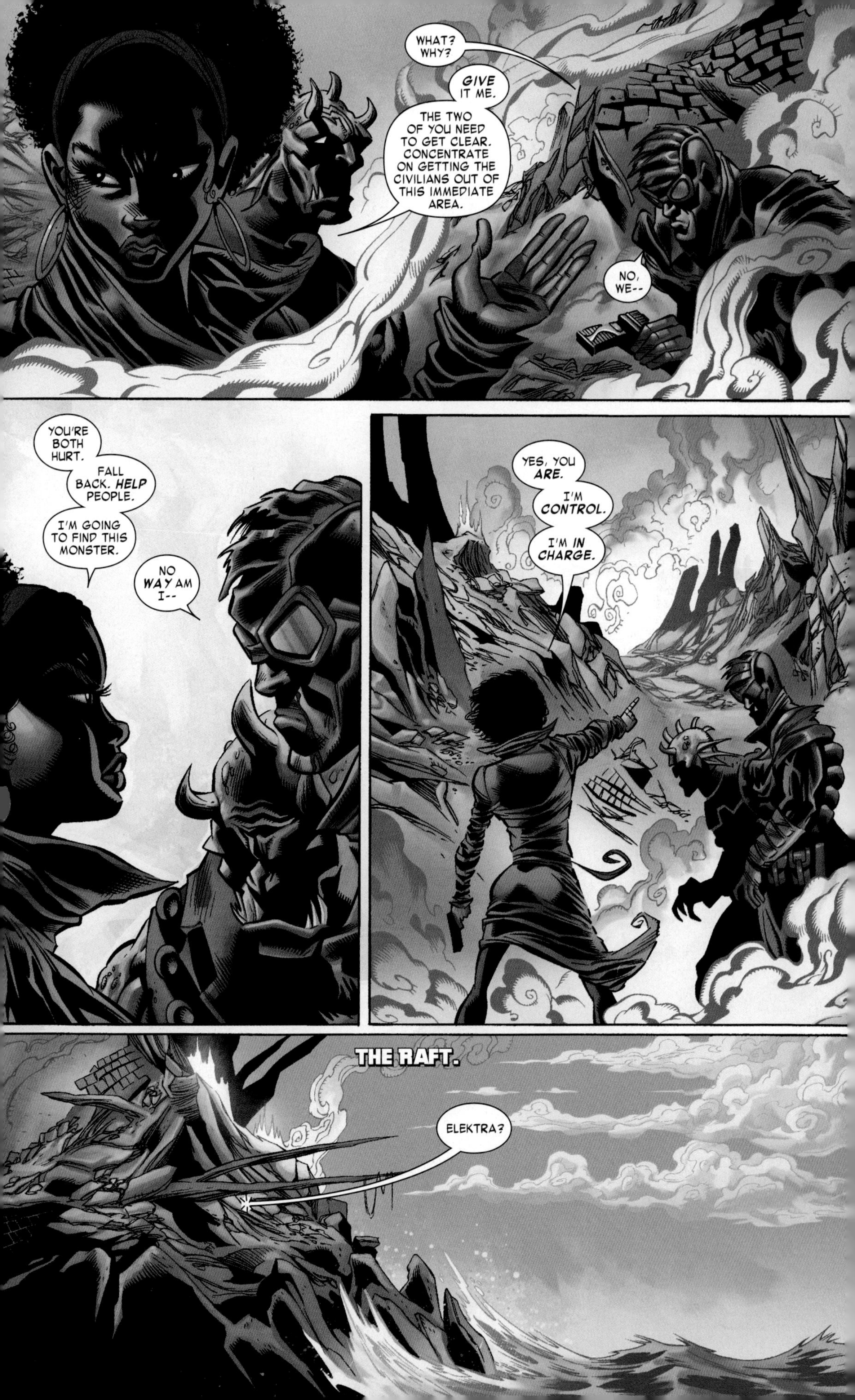
WHAT? WHY?
GIVE IT ME.
THE TWO OF YOU NEED TO GET CLEAR. CONCENTRATE ON GETTING THE CIVILIANS OUT OF THIS IMMEDIATE AREA.
NO, WE--
YOU'RE BOTH HURT.
FALL BACK. HELP PEOPLE.
I'M GOING TO FIND THIS MONSTER.
NO WAY AM I--
YES, YOU ARE.
I'M CONTROL.
I'M IN CHARGE.
THE RAFT.
ELEKTRA?

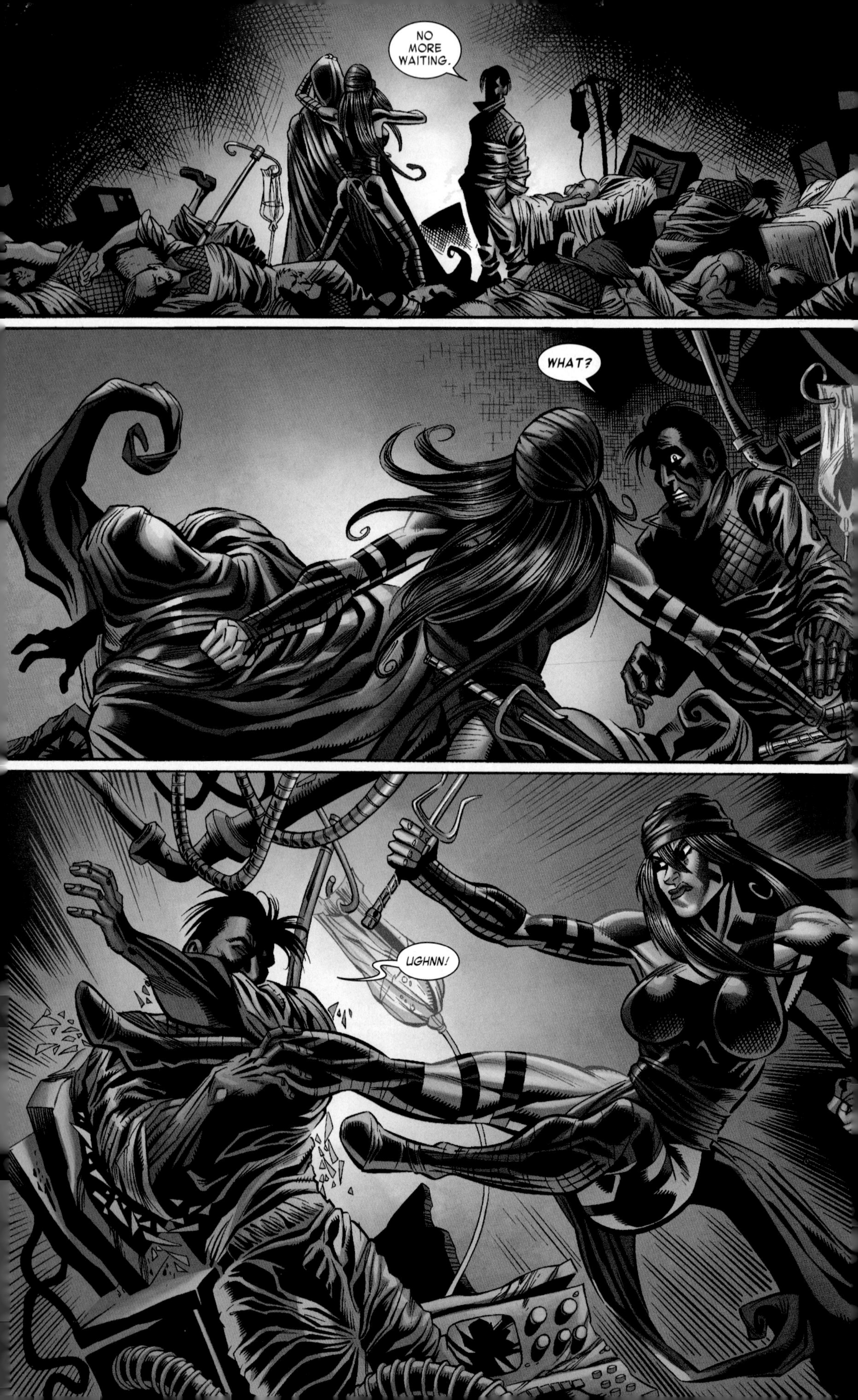
NO MORE WAITING.
WHAT?
UGHNN!

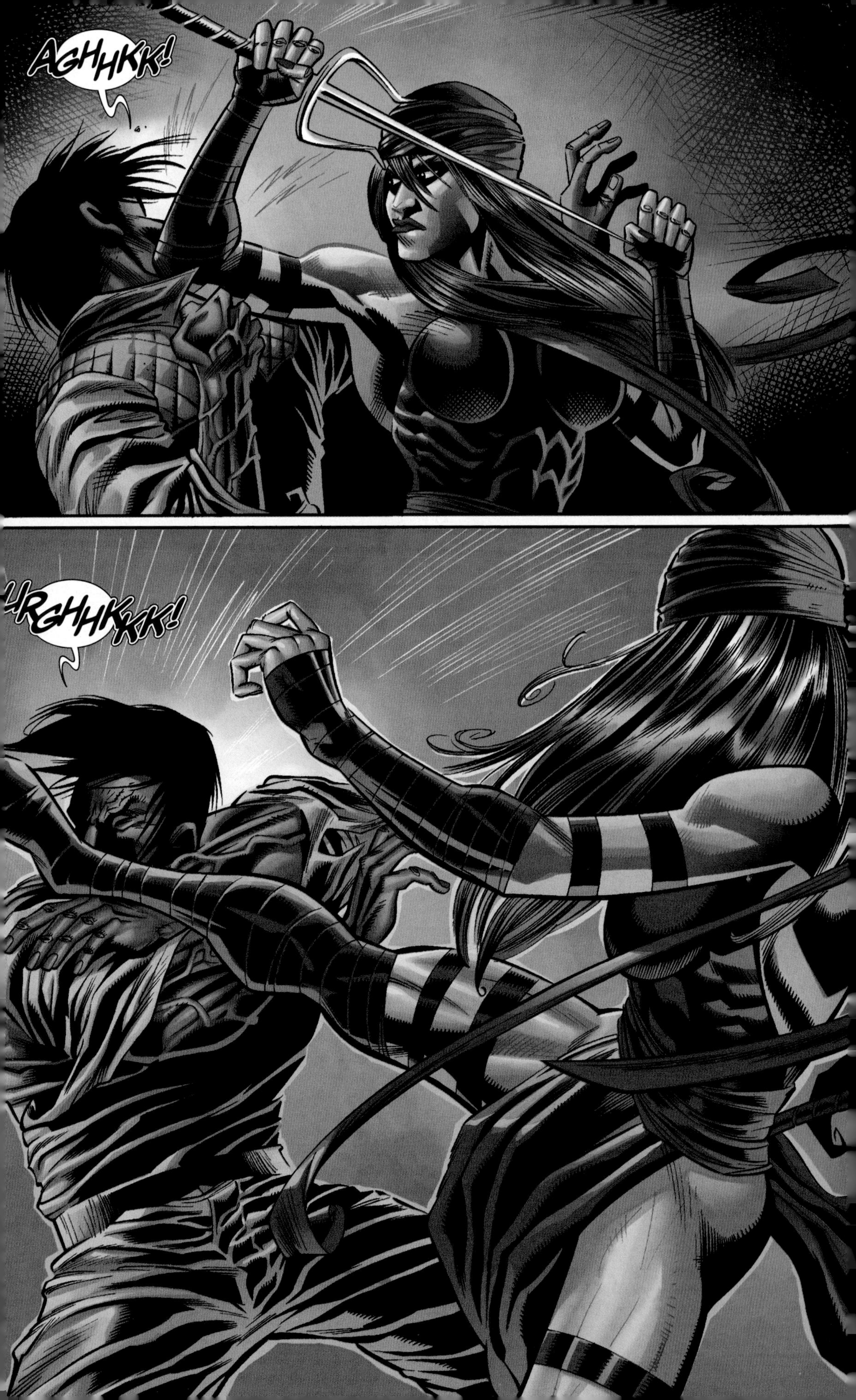
AGHHKK!
URGHHKKK!

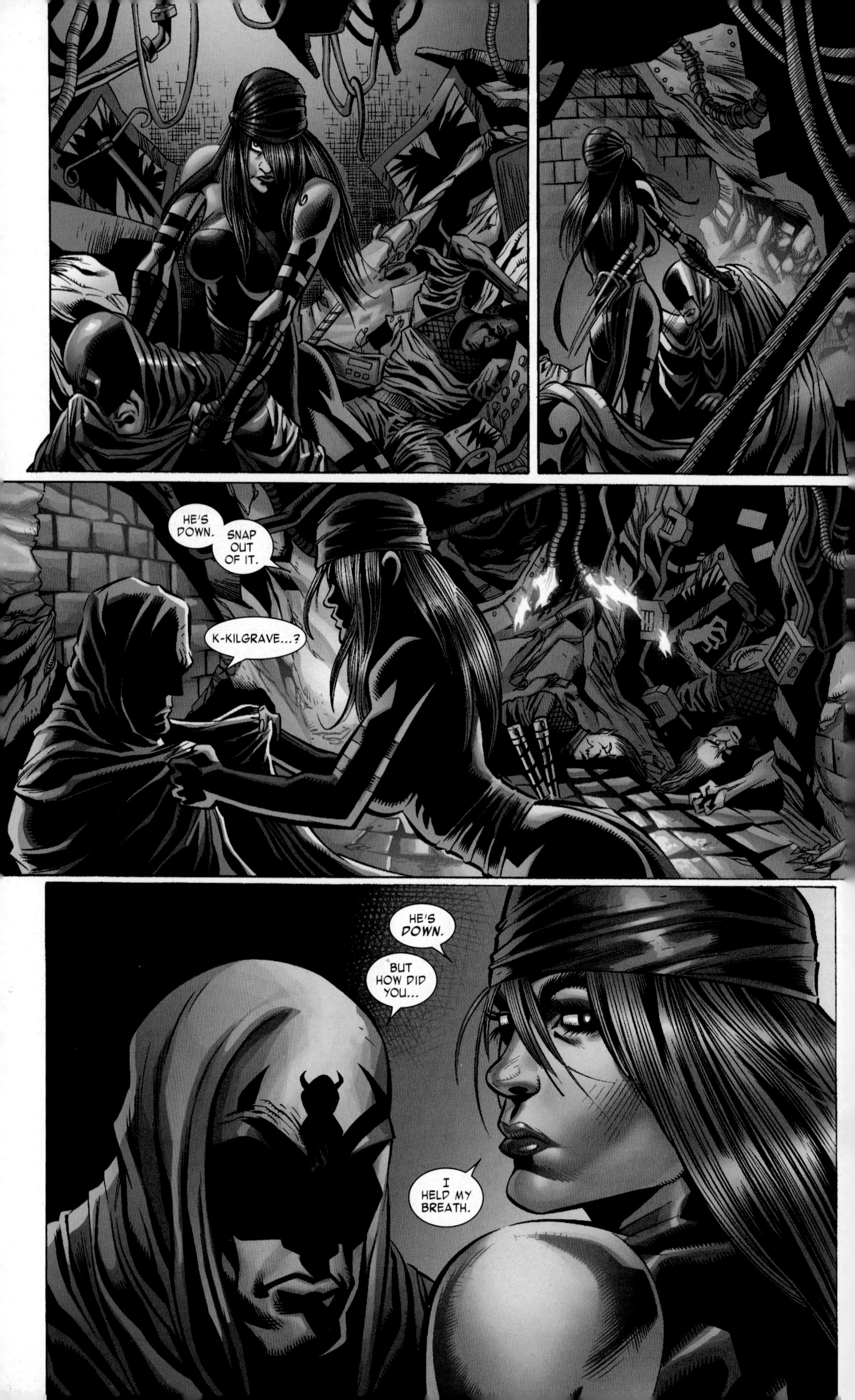
HE'S DOWN.
SNAP OUT OF IT.
K-KILGRAVE...?
HE'S *DOWN.*
BUT HOW DID YOU...
I HELD MY BREATH.

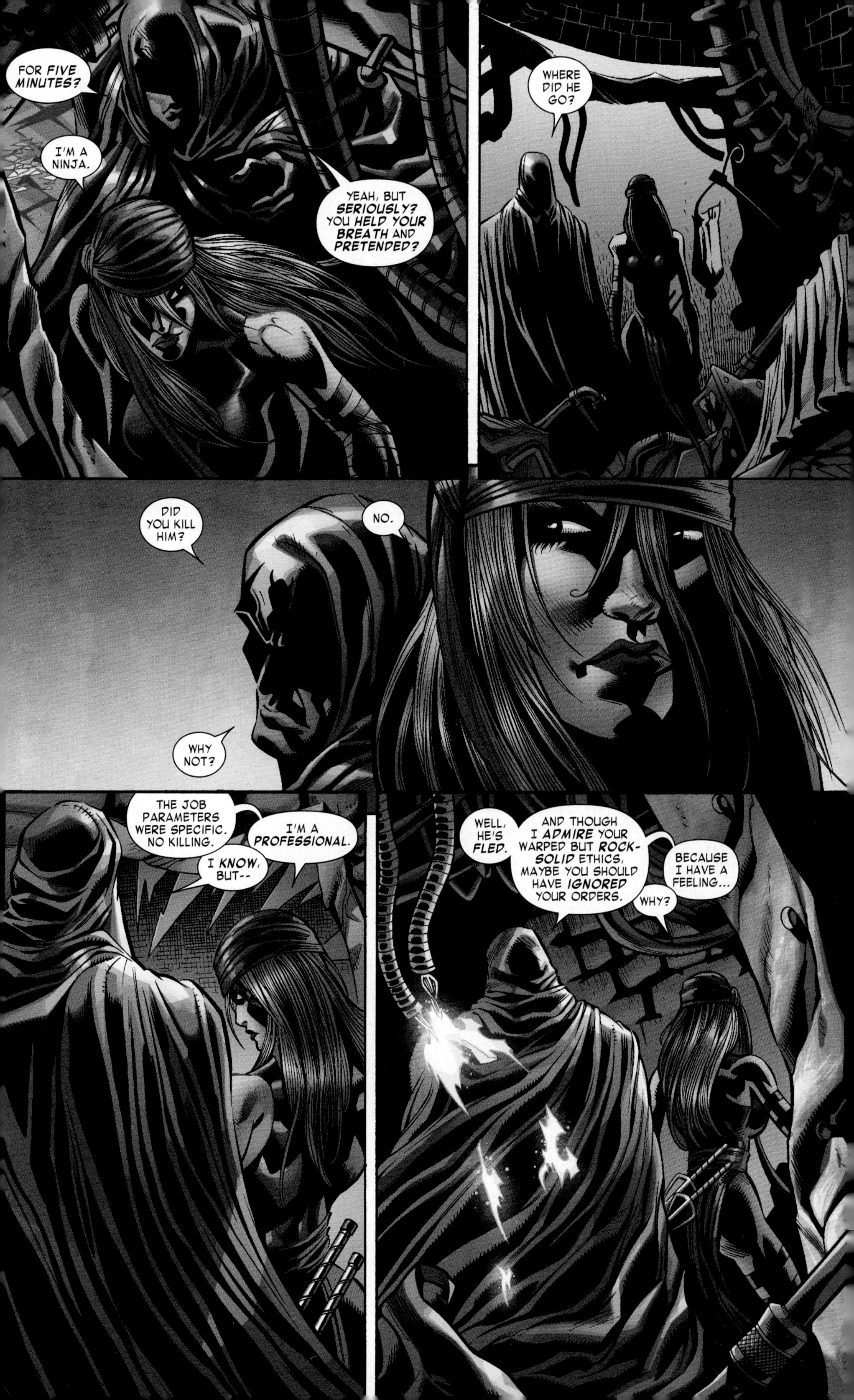
FOR FIVE MINUTES?
I'M A NINJA.
YEAH, BUT SERIOUSLY? YOU HELD YOUR BREATH AND PRETENDED?
WHERE DID HE GO?
DID YOU KILL HIM?
NO.
WHY NOT?
THE JOB PARAMETERS WERE SPECIFIC. NO KILLING.
I'M A PROFESSIONAL.
I KNOW, BUT--
WELL, HE'S FLED.
AND THOUGH I ADMIRE YOUR WARPED BUT ROCK-SOLID ETHICS, MAYBE YOU SHOULD HAVE IGNORED YOUR ORDERS.
WHY?
BECAUSE I HAVE A FEELING...

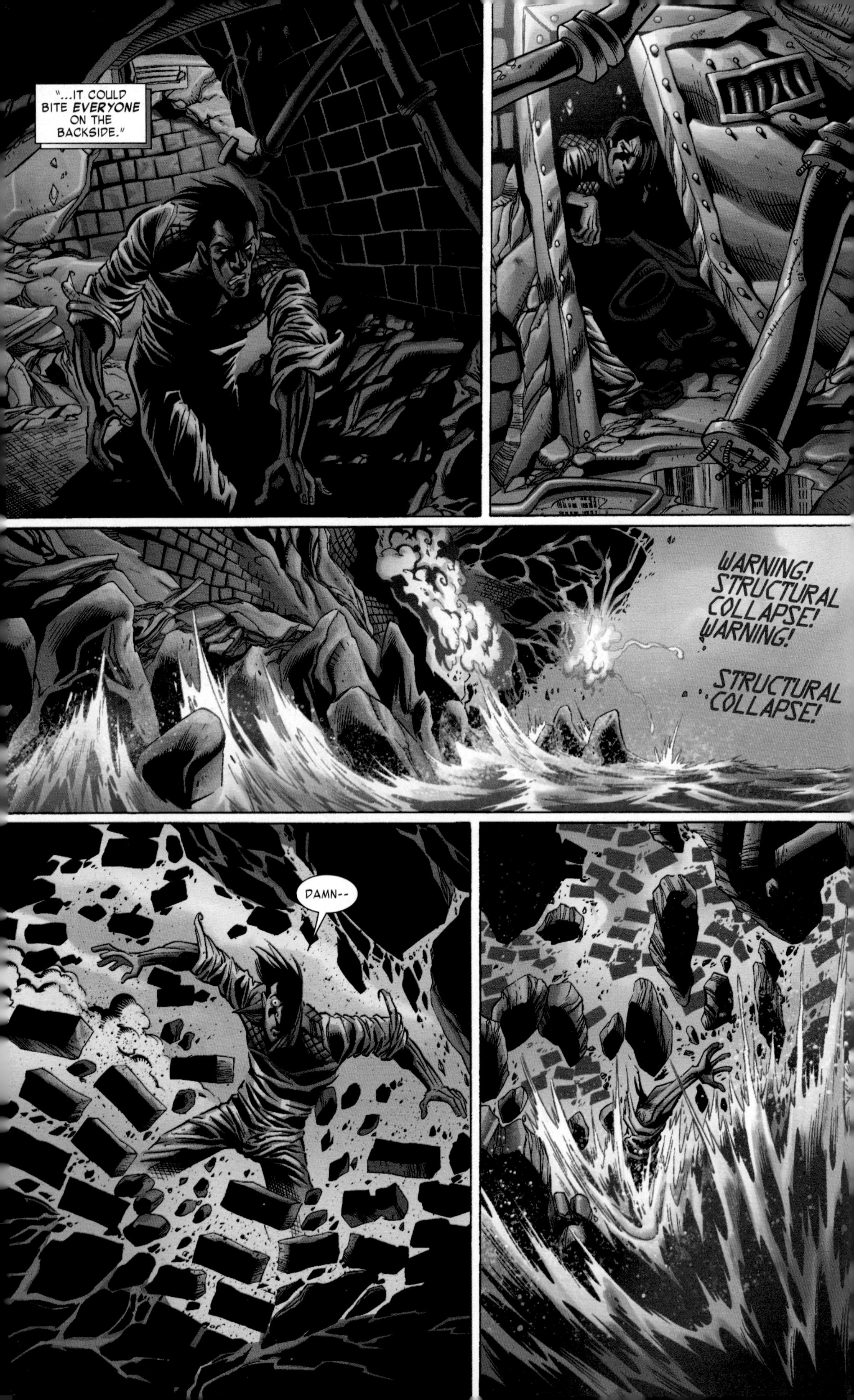
"...IT COULD BITE *EVERYONE* ON THE BACKSIDE."
WARNING! STRUCTURAL COLLAPSE! WARNING!
STRUCTURAL COLLAPSE!
DAMN--

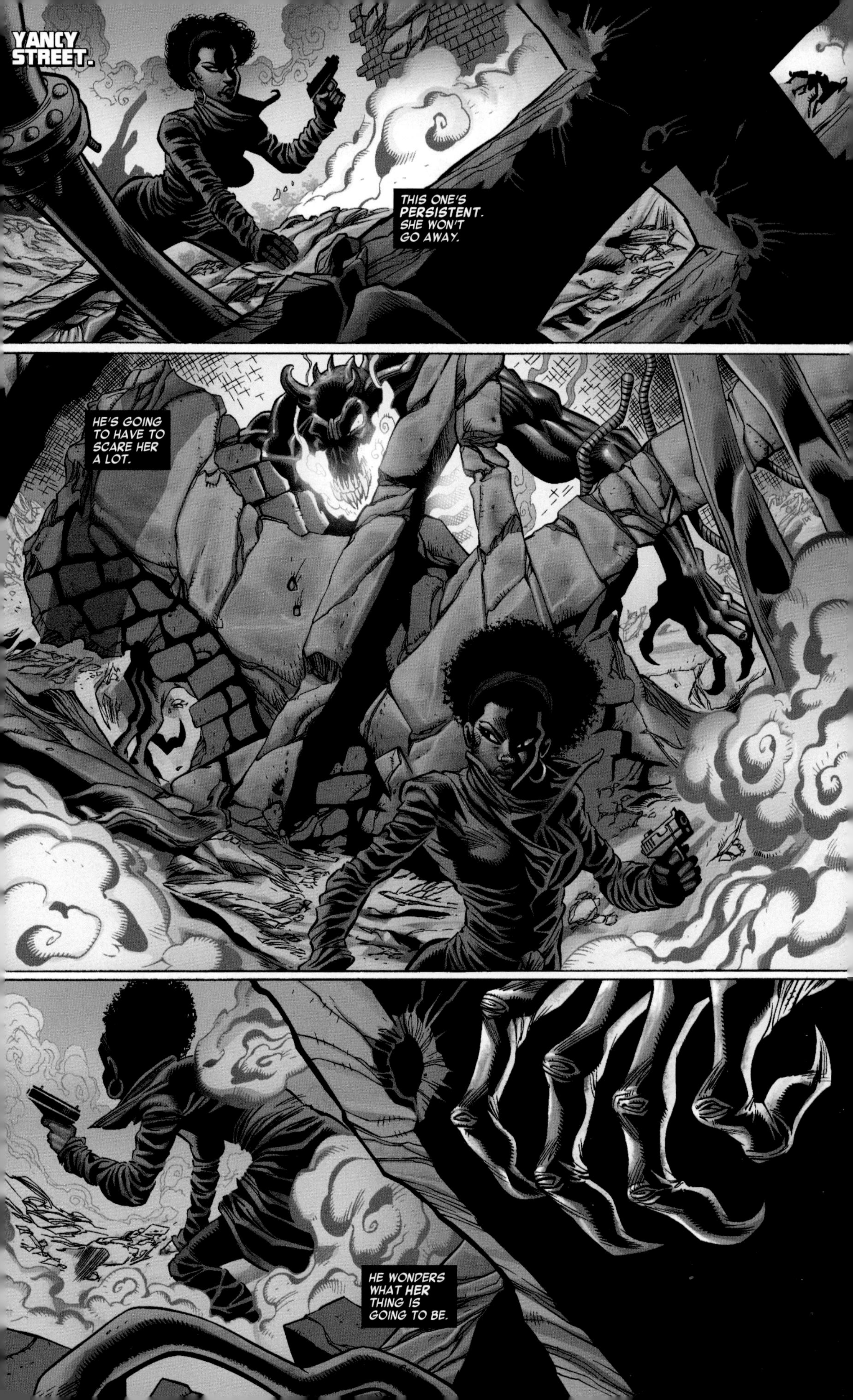
YANCY STREET.
THIS ONE'S PERSISTENT. SHE WON'T GO AWAY.
HE'S GOING TO HAVE TO SCARE HER A LOT.
HE WONDERS WHAT HER THING IS GOING TO BE.

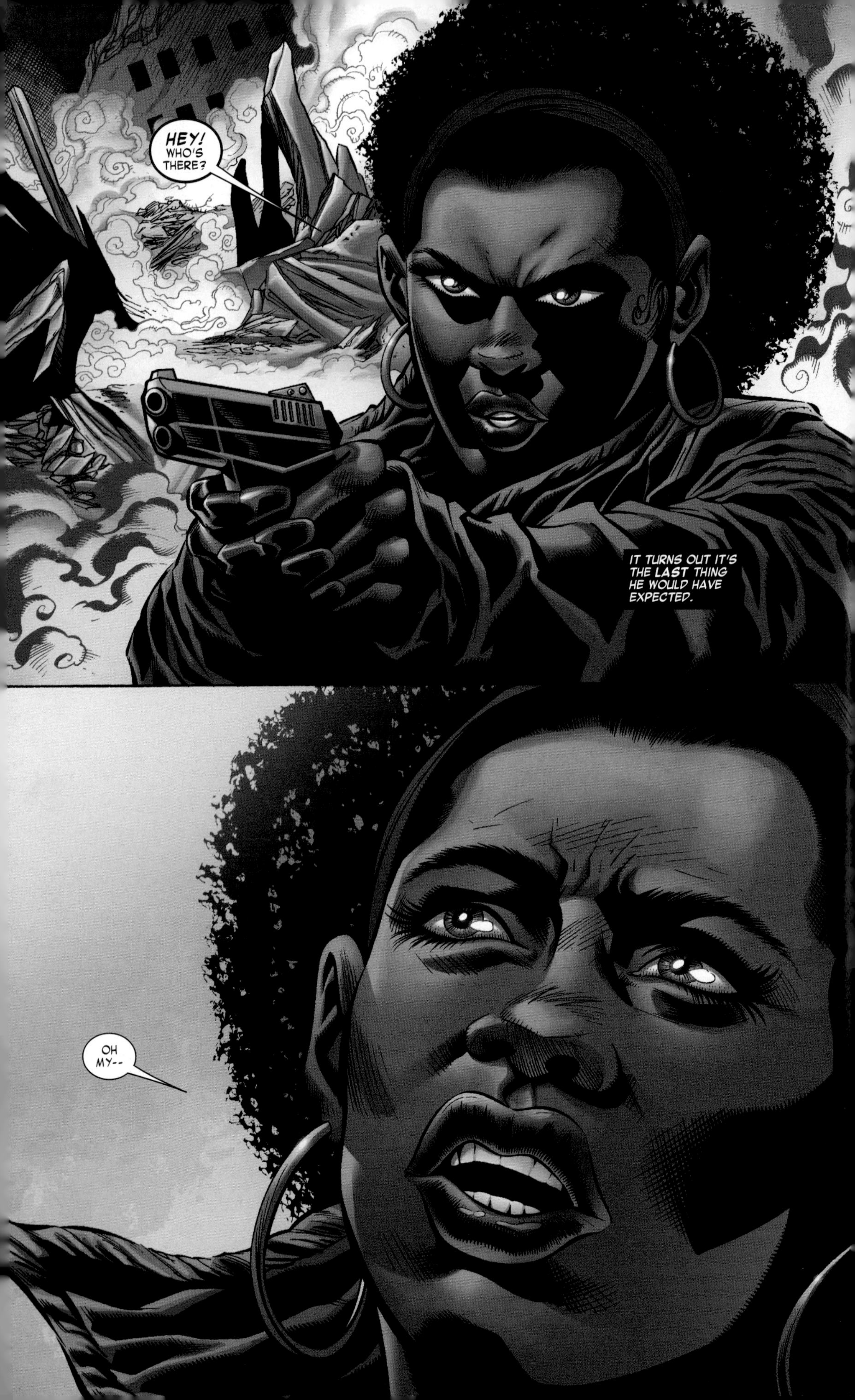
HEY! WHO'S THERE?
IT TURNS OUT IT'S THE LAST THING HE WOULD HAVE EXPECTED.
OH MY--

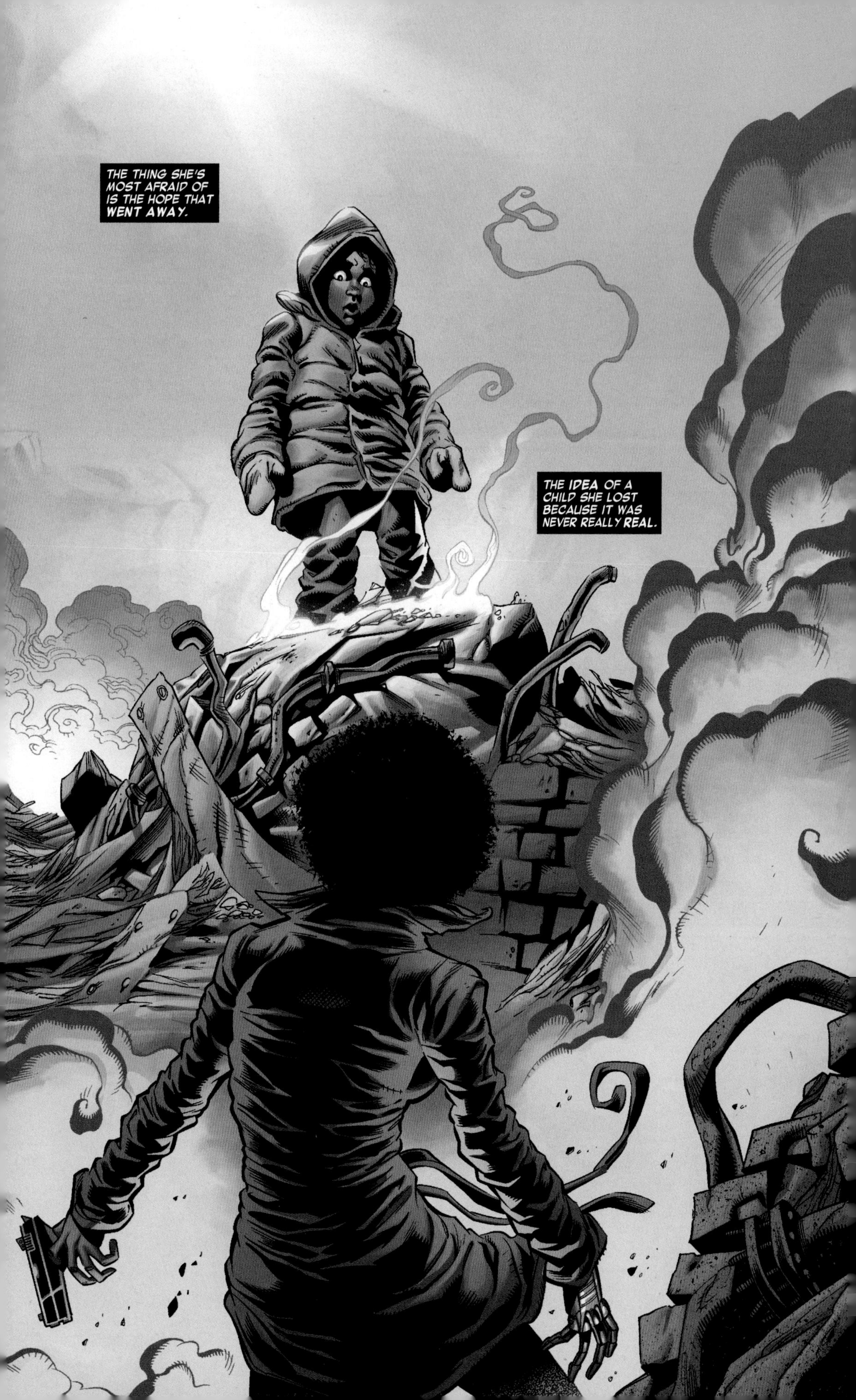
THE THING SHE'S MOST AFRAID OF IS THE HOPE THAT **WENT AWAY.**
THE **IDEA** OF A CHILD SHE LOST BECAUSE IT WAS NEVER REALLY **REAL.**

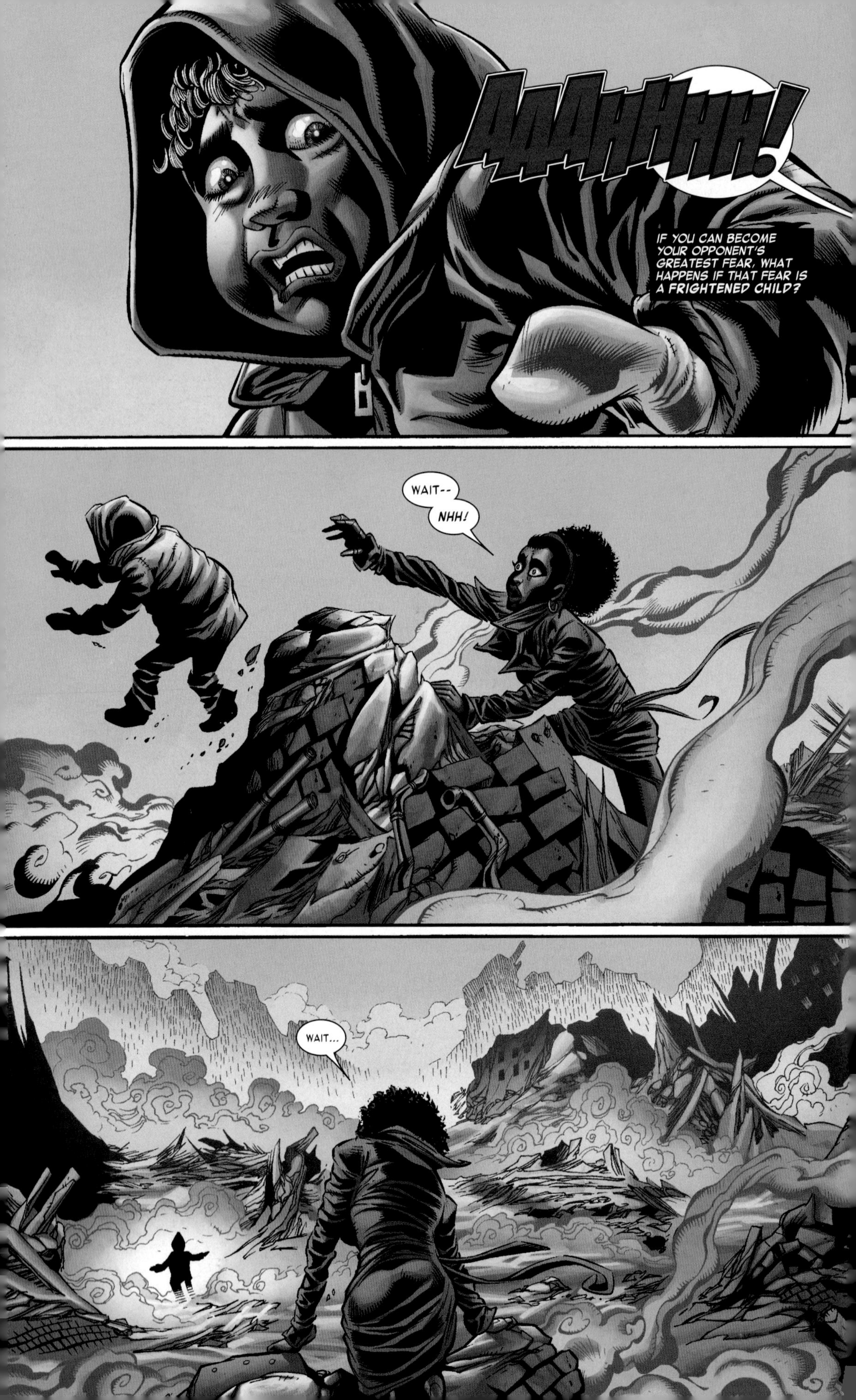
AAAHHHH!
IF YOU CAN BECOME YOUR OPPONENT'S GREATEST FEAR, WHAT HAPPENS IF THAT FEAR IS A FRIGHTENED CHILD?
WAIT--
NHH!
WAIT...

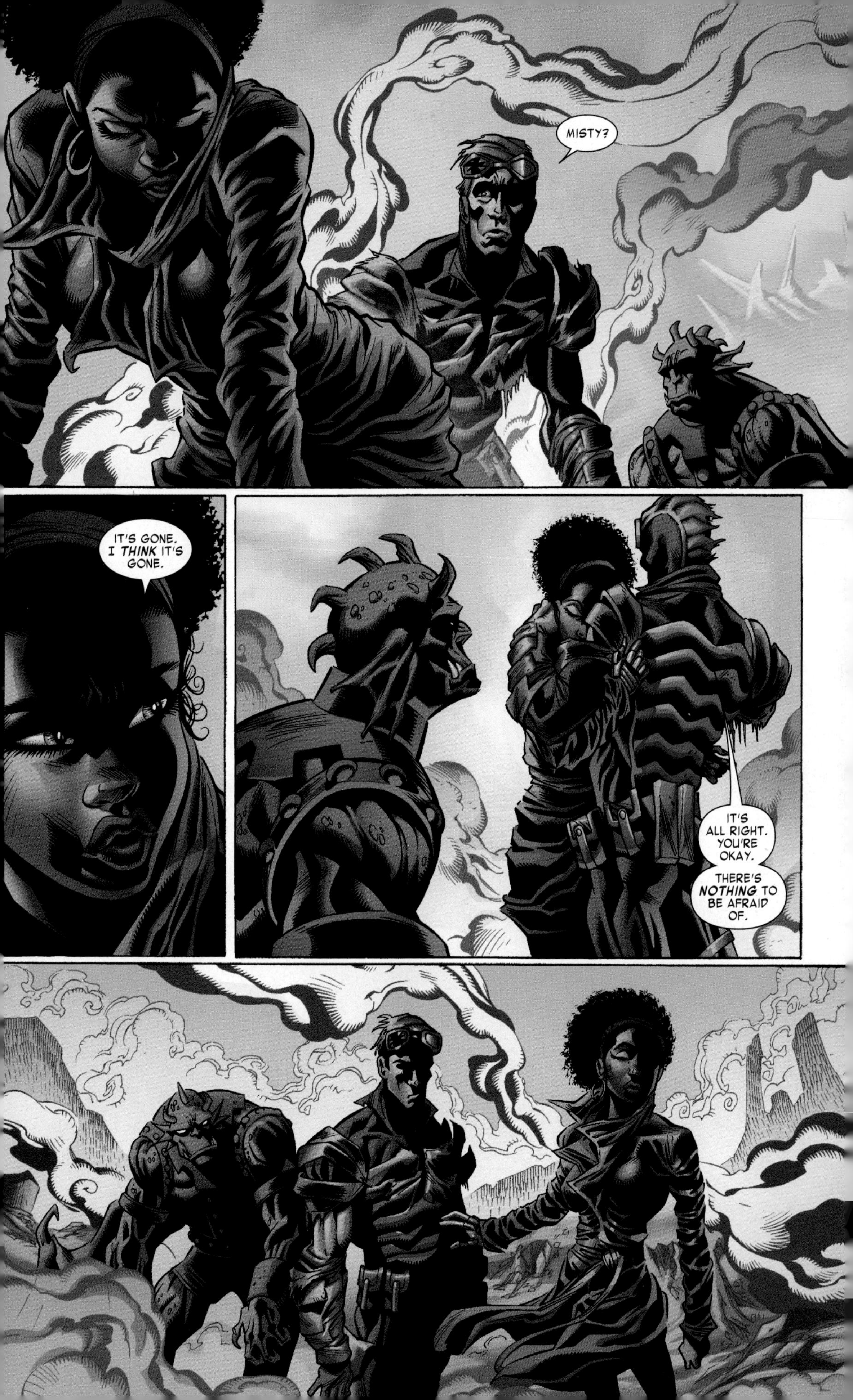
MISTY?
IT'S GONE. I THINK IT'S GONE.
IT'S ALL RIGHT. YOU'RE OKAY.
THERE'S NOTHING TO BE AFRAID OF.

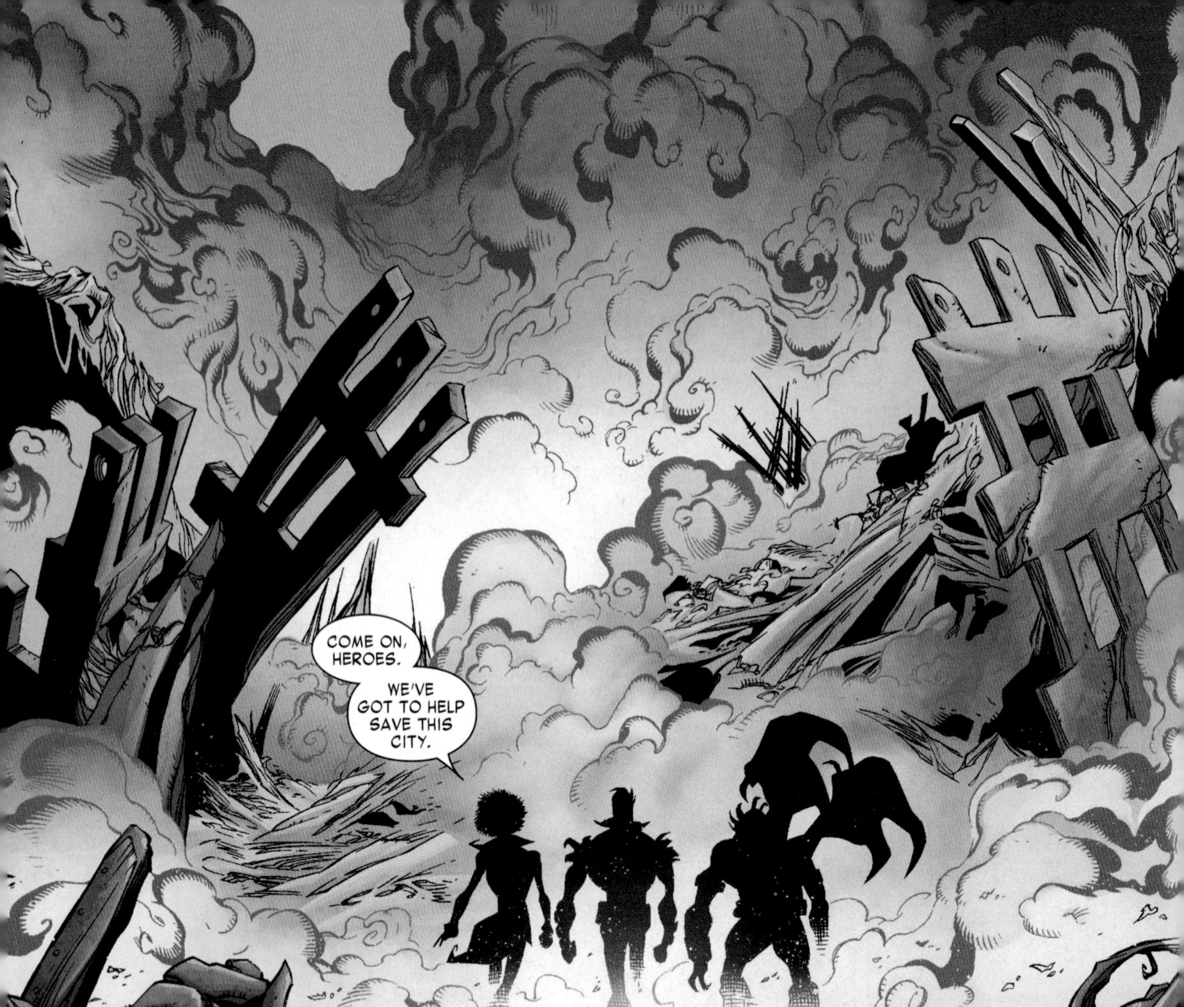
COME ON, HEROES.
WE'VE GOT TO HELP SAVE THIS CITY.

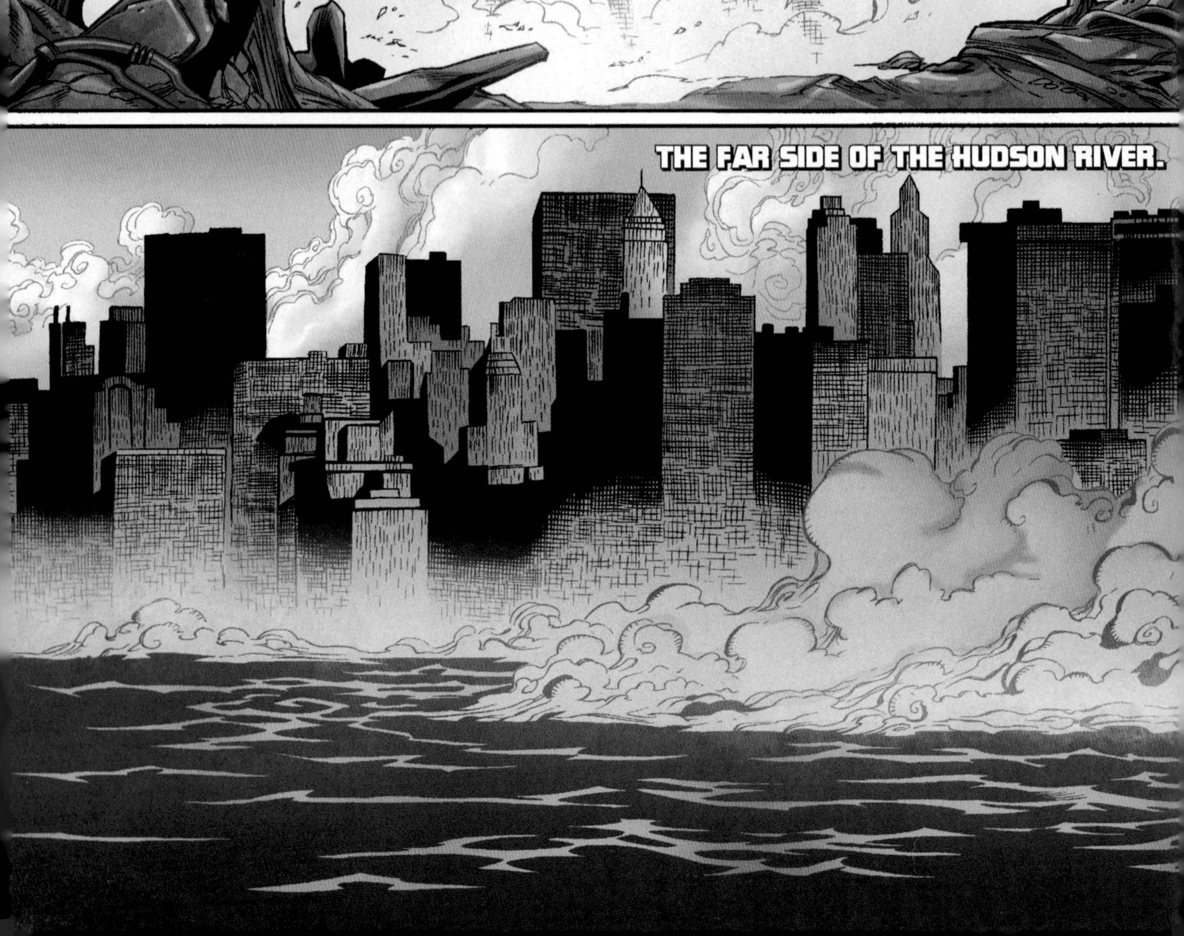
THE FAR SIDE OF THE HUDSON RIVER.

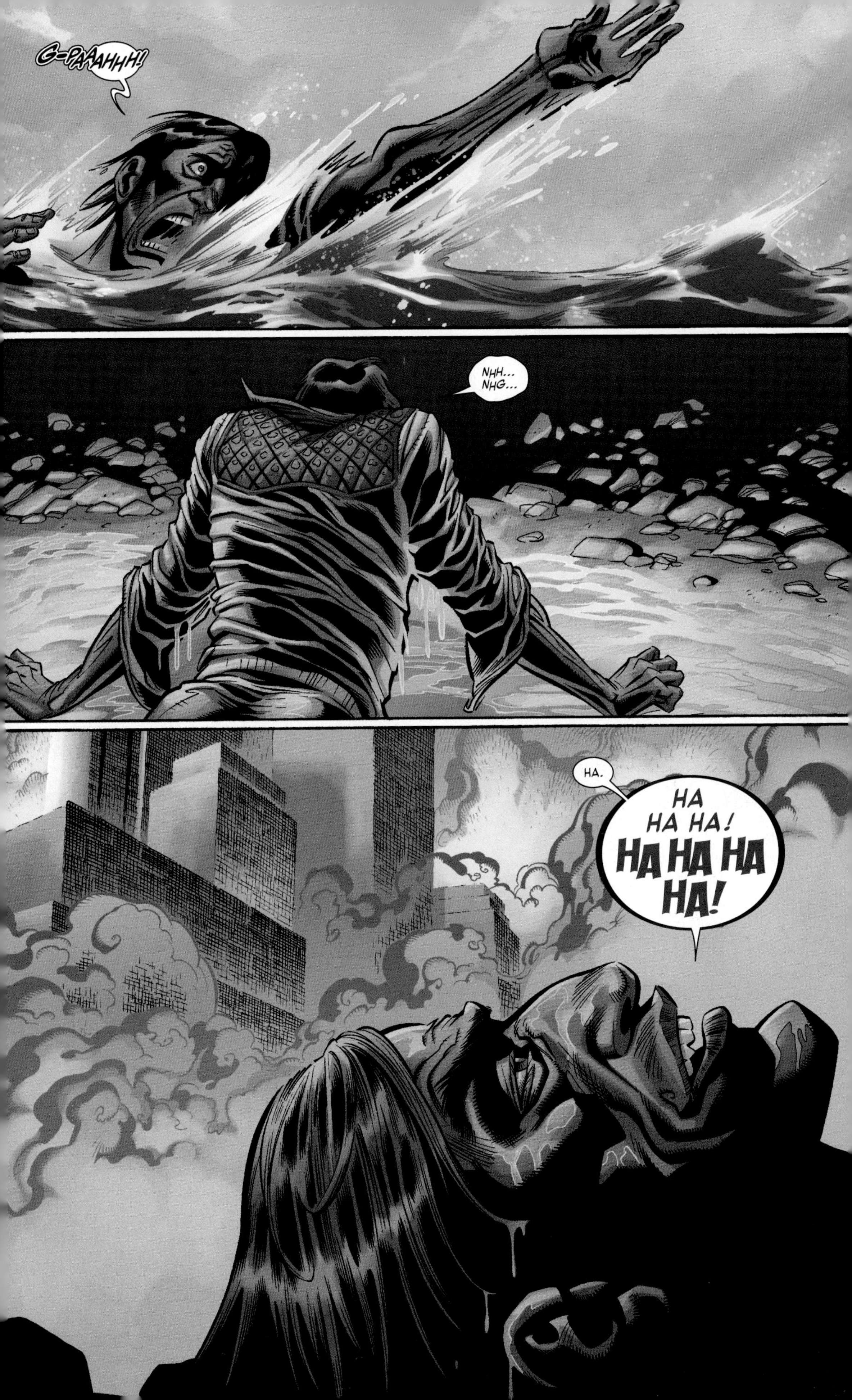
G-PAAAHHH!
NHH... NHG...
HA.
HA HA HA! HA HA HA HA!

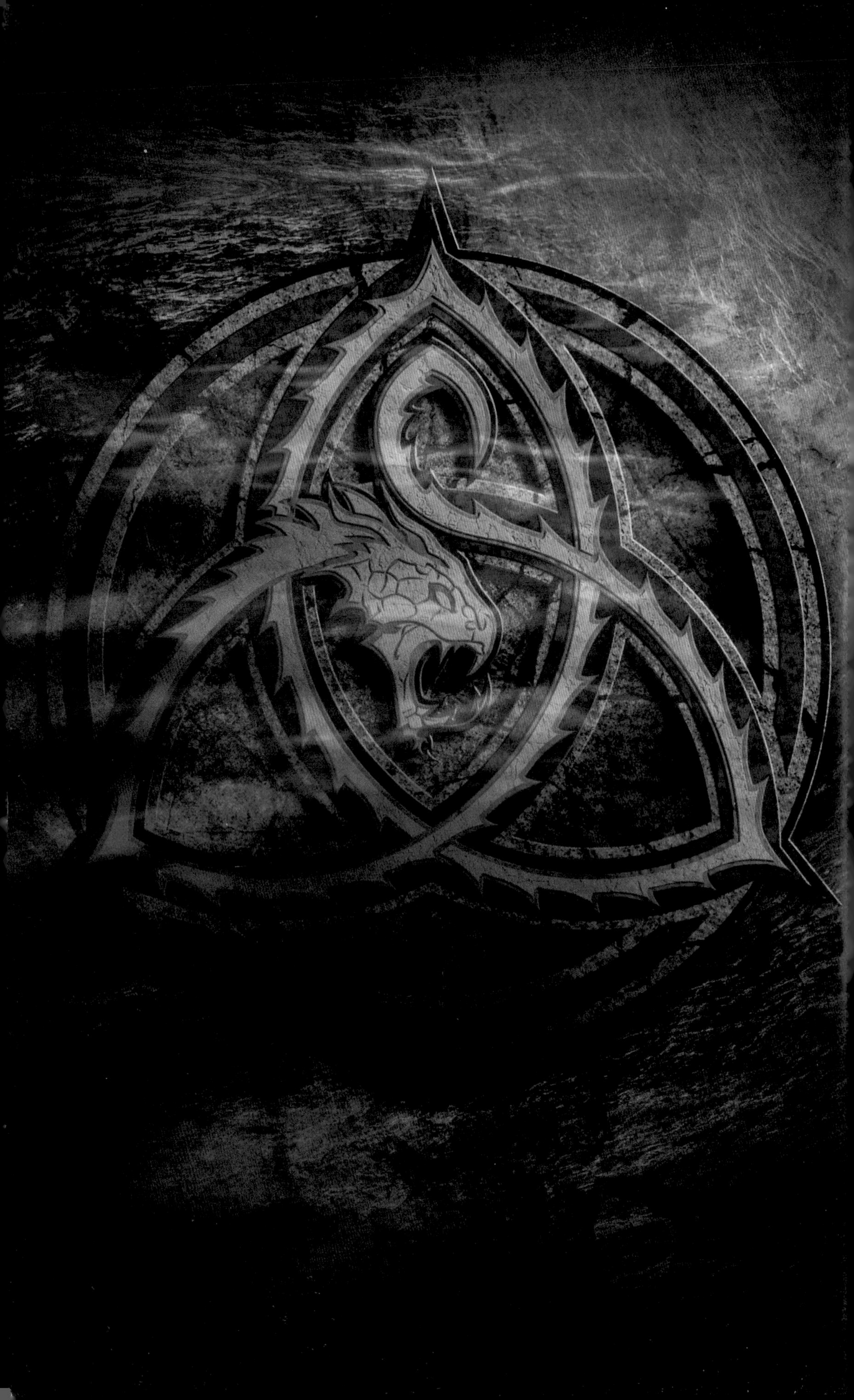

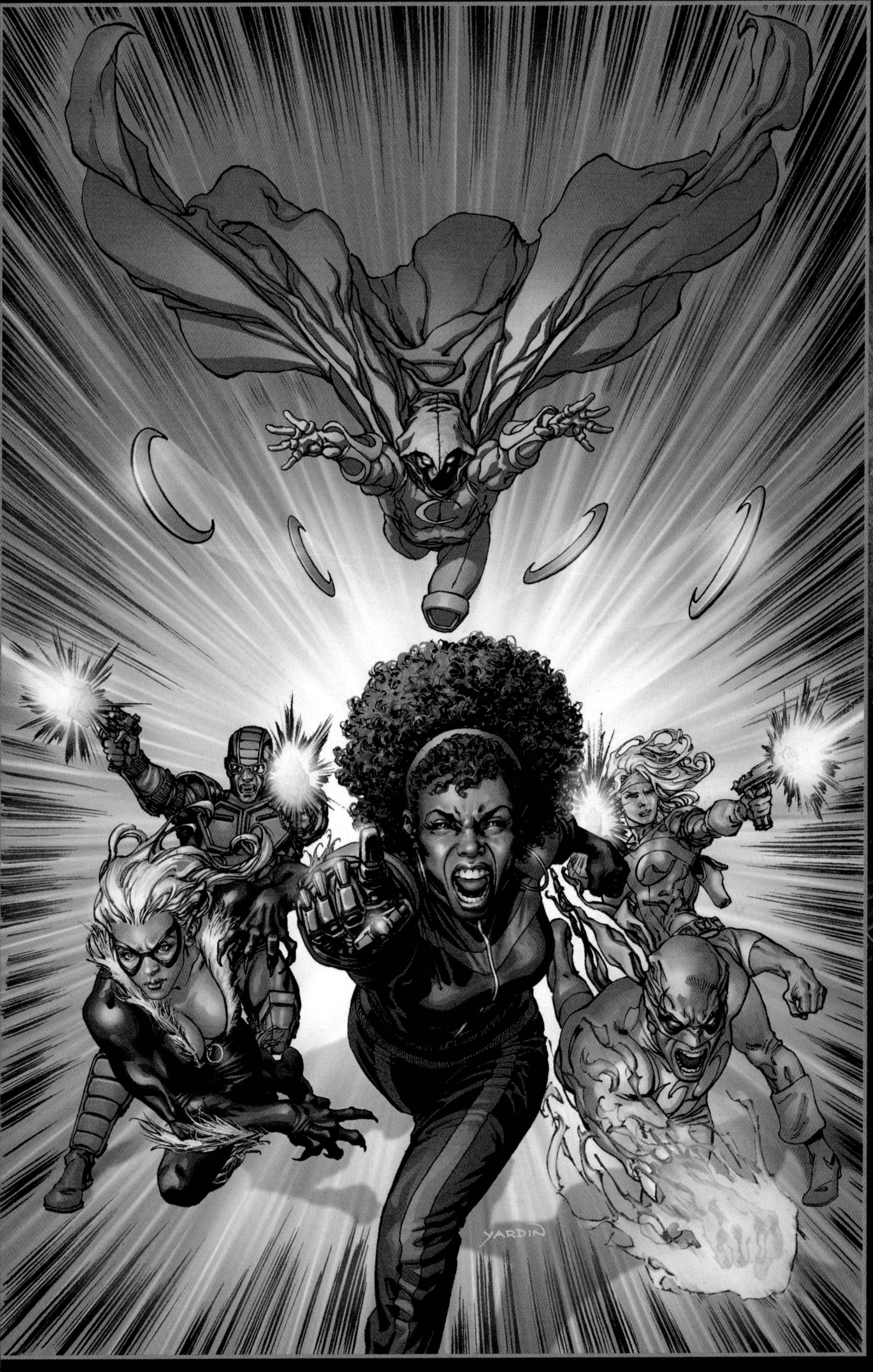
YARDIN

HEROES FOR HIRE #12

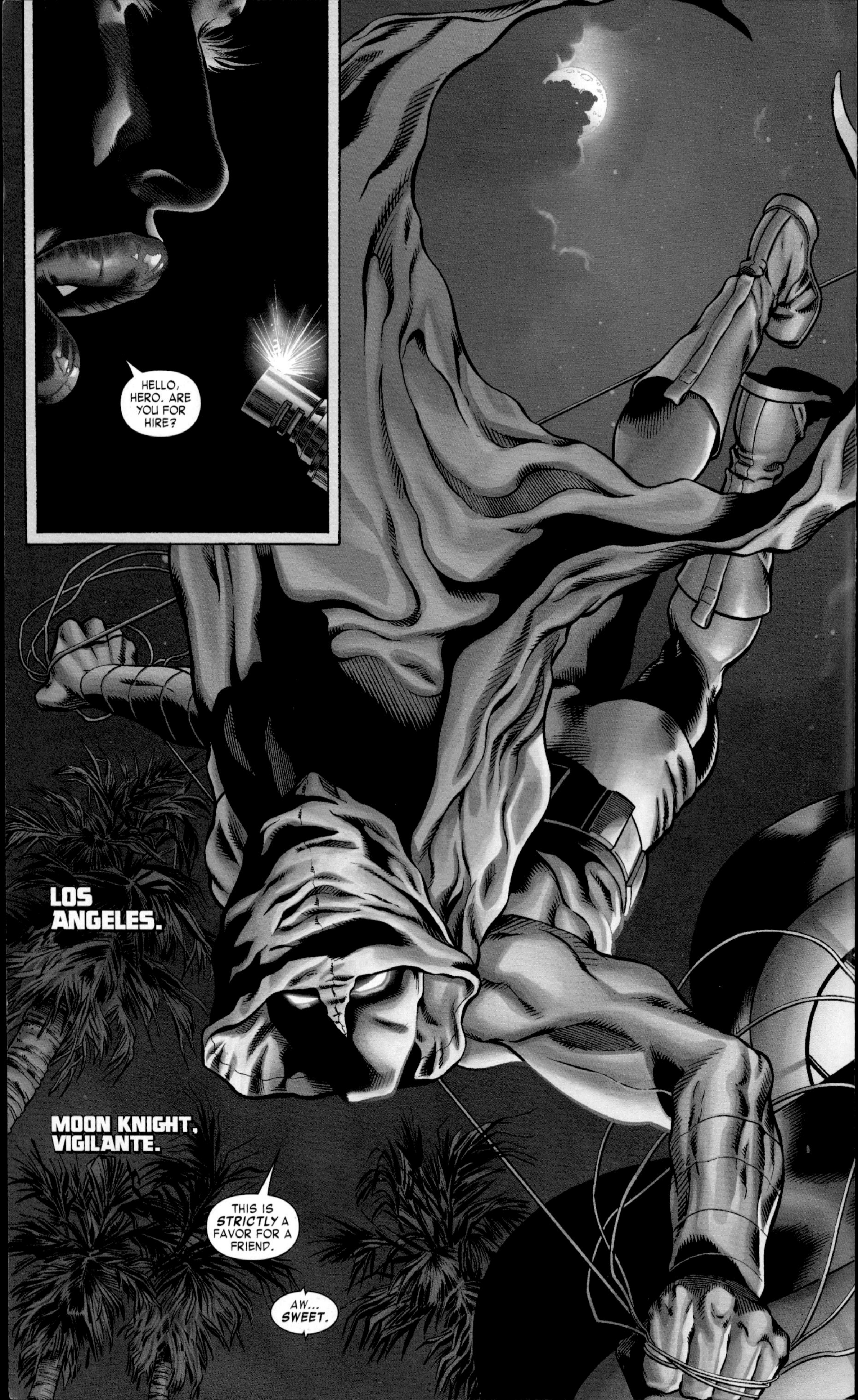
HELLO, HERO. ARE YOU FOR HIRE?
LOS ANGELES.
MOON KNIGHT, VIGILANTE.
THIS IS STRICTLY A FAVOR FOR A FRIEND.
AW... SWEET.

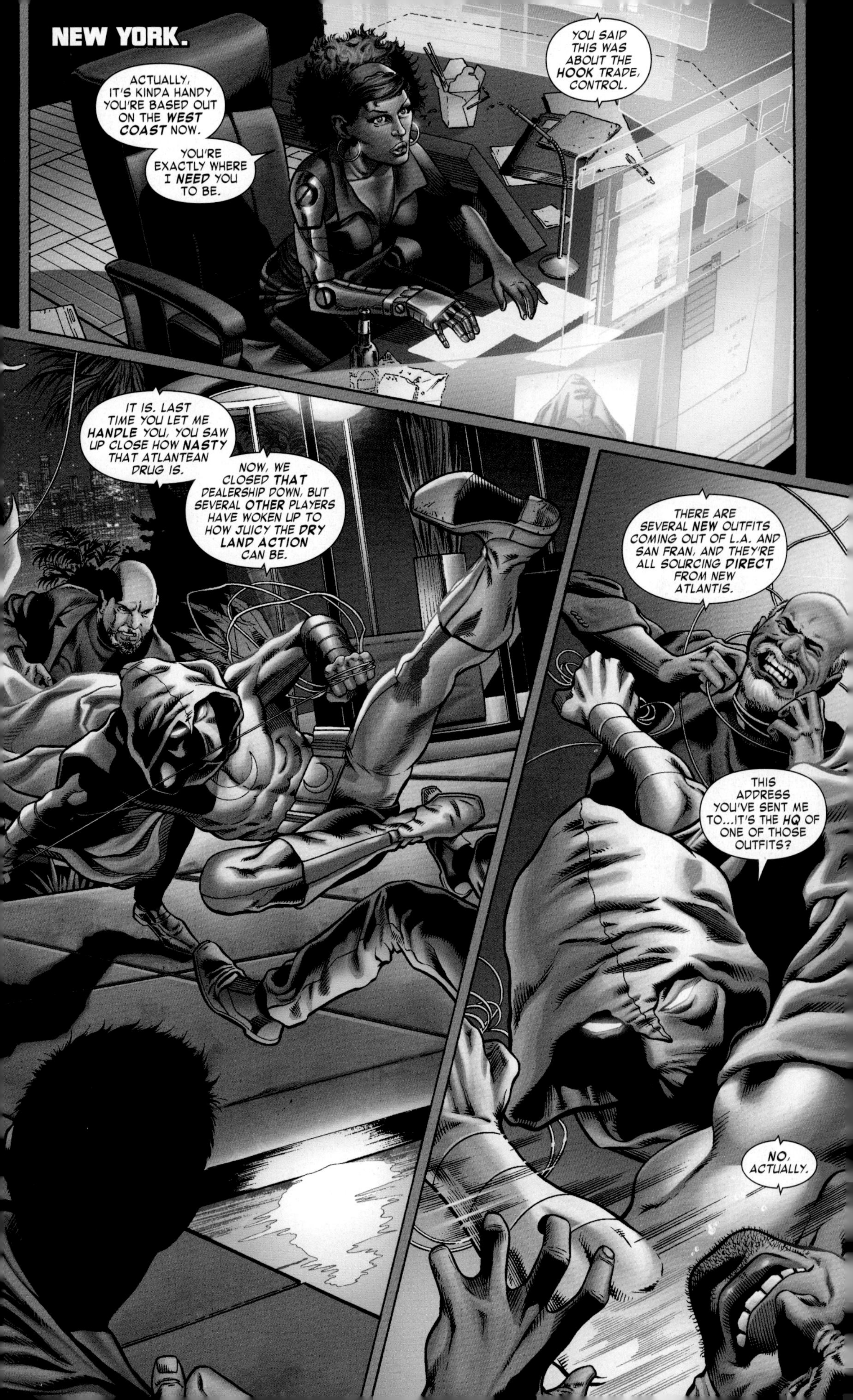
NEW YORK.
ACTUALLY, IT'S KINDA HANDY YOU'RE BASED OUT ON THE WEST COAST NOW.
YOU'RE EXACTLY WHERE I NEED YOU TO BE.
YOU SAID THIS WAS ABOUT THE HOOK TRADE, CONTROL.
IT IS. LAST TIME YOU LET ME HANDLE YOU, YOU SAW UP CLOSE HOW NASTY THAT ATLANTEAN DRUG IS.
NOW, WE CLOSED THAT DEALERSHIP DOWN, BUT SEVERAL OTHER PLAYERS HAVE WOKEN UP TO HOW JUICY THE DRY LAND ACTION CAN BE.
THERE ARE SEVERAL NEW OUTFITS COMING OUT OF L.A. AND SAN FRAN, AND THEY'RE ALL SOURCING DIRECT FROM NEW ATLANTIS.
THIS ADDRESS YOU'VE SENT ME TO...IT'S THE HQ OF ONE OF THOSE OUTFITS?
NO, ACTUALLY.

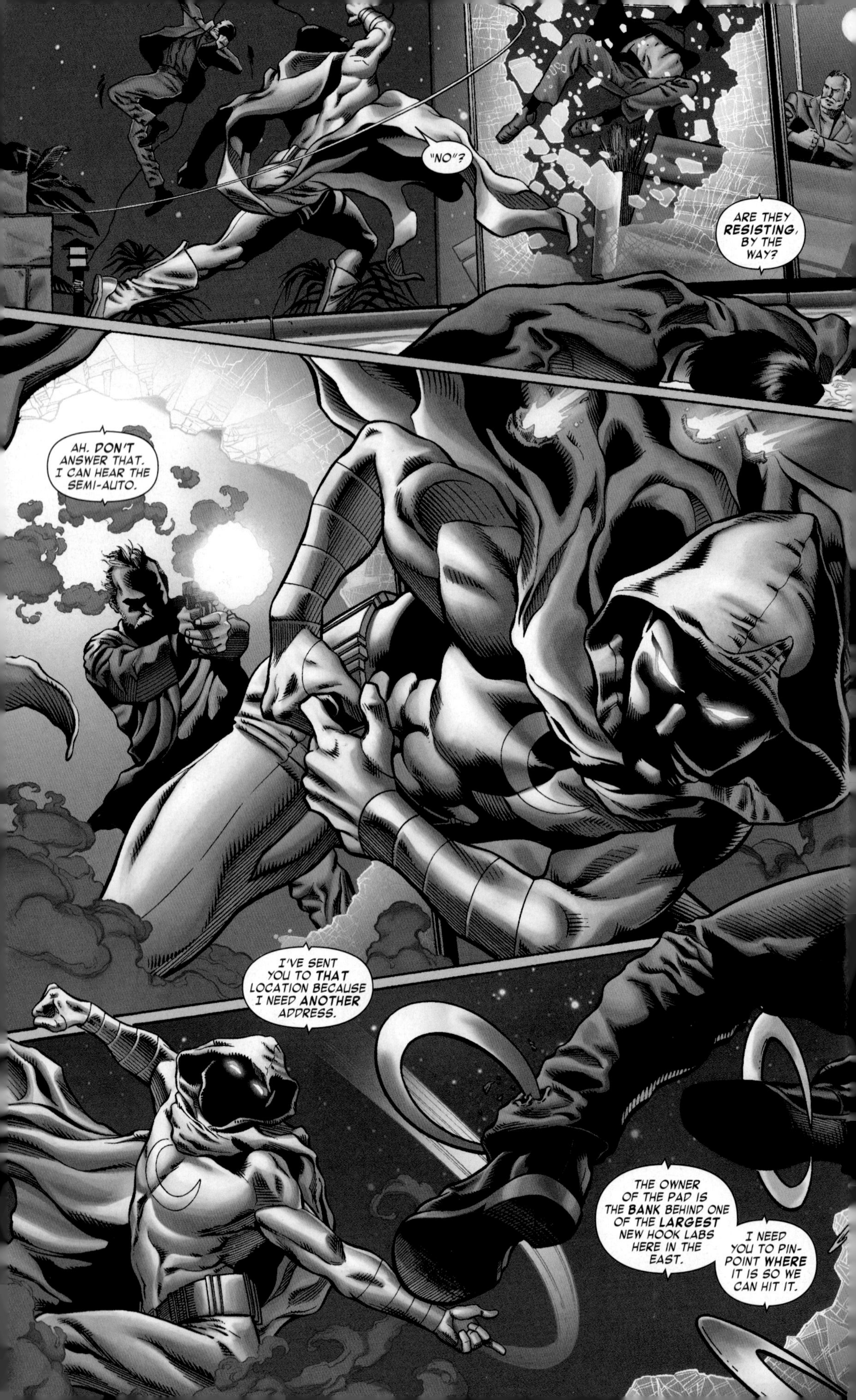
"NO"?
ARE THEY RESISTING, BY THE WAY?
AH. DON'T ANSWER THAT. I CAN HEAR THE SEMI-AUTO.
I'VE SENT YOU TO THAT LOCATION BECAUSE I NEED ANOTHER ADDRESS.
THE OWNER OF THE PAD IS THE BANK BEHIND ONE OF THE LARGEST NEW HOOK LABS HERE IN THE EAST.
I NEED YOU TO PIN-POINT WHERE IT IS SO WE CAN HIT IT.

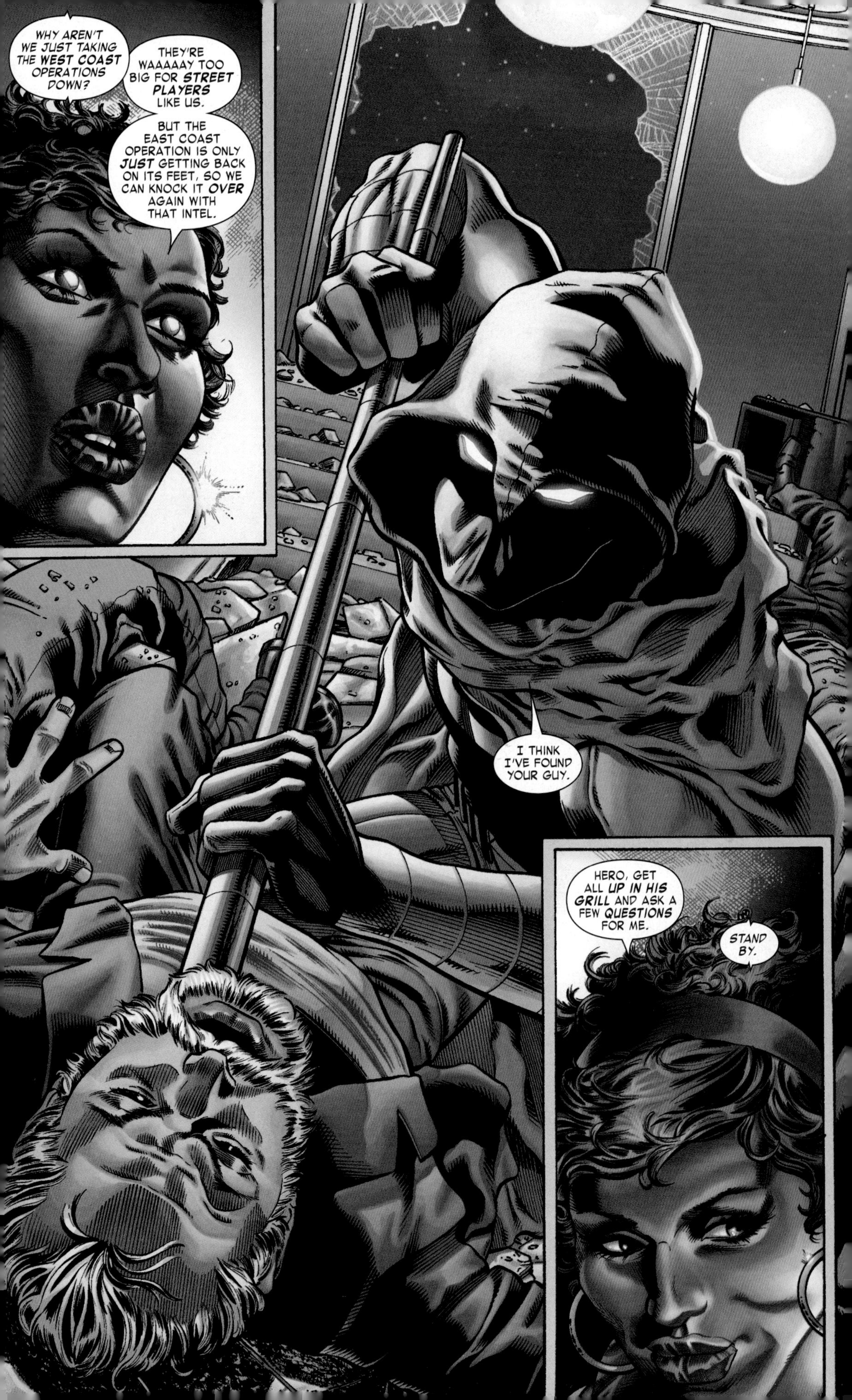
WHY AREN'T WE JUST TAKING THE WEST COAST OPERATIONS DOWN?
THEY'RE WAAAAAY TOO BIG FOR STREET PLAYERS LIKE US.
BUT THE EAST COAST OPERATION IS ONLY JUST GETTING BACK ON ITS FEET, SO WE CAN KNOCK IT OVER AGAIN WITH THAT INTEL.
I THINK I'VE FOUND YOUR GUY.
HERO, GET ALL UP IN HIS GRILL AND ASK A FEW QUESTIONS FOR ME.
STAND BY.

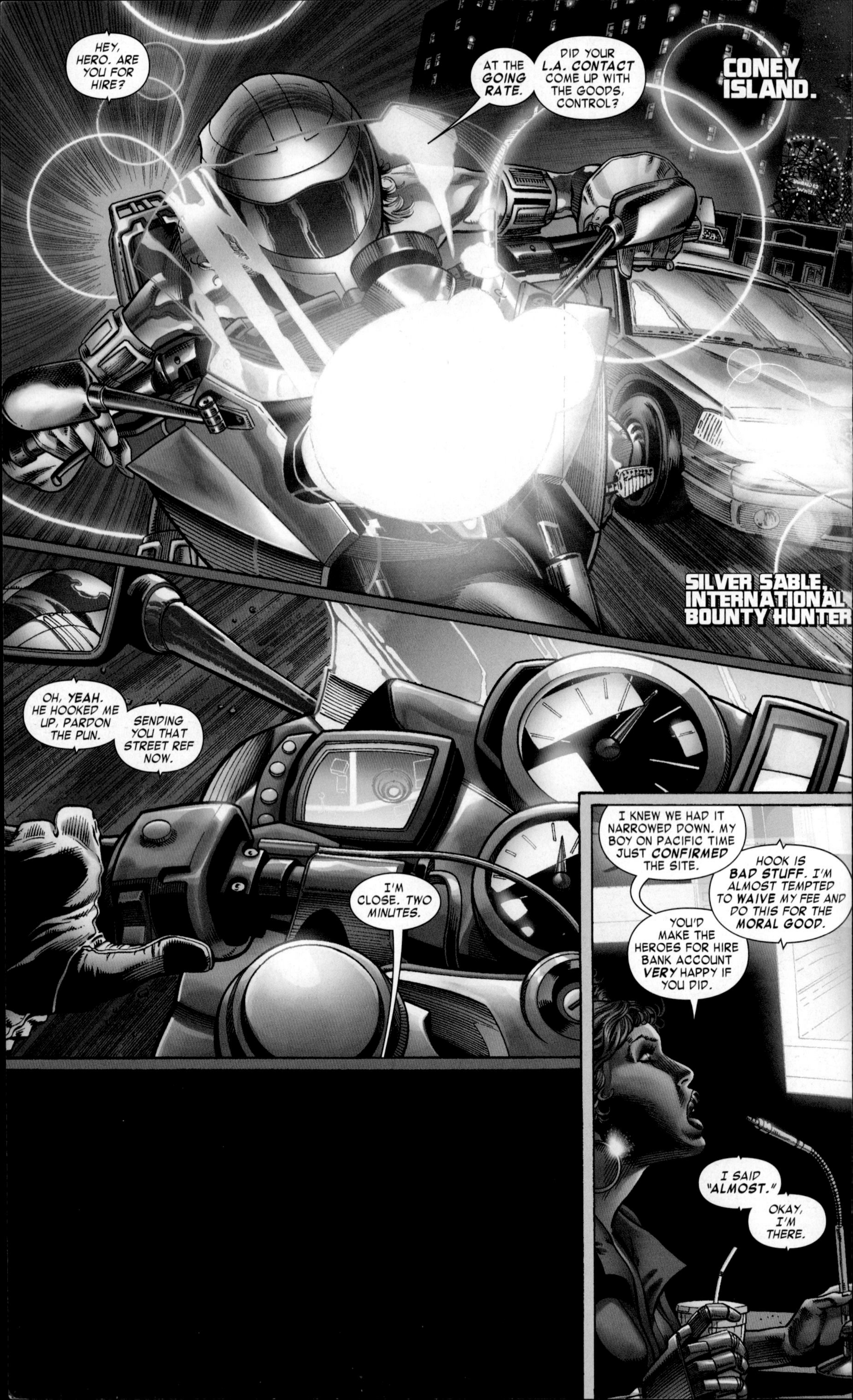
HEY, HERO. ARE YOU FOR HIRE?
AT THE GOING RATE.
DID YOUR L.A. CONTACT COME UP WITH THE GOODS, CONTROL?
CONEY ISLAND.
SILVER SABLE... INTERNATIONAL BOUNTY HUNTER
OH, YEAH. HE HOOKED ME UP, PARDON THE PUN.
SENDING YOU THAT STREET REF NOW.
I'M CLOSE. TWO MINUTES.
I KNEW WE HAD IT NARROWED DOWN. MY BOY ON PACIFIC TIME JUST CONFIRMED THE SITE.
HOOK IS BAD STUFF. I'M ALMOST TEMPTED TO WAIVE MY FEE AND DO THIS FOR THE MORAL GOOD.
YOU'D MAKE THE HEROES FOR HIRE BANK ACCOUNT VERY HAPPY IF YOU DID.
I SAID "ALMOST."
OKAY, I'M THERE.

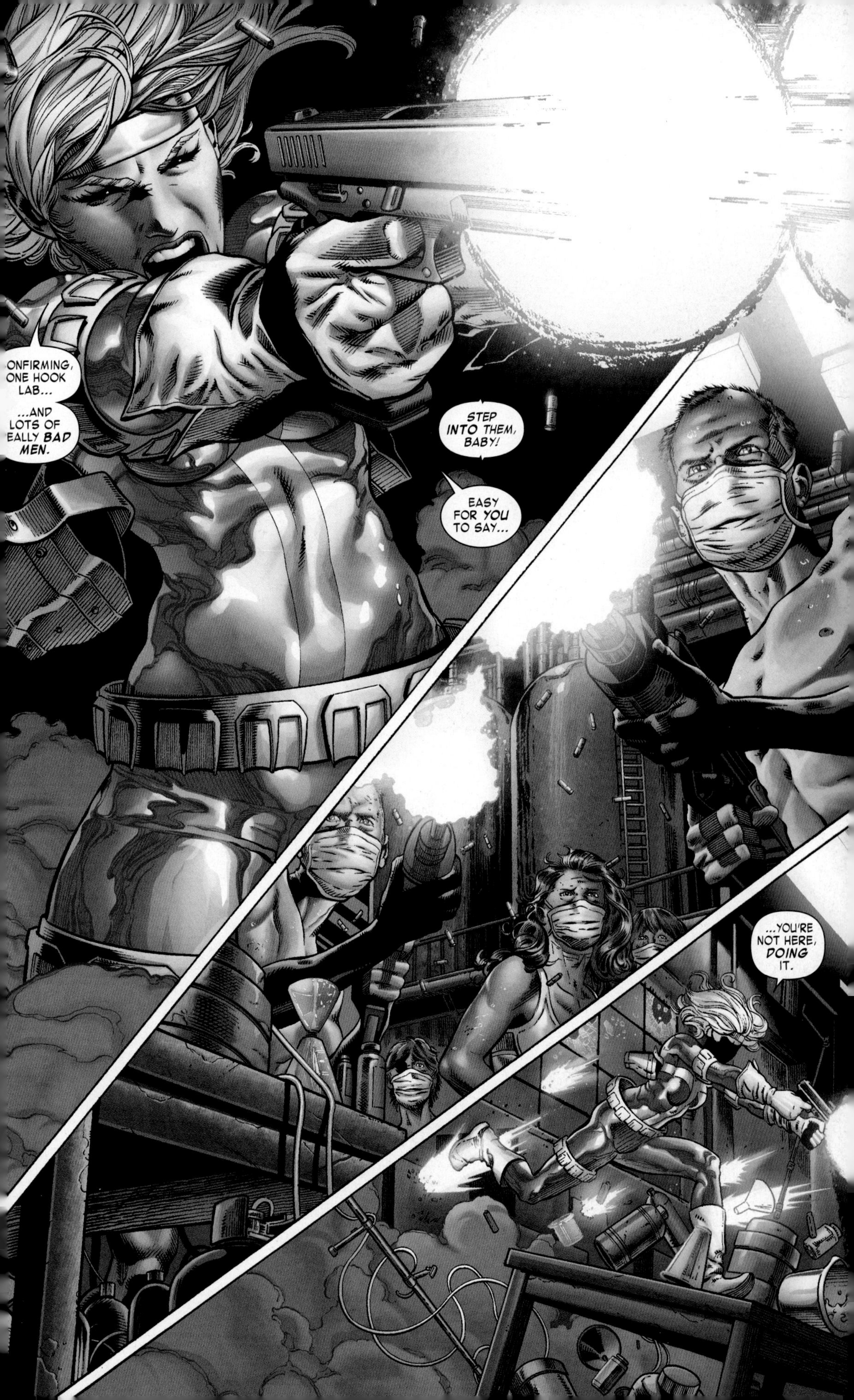
ONFIRMING, ONE HOOK LAB...
...AND LOTS OF EALLY BAD MEN.
STEP INTO THEM, BABY!
EASY FOR YOU TO SAY...
...YOU'RE NOT HERE, DOING IT.

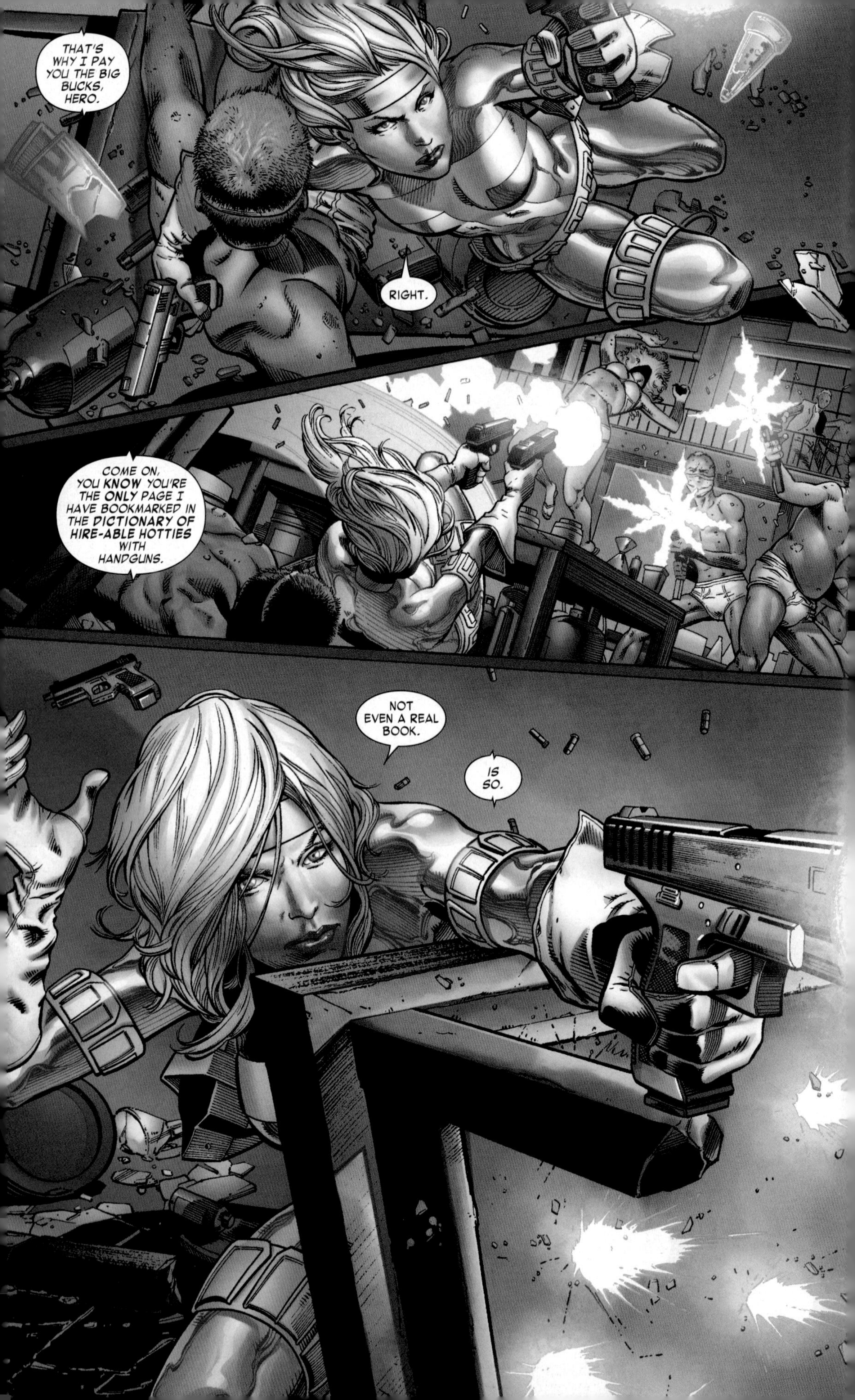
THAT'S WHY I PAY YOU THE BIG BUCKS, HERO.
RIGHT.
COME ON, YOU KNOW YOU'RE THE ONLY PAGE I HAVE BOOKMARKED IN THE DICTIONARY OF HIRE-ABLE HOTTIES WITH HANDGUNS.
NOT EVEN A REAL BOOK.
IS SO.

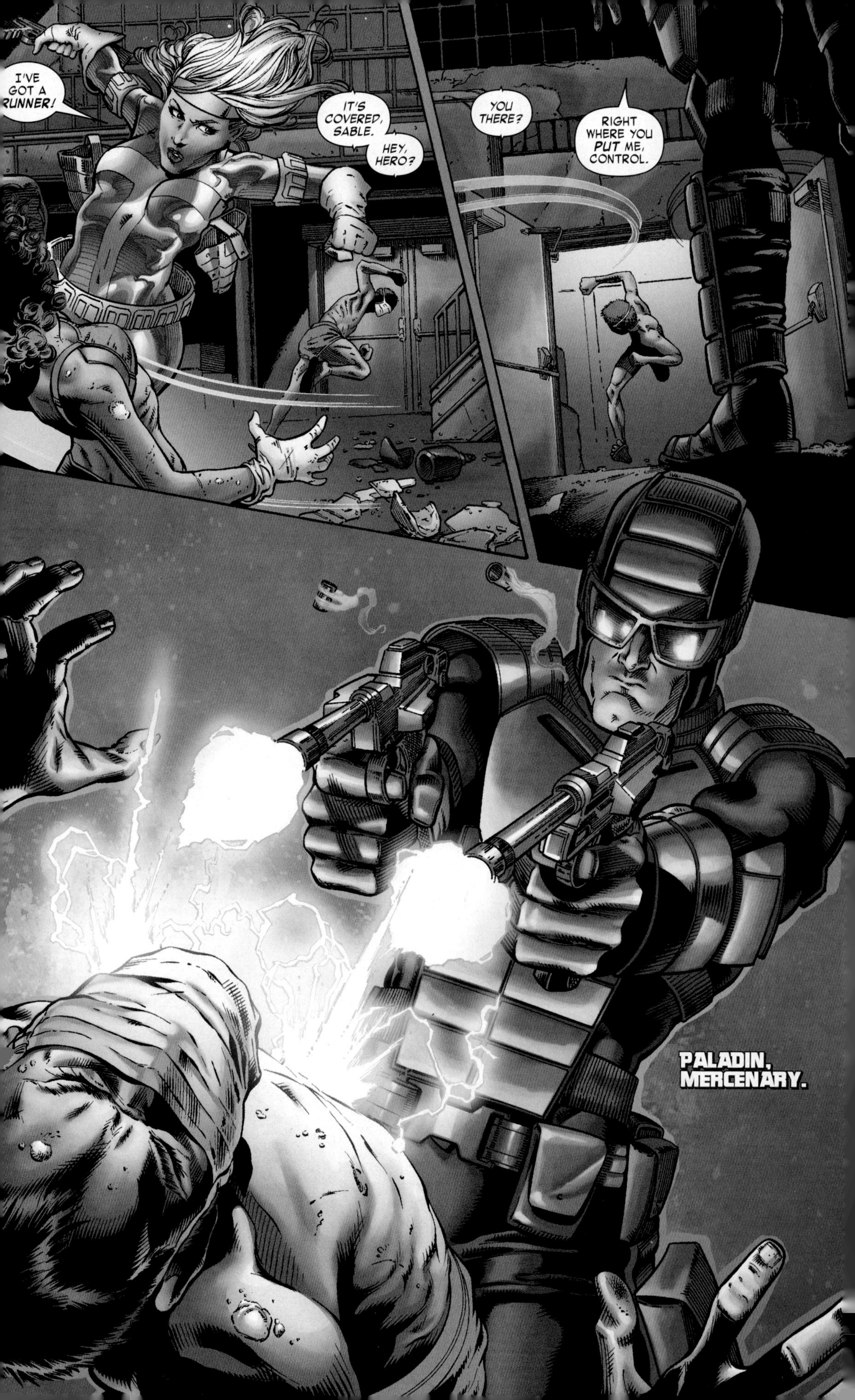
I'VE GOT A RUNNER!
IT'S COVERED, SABLE.
HEY, HERO?
YOU THERE?
RIGHT WHERE YOU PUT ME, CONTROL.
PALADIN, MERCENARY.

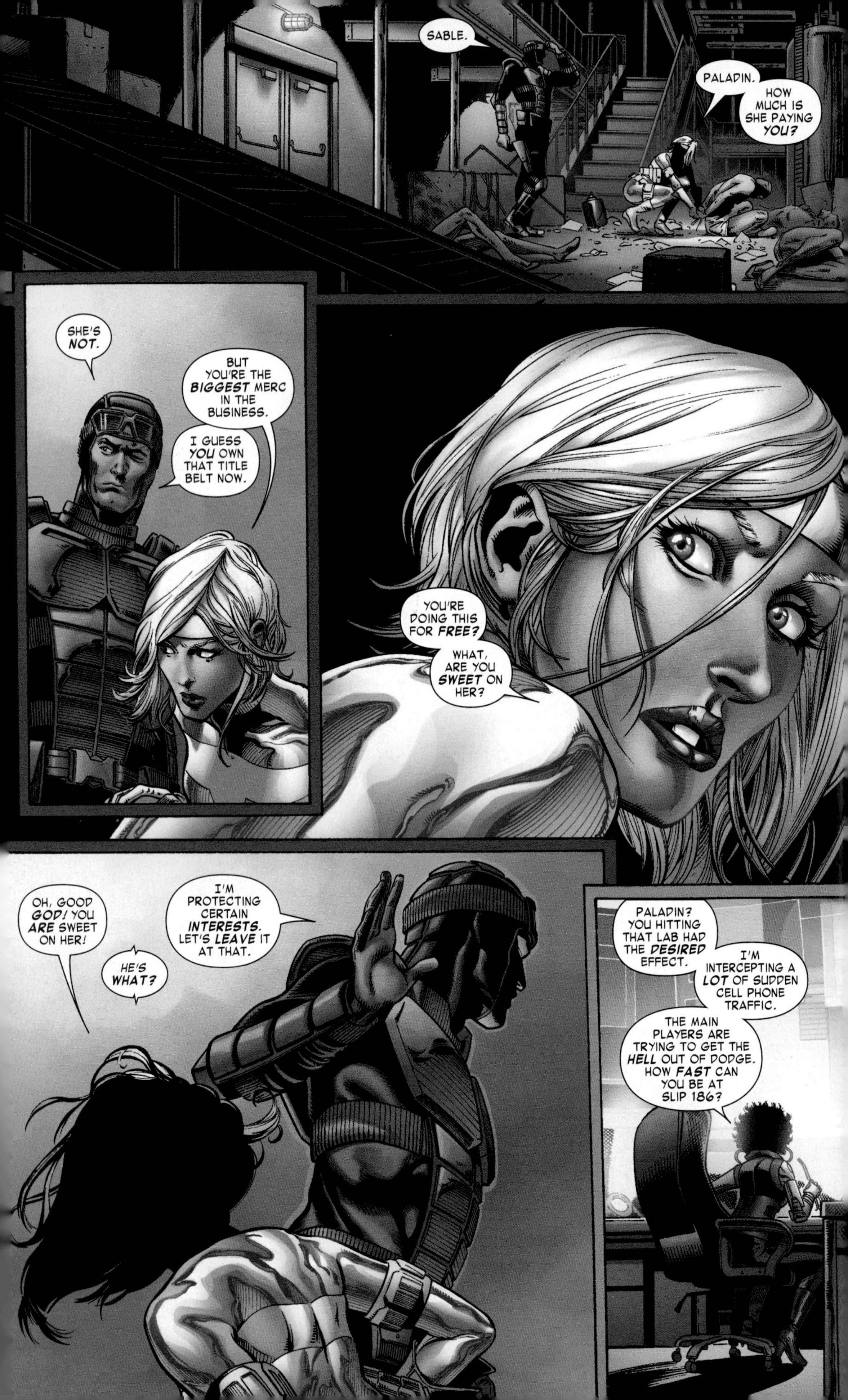

SABLE.
PALADIN.
HOW MUCH IS SHE PAYING YOU?
SHE'S NOT.
BUT YOU'RE THE BIGGEST MERC IN THE BUSINESS.
I GUESS YOU OWN THAT TITLE BELT NOW.
YOU'RE DOING THIS FOR FREE?
WHAT, ARE YOU SWEET ON HER?
OH, GOOD GOD! YOU ARE SWEET ON HER!
HE'S WHAT?
I'M PROTECTING CERTAIN INTERESTS. LET'S LEAVE IT AT THAT.
PALADIN? YOU HITTING THAT LAB HAD THE DESIRED EFFECT.
I'M INTERCEPTING A LOT OF SUDDEN CELL PHONE TRAFFIC.
THE MAIN PLAYERS ARE TRYING TO GET THE HELL OUT OF DODGE. HOW FAST CAN YOU BE AT SLIP 186?

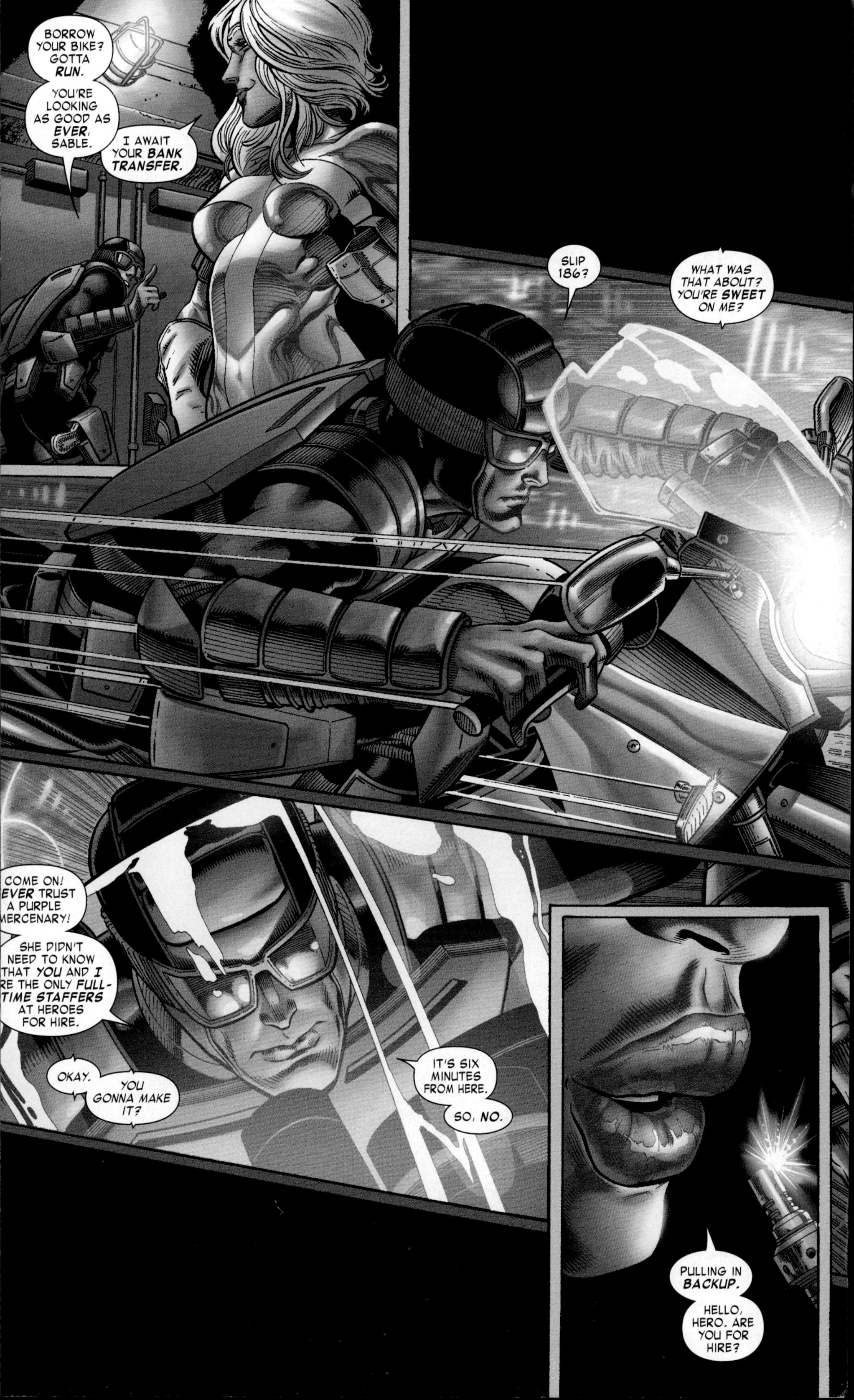

BORROW YOUR BIKE? GOTTA RUN.
YOU'RE LOOKING AS GOOD AS EVER, SABLE.
I AWAIT YOUR BANK TRANSFER.
SLIP 186?
WHAT WAS THAT ABOUT? YOU'RE SWEET ON ME?
COME ON! EVER TRUST A PURPLE MERCENARY!
SHE DIDN'T NEED TO KNOW THAT YOU AND I RE THE ONLY FULL-TIME STAFFERS AT HEROES FOR HIRE.
OKAY.
YOU GONNA MAKE IT?
IT'S SIX MINUTES FROM HERE.
SO, NO.
PULLING IN BACKUP.
HELLO, HERO. ARE YOU FOR HIRE?

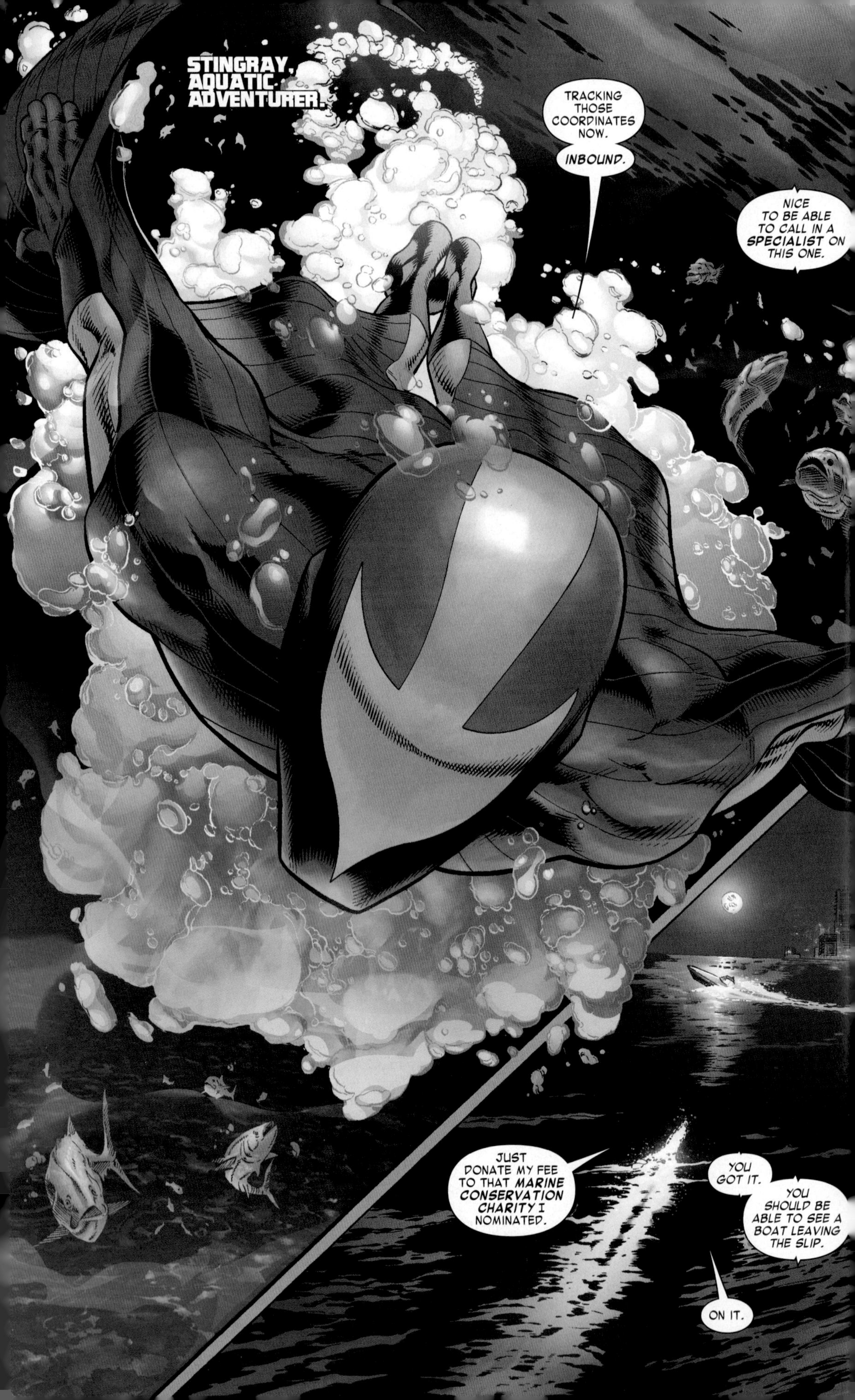
STINGRAY, AQUATIC ADVENTURER.
TRACKING THOSE COORDINATES NOW.
INBOUND.
NICE TO BE ABLE TO CALL IN A SPECIALIST ON THIS ONE.
JUST DONATE MY FEE TO THAT MARINE CONSERVATION CHARITY I NOMINATED.
YOU GOT IT.
YOU SHOULD BE ABLE TO SEE A BOAT LEAVING THE SLIP.
ON IT.

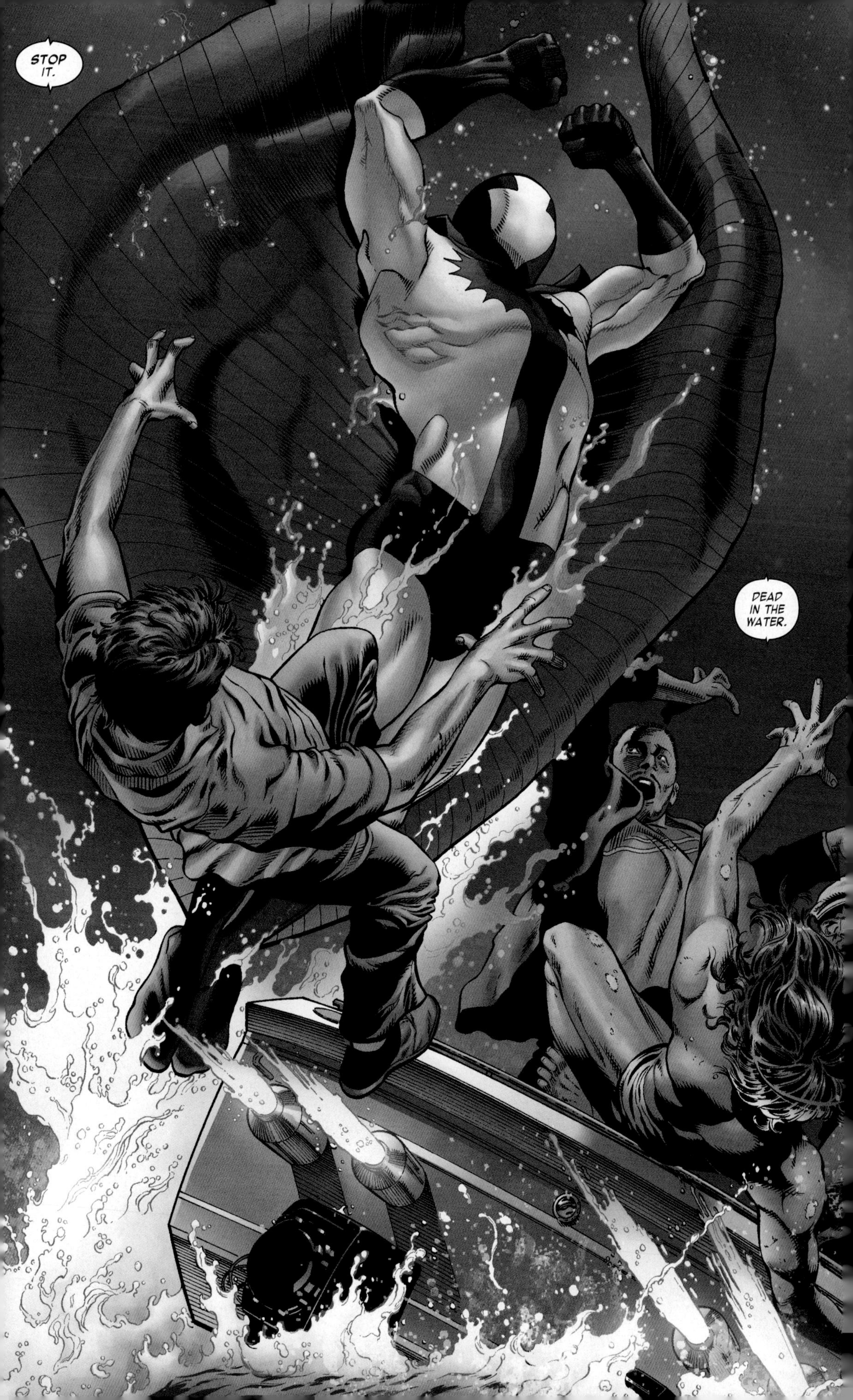
STOP IT.
DEAD IN THE WATER.

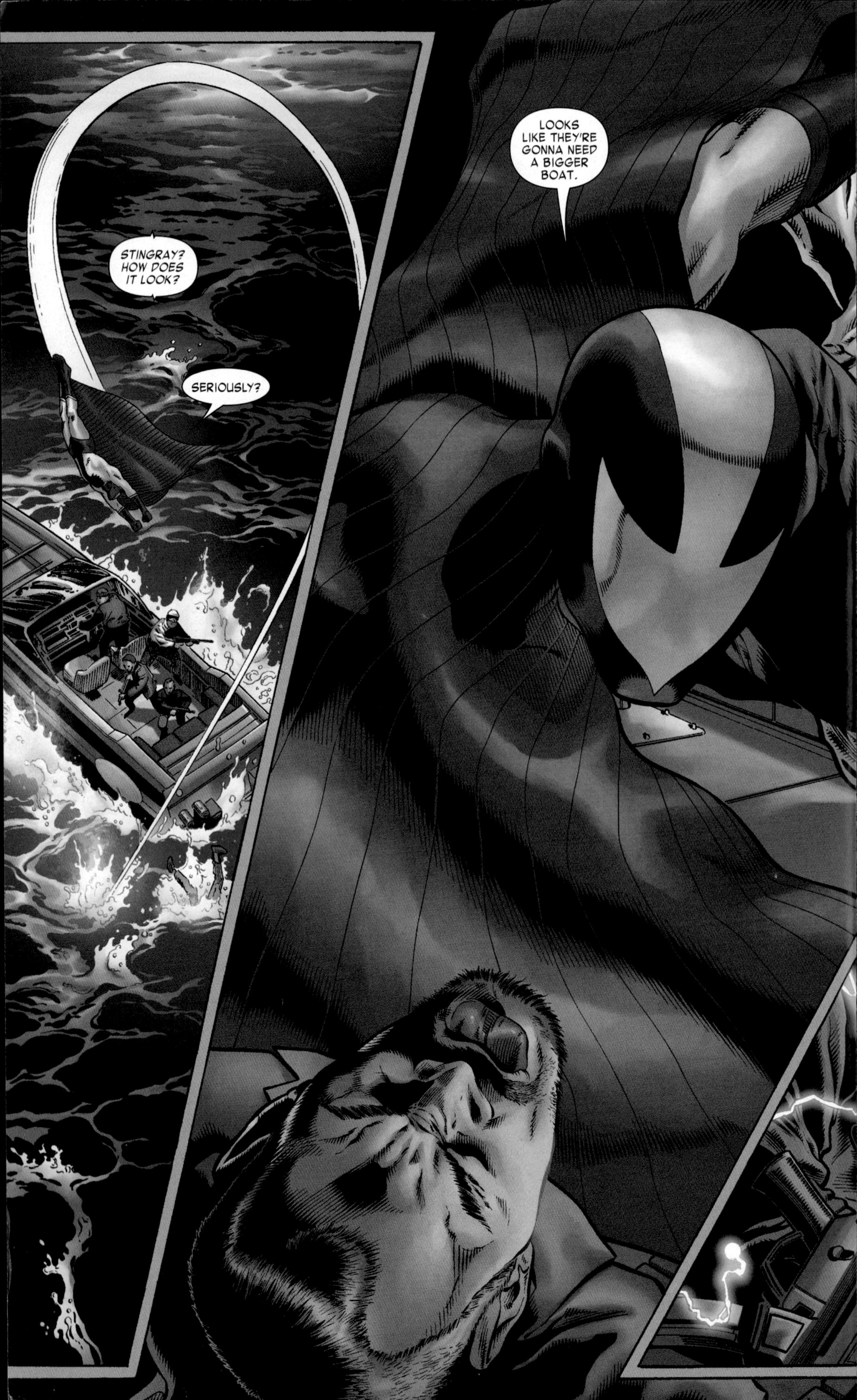
STINGRAY? HOW DOES IT LOOK?
SERIOUSLY?
LOOKS LIKE THEY'RE GONNA NEED A BIGGER BOAT.

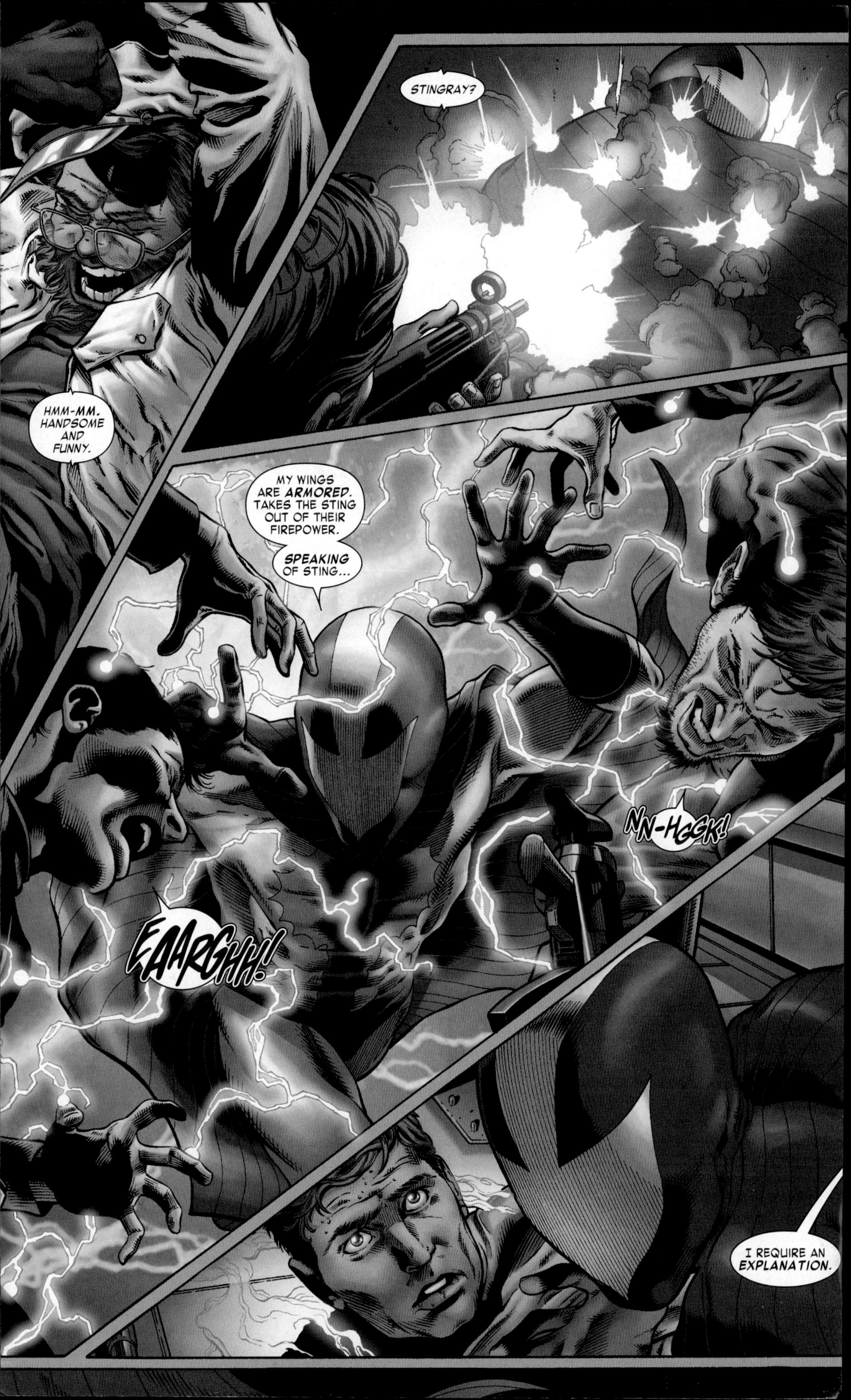
HMM-MM. HANDSOME AND FUNNY.
STINGRAY?
MY WINGS ARE ARMORED. TAKES THE STING OUT OF THEIR FIREPOWER.
SPEAKING OF STING...
NN-HGGK!
EAARGHH!
I REQUIRE AN EXPLANATION.

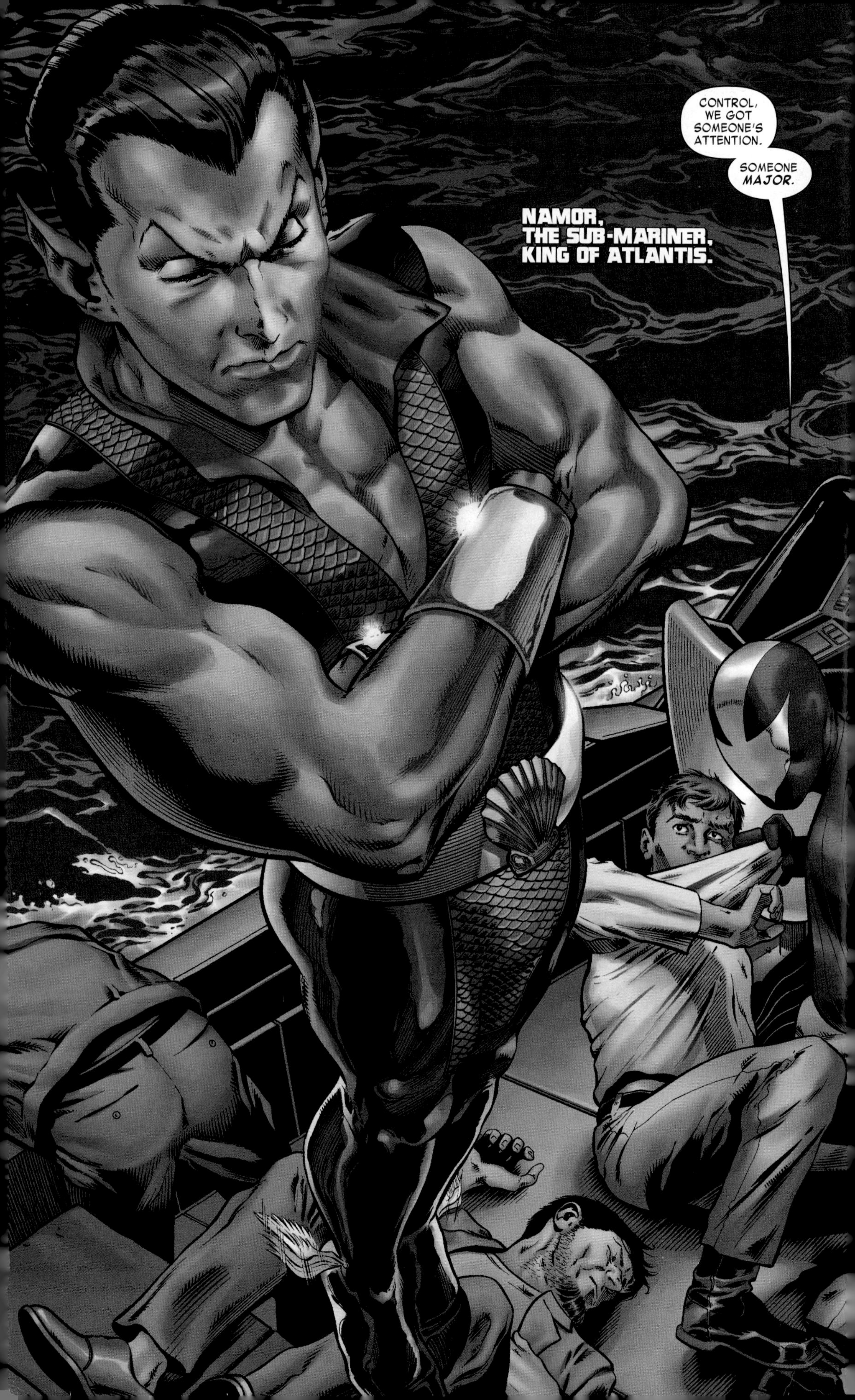
CONTROL, WE GOT SOMEONE'S ATTENTION.
SOMEONE MAJOR.
NAMOR, THE SUB-MARINER, KING OF ATLANTIS.

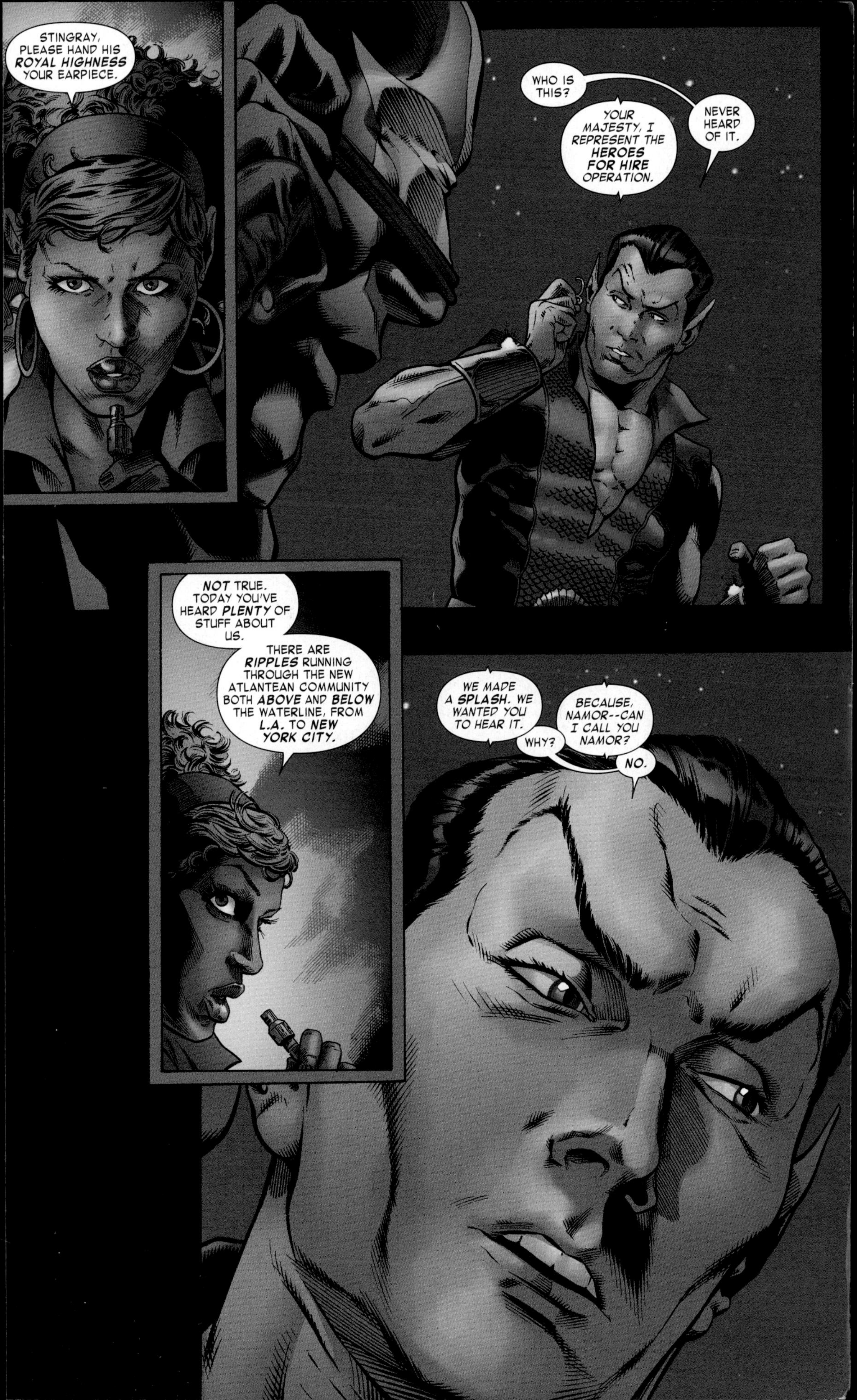
STINGRAY, PLEASE HAND HIS ROYAL HIGHNESS YOUR EARPIECE.
WHO IS THIS?
YOUR MAJESTY, I REPRESENT THE HEROES FOR HIRE OPERATION.
NEVER HEARD OF IT.
NOT TRUE. TODAY YOU'VE HEARD PLENTY OF STUFF ABOUT US.
THERE ARE RIPPLES RUNNING THROUGH THE NEW ATLANTEAN COMMUNITY BOTH ABOVE AND BELOW THE WATERLINE, FROM L.A. TO NEW YORK CITY.
WE MADE A SPLASH. WE WANTED YOU TO HEAR IT.
WHY?
BECAUSE, NAMOR--CAN I CALL YOU NAMOR?
NO.

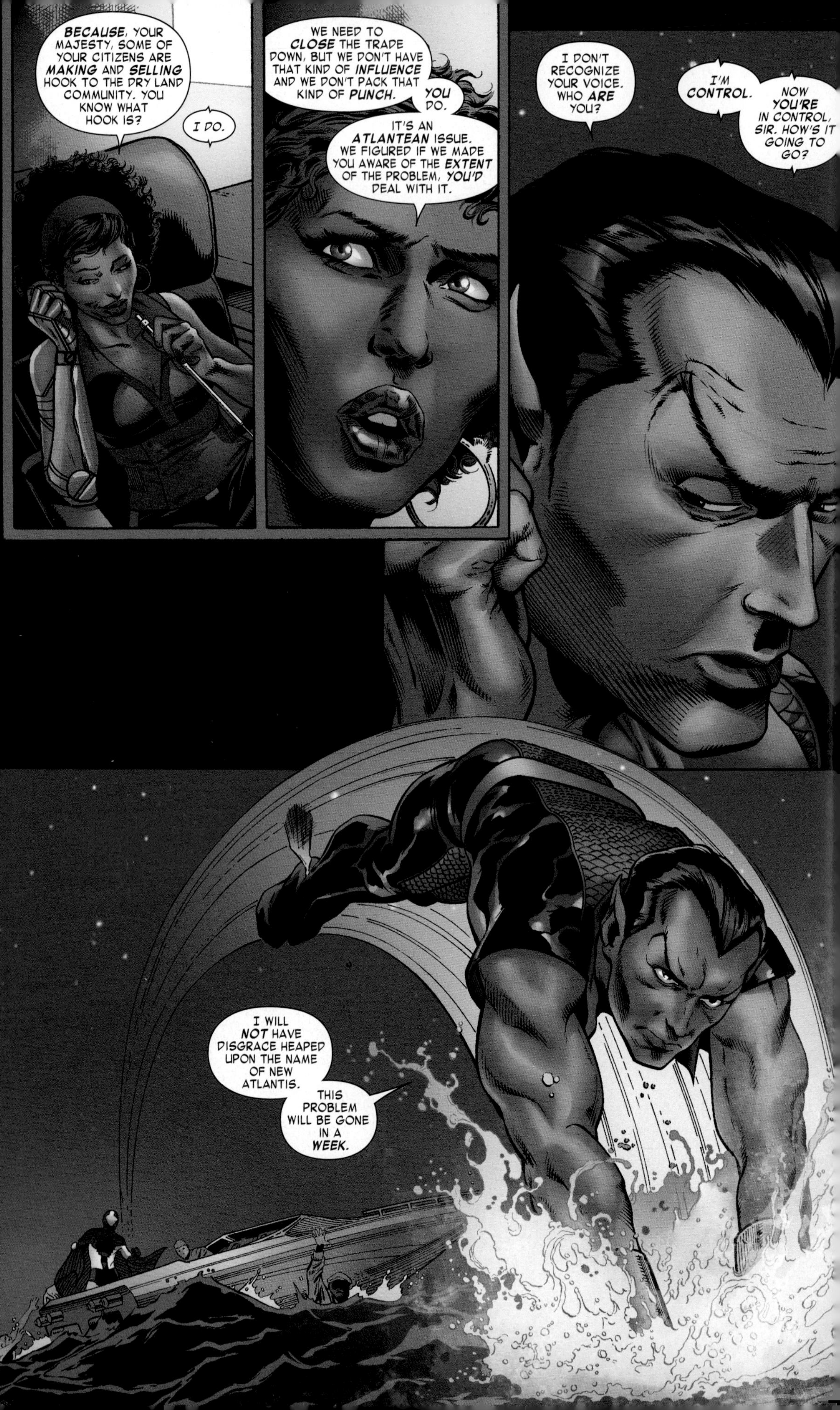
BECAUSE, YOUR MAJESTY, SOME OF YOUR CITIZENS ARE MAKING AND SELLING HOOK TO THE DRY LAND COMMUNITY. YOU KNOW WHAT HOOK IS?
I DO.
WE NEED TO CLOSE THE TRADE DOWN, BUT WE DON'T HAVE THAT KIND OF INFLUENCE AND WE DON'T PACK THAT KIND OF PUNCH.
YOU DO.
IT'S AN ATLANTEAN ISSUE. WE FIGURED IF WE MADE YOU AWARE OF THE EXTENT OF THE PROBLEM, YOU'D DEAL WITH IT.
I DON'T RECOGNIZE YOUR VOICE. WHO ARE YOU?
I'M CONTROL.
NOW YOU'RE IN CONTROL, SIR. HOW'S IT GOING TO GO?
I WILL NOT HAVE DISGRACE HEAPED UPON THE NAME OF NEW ATLANTIS.
THIS PROBLEM WILL BE GONE IN A WEEK.

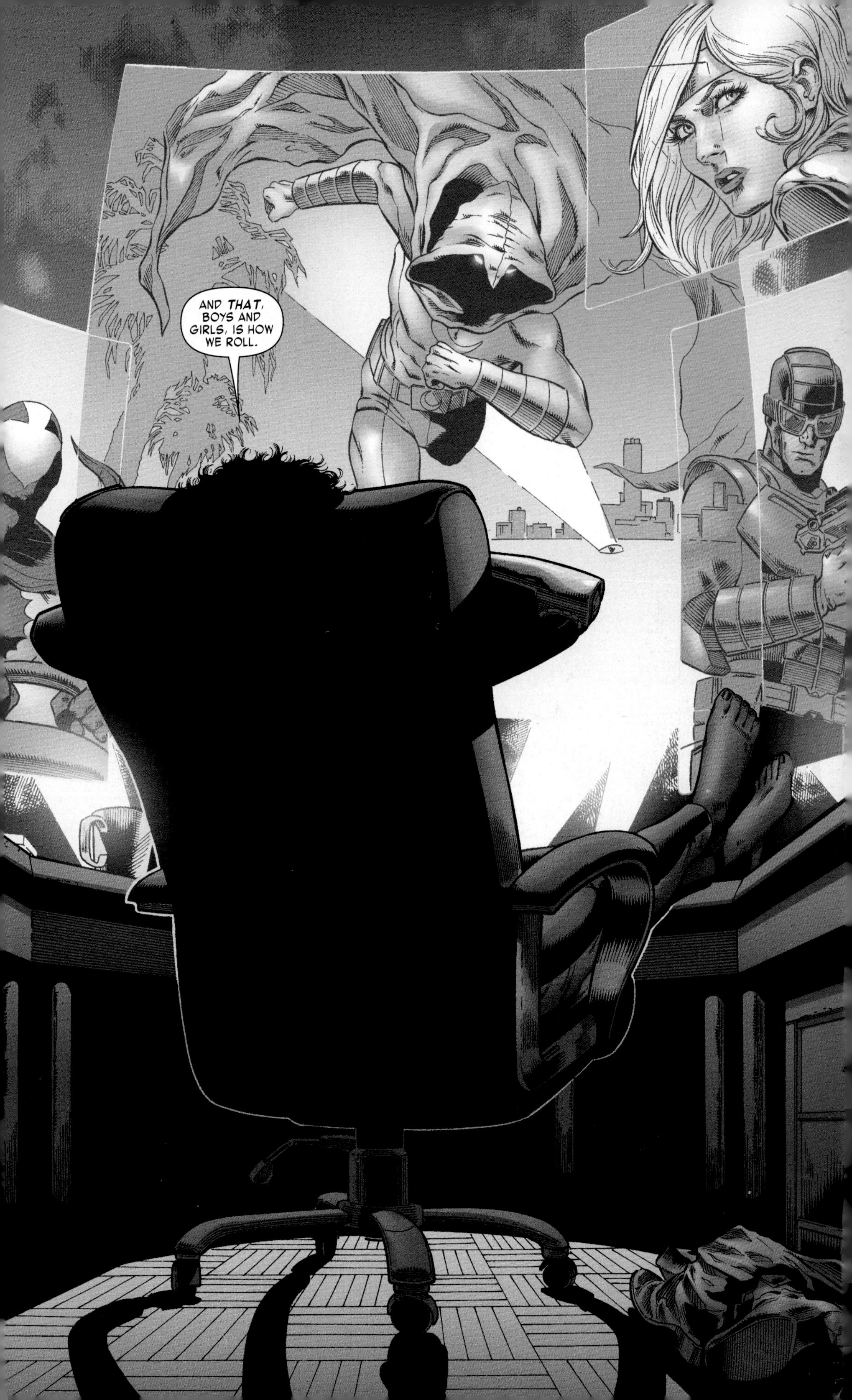
AND *THAT*, BOYS AND GIRLS, IS HOW WE ROLL.

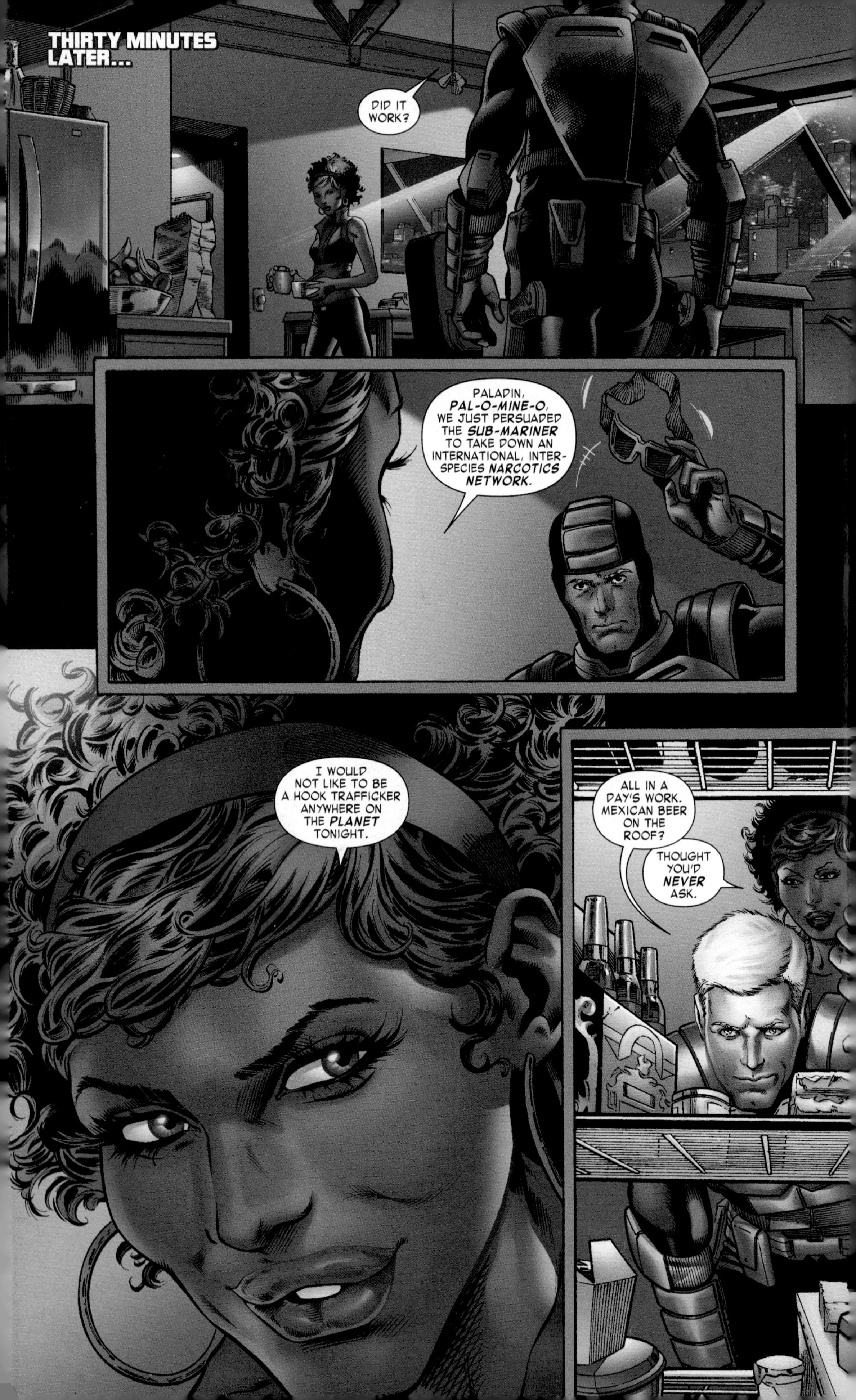
THIRTY MINUTES LATER...
DID IT WORK?
PALADIN, PAL-O-MINE-O, WE JUST PERSUADED THE SUB-MARINER TO TAKE DOWN AN INTERNATIONAL, INTER-SPECIES NARCOTICS NETWORK.
I WOULD NOT LIKE TO BE A HOOK TRAFFICKER ANYWHERE ON THE PLANET TONIGHT.
ALL IN A DAY'S WORK. MEXICAN BEER ON THE ROOF?
THOUGHT YOU'D NEVER ASK.

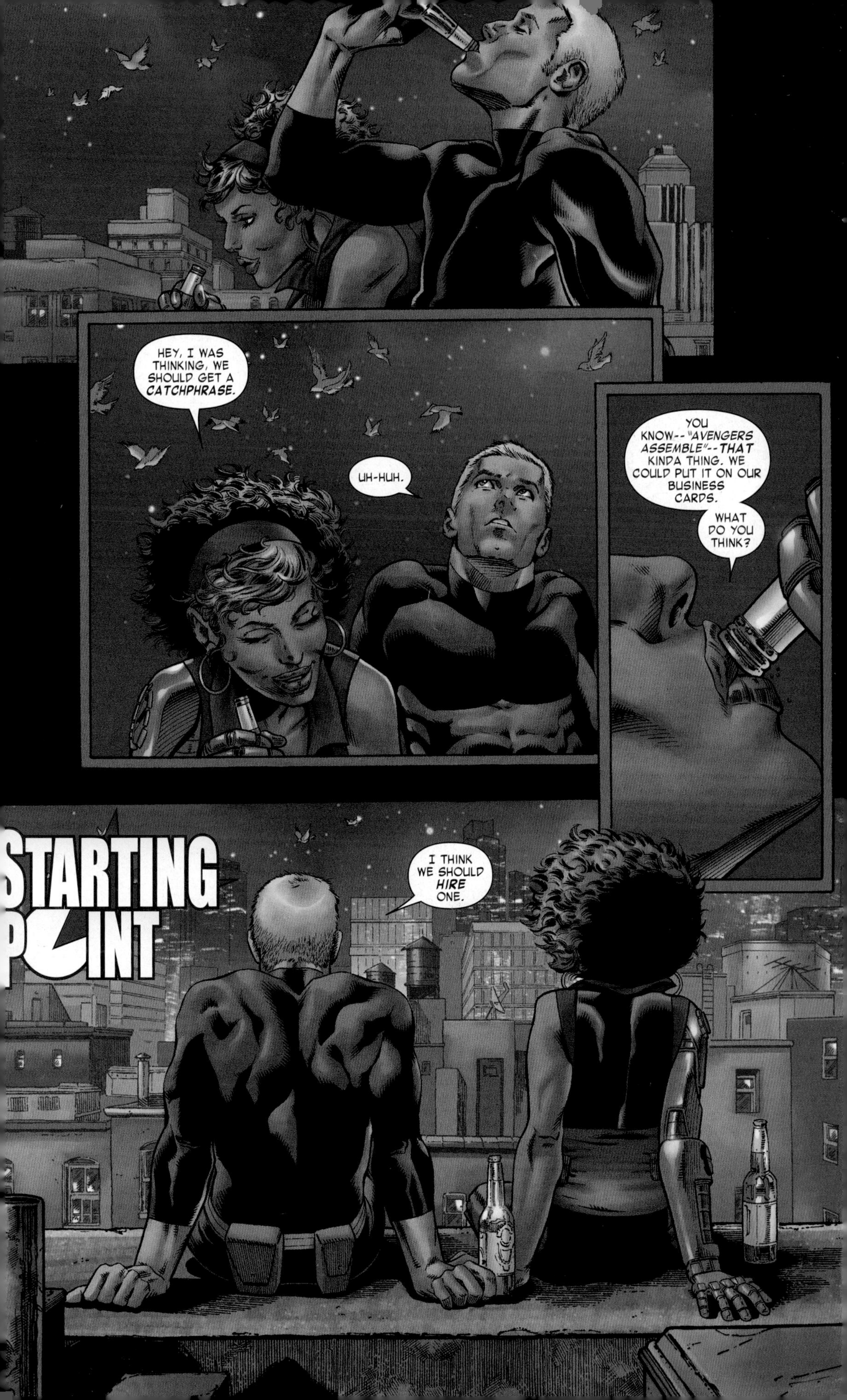
HEY, I WAS THINKING, WE SHOULD GET A CATCHPHRASE.
UH-HUH.
YOU KNOW-- "AVENGERS ASSEMBLE"--THAT KINDA THING. WE COULD PUT IT ON OUR BUSINESS CARDS.
WHAT DO YOU THINK?
STARTING POINT
I THINK WE SHOULD HIRE ONE.

PLAY MISTY F

DnA Continue Their Winning Streak With Heroes For Hir

By Jess Harrold
Design by Rodolfo Muraguchi

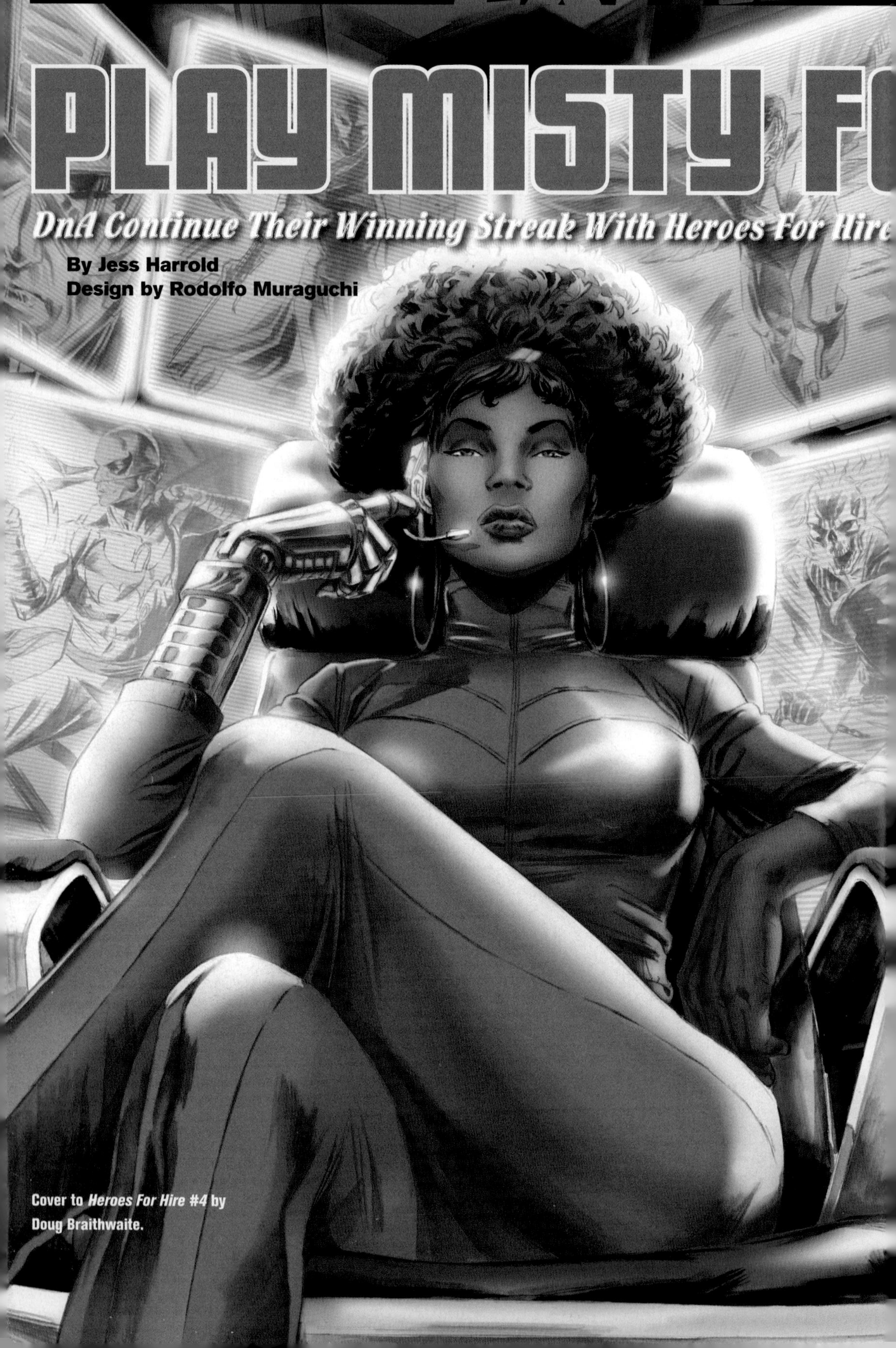

Cover to *Heroes For Hire #4* by Doug Braithwaite.

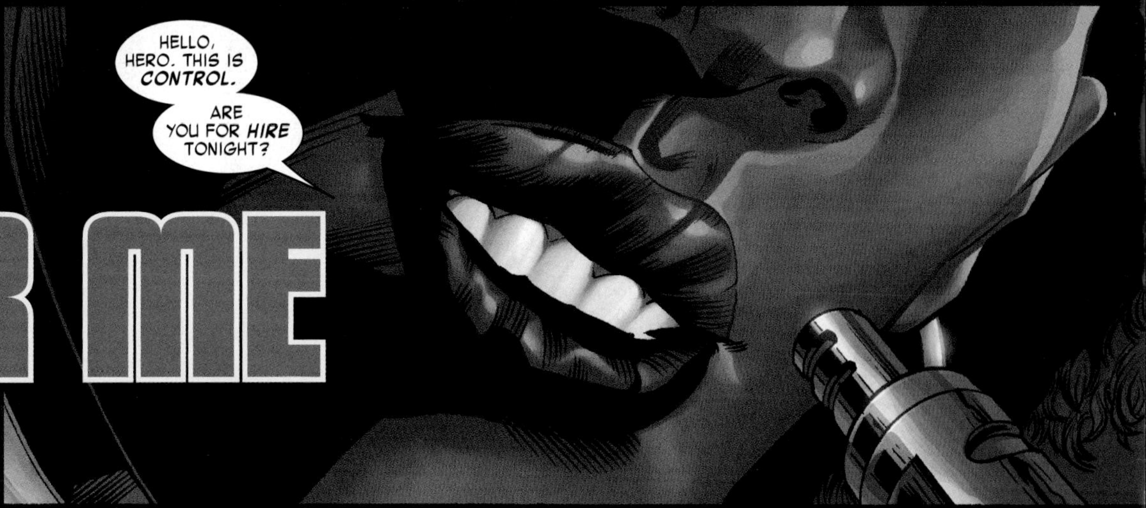
HELLO, HERO. THIS IS *CONTROL.*
ARE YOU FOR *HIRE* TONIGHT?
R ME

"HELLO, HERO." When a hero hears Misty's catchphrase, it's time for action. (Art from *HFH #4* by Robert Atkins.)

Great things come in twos. Abbott and Costello. Fish and chips. Power Man and Iron Fist. And perhaps best of all for comic readers, Dan Abnett and Andy Lanning – the writing team almost as funny as that first pair and every bit as British as the second, and who write a book that owes its name to the third: *Heroes for Hire*. And at the heart of its rotating cast of heroes, well, for hire are another dynamic duo: Misty Knight and Paladin, fighting to rebuild their operation's reputation after an early setback. Putting on our best Misty voice, we called the *Nova*, *Guardians of the Galaxy* and *New Mutants* scribes, and said: "Hey, dudes. This is *Spotlight*. Are you ready for an interview?" Together, they are DnA, they call their book H4H, they make us LOL, and this is their Q&A!

SPOTLIGHT: We here at *Spotlight* like little better than a twist ending to a #1 issue, and you guys certainly delivered! We didn't guess the Puppet Master was secretly controlling Misty Knight's Heroes for Hire operation, but now we know some as-yet-unseen master manipulator was pulling *his* strings.

DnA: It seemed to catch everyone by surprise. That was the plan. We do love us a major turn! The truth will out during *Fear Itself*, and then things will get very serious! Like our *Secret Invasion* issues of *Guardians of the Galaxy*, we wanted to do a crossover sequence that tied directly into the main event *and* advanced our own book's continuity in vital ways. And a cool new villain, too!

SPOTLIGHT: Speaking of things getting serious – is it just us, or are sparks beginning to fly between your two stars?

DnA: Well, Misty doesn't seem to notice anything, but a certain purple merc does seem to have more than financial interests in the whole deal.

SPOTLIGHT: After a trying time, it looks like Misty is stepping out of the control room and starting to kick some bottom again.

DnA: She's tough, she likes to take charge and get things done,

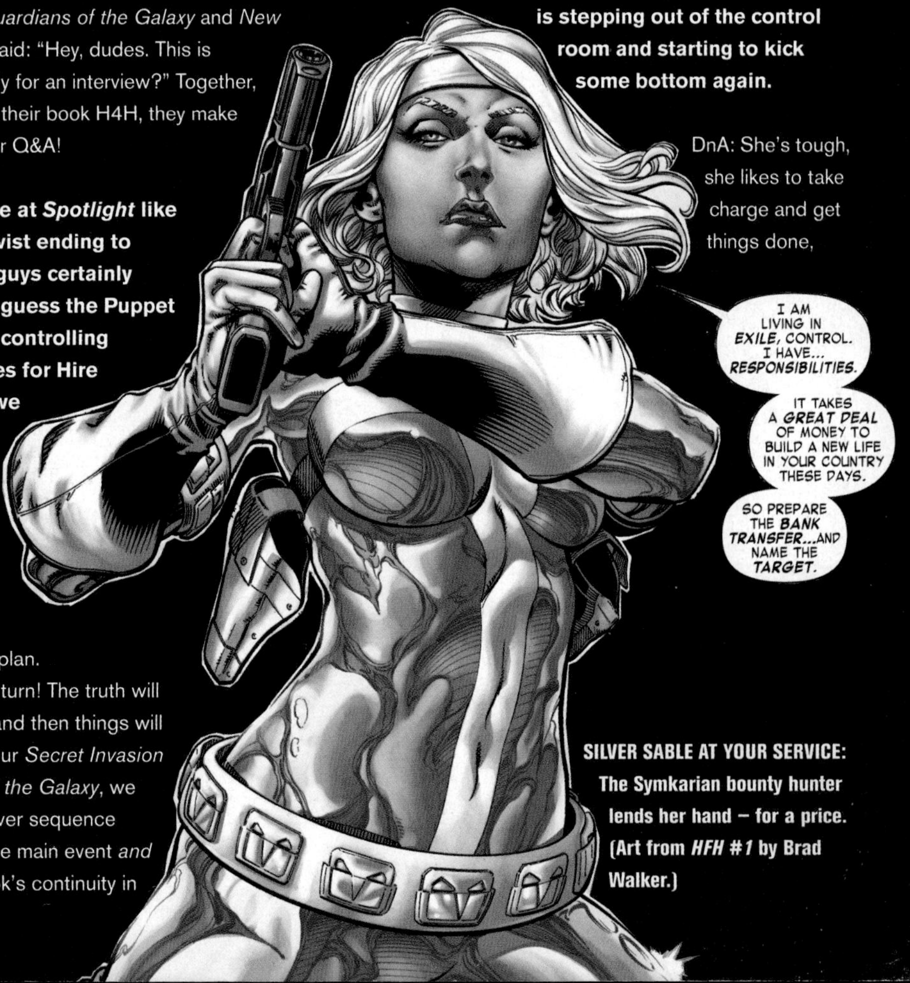
I AM LIVING IN *EXILE*, CONTROL. I HAVE... *RESPONSIBILITIES.*
IT TAKES A *GREAT DEAL* OF MONEY TO BUILD A NEW LIFE IN YOUR COUNTRY THESE DAYS.
SO PREPARE THE *BANK TRANSFER*...AND NAME THE *TARGET*.

SILVER SABLE AT YOUR SERVICE: The Symkarian bounty hunter lends her hand – for a price. (Art from *HFH #1* by Brad Walker.)

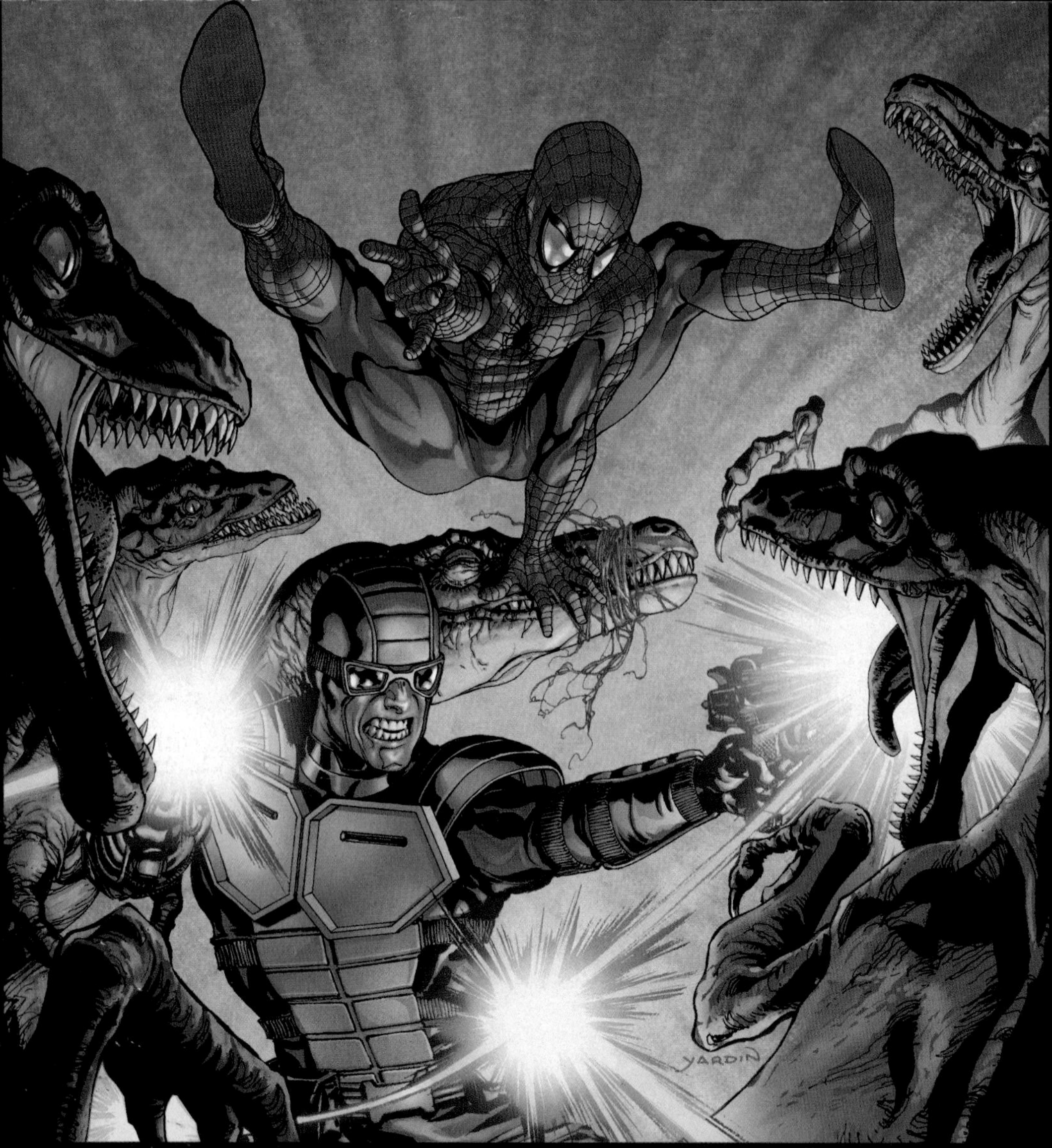
YARDIN

SPIDER-MAN FOR HIRE: Paladin – unwillingly – teams up with Spider-Man in *HFH* #6-7. (Cover to *HFH* #7 by David Yardin.)

and she's got the skills to back up her attitude. She also knows just about everybody in the hero biz. She's been through a really tough time recently with her breakup with Iron Fist and the loss of their child – which turned out not to be a real pregnancy, after all. She needs to get her health and her confidence back, and the Heroes for Hire operation is her way of easing herself back into the game.

SPOTLIGHT: You've firmly established that Heroes For Hire doesn't always mean straight cash. It's interesting the way you have Misty trading info with the heroes, offering leads on their own personal missions in return for their help. Kind of a "you scratch my back" intelligence network for the vigilante classes.

DnA: Yeah, it's got that vibe. It's informal and ad hoc, very street-level. You trade what you want to trade and pay what you're prepared to afford. It's a kind of super-hero information black market, but with a fairly strong moral code. Usually.

SPOTLIGHT: On that basis, would you like to see Control on the phone in other books?

DnA: That would be great! Part of the Marvel Universe continuity!

SPOTLIGHT: You featured Batroc, who is always a delight to read – and presumably write – as an adversary. But he, too, is a mercenary for hire. For the right trade, could he be someone Misty might find a use for? Or would that cross that moral line?

DnA: It's possible. He's a great character, a longtime favorite of ours. Apparently comical, but totally badass. The line is pretty firm, but sometimes needs must. (As we may soon see!)

SPOTLIGHT: Recent issues featured Spider-Man

and his snappy dialogue, which seems a natural fit for your writing style. Is he a character you'd like to do more with?**

DnA: We've always loved Spidey, and it was more fun than we could have imagined writing him into the book. Yes, we'd love to do more – though serious kudos to Mr. Slott for writing such a great Spidey book at the moment. Wouldn't want to steal his gig away!

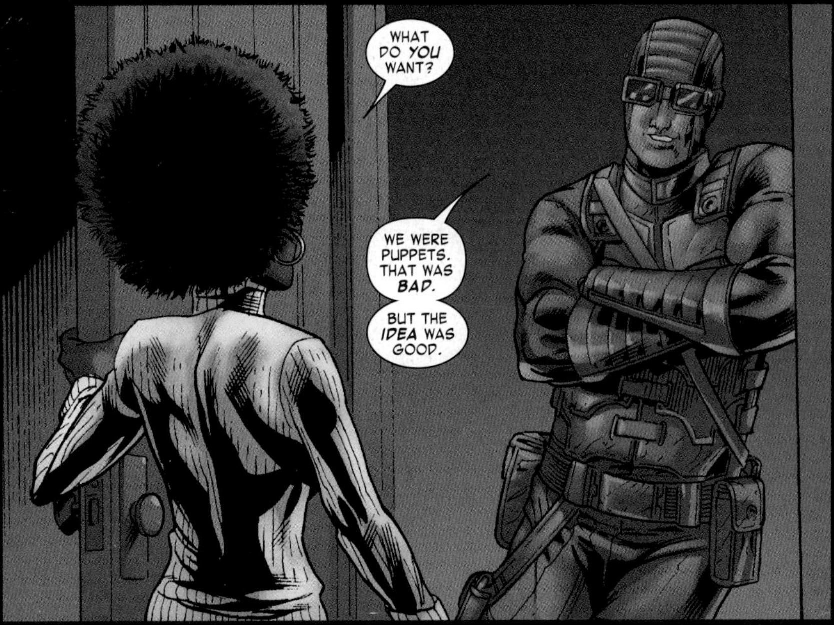
WHAT DO *YOU* WANT?
WE WERE PUPPETS. THAT WAS *BAD*.
BUT THE *IDEA* WAS GOOD.

AN ONGOING RELATIONSHIP? In the aftermath of the Puppet Master's defeat, Heroes for Hire will expand to a two-person operation – if Paladin has his way. (Art from *HFH #5* by Robert Atkins.)

SPOTLIGHT: You really got inside Paladin's head in the Spidey issues, exploring his jealousy and hero worship. Paladin seems to be a little uncomfortable in his own skin right now, maybe wanting to better himself?

DnA: Not just us feeling that, then? He's tired of the jibes and the rep, and he knows how hard and professionally he works. Maybe a change is coming.

SPOTLIGHT: Your book is going to get involved with the craziness of "Spider-Island" – what do you have lined up for that? Could Paladin get the taste of life with spider-powers he wonders about in #7?

DnA: Maybe. We can't say. "Spider-Island" is a big deal, and we're sharing some of that fun. It's going to be creepy, though. Tough and creepy.

SPOTLIGHT: With Marvel starting to kick around some TV ideas for characters like Cloak and Dagger, it strikes us that *Heroes for Hire* would make for a great show. You even have a neat catchphrase! What's your pitch? Who's your star?

DnA: Our pitch is that first issue, isn't it? A statement of intent. We try to make *H4H* a series with a jump-on point in most issues. Misty will always be Pam Grier to us, but what about Jasika Nicole (*Fringe*)? Can Freema Agyeman (*Doctor Who*) do an American accent?

"She needs to get her health and her confidence back, and the Heroes for Hire operation is her way of easing herself back into the game."

– DnA on Misty Knight

SPOTLIGHT: Good question. Maybe John Barrowman could play Paladin and teach her. Finally, in Misty's black book, who is the hardest to hire? Who works the cheapest?

DnA: Ghost Rider is hard to "hire." Plus, he melts the ear pieces. Elektra's easy to hire, but hard to focus. (On, you know, not killing people.) On the other end of the spectrum, Paladin will find a lost kitten for a bag of chips. [*That's fries to us – American Ed.*] Kidding, Paladin!

When's the last time there's been a bad DnA book? While you're fruitlessly searching to find that impossible bit of information, we'll be waiting patiently for Heroes For Hire #9, *on sale now!* •

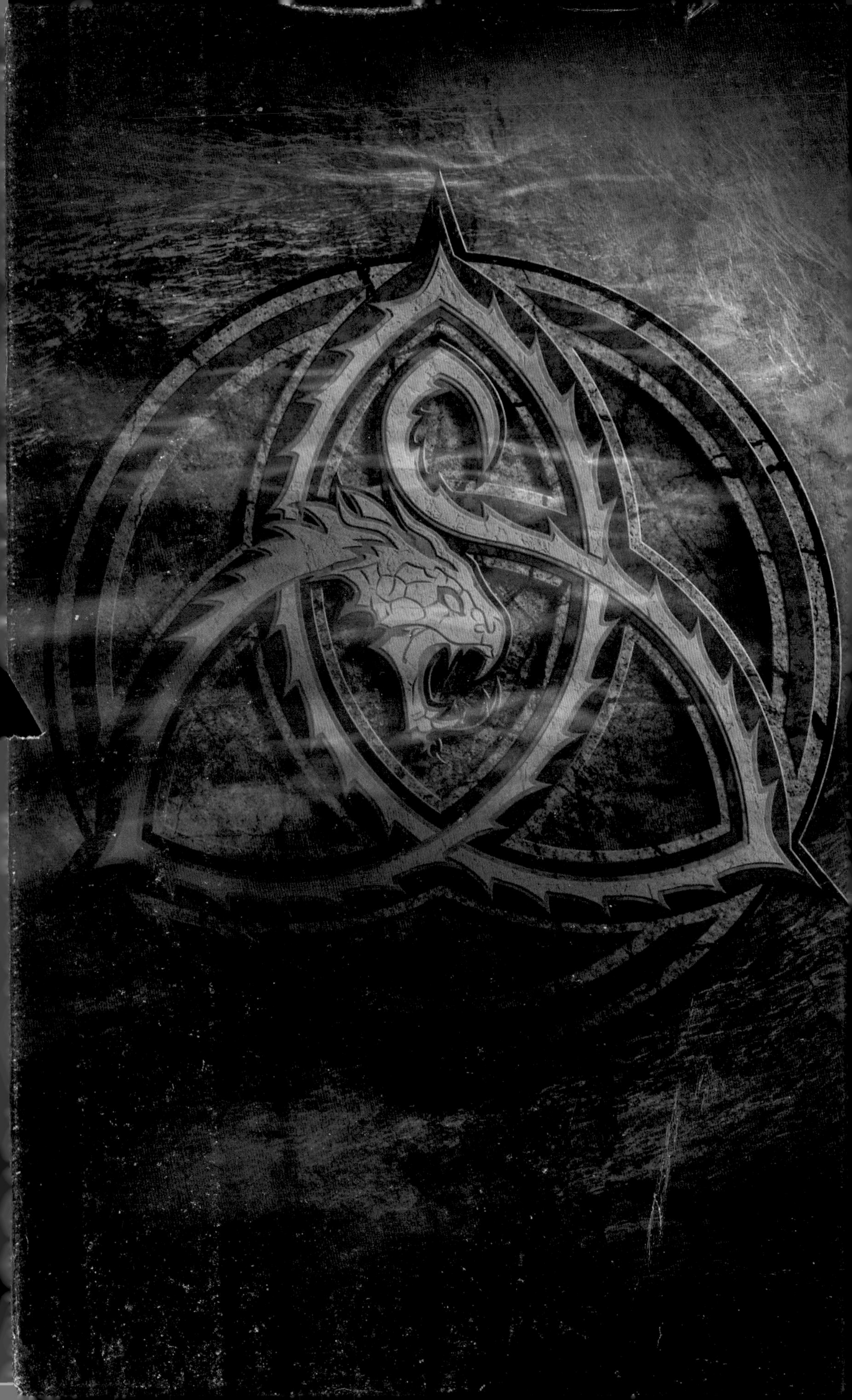